English Ethnicity and Race in Early Modern Drama

Working with both popular and elite sources from the period's drama to medical texts to historiography Mary Floyd-Wilson intervenes in the current literary scholarship on race to disembed and recover the complex basis of early modern ethnic distinctions: an interdisciplinary discourse that she terms "geohumoralism." The importance of *English Ethnicity and Race in Early Modern Drama* lies in its recognition that the English were afflicted in the sixteenth century by a profoundly unstable sense of identity derived from the British Isles' northern, marginalized status in a set of classical texts that were revered and considered authoritative. Simply put, humoralism, for the early modern English, was ethnology. Floyd-Wilson demonstrates that the English were not only driven to rearrange, discursively, this inherited knowledge in an effort to revalue those traits conventionally identified as "northern," but they also aimed to alter or remedy their northern natures through the manipulation of their environment whether that meant the air, temperature, diet, and terrain, or the effects of travel, education, rhetoric, impersonation, or fashion. To follow Floyd-Wilson's application of contemporary geohumoral theory to a succession of major canonical texts is exhilarating, surprising, and unsettling, as Marlowe, Shakespeare, Jonson and others emerge as unwittingly complicit in ways of thinking about English selfhood that enabled the growth of the Atlantic slave trade and British imperialism.

MARY FLOYD-WILSON is Assistant Professor of English Literature at the University of North Carolina at Chapel Hill. She has published articles in several journals including *English Literary Renaissance, Women's Studies,* and *South Atlantic Review* and is a contributing author to *British Identities and English Renaissance Literature* (2002). She is currently co-editing a volume of essays entitled *Reading the Early Modern Passions: Essays on the Cultural History of Emotion.*

English Ethnicity and Race in Early Modern Drama

Mary Floyd-Wilson

University of North Carolina at Chapel Hill

CAMBRIDGE
UNIVERSITY PRESS

PUBLISHED BY THE PRESS SYNDICATE OF THE UNIVERSITY OF CAMBRIDGE
The Pitt Building, Trumpington Street, Cambridge CB2 1RP, United Kingdom

CAMBRIDGE UNIVERSITY PRESS
The Edinburgh Building, Cambridge CB2 2RU, UK
40 West 20th Street, New York, NY 10011-4211, USA
477 Williamstown Road, Port Melbourne, VIC 3207, Australia
Ruiz de Alarcón 13, 28014 Madrid, Spain
Dock House, The Waterfront, Cape Town 8001, South Africa

http://www.cambridge.org

First published 2003

Printed in the United Kingdom at the University Press, Cambridge

Typeface Times 10/12 pt   *System* LATEX 2$_\varepsilon$ [TB]

A catalogue record for this book is available from the British Library

ISBN 0 521 81056 6 hardback

For Lanis and Claude

Contents

Illustrations

Acknowledgements

English Ethnicity began as a dissertation project at the University of North Carolina at Chapel Hill and benefited there from a University dissertation fellowship. Darryl Gless, whose love of Shakespeare and teaching set me on this path, provided encouragement and kind support as my adviser. I am grateful to Reid Barbour for pushing me to clarify and complicate my argument at every turn in its early stages. I was fortunate to be their student, and I am honored to return to the UNC English department as their colleague. My participation in Gail Kern Paster's Folger seminar, "Humoring the Body," helped redefine the book's direction and scope. In the years since, my scholarly, professional, and personal debts to Gail have continued to grow. Always brilliant and challenging, she is an inspiration not only as an intellect but also for her admirable integrity and generous collegiality. I completed the manuscript at Yale University, where I had the support of the Morse fellowship fund and the Hilles publication award. I am grateful as well to the Folger Shakespeare Library for granting me a research fellowship. For their gifts of time, incisive commentary, and exceptional engagement with my work, I owe profound and warm thanks to Larry Manley, Steven Mullaney, Katherine Rowe, and Garrett Sullivan. I want also to express my gratitude to the following colleagues and friends, who have helped me along the way with their advice and encouragement: David Baker, Benjamin Braude, Alan Dessen, Elizabeth Dillon, Peter Erickson, David Glimp, Kim F. Hall, Amy Hungerford, Phebe Jensen, Pericles Lewis, Ian MacInnes, Carla Mazzio, Thomas Olsen, Peter Parolin, Annabel Patterson, Joseph Roach, Ramie Targoff, and Valerie Wayne. I am indebted to Elizabeth Archibald, Jenn Lewin, Ann Moller, Ace Padian, Cecily Rose, Tracey Tomlinson, and Alice Wolfram for their indispensable assistance.

A version of chapter 5 appeared in *English Literary Renaissance* 28 (Spring 1998): 183–209. My thanks to the journal for permission to reprint it. My gratitude also to Cambridge University Press for permission to reprint a portion of chapter 7, which appeared as "Delving to the root: *Cymbeline*, Scotland, and the English Race," *British Identities and English Renaissance Literature*, ed. David Baker and Willy Maley (Cambridge: Cambridge University Press, 2002), pp. 101–15. A version of chapter 6, under the title "*Othello*, Passion, and

Race," will appear in the collection *Writing Race Across the Atlantic World, 1492–1763*, ed. Philip Beidler and Gary L. Taylor (New York: Palgrave, forthcoming). Except for silently modernizing i, j, u, and v, I have retained the original spelling of the primary texts and facsimile editions.

It is with affection and gratitude that I thank Mary A. Beard for always believing I can do it, no matter what "it" is. Thanks to Jim, Diana, and David for their support. I dedicate this book, with love, to Lanis Wilson and our son Claude, who lost me most to the study but buoyed me most when my spirits flagged.

Introduction: the marginal English

DESDEMONA: ... my noble Moor
Is true of mind, and made of no such baseness
As jealous creatures are ...
EMILIA: Is he not jealous?
DESDEMONA: Who, he? I think the sun where he was born
Drew all such humours from him.

(*Othello*, 3. 4. 24–9)[1]

Where would Desdemona get such a notion? Why does she believe that the African sun would draw out the body's humors and heated passions? Has love blinded her to the Elizabethan commonplace that hot climates create fiery temperaments?[2] For the most part critics of *Othello* ignore Desdemona's appraisal of the Moor's humoral complexion. And if they do acknowledge her assertion, her grasp of early modern climate theory is summarily dismissed. We are reassured that we know better: obviously Othello is jealous, and his jealousy substantiates the Renaissance stereotype of violently heated Africans.[3]

But do we know better? Desdemona may know more than we thought. Her statement is supported by a long line of classical, medieval, and early modern texts wherein climatic explanations of color and disposition were grounded in humoralism. Regionally inflected humoralism, reductively construed as "climate theory" by modern scholars, proves to be the dominant mode of ethnic distinctions in the late sixteenth and early seventeenth centuries.[4] Desdemona actually appeals to two widely held early modern beliefs concerning somatic differences. First, she implies that humoral theory is the foundational knowledge for comprehending a person's disposition (if Othello lacks humors, then he must not be jealous).[5] Here, she is most certainly correct. Second, she suggests that humoral theory is also the foundational knowledge for making ethnological distinctions (Othello's lack of humors is what distinguishes him from people of cooler climates). This, too, would have been accepted as an accurate claim, though it is less known to modern readers.[6]

Desdemona does in fact know what she is talking about. Her surprising conclusion that the heat of the African sun would dry and cool the body's humors is a commonplace in classical, medieval, and early modern writings on regional identities. From Pseudo-Aristotle to Albertus Magnus to Jean Bodin, writers have maintained the notion, as we find it articulated here in the sixteenth-century encyclopedia *Batman uppon Bartholome*, that the heat in Africa "burneth and wasteth humours," making the bodies cool and dry. Conversely, the cold air in the north "breedeth humours of the bodye...[the] vapours and spirites be smitten inward, [and] it maketh them hotter within..."[7] Competing with this theory of complexions was a less popular explanation derived from Hippocrates' unflattering portrait of the northern Scythians in *Airs, Waters, Places*, which maintained that cold air generated cold, moist bodies.[8] Rather than one explanation simply invalidating the other, these contradictory theories of complexion were brought together in a wide range of early modern texts to produce a "scientific" ethnology that proves, at turns, both deterministic and ideologically malleable.[9]

As the quotation from *Batman uppon Bartholome* indicates, regionally framed humoralism – what I term "geohumoralism" – applies not only to Moors but to people of all climates. Derived from the classical texts of Aristotle, Galen, Vitruvius, Pliny, and others, geohumoralism, in its inception, aimed to comprehend (and estrange) the northern and southern climatic extremes that bordered the Mediterranean. The same classical tripartite scheme that constructed ancient Greece and Rome as the civilized middle between the barbaric lands north and south also determined the logic of geohumoralism. Thus, humoral temperance, like civility, was held to be attainable only in a temperate clime.[10]

Despite Europe's contact with the New World, the classification of people and nations during this period still conformed to the ancient tripartite divisions of climatic regions – northern, southern, and temperate zones.[11] Even when latitudinal specifications shifted with the author's native bias, the basic paradigm of a temperate middle zone and its extreme boundaries was consistently invoked in the early modern period. Ideally *moderate* complexions, in both appearance and temperament, belonged to those inhabitants of the middle, temperate region. Classical geohumoral discourse had depended on a Mediterranean-centered world and relied on a logic of inversion to characterize the north and the south.[12] As the barbaric outsiders to the *polis* or *oikumene*, white northerners and black southerners, or Scythians and Ethiopians, were paired together in intemperance but opposed in particular qualities. Yet extreme climates were also recognized for the exceptional influence they had on their inhabitants: the Scythians garnered praise for their physical strength and martial prowess, while the Ethiopians were associated with natural wisdom and spirituality. Early modern geohumoralism retains the tripartite structure and rhetoric of inversion established by Herodotus and other ancient writers, but the strengths and weaknesses of the Ethiopians and Scythians are now projected onto early modern Africans and northern Europeans.

To understand how Desdemona's invocation of this knowledge has any bearing on the ethnological tensions in *Othello*, we will need to consider the general status of geohumoralism in early modern England, which is a subject I take up in part I of the book, "Climatic culture: the transmissions and transmutations of ethnographic knowledge." While scholars have recognized the continued predominance of the Herodotan schema in early modern ethnography, they have overlooked the significance of Britain's decentered position in this paradigm.[13] Rather than setting up a correspondence between England and the Mediterranean, sixteenth-century ethnography suggested, remarkably, identification between Britons and Africans.[14] The logic of inversion fixed the white northerner and the black southerner in an interdependent relationship: if the southerner is hot and dry, then the northerner must be cold and moist; if the southerner is weak and wise, the northerner must be strong and witless.

Though its appearance in England predates the early modern period, geohumoralism gained in popularity in the sixteenth century. Geohumoral theory is outlined, for example, in the English prose writings of William Harrison, Baptist Goodall, Peter Heylyn, Fynes Moryson, Thomas Nashe, John Norden, Thomas Proctor, William Slatyer, Thomas Walkington, Thomas Wright, and in the popular English translations of texts by Juan Huarte, Levinus Lemnius, Pierre Charron, Louis Le Roy, and Jean Bodin.[15] Bodin's political writing and historiography were, in particular, highly influential in England. It is his thesis in *The Six Bookes of a Commonweale* (1606) that all effective rulers must know the "diversitie of mens humors, and the meanes how to discover the nature and disposition of the people" in order to "accommodat the estate to the humor of the citisens; and the lawes and ordinances to the nature of the place, persons, and time."[16] Just as a physician applies remedies that contravene the distempers of his patient, sovereign powers can institute laws that amend the particular imbalances of their country's population.

Ranging between both popular and elite sources – from the period's drama to medical texts to historiography – *English Ethnicity* intervenes in the current literary scholarship on race to disembed and recover the complex basis of Desdemona's knowledge.[17] As we shall see, early modern geohumoralism contradicts many of the racial stereotypes concerning the behavior and capacities of non-English "others" that began to emerge in the early modern period. Part of the argument I take up in chapter 6, "Othello's Jealousy," is that the spectacular representation of the Moor's passions in Shakespeare's play rearranges the older geohumoral knowledge and that this rearrangement accommodates the ongoing construction of modern racial categories. But more centrally, it is my argument in that chapter and throughout *English Ethnicity* that geohumoralism is fundamental to early modern English conceptions of how their own, more northern, bodies and minds were shaped and influenced by external forces. The environment – whether that meant the air, temperature, diet, and terrain, or the effects of education, rhetoric, or fashion – necessarily produced and destabilized early modern English selves.[18]

As the statement from *Batman uppon Bartholome* makes clear, Desdemona's assertion about the interaction between Africa's heat and Othello's temperament would necessarily invoke for an early modern audience the homologous tenet that the cold air in northern regions generates a body's humors. The Moor's violent metamorphosis not only does the essential cultural work of exploding a conventional (though now obscure) perception of Africans – as naturally cold and fixed in their humors – but it also, by implication, helps to revalue the northerner's natural temperament. In other words, I aim in my discussion of *Othello*, as in all my readings of early modern texts, to make plain what is at stake, ethnologically, for the English.

To comprehend the English people's understanding of ethnicity – their own and others' – we must begin with the recognition that they conceived of themselves and their island as "northern." England's northern climate and the English people's northern status colored their perspective on everything from fashion to medicine to politics.[19] This is not to say simply that chilly weather compelled the English to wear wool, but that a fundamental sense of displacement – derived from the British Isles' marginalized status in a set of classical texts that were revered and considered authoritative – gave rise to the notions that their bodies were intemperate, their culture borrowed and belated, and their nature barbarous.[20] The English prove to be entangled in a web of geographical determinism as they grappled with their own subscription to classically derived medical theories and natural philosophy. In both imaginative and non-imaginative literature, late sixteenth- and early seventeenth-century English writers struggle to stabilize and rehabilitate their northern identity.

The native English investment in geohumoralism can be exemplified briefly by referring to William Harrison's characterization of the "Generall Constitution of the Bodies of the Britons" in *The Description of Britaine* (1587). Initially Harrison exalts the Britons for their northern traits: they are "white in color, strong of bodie, and full of bloud, as people inhabiting neere the north, and farre from the equinoctiall line, where the soile is not so fruitful, and therefore the people not so feeble." His tone changes however when he concedes that the northern complexion is renowned more for its deficiencies:

And for that we dwell northward, we are commonlie taken by the forren historiographers, to be men of great strength and little policie, much courage and small shift, bicause of the weake abode of the sunne with us, whereby our braines are not made hot and warmed . . . affirming further, that the people inhabiting in the north parts are white of colour, blockish, uncivill, fierce and warlike, which qualities increase, as they come nearer the pole.[21]

Harrison helps us see, I propose, that to be white and British in the early modern period was not a badge of superiority but cast one instead on the margins as uncivil, slow-witted, and more bodily determined than those people living in more temperate zones.[22]   Though I believe we can trace, in different spheres (economic, religious, colonial, for example), various strands of thought that enabled the eventual construction of race in the seventeenth century, my primary interest in *English Ethnicity* is how, given its unflattering implications, the period's dominant somatic discourses may have instilled in the English a desire to reassess and reconceptualize notions of regional influence and ethnological inheritance.[23] As we shall see, it works to the English people's advantage to challenge and revise a body of knowledge that depicts them as impressible, barbaric, and inversely defined by the traits and temperament of dark peoples on the other side of the world.

Forgetting Africa

Recognizing that geohumoralism was not simply a theory that explained the appearance and behavior of "others" is the first step toward reframing its historical significance. Much in the same way that Shakespearean scholars have dismissed Desdemona's knowledge, early modern scholars in general have written off the viability of "climate theory" by misconstruing it as nothing more than an erroneous explanation of blackness.[24] In a narrative initiated by Winthrop Jordan in his important study *White Over Black*, the argument goes that when English travelers encountered the blackness of West Africans, they were unable to accommodate what they saw with their prevailing physiological theories.[25] Jordan asserts that Englishmen viewed "blackness in human beings [as] a peculiar and important point of difference" which set the African "radically *apart* from Englishmen."[26] Further citing as evidence the Elizabethan travel writers' puzzlement over the existence of lighter-skinned Indians in parallel latitudes, Jordan and others have concluded that the Renaissance writers' skepticism toward climatic explanations of blackness can be attributed to the rise of Baconian empiricism.[27]   The inherent peculiarity of black skin, it seems, produced a scientific skepticism regarding classical natural philosophy, which then led to the distinctly unscientific conclusion that dark complexions were a phenomenon that fell outside the bounds of nature.[28]

We should recognize, however, that this narrative suppresses vital contradictions and ideological struggles. It glosses over the inherent difficulty in transforming a widely accepted conception of blackness-as-natural into something inexplicable and unnatural, and it obscures the English desire to reconceive the northerner's pale, intemperate, and marginalized complexion as civilized and temperate. There is no question that black skin *becomes* a scientific problem during this period, and once conceived as a mystery, it is the fundamentally nonscientific "Curse of Ham" which then emerges as an explanation of its origins and significance. But to attribute this conceptual shift either to bewilderment or empiricism is to underestimate the complexity, endurance, and cultural significance of geohumoral theories of complexion. We need to acknowledge that the racial stereotypes that facilitated the Atlantic slave trade were incompatible with geohumoral tenets. Thus, England's nascent expansionist ideology helped to disrupt the accepted paradigms of scientific knowledge. Seeking to reorganize early modern ethnology along newly nationalist lines, racialist thinking estranged both blackness and whiteness (and their attendant associations) from their dominant, and far-from peculiar, homologies.[29]

Crucial to this process of estrangement was the forgetting of Africa's ancient and venerable associations. Classical writers such as Diodorus, for example, had viewed the Ethiopians as wise and extremely pious "first begotten of the earth," and this perspective lingered on in the abiding cultural belief that the African climate had given rise to their favored status.[30] During the Italian Renaissance there had been, we should note, explicit connections made between external blackness and Egyptian wisdom.[31] Hence the "revival of Platonism and Neoplatonism," as Karl Dannenfeldt has observed, "enhanced the role of Egypt as the original land of theologians and philosophers."[32] As I shall demonstrate in chapter 3, "An inside story of race: melancholy and ethnology," early modern geohumoralism associated the blackness produced by hot climates with prophecy and genial melancholy. Despite their reputed savagery, West Africans were not initially perceived as different in kind, but in terms of the more familiar Moors, Ethiopians, and Egyptians.[33] In *The Second Voyage to Guinea* (1554) for example, Robert Gainsh links the West Africans to North Africa and Ethiopia: "the people which now inhabite" the western coast, as well as in "the midle parts of Africa, as Libya the inner, and Nubia, with divers other great & large regions about the same, were in old time called Æthiopes and Nigritæ, which we now call Moores, Moorens, or Negroes, a people of beastly living..."[34] The implication is that the "old time" Ethiopians have degenerated into beastly "Negroes." Indeed, it was this residual sense of Africa as an ancient civilization that gave shape to the English writers' ambivalent construction of blackness as both noble and monstrous, civil and barbaric. Thus Othello can be both an "old black ram" and a noble Moor. And as the Atlantic slave trade gained momentum, Europeans began to deny Africa its place in classical history, and they accomplished this in part by establishing a fixed boundary between North and West Africa.[35]

I think we would do well to unsettle Jordan's thesis that blackness set Africans "radically *apart* from Englishmen." As I have begun to suggest, the tripartite structure of geohumoralism not only estranged northern whiteness and southern blackness but it also tended to intertwine the two as inversions of the other. We can see this plainly in William Harrison's portrait of his own countrymen, wherein he characterizes the bodies of the Britons by describing their dark southern counterparts. Unlike the Britons, the people living near the equator are warmed by the sun and possess the "contrarie gifts" of "blacknesse, wis-dome, civilitie, weakenesse, and cowardise." Indeed, it is the Britons' inverse, or "contrarie," relationship with the Africans that compels Harrison to reinter-pret the southerner's natural traits as corrupted qualities, declaring that these "gifts of theirs doo often degenerate into meere subtiltie, instabilitie, unfaithful-nesse, & crueltie."[36] Harrison's portrait of the early Britons illustrates how the classical tripartite structure is translated into an English binary of the northern self and the southern Other. Yet we must not confuse this binary relationship with the familiar racial hierarchy of "white over black." In modern racial bi-naries, the white "self" derives an assumed sense of stability and superiority from fixed, hierarchical categories of difference. For Harrison and his fellow countrymen, Britain's northern location excluded its inhabitants from the su-periority of temperance and moderation and positioned them as "other" to the normative middle. Moreover, the strange intimacy implied by the repeated pair-ing of northerners and southerners in geohumoral discourse makes objectifying and demonizing the darker "other" a deeply ambiguous impulse in Elizabethan and Jacobean England. Since blackness reflected the northerner's intemper-ance, its representation not only elicited fear and condemnation but also the Englishman's desire to appropriate and incorporate the properties of a southern complexion. As I discuss in chapter 3, England's late sixteenth-century vogue of melancholia serves as a prime example of the northern nation's ambivalence toward a temperament recognized by many to be indigenous to the south; while some northerners aimed to cultivate the inward blackness of melancholy, others condemned its appearance in England as a foreign affectation or infection.

In making his argument that blackness struck English travelers as both novel and inexplicable, Jordan turns again to Hakluyt's report of Robert Gainsh's account of the second voyage to Guinea (1554), which stands as one of the earliest records of England's involvement in the Atlantic slave trade. Gainsh provides a description of black slaves that employs the rhetoric of inversion that we saw in Harrison, but to highly different ends:

> [The English voyagers] brought with them certaine blacke slaves, whereof some were tall and strong men, and could wel agree with our meates and drinkes. The colde and moyst aire doth somewhat offend them. Yet doubtlesse men that are borne in hot Regions may better abide colde, then men that are borne in colde Regions may abide heate, forasmuch as vehement heate resolveth the radicall moysture of mens bodies, as colde constraineth and preserveth the same.[37]

It is not my intention to minimize the odious nature of this writer's intentions in assessing the value of the "black slaves," but I do want to suggest that this appeal to geohumoralism indicates not only a surprising familiarity with dark complex-ions but also some anxiety about the northern body's vulnerabilities. Interest in how northern "meates and drinkes" may "offend" the African's complexion echoes the advice manuals of the period, which dwell on the Englishman's notorious susceptibility to the effects of travel.[38] Certainly, the author's reflexive consideration of northern bodies is overshadowed by what appears to be a crude estimation of the slaves' prospective value as laborers, but this too is framed by the inverted logic of geohumoralism: the "tall and strong men" receive greater scrutiny not simply for the intrinsic value of strength and height but also for the compatibility between "tall and strong men" and English "meates and drinkes." Geohumoral tenets held that northerners were physically hearty and well-nourished by their equally hearty native diets; southern air, meat, and drinks, on the other hand, were noted for producing weak, but wise inhabitants. Ironically, the English observer presumes that those black slaves who reflect the Englishman's alleged body type will prove to be the more adaptable and worthy investments. In short, this encounter should not be read as an awakening of empiricism or scientific curiosity but as a reshuffling of old knowledge under new pressures.

Where geohumoralism and empiricism seem to collide most dramatically for modern scholars and early modern skeptics is when faced with the facts that blackness remained black in colder climates and could be transmitted from parent to child. The most frequently cited text in historical accounts of early modern racialism in England, George Best's *A True Discourse* (1578), raises these very points to assert that blackness should not be ascribed to environmental forces:

> I my selfe have seene an Ethiopian as blacke as a cole brought into England, who taking a faire English woman to wife, begat a sonne in all respects as blacke as the father was, although England were his native countrey, and an English woman his mother: whereby it seemeth this blacknes proceedeth rather of some natural infection of that man, which was so strong, that neither the nature of the Clime, neither the good complexion of the mother concurring, coulde any thing alter, and therefore, wee cannot impute it to the nature of the Clime . . . And the most probable cause to my judgement is, that this blacknesse proceedeth of some naturall infection of the first inhabitants of that Countrey, and so all the whole progenie of them descended, are still polluted with the same blot of infection.[39]

Though scholars have long focused on the incipient racism of Best's argument, which appears fairly obvious, they have neglected to appreciate his immediate motives for identifying blackness as a "natural infection."[40] Best, we should understand, is contributing to a genre of promotional tracts aimed at persuading the English that they would not be ineluctably altered by moving to and residing in a foreign climate. However troubling their native environment was perceived to be, travel, it was understood, exacerbated the English people's imperfections.[41] In 1585, for example, the Barbary Company attempted to reassure English representatives bound for Morocco that the country's air "is as holsome as can be, and yourself not altered neither in favor nor person, but helthful and in as good likinge as you were at your departure." But at least one ambassador, Henry Roberts, was purported to be "undon by the unaturall clyment in that countrie."[42] Addressing the "Merchants of London," Best argues aggressively that Africa is an "earthly Paradise" where English travelers can easily "abide the heat."[43] Observing that the cold air in England threatens "injury" (which is why the English natives must wear "so many clothes"), Best maintains that Africa is more temperate than England.[44] Thus, Best embraces the basic principles of geohumoralism, conceding that a "certeine agreement of nature... [exists] betweene the place and the thing bred in that place," but he also recognizes that the English people's fears of their own vulnerability may be assuaged by interpreting blackness as anomalous and peculiar.[45]

Though it works to Best's advantage to cast blackness as an infection, and thereby as a phenomenon unrelated to the effects of the environment, many of Best's contemporaries had little trouble reconciling the transmission of traits with geohumoral influences.[46] Reaching more audiences than Best's *Discourse*, for example, was Shakespeare's *Titus Andronicus* (1594), wherein the pairing of Aaron the Moor and Tamora the Goth produce a dark-skinned baby while in Rome. Significantly, the play makes clear that the child's blackness was not presumed to be an inevitability. As Aaron is heard to explain, if the "bull and cow are both milk-white / They never do beget a coal-black calf" (5. 1. 31–2), but when one parent is white and the other black, Nature might give the baby his father's or his "mother's look" (line 29). In fact, Aaron's own "countryman" Muliteus and his light-skinned wife have also had a baby in Rome, and "[h]is child is like to her, fair as [the Goths] are" (4. 2. 152–4). Aaron's skin color or "seal" may be stamped in the baby's face (line 69) but if Tamora's "seed" had been dominant, the child would have resembled his mother. Climate determines the color and temperament of general populations, but the transmission of traits also depends on the parents.[47]

These are the conclusions of Spanish physician Juan Huarte in his treatise on humoralism and education, *The Examination of Men's Wits* (1594).[48] What Best had identified as a "natural infection," Huarte terms a "rooted quality." Though a people's shared humoral complexion is shaped by their native environment, these circumstances still allow for certain traits – or rooted qualities – to pass from parent to child. It remains indisputable, Huarte observes, that over very long periods of time people become "conformable to the countrey where they inhabited, to the meats which they fed upon, to the waters which they dranke, & to the aire which they breathed." But once the environment has produced certain ingrained characteristics, generations of descendants are able to maintain and transmit these same traits even when residing outside their ancestral region (p. 195). Notably, it is the dark skin and admirable wisdom of the Egyptians that stands as Huarte's most powerful example:

though 200 yeares have passed . . . sithens the first Aegyptians came out of Aegypt into Spaine, yet their posterite have not forlorne that their delicacie of wit and promptnesse, nor yet that rosted colour which their auncestors brought with them from Aegypt.

Just as the Moors may "communicate the colour of their elders, by means of their seed, though they be out of Aethiopia," so does "the force of mans seed . . . receiveth thereinto any well rooted qualitie" (p. 199). Moreover, Huarte explains, blackness is not the only quality that may prove "well rooted":

in the engendering of a creature, two seedes should concurre; which being mingled, the mightier should make the forming and the other serve for nourishment. And this is seen evidently so to be: for if a blackamore beget a white woman with child, & a white man a *negro* woman, of both these unions, wil be borne a creature, partaking of either qualitie. (p. 316)[49]

We must keep in mind, I submit, that in rejecting the possibility that blackness is a consequence of the kind of geohumoral effects that Huarte describes, George Best not only reframed the African's complexion as a scientific mystery, but he also swept away an inherited knowledge that had long identified blackness with wisdom and constancy. Notoriously, Best displaced geohumoralism with a unique exegesis of Genesis, so as to attribute black skin to the "Curse of Ham."[50]

As historian Benjamin Braude has demonstrated, the curse of Ham – as an explanation of blackness – had not yet become a dominant cultural belief at the time of George Best's writing.[51] A quick survey of the editorial changes to Peter Heylyn's geographical survey, *Microcosmos*, attests to its growing popularity during the seventeenth century: the 1621 edition makes no mention of the curse; in 1627, the text introduces the explanation as a "foolish tale," but by 1666, it tentatively endorses the legend.[52] What the Hametic curse provides for western critics today, and provided for European authors in the past, is a simplification of the meaning of blackness: blackness signifies sin and servitude. As Jordan has observed, "it is suggestive that the first Christian utilizations of this theme came during the sixteenth century – the first great century of overseas exploration," as well as the first century of England's involvement in the Atlantic slave trade.[53] It is also important to recognize that its emergence during this period worked in tandem with ideological erasures taking place in more "scientific" discourses. As natural philosophy shifted the focus away from theories of color variation to the mystery of blackness, religious discourse responded with a scriptural explanation of that mystery. Dislodged from the realm of natural "science" and its association with humoralism, blackness was reinvented as a sign of inferiority to justify a growing slave economy.

It was only during the early modern period that writers began to trace Ham's lineage strictly to Africa.[54] Indeed, as late as 1548, the links between Noah's sons and particular regions were tentative enough for John Bale to trace the ancestral line of "Albion," King of Britain, to Ham in his 1548 catalogue of

British authors.[55] And apparently this genealogy was not as outlandish as it might seem to us: as Denys Hay explains, "There were two quite contrary accounts of the origin of the British" in the medieval text *Historia Britonum*:

One of these represents Brutus, the eponymous founder of the Britains, as descended from Ham; the other as descended from Japheth. The generations are traced back in the first case to Silvius (Brutus's father), who was the son of Aeneas and descended from Jupiter and Saturn, themselves deriving from Zoroaster the grandson of Ham.[56]

Modern attachments to the myths of racial lineage have made it difficult for us to recognize the global fluidity of sixteenth-century British genealogies. In one version of *A View of the State of Ireland*, for example, Edmund Spenser suggests that the Irish have Carthaginian roots. In a similar vein, the Scots countered England's Brut mythography with their own claim to an Egyptian ancestry. And the antiquarian John Twynne argued that the Welsh were descendants of the dark-skinned Phoenicians. As Twynne explains it, Britain's northern climate had lightened the skin of subsequent generations, yet their long-held custom of painting themselves denoted their southern lineage.[57]

There is no question that Best's *Discourse* provides a dramatic example of how Europe's growing investment in the Atlantic slave trade was inextricably tied to the early modern construction of race. Moreover, his text is part of a long tradition of negative associations with blackness – particularly in the discourses of religion and aesthetics – associations that would become crucial matter in eighteenth- and nineteenth-century constructions of the racialized "other."[58] But these issues, which have been ably demonstrated by others, are not the subject of my study. I am, instead, interested in heeding Emily Bartels's reminder of

how experimental and disjointed England's overseas activities were, how fractured its visions and random its advances. The instance of Africa . . . makes us question the predictability and inevitability of the outcome – the long history of oppression that was, when viewed through what preceded, not always in the cards.[59]

In focusing on England's eventual commitment to the Atlantic slave trade and on those aspects of early modern discourse that subjugated Africans, denigrated blackness, and helped to naturalize a link between color and slavery, we have overlooked an ethnological history that failed to predict the outcome that we now know. *English Ethnicity* resists recapitulating the accession of white over black. It attempts instead to retrieve the counterintuitive notions of ethnicity and "race" that the now-dominant narrative of oppression aimed to erase: the representations of northern "whiteness" and English identity as barbaric, marginalized, and mutable, and the long-neglected perceptions of "blackness" as a sign of wisdom, spirituality, and resolution. Readings that ignore such expressions of ethnic and racial differences risk confirming, rather than historicizing, the normative status of whiteness and Englishness.

Northern perspectives

It is my argument in the first half of this book that in sixteenth-century England humoralism is ethnology. Estranged and marginalized from the middle, temperate climate of the Mediterranean, the English were compelled to interpret their classically derived natural philosophy from a northern perspective. Medical advice in Thomas Cogan's *The Haven of Helthe* (1584), for example, is filtered through the understanding that England has a cold, moist climate. In the preface to *The Passions of the Minde in Generall* (1604) – a handbook on rhetoric and the management of one's emotions – Thomas Wright advises his countrymen to use his book to ameliorate their northern inclinations.[60] And, as we shall see, English efforts to reconstruct their own ethnic identity as the norm is what helps elevate the sanguine complexion to its ideal – but markedly regionalized – status in the Renaissance.[61]

In reading early modern humoral discourse as culturally inscripted with ethnic interests, I am following the model of Gail Kern Paster's work, which has shown that humoral texts are never socially neutral but deeply inflected with narratives of gender and class distinctions. In much the same way, the larger framework of geohumoralism is organized by the hierarchies of gender and class.[62] The tripartite mapping of northern, southern, and temperate zones establishes correspondences between temperance, masculinity, and good governors. Laborers and effeminate men prosper in the extreme regions. Indeed, much of England's anxiety regarding geohumoralism stemmed from the troubling implications it brought to bear on English constructions of the elite male. When read through the grid of classical gender distinctions, the northerner's fleshiness, fluidity, temperature, and even color could be cast in feminine, or barbaric, or other socially subordinate terms. It mattered, for example, that the ideal somatic type for the male in classical Roman culture was "*inter nigrum et pallidum*" and that a "pale, white skin in a male indicated a lack of manliness."[63]

Distinct from modern racial thinking, which relies on fixed categories and a fixed hierarchy, early modern ethnology values the good of *temperance* – an elusive, but theoretically achievable, balance of humors. There is a crucial correspondence, I maintain, between the elusiveness of ethnological temperance – the ideally moderate, humorally balanced complexion that the English lacked and coveted – and the precarious balancing act of elite male identity. Paster has illustrated that there was "small sanction within the codes of humoral masculinity for the cold male and even less sanction within humorality in general for the choleric or sanguine woman."[64] But, in fact, the contradictions and conflicts in early modern humoralism indicate that none of the four complexions could ensure a stable masculine subject. To embody and express masculinity successfully, the classical ideal male must sustain *crasis* or temperance, a harmonious mixture of all four qualities, warm, cold, dry, and moist.[65] Masculinity and social superiority, maintained by temperance, could be undone by the predominance of any one humor. Even within temperate regions, minor "differences of style of life, climate and diet" produced puzzling questions, for example, about the body's gendered identity, such as whether the "hottest female is colder than the coldest male."[66] Once translated to the north and south, however, the conflicts in the discourse were exacerbated. On a local level, English gentlemen would work to distinguish themselves from women and the lower orders as more temperate and self-contained, but on the world stage, they found themselves character-ized as excessively pale, moist, soft-fleshed, inconstant, and permeable.[67] The English, in a geohumoral context, were defined by intemperance.

We would do well to remember that Pico della Mirandola's famous affir-mation of the Renaissance man's freedom and exceptionality, his ability to fashion himself "in whatever shape [he] shalt prefer," is premised on a cosmic order which places man "at the world's center that [he] mayest from thence more easily observe whatever is in the world."[68] Thus, before the Renaissance *Englishman* could fashion himself "in whatever shape" he preferred, he first had to counter or accommodate the effects of his placement at the world's edge. Much of *English Ethnicity* is concerned with revealing and exploring how the English sought to rectify their marginal status, and it is my argument that these efforts took two basic, sometimes contradictory, forms: (1) a discursive rearrangement of the inherited knowledge, which aimed, for example, to locate value in "northernness"; (2) a manipulation of a whole range of environmental influences (from diet to education to fashion) that aimed to alter or remedy "northernness."

Turning once again to William Harrison's discussion in *The Description of Britaine* (1587) of the Britons' natural "constitution," we find an apt example of what I mean by discursive rearrangement. It is in Harrison's interest to establish the ultimate virtue and strength of his own people's complexion and to detach white, northern complexions from their "uncivill" and "blockish" associations. Rather than suggesting that the Britons should change themselves, Harrison chooses, instead, to defend humoral excesses:

by this meanes therefore it commeth to passe, that he whose nature inclineth generallie to phlegme, cannot but be courteous: which joined with strength of bodie, and sinceritie of behavior (qualities universallie granted to remaine so well in our nation, as other inhabitants of the north) I cannot see what may be an hinderance whie I should not rather conclude, that the Britons doo excell such as dwell in the hoter countries, than for want of craft and subtilties to come anie whit behind them.[69]

What proves comic here, of course, is that phlegm carries few, if any, positive qualities in humoral discourse. Though he makes a valiant effort, Harrison's attempt to invest phlegm – a traditionally weak and effeminate humor – with "courtesy" and "sinceritie" was one of many failed tactics in the ongoing construction of Englishness.[70]

As I demonstrate in chapter 2, "British Ethnology," the question of how to remedy, reform, or regenerate their native complexion was a point of controversy for the early modern English. A treatise published in England in 1591 advocated a cathartic method, advising northerners to purge the "grosse humour ingendred in them, by reason of the grossness and coldnes of the aier."[71] In *The Passions of the Minde in Generall* (1604), Thomas Wright entreated his countrymen to bolster their protean and vulnerable natures by judiciously adopting a kind of "southern" wariness in their carriage. In a similar vein, John Milton urged his nation to temper their northern excesses and "natural political deficiencies" by "import[ing] civil virtues from the 'best ages' and those situated in more favorable climates."[72] Those following in the footsteps of Roger Ascham's *The Scolemaster* (1570), however, proved concerned that the Englishman's impressible nature (and naturally spongy brain!) would lead him to absorb foreign vice indiscriminately.[73] In *The English Ape* (1588), for example, William Rankins maintains that his countrymen had been created "perfect" by their climate but their incessant importation of foreign customs and fashions had succeeded in tainting their innately malleable complexions. Travel, education, literature, government, religion, diet, custom, fashion, and the theater were all cited in the early modern period as sources of both remedy and further corruption in the Englishman's pursuit of a temperance that belied his natural complexion.

We may be compelled to ask at this point why England had become so acutely aware of its northern identity in the sixteenth and early seventeenth centuries. Kim F. Hall recently attributed the development of "racialism" during this period to England's loss of "its traditional insularity" as it moved from "geographic isolation into military and mercantile contest with other countries."[74] Yet at the same time that England became more of a presence internationally, the nation's symbolic ties to the Mediterranean – the perceived center of the world – were severed by its break with Rome. In addition to a realignment of theological and political affiliations, the Reformation compelled England to imagine its identity in terms of detachment and division from the center.[75] In various ways Elizabethan and Jacobean England continued to understand its historical significance through Rome and Roman values, but the British people's status as northerners became increasingly important – as a source of both anxiety and pride.

When the Reformation ignited interest in the origins of the English church, it also turned the focus of English historiography northward. Early modern scholars such as William Camden did not simply reject Geoffrey of Monmouth's fiction that the Britons were descendants of ancient Troy, they looked to Caesar's *Commentaries on the Gallic War* as the official beginning of Britain's recorded history, and this shift in historiography emphasized the northern barbarity of Britain's origins.[76] Jean Bodin's *Methodus*, the influential guide to historiographic writing in the sixteenth century, classified all northerners – be they Picts, Scots, Celts, Goths, or Britons – as Scythians; they shared a climate, a genealogy, and a set of barbaric traits associated with the classical northern stereotype.

As descendants of Troy, the Britons had claimed a noble lineage, which could be accommodated to the traditional terms of classical ethnography: as Giraldus Cambrensis explained, the "Britons...transplanted from the hot and parched regions...still retain their brown complexion and that natural warmth of temper from which their confidence is derived...from thence arose that courage, that nobleness of mind, that ancient dignity, that acuteness of understanding."[77] Thus, the warm Mediterranean climate had implanted the Trojans' innate virtues, which succeeding generations maintained despite Britain's northern environment. By tracing its earliest ancestors to the Mediterranean, England's myth of a Trojan genealogy had circumvented the embarrassments of a northern descent. But as the myth rapidly lost ground, English writers were compelled to acknowledge the implications of their barbaric ancestry.[78]

While faith in the westward and northward translation of empire was eased by the Trojan mythography, the Englishman's autochthonous roots constituted a more estranged relationship with the classical world and humanist studies. The northern appropriation of Mediterranean texts and values also carried the terms of England's displacement from the center of the world. For if the English no longer see themselves as descendants of Troy, it is the classical portraits of northerners, rather than Mediterraneans, who come to represent the English people's ancestral roots. What Camden and his followers found in the classical texts were accounts of northern savagery that proved indistinguishable from the descriptions of barbarians in the south – particularly when it came to sexual mores. In *Forms of Nationhood* Richard Helgerson turned our attention to the Elizabethan writers' efforts to purge or transform the perceived barbarism of their own language and laws, but his analysis also gestures toward the deeper cultural fear that the "English nature [itself was] unalterably resistant to the nurture of civility."[79] In facing their northern roots, the English confronted the possibility that they were the barbaric progeny of a dissolute, mingled, and intemperate race.

Without the Brutish myth attesting to England's inherent nobility, William Camden made the argument that the English people's native barbarism had been purged by the Roman conquest. In this context, the English could still lay claim to civility – but not an innate civility. Whereas the Brut mythography had allowed the Britons some identification with the greatness of their conquerors, Camden's narrative tells the story of domestic barbarism extirpated by the triumph of a foreign civilization. Submission to an alien authority supplanted a glorious ancestry. Camden implies further that, in addition to martial prowess and bodily strength, the need for subjugation and reformation may also be intrinsic to the northerner's natural complexion. At the same time, his account suggests that the English people may be predisposed to embracing foreign cultures. In other words, the historical perspective of Camden's *Britannia*, in which the horizontal transplantation of customs and culture may, or may not, redress the lineal transmission of ignoble traits – this perspective can be construed as a framework to the local controversies over fashion, travel, and diet.[80] Faced with the uncertain implications of an obscure past, sixteenth- and seventeenth-century English writers struggled with the possibility that their countrymen were exceedingly impressionable, a quality that promised either their salvation or their ruin.

Northern "racialism," I contend, emerged in part out of a desire to relocate and secure the generative sources of greatness, and the first impulse toward the construction of an English race manifests itself in the form of philobarbarism. Rather than lamenting the deficiencies of the northern subject, English writers began to embrace the stereotype. We can even detect in Edmund Spenser's condemnation of the Irish-Scythians a grudging admiration of their northern barbarism: "very valiaunt, and hardie, for the most part great indurers of colde, labour, hunger, and all hardnesse, very active and strong of hand, very swift of foot..."[81] To cite a crucial example in the history of racial construction, Richard Verstegan's *A Restitution of Decayed Intelligence* (1605), renowned for its argument that the English are primarily descended from the Saxons, reveals the racialist bias of philobarbarism.

In privileging Tacitus over Caesar as the primary classical source of English genealogy, Verstegan aims to establish two significant points: (1) the English are not the progeny of Caesar's promiscuous and mingled Britons; (2) the heroic qualities of the Germans necessarily repudiate the less flattering tenets of climate theory.[82] Verstegan emphasizes Tacitus' praise of the Germanic northern tribes for their chastity and ethnic purity. These ancient Germans were never subdued, they remained "unmixed with forrain people" and "that of all barbarous people, they only did content themselves one man with one woman."[83] Yet geohumoralism threatens to undermine Verstegan's construction of Germanic virtue :

And as touching the knowledge of the people, what learning or skil is there among men that they [the Germans] exceed not in? It is a meer imaginarie suposal, to think that the temperature of the ayr of any region, doth make the inhabitants more or lesse learned or ingenious ... I do confesse that certain nations have certain vertues & vices more apparently proper to them then to others, but this is not to bee understood otherwise to proceed, then of some successive or heritable custome remaining among them, the case concerning learning and scyence beeing far different: for where was there ever more learning and scyence then in Greece, and where is there now in the world more barbarisme? What moste excellently learned men, & great doctors of the Churche, hath Africa brought foorth, as Tertulian, Optatus, Lanctantius, S. Cyprian, and S. Augustyn? And with what learned men is Africa in our tyme acquainted? Contrariwise in the flowrishing dayes of the Romans, how utterly without the knowledge of letters, scyences and artes, were the Germans; and how do the Germans now a dayes flowrish in all learning and cunning.[84]

That Verstegan feels the need to make this impassioned refutation of traditional climate theory reveals the degree to which the temperature of the air was perceived to determine English identity. Shedding the tripartite structure of geohumoral discourse, however, does not prove easy: by insisting that the decline of southern greatness confirms its emergence in the north, Verstegan still relies on the logic of geohumoralism. Yet his text also registers the first stirrings of an English identity that is both "peculiar" and "pure" – hence, racialized. He essentializes the English people's northern nature by detaching them from the less flattering, and more unsettling, effects of a cold, harsh climate.[85]

It is significant that Verstegan's historiographical "discovery" of England's Germanic origins emerged amidst the ethnic tensions of the Jacobean union project. In chapter 7 I consider how Shakespeare's *Cymbeline* is framed by these concerns. Performed around 1610, when Camden first published an English translation of *Britannia* and informed by Camden's revisionary historiography, *Cymbeline* spins out an ethnological fantasy in which the Scots submit to Anglo-British rule and the English emerge as a race bolstered by their climate but unaffected by Britain's early history of mingled genealogies and military defeats. The embrace of Posthumus promises a unified Britain and a civilized Scotland, but the rediscovery of Arviragus and Guiderius – who prove to be the Saxon branches – provides the English with a "racially" pure ancestry.

As a rather dubious pastime of "civilization," the English theatre became a lightning rod for the ethnological concerns that I have outlined here. It is my contention that the prominent dramatists of the period, Christopher Marlowe, Ben Jonson, and William Shakespeare, were all profoundly engaged not only in the discursive rearrangement of classical geohumoralism – as my arguments regarding both *Othello* and *Cymbeline* should indicate – but also in theatre's potential for tempering or corrupting the northerner's humors. The multivalent nature of theatrical power nourished and fed on the English people's perception of their natural complexion as defective, in need of amelioration, and exceedingly susceptible to all kinds of external influences, from the heat of rhetoric to the chill of their own climate.[86]

As Thomas Wright suggests in *The Passions of the Minde in Generall* (1604), the English people's proclivity for fashion, aping, and imitation made them not unlike "Stage-players."[87] And yet, Wright himself would draw a distinction, I propose, between the English people's susceptibility to imitation and the subtle southerner's capacity (as he is characterized in Wright's preface) to "dissemble better his owne passions, and use himselfe therein more circumspectly."[88] At first glance we might mistake both these figures for an empowered Proteus – that sometimes positive icon of Renaissance aspirations that Jonas Barish describes in *The Antitheatrical Prejudice* – but the constitutional difference between the Italian and the northern Englishman marks a crucial boundary between those shape-shifters who are "directing [their] own transformations" and those who are "passively submitting to them."[89] My fourth chapter, "*Tamburlaine* and the Staging of White Barbarity," takes up the problem of English impressibility as it is censured by the period's anti-theatricalists. Critics of the English playhouses, I argue, express nostalgia for the hearty, tough complexions of their barbaric "Scythian" ancestors, and they identify the theatre, in particular, as a source of their nation's current state of softness and vulnerability. By staging a barbaric Scythian hero, Christopher Marlowe not only taps into the ethnological anxieties of the period, but he also transforms the anti-theatrical ideal – the hardened Scythian soldier – into the epitome of theatricality.

Though we can, as Barish has done, easily discern anti-theatrical prejudices in Ben Jonson's writings, we should also recognize that Jonson took seriously the theatre's power for remedy and humoral reform. In chapter 5 "Temperature and Temperance in Ben Jonson's *The Masque of Blackness*," I suggest that Jonson wrote his first masque for the Jacobean court with dual motives: to fasten his theatrical forces to the King's capacity as governor to temper his unruly citizens and to offer up a mythopoetic remedy to the vulnerabilities associated with northern complexions. Upon King James' accession in 1603, the proposed union with Scotland threatened to remove the English nation further north and further away from the civility of temperance. By foregrounding the subject of "complexion" in relation to the geohumoral component of King James' political theory and the Scottish claim to southern origins, Jonson aims to re-dress the inherent barbarism of England's northern neighbors. *The Masque of Blackness*, like *Othello*, is on the cusp – between older ethnological values and emergent racial ones. Though we have recognized an incipient racialism in the Ethiopians' quest for a physical metamorphosis from black to white, we have missed how the masque also equates the transmission of ancient wisdom northward – from Ethiopia to Egypt to Britannia – with the incorporation of internal blackness.

It should strike us as more than a coincidence that external "blackness" is severed from the positive effects of the southern climate and reinterpreted as a sign of depravity at the same time that the English people's northern roots are the subject of great scrutiny. Just as the English were coming to terms with their own inherent barbarism, their contact with other "barbarians" increased. We need to reinterpret the Englishmen's encounters in West Africa with the understanding that their own sense of whiteness and ethnicity was in flux. And we need to recognize how the erasure of Africa from the civilized world, and the reinterpretation of "blackness" as monstrous and unnatural, allowed for the construction of a European race that united a wide range of colors and complexions under an invisible badge of inherited superiority. *English Ethnicity* aims to recover Desdemona's knowledge, but more than that, this book seeks to understand how and why Desdemona came to be proven wrong.

Part I

Climatic culture: the transmissions and transmutations of ethnographic knowledge

[The Elizabethans] had to know themselves as the barbarous or inferior other, know themselves from the viewpoint of the more refined or more successful cultures of Greece, Rome, and contemporary Europe, before they could undertake the project of national self-making. In this sense, to be English was to be other – both before their work began and after it had been accomplished. Before, it was the otherness of the barbarian, the inferior. After, it was the otherness of the model of civility into which they had projected themselves.

Richard Helgerson, *Forms of Nationhood*[1]

...Hippocrates' *Airs, Waters, and Places*, rather than the histories of Herodotus, became a key text as well as a blueprint, albeit inaccurate, for the origins of what came to be termed as 'the Caucasian races' of Europe.

Ivan Hannaford, *Race: The History of an Idea in the West*[2]

But of all the ancient authors, Hippocrates ... exercised the greatest influence on Rabelais ... all the works contained in the [Hippocratic] anthology present a grotesque image of the body; the confines dividing it from the world are obscured, and it is most frequently shown open and with its interior exposed. Its exterior aspect is not distinct from the inside, and the exchange between the body and the world is constantly emphasized.

Mikhail Bakhtin, *Rabelais and His World*[3]

The ghost of Hippocrates: geohumoral history
      in the West

What do most people assume about the relationship between climates and temperaments? Our intuition seems to tell us that soaring thermometers make people passionate and testy, while chilly climes tend to breed reserved, chilly people. Thus, however antiquated early modern notions of climatic influence may seem, some part of us finds it logical or natural, for example, that the early moderns would believe that the "intense heat" of Africa produced intemperate lust.[1] What we fail to see is that our "intuition" is, in fact, the product of a long history of racialist thinking. The central aim of this chapter is to provide readers with a primer on classical climate theory and on the complex ways early moderns negotiated and synthesized this revered and authoritative knowledge for their own ethnological purposes. It just so happens that in exploring the transmission of this classical discourse, we will also unsettle the association that scholars have long presumed to be an unshakeable early modern commonplace: the presumed link between sexual desire and hot climates. In the course of this chapter, I will suggest that sexuality became a central focus of the racializing process in the Renaissance in part because it was an issue almost entirely absent from the classical texts. In the ancient texts on geographical differences, courage or wit, rather than sexuality, tended to be the indices of a people's predominant temperament. The one exception is Hippocrates' *Airs, Waters, Places*, which ascribes effeminacy and impotence to the "Scythians," the tribe of people residing in the frigid north.

It is also my argument in this chapter that by attending to the traces of Hippocrates' shadowy and often indirect influence on Renaissance geohumoralism we can discern some of the ideological impulses – sexual stereotyping being one – at work in early modern ethnological thought.[2] We need to recognize that *Airs, Waters, Places* plays a crucial yet peculiar role in the history of environmental theory. It is the first classical text to establish that particular climates have particular effects on the body's humors, and then to frame this "medical" or "biological" knowledge as a system for understanding the culture and innate behavior of a particular group of people: "Climates differ," Hippocrates writes, "and cause differences in character."[3] But, significantly, *Airs, Waters, Places* is

Figure 1 Ancient Britons, a watercolor (1574) by Lucas de Heere, *Corte beschryuinghe van Engheland, Schotland, ende Irland* (1660).

also an incomplete text: the portions that describe Africa, including Libya and Egypt, were lost well before the Renaissance.

As I noted in the introduction, most classical ethnographic discussions of one region are paired with a description of that region's antipodal twin: an account of the north is presented as an inversion of the south, and vice versa – a pattern identified as the "Egyptian and Scythian *logoi*" of Herodotus.[4] Indeed, we know that Hippocrates initially followed this logic and understood the Scythians to be antithetical to the Egyptians, whose "peculiarities," he notes in passing, are due to the heat instead of the cold.[5] However, since Hippocrates' description of Africa is missing, the first and most complete articulation of geohumoralism leaves a one-sided legacy. We cannot underestimate the importance of the fact that our earliest theory of a somatically based concept of ethnicity accounted for the strange habits, temperament, and excessively white appearance of a tribe of northerners.[6] For early modern northern Europeans, the alterity of their own ancestors, as Hippocrates described them, would prove to be a persistent problem as they labored to construct their ethnic identity. And, as we shall see, Renaissance geohumoralists could only infer from Hippocrates' portrait of the north what the ancient writer may have concluded about the south.

Airs, Waters, Places is also unique in that it is the only significant classical text to maintain that the relationship between the atmosphere and a person's humors is analogous: in the Hippocratic paradigm, cold, moist air engenders cold, moist bodies. Indeed, Hippocrates' conclusions most resemble modern "intuitive" assumptions about regional traits (that cold environments would breed cool dispositions), and yet he stands alone among the ancient climate theorists on this point. Other classical writers will consistently argue for a counteractive relationship between internal and external temperatures, that is, cold air makes for hot blood. Given that Hippocrates is in the minority, it is not surprising to discover that most (but not all) early modern writers reject his theory of thermodynamics.

It may also be true that Hippocrates' theory of temperatures gains few sixteenth-century adherents because it proves so unflattering to those early modern Europeans identified as "northern." The northerners in *Air, Waters, Places* are a phlegmatic tribe of people – exceedingly, and unappealingly, pale and soft – the very embodiment of their cold, wet surroundings:

The body cannot become hardened where there are such small variations in climate; the mind, too, becomes sluggish. For these reasons their bodies are heavy and fleshy, their joints are covered, they are watery and relaxed. The cavities of their bodies are extremely moist, especially the belly, since, in a country of such a nature and under such climatic conditions, the bowels cannot be dry.[7]

Moreover, for Hippocrates, the extreme force of Scythia's environment trumps normative gender differences: "All the men are fat and hairless and likewise all the women, and the two sexes resemble one another" (p. 164). This lack of gender distinctions is, in fact, the Scythians' predominant trait: they are, Hippocrates posits, the "most effeminate race of all mankind" (p. 166). Lacking the generative heat necessary for procreation, Scythian men suffer from impotence, or what became known in later texts as the "scythian disease," for they "lack sexual desire because of the moistness of their constitution and the softness and coldness of their bellies," making it "impossible for the Scythians to be a prolific race" (p. 165).[8] In this topsy-turvy world, the dominance of phlegm not only determines the nature of a people but their customs as well. The men "accept their unmanliness and dress as women, act as women and join with women in their toil" (p. 166). Male submissiveness, in turn, produces a female-dominated society: the women behave as Amazons – searing off their right breasts so that they can "ride horses and shoot arrows and hurl javelins" (pp. 162–3). We have to wonder if the classical interest in Britain's warrior women, represented in Caesar and Tacitus, was fed not only by the ancient associations between Amazons and Scythia but also by Hippocrates' contention that northern men were effeminate.

Though most northern Europeans were inclined to reject its tenets and its unflattering characterization of the northern temperament, *Airs, Waters, Places* still proved a powerful force in early modern geohumoralism. Certainly the recurrent presence of fierce northern women in Shakespeare's canon – Lady Macbeth, Tamora, Cymbeline's queen, Goneril, and Regan, to name a few – suggests that the naturalized link between northernness and female savagery established by *Airs, Waters, Places* eventually assumed local significance on the early modern English stage.[9] But it is, I maintain, the anomalous status of Hippocrates' treatise that makes it a perverse progenitor of early modern western ethnology.[10] Hippocrates' conclusion, for example, that northerners were phlegmatically passive – though often rejected in the Renaissance as humorally inaccurate – is what gives Renaissance writers the "scientific" opening they needed to refute the dominant classical portrait of *dispassionate* southerners. That is to say, inverting Hippocrates' vision of the north supported the early moderns' growing interest in characterizing Africans as excessively passionate, and thereby in need of subjugation. As we shall see, Hippocrates' thesis that extreme climates produced men and women whose sexual practices and gendered behavior challenged the temperate "norm" becomes a dynamic component of early modern ethnology.

Classical legacies

Sometime between 1605 and 1607, Thomas Walkington's *The Optick Glasse of Humors* was printed in London and subsequently reissued four times over the next fifty years. Recognized by scholars as a popular but fairly late contribution to early modern Galenic physiology, *The Optick Glasse* stands as an excellent example of the skewed but powerful influence of Hippocrates' treatise – an influence that, once detected, helps us see some of the ethnological interests of English humoralism.[11] Not unlike other humoral writers of the period,

Walkington devotes some serious discussion to whether the "soule sympathizeth with the body and followeth her crasis and temperature."[12] As Michael C. Schoenfeldt has suggested, the following passage in *The Optick Glasse* typifies the dual interests of early modern humoralism: the acknowledged possibility of material influences on the soul and the anxious insistence upon an "immaterial core self"[13]:

> We must not imagine the minde to be passible, being altogether immateriall that it selfe is affected with any of these corporall things, but onely in respect of the instruments which are the hand-maids of the soule: as if the spirits be inflamed, the passages of the humors dammed up, the braine stuffed with smoakie fumes, or any phlegmaticke matter, the blood too hote and too thicke, as is usuall in the *Scythians* & those in the septentrionall parts, who are of all men endowed with the least portion of witt and pollicie . . .[14]

What fascinates me about this passage is that for Walkington the question of whether or not the soul follows the temperature of the body transmutes into a discussion of how Scythians are determined by the "temperature of the ayre." Indeed, it is the intemperate example of the Scythian's complexion that best exemplifies for Walkington the potential encroachment of the body on the soul for the very reason that the climatic conditions in the north inflame the spirits (those subtle communicators between the soul and the body), dam up the humors, and heat the blood.[15] Thus, Walkington's uneasiness that the soul may be influenced by the body has been translated into the narrower concern that the northern Scythian's soul, by virtue of its being so deeply enmeshed in a body of inflamed spirits, may be affected with "corporall things." Walkington need not have read *Airs, Waters, Places* to manifest Hippocrates' imprint; indeed, his appeal to climate theory actually counters Hippocrates' concept of an analogous relationship between internal and external temperatures. But we can still see, I contend, the Hippocratic legacy in Walkington's identification of northern people as "Scythian," humorally imbalanced, and determined by their climate.

We need to ask why these "Scythians" hold such fascination for Walkington. Seemingly distinct from the eastern populations that we may associate with Herodotus or with Marlowe's *Tamburlaine*, these Scythians are simultaneously exotic and familiar:

> What reason can be alleag'd that those who dwell under the pole, neare the frozen zone, and in the septentrionall climate, should have such gyantly bodies and yet dwarfish wits, as many authours doe report of them? And wee see by experience in travaile, the rudenesse and simplicity of the people that are seated farre north. (p. 29)

I want to suggest that Walkington's Scythians dwell in two worlds. They are the barbarians described in the classical texts by those "many authours," such as Hippocrates, Virgil, and Dio Cassius, and they are Walkington's contemporaries, his neighbors, and the very people his readers may encounter "by experience in travaile."[16] As I will argue below, the Scythians' proximity – that they are the Englishman's nearby neighbors, if not kin – is at the heart of Walkington's attention to their unique complexion. Quite simply, the Scythians' humoral excesses matter because they may also be the Englishmen's humoral excesses.

Demonstrating a profound interest in the Scythians' physiology, Walkington abandons his discussion of the soul's relationship to the body to "treat a little of" northerners and their natural temperament (p. 25). And with elaborate detail, he meditates on how the Scythians' body and mind are constituted by the profoundly material effects of their northern environment:

> The Philosophers to this question have excogitated this reason: to wit the exceeding chilnesse of the air which doth possesse the animal spirits . . . others affirme and with more reason that they are dull-witted especially by the vehement heat which is included in their bodies, which doth inflame their spirits, thicken their blood, and therby is a cause of a new grosse, more then ayry substance . . . the externall frigidity of the ayre that dams up the pores of the bodies so greatly, that hardly any heat can evaporate . . . Now to prove that where the blood is thickned, and the spirits inflamed there usually is a want of witt . . . such creatures as have this humour thicke, are commonly devoid of witt, yet have great strength, and [unlike] such living things as have attentuated blood and very fluid [who] doe excell in witt and policy. (pp. 29–31)

To paraphrase, the cold northern air seals up the body, thus heating and thickening the blood, which strengthens the Scythians' ("gyantly") bodies and weakens their ("dwarfish") minds. Far removed from the temperance of the Mediterranean, the Scythians' geographical positioning determines their humorally marginalized status. Given the extreme nature of their somatic disproportions, Walkington implies, it seems unlikely that these barbarians can achieve a more refined state, much less *crasis* – that ideal golden mean where all four humors are in balance.

Having positioned the Scythians as monstrous outsiders, Walkington then turns his attention to the geographical location of his own country – England – and unwittingly reveals the roots of his preoccupation with these northern barbarians. It is his underlying fear that there may be very little to distinguish the Scythians from the English. In a grand effort to exonerate England from the ill effects of a cold climate, Walkington swells with nationalism, echoing John of Gaunt's praise of the "happy" isle:

> Wee must note here, that this is spoken of the remoter parts neare unto the pole, lest wee derogate any thing from the praise of this our happy Iland; (another blisfull Eden for pleasure) all which by a true division of the climes is situated in the septentrionall part of the world, wherein there are and ever have beene as pregnant wits, as surpassing politicians, as judicious understandings, as any clime ever yet afforded under the cope of heaven. (p. 31)

Ironically, this protest is what alerts us to England's northern status. Unable to deny that a "true division of the climes" situates England "in the septentri-onall part of the world," Walkington can only entreat his reader to view the English people as exceptional. English natives are as politic and wise as any other climate, he asserts, despite the disadvantages of their northern location. At the same time, it is his insistence on the difference between England's north-ern climate and Scythia that acknowledges a viable and disturbing correspon-dence between them.[17] The move that Walkington makes in *The Optick Glasse*, wherein seemingly general or universal issues of humoralism are reframed as geohumoralism, is standard practice in sixteenth-century English writings on physiology. As I hope to demonstrate in this chapter and the next, when the English recognize their northern status, they find themselves marginalized by their own classically based discourses on physiology, psychology, and emotion – discourses that held that the pursuit of health was premised on a temperate cli-mate. Hence, as we shall see, humoral theory was, for many early modern Europeans, ethnological knowledge.

In characterizing the northerners as excessively heated, big-bodied, and slow-witted, Walkington draws on the dominant classical theory of climatic effects – a tradition I refer to as Aristotelian. Subsequent to the writing of Hippocrates' treatise, the Aristotelian writers held that human nature counteracts the effects of locale and climate, and this view prevailed well into the early modern period. Aristotle's *Problems*, a central text in this discourse, explains the theory of counteraction as follows:

The effect of hot regions upon their inhabitants is to cool them (for, their bodies having rarities [thinness of composition], the heat escapes out of them), but those who live in a cold climate become heated in their nature, because their flesh is densified by the external cold, and when it is in this condition the heat collects internally.[18]

Clearly these assertions contradict Hippocrates' theory of temperatures, and yet it is important to note that the relationship between the environment and the body's degree of *moisture* remains consistent across the classical canon of texts.

Hippocrates had suggested that the Scythians embodied the moisture of their climate, and he attributed this "internal" state to the porous flux of their bodies. Indeed, the demarcation between human and environment was only faintly drawn in *Airs, Waters, Places*. The Aristotelian tradition also maintains that northerners are excessively moist, but the explanation for this imbalance is reconciled with the counteractive theory of temperatures. As the above quotation from Aristotle indicates, heat collects internally because cold air *densifies* the flesh, thus sealing in the body's moisture. According to Vitruvius:

For in those regions where the sun pours forth a moderate heat, he keeps the body duly tempered; where he comes near and the earth scorches, he burns out and removes the moisture; whereas in the cold regions, because they are far distant from the south, the moisture is not drawn out from their complexions, but the dewy air from the sky pours moisture into the body, enlarges the physique and deepens the voice.[19]

More than temperature, it is the excess or dearth of moisture in the body that determines the appearance and character of northerners and southerners. The drying effects of the sun thin the blood and give the southerner "a smaller stature, dark complexion, curly hair, black eyes, [and] strong legs." And since southerners are not weighed down by excessive moisture or blood, they prove exceptionally wise and timid. Cold environments, however, generate a "fullness" of blood, thus northerners possess courage, a "tall stature, fair complexion, straight red hair, blue eyes."[20] And it is their excessive moisture that burdens them with "sluggish minds."[21]

We should recognize at this point, I propose, that the Aristotelian theory of counteraction lies at the base of what modern scholars have misconstrued as the "sunburn" explanation for blackness.[22] Rather than scorching the surface of the skin, the sun's heat burns out the body's heat and moisture, leaving only a black earthy element that darkens the outer flesh. Thus, external blackness signifies the body's degree of moisture and heat. In attaining only a superficial knowledge of this theory, we have not only distorted the meaning of blackness in pre-racialized cultures, but we have forgotten the other half of the doctrine: exceedingly pale skin is the outward appearance of flesh that has been suffocated or "densified by the external cold."[23] So whiteness and blackness signify the body's degree of moisture and heat. Since temperance and a medium color were the classical ideals, ancient writers found what Pliny termed "white frosty skin" to be just as strange and unappealing as the "scorched appearance" of southerners.[24]

As a Mediterranean-centered discourse, the primary goal of classical climate theory was to establish Greece and Italy as the only locales where a balance of mental and physical strengths was an achievable goal. The writings of Aristotle, Pseudo-Aristotle, Vitruvius, and Pliny all construct a binary between the north and south that frames their home locale as the idealized and temperate middle zone. In Aristotle's *Politics* the Greeks are contrasted with those "who live in a cold climate and in Europe [where people] are full of spirit, but wanting in intelligence and skill" and with the "natives of Asia [who] are intelligent and inventive, but they are wanting in spirit..." The "Hellenic race ...[since it] is situated between them, is likewise intermediate in character, being high-spirited and also intelligent. Hence it continues free, and is the best-governed of any nation."[25] Similarly, in Pliny's *Natural History*, residing in the "middle of the earth" is what ensures the "healthy blending" of all physical and intellectual qualities. Middle zone "men are of medium bodily stature, with a marked blending even in the matter of complexion; customs are gentle, senses elastic, intellects fertile and able to grasp the whole of nature; and they also have governments, which the outer races never have possessed."[26] As we shall see, once these ancient notions are translated to other regions in the Renaissance, the pursuit of temperance becomes more clearly an ethnological issue – its elusiveness marking the outsider as stubbornly intemperate.

Intemperance is equivalent to barbarism in this discourse, and the tripartite structure of ancient climate theory is indistinguishable from the spatialized interpretations of barbarism and civility. For the ancient Greeks, any outsider to the *oikumene*, whether north or south, was identified as a barbarian. In the same way, for the Romans, those peoples living outside the *polis* inhabited inferior climates that defined the boundaries of civilization.[27] As Pliny maintains in his discussion of climatic effects, the "outer races" are "quite detached and solitary on account of the savagery of the nature that broods over those regions."[28] And when Aristotle poses the question, "Why are those who live under conditions of excessive cold or heat brutish in character and aspect?" he assumes a correspondence between somatic intemperance and barbarism.[29] Thus, classical climate theory provided physiological explanations for the Greeks' and Romans' potential for civility and temperance, as well as for the barbaric excesses of those outside the Mediterranean. As Aristotle explains it, extreme temperatures have adverse effects on the mind and body:

Why are those who live in warm regions wiser than those who dwell in cold districts? Is it for the same reason as that for which the old are wiser than the young? For those who live in cold regions are much hotter, because their nature recoils owing to the coldness of the region in which they live, so that they are very like the drunken and are not of an inquisitive turn of mind, but are courageous and sanguine; but those who live in hot regions are sober because they are cool.[30]

And yet, as this quotation intimates, not all classical barbarians are created equal. Ancient ethnography constructs its northern and southern barbarians with opposed traits: those in the north are white, ignorant, dull-witted, brave, and physically strong; southerners are black, learned, wise, cowardly, and physically weak.

Though "barbarous" in the sense that they are non-Greek or non-Roman outsiders, Egyptians and Ethiopians were recognized by the ancient writers to be the descendants of advanced and once-revered civilizations.[31] Indeed, Herodotus, arguably the West's first ethnographer, relies on his knowledge of Egypt's antiquity to infer the nature of those savage lands north of Greece. As John Gillies explains in *Shakespeare and the Geography of Difference*:

Herodotus was able to invent an entire ethnography for Scythia (an extreme northerly region of which he knew very little) by systematically inverting everything which he knew about Egypt (an extreme southerly region). Hence where the Egyptians are the most ancient and learned of men, the Scythians are the "youngest," the most ignorant and the most savage. Where nature in Egypt is dominated by heat, that in Scythia is controlled by cold.[32]

As we shall see in our discussion of Jean Bodin's sixteenth-century ethnography, it is an abiding interest of the early moderns to outline the differences between the barbarity of a learned but declining south, and the brutishness of northerners who are entirely lacking in wisdom, culture, and history. As a case in point, these classical distinctions are manifest in the barbarians of Shakespeare's *Titus Andronicus*, in which the northern Goths are "warlike" and crudely impolitic, while Aaron the Moor excels in his behind-the-scenes role as "[c]hief architect and plotter of these [Roman] woes" (5. 3. 121).

In its transmission to medieval Britain, classical climate theory remains resolutely Aristotelian. What changes, of course, is that in describing their native temperament, northern writers displace themselves from the temperance of the middle regions. Consider, for example, the implications of Ranulph Higden's description of "men in Europe" in the fourteenth-century chronicle *Polychronicon*:

men in Europe be more grete in body, more myghty in strenghte, moore bolde in herte, more feire in beaute, then in Affrike. For the beame of the sonne beenge continually by contynualle permanence on men of Affrike consumenge theire humores, causethe theyme to be more schorte of body, more blacke of skynne, more crispedde in heire, also more feynte in hearte by the euaporacion of spirites: hit is in contrary wyse of men beenge in the northe partes; for colde casuenge opilacion and stoppenge the poores exterially causethe humores to be fatte, that makethe men more of body, more whyte, more hoote interially, and by that moore bolde.[33]

By letting the temperate middle zone drop out of the equation, we may detect in Higden a chauvinistic impulse to move Britain toward the center, for he is able to locate the British within the broader category of "men in Europe."[34] And his omission of any reference to the northerner's dullness and the African's mental acuity anticipates the ways in which Britain's marginalized northern perspective will engender a more extensive restructuring of classical ethnographic discourse in the early modern period. At the same time, the absence of a temperate ideal means that Higden must also construct European whiteness in the intemperate mold of the Scythian's northern complexion. Indeed, the northerly translation of geohumoral discourse compels the British writer to identify his people as peripheral – and as necessarily homologous to the Ethiopians. In light of the still-dominant notion among modern scholars that the early modern English viewed African blackness as an inexplicable marvel, Higden's statements are remarkable. For Higden, the presence or absence of actual Africans in medieval Britain is a moot point. He asks his readers, instead, to imagine themselves as the extreme counterparts of the darker, cooler, drier peoples at the other end of the world. The somatic nature of his own countrymen is understood in the inverted, and surprisingly familiar, terms of the African's physiological status. As I shall argue later in chapter 3, the British people's shared marginalization with the dark peoples of Africa manifests itself in the Renaissance period not simply as a binary but as an ambivalence that mingles both an antipathy toward external blackness and an affinity for the inward, and tempering, qualities of black humors.

That northerners would necessarily filter ancient ethnography through their own temporal and spatial perspective comes through even more clearly in Albertus Magnus or Albert the Great's thirteenth-century text, *The Nature of Places*.[35] Naming Aristotle and Vitruvius as his sources, Albert initiates a process of synthesizing the ancient sources that will typify early modern ethnological discourse. Although Hippocrates has not yet reemerged to trouble this synthesis, Albert's articulation of climate theory proves to be, as Clarence Glacken puts it, "the most elaborate discussion of geographical theory with relation to human culture since the Hippocratic *Airs, Waters, Places*."[36] Albert's central conclusions are, by now, familiar: the heat in Ethiopia causes the body to radiate "a fine moisture," burning "the earthly mass which remains," which "generates blackness...And because their bodies are surrounded by very hot air, it is necessary that they be porous and dry, since the moisture evaporates continually from them" (p. 101). Ethiopians "excel more in ingenuity on account of the moving heat, and the keenness of their spirits" (p. 102). Free of excess humors, these southerners possess "light" hearts (p. 104) and "political acumen" (p. 105). In direct contrast, those living in cold regions abound in blood: "[t]heir humor is thick and bodily spirit does not respond to the motion and receptivity of mental activity. Therefore, they are dull-witted and stupid" (p. 104). Characterized by more corporeal attributes, northerners "have beautiful faces, smooth features, and joints well hidden, and they are heavy and well-fleshed." They "are bold on account of their fiery hearts" (p. 106), and their customs are "wolfish" (p. 104).

It is in Albert's description of the middle zone, however, where one can detect both the belated and displaced effect of identifying with northern Europe. Albert presents the temperance of the Roman people as a glorious stage in history – an interpretative move that anticipates the early modern use of geohumoralism as a tool in the construction of historical narratives:

The middle people, however, between these easily cultivate justice, keep their word, embrace peace, and love the society of men. For this reason Vitruvius, the architect, says that the rule of the Romans had endured longer than other reigns; because as the exposed middle has lain between the southerners who contrive with keenness of ingenuity and reason, and the northerners who lay hold of things, with eagerness and without discretion, the northerners on the one hand having audacity, and on the other, the southerners having political acumen; so they equaled the former and the latter in those things by which they sought to shake the Roman kingdom. (pp. 104–5)

Unlike the Greeks and Romans, whose writings aimed to delineate their position at the center of the known world, Albert's admiration for the "Roman kingdom" subtly registers his disaffiliation with its triumphs. Implicit in his observation that Roman temperance ensured the longevity of their power is the recognition that temperance is always vulnerable ("as the exposed middle") to the threat of more extreme forces. And what remains unspoken here is the historical understanding that Rome was indeed shaken to the ground by the audacity and indiscretion of wolfish northerners.

While Albert's geohumoral perspective on Rome's decline anticipates the ways in which climate theory will be put to historiographical and political uses in the sixteenth century, it is Albert's discussion of sexuality that most sharply differentiates his text from its Aristotelian predecessors. As we have seen, the Aristotelian writers tended to draw on climate theory to establish whether the barbarians they faced, north or south, were political or military threats. They do not address the relationship between the environment and sexual behavior. This is not to say that after Hippocrates classical writers showed no interest in the marriage customs or sexual behavior of others, but it is to observe that the relative temperature or degree of moisture thought to engender sexual desire was not a primary consideration. Scholars have long cited the classical descriptions of polygamous tribes in Ethiopia as evidence that Greek and Latin writers viewed Africans as sexually wanton, but this generalization not only ignores rival descriptions of inordinately chaste African tribes, but it also detaches southern behavior from the north–south binary of classical barbarism. "Barbarians" of all complexions, both north and south of the Mediterranean, were characterized by the ancients as sexually aberrant – aberrance taking the form not only of licentiousness but sexual inadequacy and frigidity.

To offer a representative example of modern views, J. P. V. D. Balsdon concludes in *Romans and Aliens* that Roman writers classified all Africans as "over-sexed" on the basis of Livy's specific references to the Numidians: "est genus Numidarum in Venerem praeceps" and "sunt ante omnes barbaros Numidae effusi in Venerem," together with scattered descriptions of the polygamous practices of certain African tribes.[37] We need to balance Balsdon's assertion, however, with the recognition that classical writers also characterized northern tribes – including the Britons – as sexually promiscuous. Solinus, for example, described a British king who "is not suffered to have anie woman to himselfe, but whomsoever he hath minde unto, he borroweth for a tyme and so others by turnes. Wherby it commeth to passe that he hath neither desire nor hope of issue"; the people of Thule "use their women in common, and no manne hath any wife."[38] Strabo claimed that the Irish were notorious for having "intercourse, not only with other women, but also with their mothers and sisters."[39] And of course, Caesar discovered that the Britons practiced polyandry: "Groups of ten or twelve men share their wives in common, particularly between brothers or father and son. Any offspring they have are held to be the children of him to whom the maiden was brought first."[40]

Another twentieth-century historian, J. W. Johnson maintains that the ancients developed "the view that climate directly affected human sexuality" by citing Hippocrates as his primary support and noting that *Airs, Waters, Places* imputes sexual impotence to the Scythians. But Johnson also extends this argument to contend that Hippocrates had "reversed the coin by correlating hot climates and lustful behavior."[41] While this error may be excusable, Johnson's biases are telling in his discussion of Herodotus, where he finds "that Africans as a whole were of a highly sensual and passionate nature and were notorious for sexual promiscuity."[42] While it is true that Herodotus identifies several Libyan tribes as polygamous, it is also true that he says the same thing about the relatively northern Thracians.[43] Moreover, Herodotus describes Egyptians as notably decorous in their sexual relations.[44] Nowhere does this classical ethnographer typify Africans as "highly sensual" or "passionate."

By expanding his geohumoral discussion to the subject of sexual desire, Albert the Great moved in a different direction from the Aristotelian climate theorists who came before him. Albert follows the logic of medieval humoralism, and his northerners are full of blood – heated and replete with moisture – possessing a sanguine complexion typically associated with sexual appetite. It is "on account of the heat of their stomach and humors," which "produce tumescence in the genitals" (p. 106), that northerners, Albert reasons, "desire women."[45] Given the ancient tradition of identifying the northerner with physicality, it seems that this medieval writer has extended Aristotle's counteractive tenets to characterize the northerner as libidinous. It is an easy deduction, and one that early modern European writers will struggle to combat.

Mapping early modern humoralism

There seems to be little question that climatological theory gained "new currency" in the sixteenth century, and as Waldemar Zacharasiewicz has argued, we can attribute this widespread engagement in part to the "dramatically increased availability of Hippocrates' *De aere, aquis et locis*."[46] And yet, the Aristotelian notion of counteraction dominated ethnology. Indeed, what we find in early modern ethnography is an effort to synthesize not only the conflicting Hippocratic and Aristotelian traditions but also to integrate contemporary writings on history, politics, medicine, and travel. Counter to what we might assume, the classical/medieval geohumoral arguments become more elaborate and more comprehensive in the early modern period. Jean Bodin, for example (whose *Methodus* (1566) and *The Six Bookes of a Commonweale* (1576) influenced countless English writers), produced a systematic ethnological theory that brought together the diverse writings of Hippocrates, Aristotle,

Pseudo-Arisotle, Galen, Polybius, Pliny, Caesar, Tacitus, Vitruvius, Vegetius, Leo Africanus, Scaliger, Sebastian Munster, and Francis Alvarez, among others.[47] By the mid-sixteenth century it was an unquestioned commonplace that environmental factors – the temperature, water, soil, and terrain – necessarily conditioned the appearance, complexion, temperament, and potential of all people.

Bodin calls all northerners "Scythians," including the Britons, Irish, Scots, Germans, and Danes, and he designates Hippocrates as the "highest authority" on climatic matters, and yet the foundation of Bodin's ethnological theory is firmly Aristotelian: cold air seals in heat and moisture, while hot air dries up the body's humors. Like Walkington, Bodin maintains that the Scythians are "warm and wet," but unlike his English successor, it is his claim that "Scythians" reside in Britain, as well as in other northern locales (p. 104). To account for Hippocrates' contradictory theory, Bodin suggests that *Airs, Waters, Places* must refer to the "furthest places of the north" but not to northern Europeans (p. 89). Bodin, in fact, modifies the classical tripartite geography by expanding the temperate zone to include not only Italians, but also the Spanish, "Asiatics," and of course, the French. In the south, he places, among others, Sicilians, Arabs, Persians, Numidians, Egyptians, Libyans, and Moors. And in the north, he locates Britain, Ireland, Gothland, Denmark, lower Germany, Scythia, and Tartary (pp. 95–6).

Bodin does not, however, dismiss Hippocrates' description of the Scythians entirely, for he cites *Airs, Waters, Places* to establish his argument about the sexual nature of various peoples. In spite of the Scythians' internal heat, Bodin maintains that northerners are naturally chaste. And in spite of a lack of heat, southerners are lustful. Clearly, Bodin contends, Hippocrates' theory of temperatures was wrong: "I do not know why Hippocrates thought the Scythians were cold ventrally. Nature itself demonstrates that that is false" (p. 104). Hippocrates did, however, get something right, for it is his description of Scythian impotence that attests to the northerners' extraordinary chastity. In every way but sexually Bodin's northerners are defined by the heat and moisture of their complexions: they are voracious, fierce, slow-witted, and given to great bouts of drinking, eating, and fighting. And yet they lack sexual desire. Conceding that this is a mystery, Bodin observes:

this [chastity] can in no way be attributed to self-control, since we have already shown that the northerners, by their own nature, are most intemperate in drinking, food, wrath, gaming, and stealing. It is the temperate man who is also continent, not the opposite. (p. 105)

Conversely, southern behavior is determined by their cool, dry complexions; they are, therefore, abstinent, wise, politic, and fearful. And lascivious. Thus,

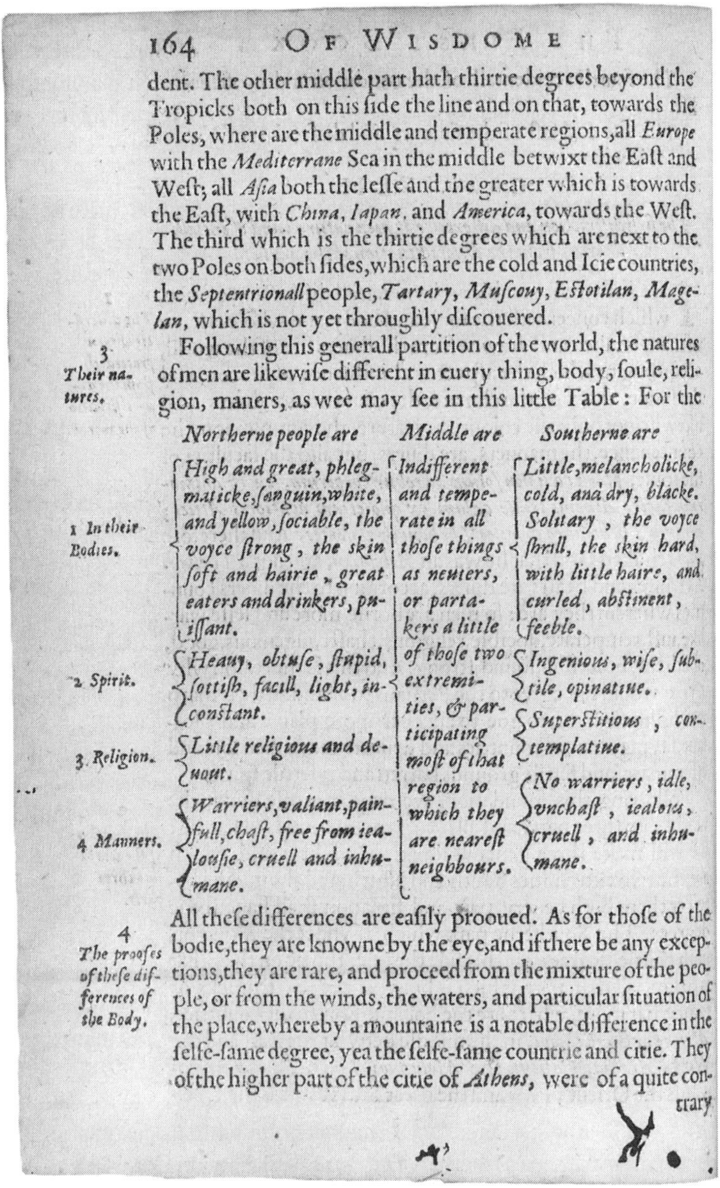

164   OF WISDOME

dent. The other middle part hath thirtie degrees beyond the Tropicks both on this side the line and on that, towards the Poles, where are the middle and temperate regions, all *Europe* with the *Mediterrane* Sea in the middle betwixt the East and West; all *Asia* both the lesse and the greater which is towards the East, with *China, Iapan,* and *America,* towards the West. The third which is the thirtie degrees which are next to the two Poles on both sides, which are the cold and Icie countries, the *Septentrionall* people, *Tartary, Muscouy, Estotilan, Magelan,* which is not yet throughly discouered.

3 Their natures.

Following this generall partition of the world, the natures of men are likewise different in euery thing, body, soule, religion, maners, as wee may see in this little Table : For the

Northerne people are	Middle are	Southerne are
1 In their Bodies. High and great, phlegmaticke, sanguin, white, and yellow, sociable, the voyce strong, the skin soft and hairie, great eaters and drinkers, puissant.	Indifferent and temperate in all those things as neuters, or partakers a little of those two extremities, & participating most of that region to which they are nearest neighbours.	Little, melancholicke, cold, and dry, blacke. Solitary, the voyce shrill, the skin hard, with little haire, and curled, abstinent, feeble.
2 Spirit. Heauy, obtuse, stupid, sottish, facill, light, inconstant.		Ingenious, wise, subtile, opinatiue.
3 Religion. Little religious and deuout.		Superstitious, contemplatiue.
4 Manners. Warriers, valiant, painfull, chast, free from iealousie, cruell and inhumane.		No warriers, idle, vnchast, iealous, cruell, and inhumane.

4 The proofes of these differences of the Body.

All these differences are easily prooued. As for those of the bodie, they are knowne by the eye, and if there be any exceptions, they are rare, and proceed from the mixture of the people, or from the winds, the waters, and particular situation of the place, whereby a mountaine is a notable difference in the selfe-same degree, yea the selfe-same countrie and citie. They of the higher part of the citie of *Athens,* were of a quite contrary

Figure 2 A chart on the natures of men, from Pierre Charron, *Of Wisdome* (1612?).

Bodin implies, chastity in the north and promiscuity in the south are inexplicable signs of monstrosity – in the Renaissance sense of the word. I will return to Bodin's mystery (a mystery made possible in part by his selective appeal to the "authority" of Hippocrates) at the end of this chapter, to underline my point that the ethnological significance of lust was undergoing a radical transition in the late sixteenth century.

But for now I would like to assess other ways in which early modern geo-humoralism is "early modern." We can see at a glance in the following chart from Pierre Charron's *Of Wisdome* (1612) how the sixteenth-century integration of Hippocratic and Aristotelian theories led to the establishment of new regional typologies and the affirmation of old ones:

NORTHERNE PEOPLE ARE: [In their bodies] High and great, phlegmaticke, sanguin, white, and yellow, sociable, the voyce strong, the skin soft and hairie, great eaters and drinkers, puissant. [in spirit, they are] Heavie, obtuse, stupid, sottish, facill, light, inconstant. [in religion, they are] Little religious and devout. [and in manners they are] Warriers, valiant, painfull, chaste, free from jealousie, cruell and inhumane.

MIDDLE ARE: Indifferent and temperate in all those things, as neuters or partakers a little of those two extremities, & participating most of that region to which they are nearest neighbours.

SOUTHERNE ARE: [In their bodies] Little, melancholicke, cold, and dry, blacke, Solitarie, the voyce shrill, the skin hard, with little haire, and curled, abstinent, feeble. [spirit] Ingenious, wise, subtile, opinative. [religion] Superstitious, contemplative. [manners] No warriers, idle, unchast, jealous, cruell, and inhumane.[48]

As Charron illustrates, sixteenth- and seventeenth-century climate theory was not only humoral in that the air affected the body's heat and moisture but also in its transformation of complexions (sanguine, phlegmatic, melancholic) into regional identities. In deference to both Hippocrates and Aristotle, Charron locates the phlegmatic and the sanguine in the north. Note as well that he identifies the southerner as a "cold" melancholic without designating the internal temperature of the northerner. The choleric are not on Charron's chart; however, he does suggest elsewhere that the "middle regions are sanguin and cholericke, tempered with a sweete, pleasant, kindly disposed humor; they are active."[49] For the most part, Charron follows Bodin in maintaining that all differences among people, whether in appearance, intellect, strength, or weakness, can be attributed to a "lack of proportion in the mixing of humors" (*Method*, p. 102).

It is these (dis)proportions, Bodin maintains, that give people throughout the world their varied skin tones:

Under the tropics they are unusually black; under the pole, for the opposite reason, they are tawny in color. After that, down to the sixtieth parallel, they become ruddy; thence to the forty-fifth they are white; after that to the thirtieth they become yellow, and when the yellow bile is mingled with the black [melancholy], they grow greenish, until they become swarthy and deeply black under the tropics. (p. 89)

Southerners, who "abound in black bile," are melancholic (p. 102). "Scythians" possess an excess of "blood and humor" and are thereby sanguine (p. 111). People inhabiting the temperate zone (which includes France) display "an infinite variety blended from the extremes," though they often prove choleric (p. 91). In identifying the French and "middle" natures as choleric, and then claiming that choler is a kind of temperance, Bodin and Charron are transparently chauvinistic. But they are not alone in their biases. Where temperance or *crasis* comprised a classical ideal – as a balance or melding of all four humors – the early moderns betray an ethnological interest in their ranking of the four complexions. The Elizabethan debate over the effects and symptoms of melancholia, as I shall argue in chapter 3, cannot be fully understood without recognizing this ethnological context.

It is no accident that Thomas Walkington in *The Optick Glasse*, with his English biases, ranks the sanguine and phlegmatic complexions as superior to the choleric and melancholic – a hierarchy that reverses Bodin's continental perspective. Indeed, the sanguine man in *The Optick Glasse* comes close to perfection:

[T]his happy temperature, and choise complexion, this sanguine humor, is worthy of a panegyricall toung... if there were a monarch or prince to bee constituted over all temperatures, this purple sanguine complexion should, no doubts, aspire to that hie preheminence of bearing rule: for this is the ornament of the body, the pride of humors, the paragon of complexions, the prince of all temperatures... hee which is possessed with a sanguine pure complexion is graced with the princeliest and best of all. For the externall habit of body, for rare feature they goe beyond all that have this temper, being most deckt with beautie which consists in a sweet mixture of these two colours white and redde, and for the gifts of the minde, it is apparent likewise to our understanding, that they doe surpasse al, having such pure tempered & refined spirits. (pp. 110–13)

Rather than questioning the motive for Walkington's extravagant praise here, scholars have traditionally cited this passage as support for the notion that the sanguine temperament is a recognized Renaissance ideal rather than a more local Anglicized one. In Lawrence Babb's *The Elizabethan Malady*, for example, *The Optick Glasse* proves to be his *sole* source for the assertion that the "sanguine complexion is considered the most desirable... [and] The melancholy temperament... least enviable."[50] Yet if we abandon the conventional notion that early modern humoralism was a coherent body of universally applicable knowledge, then an ethnological pattern begins to emerge. While the classical texts had established the sanguine complexion as "most desirable" in terms of bodily strength – for heat and moisture ensured one's physical health – they also maintained that a predominance of blood made men reckless, rash, overly amorous and slow-witted. In their classic study of humoralism, *Saturn and Melancholy*, Raymond Klibansky *et al.* acknowledge that the sanguine complexion underwent a significant transformation over time:

> The sanguine person in the genuine Galenian writings was still merely the simpleton, [he] gradually became what he was already to remain – a merry, light-hearted, good-tempered, handsome person of an altogether good disposition.[51]

As it turns out, Walkington's sole source for his own humoral hierarchy is an unnamed "*Antiquary*" whom we may presume to be Galen (p. 113). But in Galen's system, it was, in fact, "the choleric [temperament which]...produced keen perceptions and wit."[52] As for the writers who have classified the sanguine as dull-witted, Walkington refutes them by name: "neither do I thinke [he asserts] that either melancholick men according to *Aristotle*, or cholericke men according to the opinion of *Petrus Crinitus* are inriched with a greater treasury of wit..." (p. 113). Those who find the sanguine "to be dullards and fooles," he concludes, "do erre [against] the whole heavens" (p. 114).

Even more suggestive than Walkington's defense of the sanguine constitution is his favorable treatment of phlegm – a move that we may interpret as an accommodation of Hippocrates' characterization of northerners. Contradicting convention, Walkington maintains that after the sanguine complexion, "of all the humors, the physitions say, and it is not improbable, [the phlegmatic complexion] commeth nearest unto the best, for it is a dulcet humor" (p. 118). Significantly, the other prominent defense of phlegm in the period, as we saw in the introduction, is William Harrison's *Description of Britaine* (1587):

> by this meanes therefore it commeth to passe, that he whose nature inclineth generallie to phlegme, cannot but be courteous: which joined with strength of bodie, and sinceritie of behaviour (qualities universallie granted to remaine so well in our nation, as other inhabitants of the north) I cannot see what may be an hinderance whie I should not rather conclude, that the Britons doo excell such as dwell in the hoter countries...[53]

Unlike most geohumoral writing of the period, Harrison adheres here to the Hippocratic theory of temperatures and labors to rehabilitate phlegm as a predominant humor.[54] Given that northerners were deemed barbaric whether they were heated or cold (a point Harrison acknowledges), it makes sense that he would invest phlegm with the virtue of courtesy. But we may also detect, I propose, the effeminacy conventionally linked with phlegm in Walkington's use of the descriptor "dulcet" and in Harrison's bid for its innate civility.

As for these gendered implications of different complexions, Charron and Bodin appear to have the classical advantage; as naturally choleric, the French national complexion corresponds with the ideal measure of masculinity, for Galenic humoralism typically establishes men as the hotter and drier sex.[55] Indeed, ethnological typologies, like those outlined by Charron, derive much of their power as invective from their crucial intersections with prevailing social hierarchies of gender and class. It is implicit, for example, in Charron's schematic designations, that since the northerners' minds and bodies are ruled by bodily appetites, they can be easily conflated with women and the lower orders: heavy, obtuse, stupid, and sottish as the stereotypical rural clown, or facile, light, and inconstant as women. At the same time, it is their healthy bodies ("high and great") that ensures the northerners' masculine strengths of puissance and valiance. Inversely, the southerner's contemplative nature identifies him with the masculine half of the spirit/matter binary.[56] And just as clearly, southerners prove effeminately frail in body and mind, and their susceptibility to superstition and opinion conflates them with the misguided lower orders.

In part, I am proposing that the same tripartite logic that attaches values to regions helps organize the early modern social hierarchies of rank and gender. Achieving "racial" temperance, in other words, is analogical to securing masculinity or to cultivating nobility. Given that "race" has emerged in early modern scholarship as a "major organizing category for the period as a whole" (and that it has done so largely through an analysis of gender), it is crucial that we understand, in a historical sense, how and why distinct social categories are interimplicated in the humoral body.[57] I am not suggesting that people raced, ranked, or gendered in this period share a "common history," but I am arguing that in their reliance on the discourse of humoralism, ethnological distinctions depended on the same intemperances that helped define the still-porous boundaries of rank and gender.[58] For the early moderns, the privileged position of a noble, tempered man of a medium complexion proves impossibly elusive. To avoid lapsing into the excesses of effeminacy or degeneracy, masculinity and gentility require constant labor. As Charron's chart suggests, the excesses of effeminacy and incivility lurk everywhere, threatening to undermine the moderate ideal of aristocratic manhood. And regional disadvantages make the lapses inevitable. However fragile temperance or masculinity or nobility may be, those residing in "temperate" climes, as "partakers a little of those two extremities," possess the natural bodies best suited for the incessant pursuit of balance. In other words, the determinism of early ethnology applies more strictly to northerners and southerners, and it is manifested in the fixed traits conventionally attached to those oppressed on the basis of class and gender.

Another significant effect of geohumoralism's tripartite structure is that an intimate link exists between the outlying borders – the extremes of north and south. Classical writers deemed both the Scythians and Ethiopians as intemperate barbarians, and it is in the very pairing of these oppositions that they both become, in a strange way, lumped together by their inverted qualities. As we have seen, temperance is defined by Bodin and his followers by the invocation of a series of north-south binaries: the "body and mind are swayed in opposite directions," so that "southerners excell in intellect, the Scythians in body... Africans, however, have more than enough wisdom, but not enough strength" (*Method*, p. 98). When Juan Huarte in *The Examination of Men's Wits* notes "how far different...[the] *Aethiopians* [are] from *English*," he marks them both as equally distant from the temperate middle.[59] As Debora Shuger has recognized in her reading of Louis Le Roy's *Of Vicissitude, or the Variety of Things* (1594), these paired oppositions have the surprising and odd effect of "conflat[ing] 'black' and 'white' peoples."[60] Astonishingly, part of the humoral logic at work in these conflations is the presumption that the offspring of such extreme pairings would prove temperate. As Bodin indicates: "if the Scythians were crossed with the Ethiopians, there is no doubt but that a varied and different kind of man would be produced... In this way, then, it came about, I think, that Danes, Saxons, and English mingled with Britons, making them more ferocious, while they themselves became more kindly" (*Method*, p. 144).

That the bodies and temperaments of black and white peoples are humorally entwined is made plain in the Prince of Morocco's courting of Portia in *The Merchant of Venice*. Our critical impulse has been to view the Prince through European eyes, assuming that an Elizabethan audience would adopt a Venetian – or Belmontian – perspective (this seems to hold true even when our reading is qualified by England's more judgmental views of Venice).[61] The Prince of Morocco, however, realizes that his Belmont audience understands themselves as distinguished in physiology and temperament not only from his own but also from those fair "creature[s] northern born." Acknowledging his southern origins, the Prince ascribes his appearance to his native climate (the "shadowed livery of the burnished sun" [2.1.2]). It is his bid for Portia's affections, however, that leads him to counter the humoral corollary that Africans have "less blood within"[62]:

> Bring me the fairest creature northward born,
> Where Phoebus' fire scarce thaws the icicles,
> And let us make incision for your love
> To prove whose blood is reddest, his or mine.
>
> (2.1.4–7)

Here, and later when he claims that he can "[o]utbrave the heart most daring on the earth" (line 28), Morocco recognizes that the Venetians would deem him temperamentally incapable of heated actions. Morocco's fantasy of displayed blood articulates a desire to disrupt the same classical homologies that associate the English with those fair but estranged northern creatures. Shakespeare may be sympathetic to Morocco's wish to challenge Venetian assumptions, for the Moor's frustration with the determinism of geohumoralism mirrors what the English felt themselves. Indeed, we should not forget that England's marginalization from Belmont has already been established in the play by Portia's mockery of her English suitor in an earlier scene.

Given that Morocco is seeking marriage, scholars have also read this scene by drawing on long-held associations made between blackness and sexuality. Anthony Barthelemy, for example, maintains that "Morocco... presents an obvious and unwelcome sexual threat to Portia."[63] But if we consider the Prince's complexion within a geohumoral framework, there is some evidence to suggest that Portia perceives him, instead, to be sexually deficient. Consider Portia's disdain when she first hears of the Prince of Morocco's imminent arrival: "If he have the condition of a saint and the complexion of a devil, I had rather he should shrive me than wive me" (1. 2. 109–10). In noting a discrepancy between appearance and inward character, critics contend, Portia merely reverses the usual association between black men and devils, to jest that "inner goodness cannot compensate for external foulness."[64] But if we entertain the possible correspondence between blackness and the "*condition* of a saint," the tenor of Portia's mockery is altered. While it remains indisputable that Elizabethan discourse equated blackness with a lack of beauty, we should also recognize that the cold, dry temperament of a dark complexion presumably promoted constancy and faith. Allowing herself to be led by the eyes, Portia views the Prince's color with distaste, but her reluctance to "wive" the Prince may stem from her assumption that he lacks sexual heat. Portia has expressed frustration that she must curb her sexual "will" and "hot temper" to her father's "cold degree" (1. 2. 16–21). But the Prince's "condition," it seems, fails to provoke any "warmth" in her "affection" (lines 29–30).

I realize that my suggestion that Morocco's blood may be cold rather than warm contradicts the standard take on Renaissance views of African sexuality, summarized here by Ian Smith:

> The Moors' sexual excess, their rabid lust and unbridled sensuality, is a commonplace of Elizabethan literature, being effectively dramatized in the relationships between Aaron and Tamora, queen of the Goths [in *Titus Andronicus*], and Eleazar and the Queen Mother in the pointedly titled *Lust's Dominion*... The geography of Africa, especially the intense heat, explained both the extremes of lust and jealousy, for "the sun was believed to create passionate furies, not dry them up."[65]

These ideas are widely accepted in modern scholarship on Elizabethan culture, and no one, as far as I am aware, has attempted to question the sexual assumptions attached to our perceptions of early modern "racialism." But, significantly, Smith's primary example of this stereotype, Aaron the Moor in *Titus Andronicus*, is a character who explicitly claims that he lacks sexual desire.

Indeed, Aaron argues that his dispassionate temperament is naturally opposed to the lascivious northern Goths'[66]:

> Madam, though Venus govern your desires,
> Saturn is dominator over mine.
> What signifies my deadly-standing eye,
> My silence, and my cloudy melancholy,
> My fleece of woolly hair that now uncurls
> Even as an adder when she doth unroll
> To do some fatal execution?
> No, madam, *these are no venereal signs.*
>
> (2. 3. 30–7)[67]

By denying any link between blackness and sensuality, Aaron has of course acknowledged that his complexion may be misconstrued. But, more to the point, Aaron's claim rests on the logic of classical humoralism.

Rather than a "venereal sign," blackness denotes the cool, dry qualities of Aaron's melancholic complexion. And by drawing on the rhetoric of inversion, Aaron suggests that it is the white Goths who are ruled by the excessively heated passions of Venus, as exhibited not only in Tamora's desires but also in her sons, Demetrius and Chiron, who have inherited "[t]hat codding spirit" from their libidinous mother. We should also note that Smith's second literary example of Eleazar the Moor and the Queen in Dekker's *Lust's Dominion* provides a similar ambiguity: it is the subtitle of *Lust's Dominion* – "*the Lascivious Queen*" – which reminds us that it is not the Moor, but the Queen mother who is sexually aggressive. Eleazar initially resists the Queen's advances, complaining that he feels "sick, heavie, and dull as lead" (1. 1. 20), and when he does give in to "feed [her] lust" (line 81) it is only with the hope that such compliance will heat his cooler blood (lines 24–5).[68]

The emerging colonialist constructions of hyper-sexualized Africans have been accepted without great scrutiny as preexistent "knowledge" in part because these constructions square so well with our intuitive understanding of climate theory – that hot climates should raise internal temperatures. And once early modern travel literature began to cast doubt on the notion that the sun produced blackness, nascent colonizers were free to reinterpret the geohumoral effects of environmental heat in more accommodating terms. Consider, for example, how the portrait of Africans in *A description and historicall declaration of the golden Kingdome of Guinea* (1600) actively reworks the older tenets of geohumoralism:

they are great Drinkers, and use no lesse unseemelinesse in their feeding, but eate as unmannerly and greedily, as if they were a companie of Hogs ... They are always hungrie, and would willingly eate all day long, which shewes that they have very hot mawes, and although the Countrey is very hot, whereby the heate of the Aire commonly should fill mens stomakes, yet they are hungrie, and wee Netherlanders are not weake stomaked there, but alwaies have good appetites, whereby I am of opinion, that heate in those Countries makes men hungrie: but because I am no Doctor of Physicke, I will not intreate thereof.[69]

Although he is "no Doctor of Physicke," he seems aware of the humoral commonplace that hot climates quell appetites – it is, he implies, the particular heat of *those* countries that makes men hungry. He also understands that people who are greedy for food and drink necessarily have "hot mawes." But by citing his own experience and what he claims to have seen, he is able reject the counteractive theory of temperatures. In so doing, this writer projects what were conventionally northern traits onto the Africans and succeeds in portraying them as savages in need of strict control. Not surprisingly, the natives' most dissolute behavior is lechery, which this author, unlike Bodin, corroborates with infertility and a hot climate: "they are not over fruitfull... which I thinke proceeds from their hot natures, and the aire of the Countrey, and secondly, because their husbands have so many wives."[70]

My point is simple: before the Atlantic slave trade gained real momentum, the significance of the African body, for the English, was in flux. However, some modern scholars have arrived at the questionable conclusion that representations of blackness in the sixteenth century set Africans apart as a "special category of humankind," by focusing solely on descriptions of dark non-European "Others" and by ignoring the tripartite framework that structures early modern ethnology.[71] We might, however, temper such suppositions with Emily Bartels' observation that these same "negative stereotypes were commonly applied to such a broad range of Others – from Africans to black magicians to sodomites to Jews – that their validity had to be suspect."[72] Not only is the validity of negative stereotypes subject to suspicion, but we should also be cautioned against infusing blackness with racialized characteristics without recognizing the necessary rearrangement of knowledge that preceded the production of "special categor[ies] of humankind." It should still matter, for example, that almost all the negative terms applied to Africans in sixteenth-century travel literature were also used to describe England's latitudinal neighbors – the Irish. Indeed, the disparaging rhetoric applied to all "barbarous people," both north and south, tends toward sameness rather than difference: all barbarians are "wild and idle," "savage," and strange or excessive in their sexual relations.

As Lynda Boose has observed, "for the English the group that was first to be shunted into this discursive derogation [of inferior other] and thereafter invoked as almost a paradigm of inferiority was not the black 'race' – but the *Irish* 'race.'" It is also Boose's argument that in such tracts "as Spenser's *A View of the Present State of Ireland*, the derogation of the Irish as 'a race apart' situates racial difference within cultural and religious categories rather than biologically empirical ones."[73] Whether or not we categorize the qualities noted in these tracts as "biological," "cultural," or "religious," we should acknowledge that the rhetoric applied to both Africans and Irish during this period is virtually indistinguishable. Compare Robert Gainsh's observation that the Moors held women in "common; for they contracte no matrimonie, neyther have respect to chastitie" with Sir John Davies' statement that the Irish should be condemned for "their common repudiation of their wives; their promiscuous generation of children; their neglect of lawful matrimony; their uncleanness in apparel, diet, and lodging; and their contempt and scorn of all things necessary for the civil life of man."[74] While the Dutch writer Linschoten claimed that the women of Guinea were "much given to lust and uncleanenesse, specially with straungers, which among them is no shame," Edmund Campion, in his *Two Bokes of the Histories of Ireland* (1571) pronounced all the Irish to be exceedingly amorous, while the "lewder sorte, bothe clerkes and laye, [were] sensuall and loose to leacherye above measure."[75] Consider how Irish women, in a description taken from William Lithgow's *The Total Discourse of His Rare Adventures* (1632), were portrayed in physiological terms that would later become almost exclusively associated with African women:

[The women]...carry their Infants about their neckes, and laying the dugges over their shoulders, would give sucke to the Babes behinde their backes, without taking them in their armes: Such kind of breasts, me thinketh were very fit, to be made money bags for East or West-Indian Merchants, being more then halfe a yard long, and as wel wrought as any Tanner in the like charge, could ever mollifie such Leather.[76]

As historian Jennifer Morgan has shown, such language and imagery was increasingly deployed later in the century to justify the subjugation of Africans.[77]

By the seventeenth century a reformulated geohumoral discourse catches up to the racializing impulses of early modern European writings and allows for the now familiar correlation between heated climates and heated passions that obscures the older theories. But in sixteenth- and early seventeenth-century writings, it is still possible to discern how the transmission of classical knowledge troubled the European constructions of ethnicity and sexuality. As I mentioned earlier, Jean Bodin's effort to reconcile Aristotle with Hippocrates produces the startling argument that internal heat has no relation to sexual desire. Citing Hippocrates' impotent Scythians and Caesar's description of "Englishmen...[who] had but one woman to ten or twelve men," Bodin observes that it is puzzling that such "chastity" would thrive among the well-heated northerners.[78] And in a move that has proven unrecognizable to modern scholars, Bodin suggests the sexual desire of black Africans is extravagant in part because it does *not* originate in their cold, dry bodies.[79]

Bodin concedes that it is surprising to find that the cold-tempered southerners are lustful and the hot-natured northerners are passionless, and he suggests that it is only "through the highest wisdom of God" that this holds true:

[t]hose [northerners] who have sufficient ability to beget, passion is not very necessary;
but those [southerners] who have less humor and heat, the best parent, Nature, gave the
greater stimuli of desire. Otherwise they would not wish to propagate their kind or to
establish societies. (*Method*, p. 104)

Since heat is no longer interpreted as the stimulus for desire, Bodin reasons
that it must be engendered by "both biles...In the case of yellow bile [or
choler], lust is probably due to irritation [rather than heat,] but in black [bile],
lust is caused by froth and gaseous matter, very abundant in this kind of bile"
(*Method*, p. 106).[80] Yet this argument is further complicated by Bodin's peculiar
proposal that it is ultimately the southerners' superior wisdom and "reasoning
power" that has led them to "sin more freely for the sake of pleasure" (*Method*,
p. 105) – a proposal generated, in part, by his attempt to accommodate the
portrait of heated Africans in Leo Africanus' *History and Description of Africa*
(which I address in chapter 6).

Echoing Bodin's strange logic in *Relations of the Most Famous Kingdomes
and Common-wealths* (1630), Giovanni Botero maintains that it is the very
incompatibility of innate coldness and sensuality that attests to the prodigious
nature of the southerners' sexual passions.[81] The paradox of cold lust is, he
writes, the "handi-worke of God; that those...which wanted of that measure
of heat and moisture, should delight in wantonnesse, to raise their appetites"
for generation.[82] Remarkably and counterintuitively, it is the Africans' lack of
internal heat and moisture that leads to sexual excess, for they must labor to
achieve arousal itself. Preceding any feelings of desire is the will to pleasure. In
the experience of passion in general, Botero and Bodin agree that "the Southerne
man is not easily provoked; nor once in passion, is [he] easily to be reconciled."[83]
But on the question of sexual desire, Bodin and Botero deny its somatic origins,
and the southerner's physiological state – his cold, dry complexion – loses its
significance.

In a sense this rift between sexual passion and physiology perversely anticipates the Cartesian split between the mind and body, for it is a disavowal of
both environmental and somatic influences on the mind that will allow for the
formation of the autonomous – and white – subject. Indeed, I am suggesting
that the construction of bounded selves goes hand in hand with the construction
of racial boundaries. We can detect in Bodin and Botero emergent signs of a
discrete racialized "Other" whose complexion no longer invokes the troubling
homologies of climate theory. By assigning ethnic traits that exceed the logic of
classical humoralism, Bodin and Botero lay the groundwork for the construction of racialism. And the discursive fissure produced by the claim that cold
temperaments engender lust marks a crucial division between the old knowledge and the newer ideological impulses generated by colonization and the
growing Atlantic slave trade – a division that gets explored and complicated by
the imaginative writings of the period.

I heard them all have a conceite of an Englishman, a strange people, in the
westerne Islands, one that for his variety in habit, humour and gesture, put
downe all other nations whatsoever ...

Thomas Heywood[1]

The *Sunne* lights not a *Nation*
That more addicteth *apish imitation*
Then do we *English* ...

George Wither[2]

As I suggested in the last chapter, Britain's recognition of its marginalized position in the classical texts meant that humoralism was understood as a form of
ethnological knowledge. Expanding on this thesis, I will argue in this chapter
that in the late sixteenth and early seventeenth centuries, between the waning of
Britain's mythological origins and the emergence of racialism, British ethnicity
was conceived primarily in geohumoral terms. In a sense, Britain's Trojan lineage and the emergent myth of Anglo-Saxon purity satisfied the same desire –
the longing for a narrative that sustained and fixed English identity over time.[3]
Both narratives, as we shall see, claimed a transmission of traits from one generation to the next that eluded or withstood the threats of migration, mingling,
and conquest. During this liminal period, when originary narrative was entirely
secure, geohumoralism was predominant. Although I have been emphasizing
the ways in which early modern writers stressed the determinism of geohumoral theory, ethnicity was in fact perceived to be the result of a "conspirac[y]
of causes."[4] A generational, or vertical, transmission of traits could be altered
or enhanced not only by the nature of a place, but also by other lateral forces,
such as moving, mingling, or the importation of cultural practices.[5] Hence, what
constituted ethnological identity was exceedingly fluid and malleable – shaped
not only by the environment but also by other horizontal, synchronic, and "civilizing" forces, such as government, law, travel, diet, fashion, and education. As
I shall suggest, these shaping influences played a particularly significant role in
the conception and formation of English ethnicity because "Englishness" itself
was understood primarily as a collection of markedly fluid qualities. On the

Figure 3 Picture of Englishman from Andrew Boorde, *The Fyrst Boke of the Introduction of Knowledge* (1562?).

continent and at home, the English body and mind were cast as exceptionally impressible, vulnerable, and inconstant.

Civilizing Britain

In looking to the classical discourse, we might construe humoralism as a form of ethnology if we recall that Galen and ancient writers premised their discussions of physiology on the temperance of their home climate. As Juan Huarte jokes in a sixteenth-century manual on education, "*Galen* said verie well, That out of Greece, nature not so much as in a dream, maketh any man temperat, or with a wit requisit for the sciences."[6] When we shift our attention to early modern humoralism, as it is conceived and translated by English writers, we are compelled to acknowledge, I propose, that its displacement in the north necessarily reframes the discourse as ethnology. It is, we need to realize, during the sixteenth century that the English directly confronted and wrestled with their identity as northerners.[7] Not only did writers increasingly pay attention to England's northern marginalization from the rest of the civilized world, but English historians also recognized, without the older equivocations, that the Britons, the island's early settlers, were of northern descent. To make such an acknowledgement was, of course, to let go of the Medieval myth that the Britons had a Trojan lineage.

Sixteenth-century changes in historiography helped give rise to geohumoralism in the early modern period. Jean Bodin's historical analysis of environment, migration, language, and classical texts, for example, was perceived to be a direct challenge to the older genealogical myths of national origin. As Leonard F. Dean has observed, "Bodin was often attacked . . . as one of the 'learned clerks' attempting to discredit Geoffrey's account of early British history."[8] In England, this new historical approach was represented most prominently in William Camden's *Britannia* (1586) and Edmund Spenser's *A View of the State of Ireland* (1633) – two texts that give us a complex look at early modern English articulations of ethnic identity.[9] But before Bodin reached England, Tudor historians tended not to acknowledge, as Debora Shuger has noted, their nation's "barbarian origins, preferring the more respectable national pedigree provided by Brutus' Trojan band and the offspring of Old Testament patriarchs."[10] With the publication of Camden's *Britannia*, however, England was provided with what Shuger has called a "radically different model of English prehistory."[11] Drawing on the same classical portraits that informed Bodin's perspective, Camden depicts the early Britons as northern barbarians, giving his English readers a stark and novel picture of their ancestors as rude, uncivil, and warlike.[12] We can see this same pattern played out in *A View of the State of Ireland* (1633), when Spenser's dismissal of the "Tale of Brutus" leads to his acknowledgement that all northern nations were originally settled by northern barbarians or some branch of "Scythian."[13] Though Spenser's Irenæus expends a good deal of energy tracing and assessing possible genealogies of the Irish people, it turns out that even the Irish settlers from Spain, who may have been Spaniards, Goths, Gauls, or Africans, were in all likelihood Scythian descendants who left the south upon discovering that they "tooke no felicity in that countrey," when they found the "nature of the soyle, and the vehement heat thereof farre differing from their constitutions . . ."[14] As Shuger has argued, Spenser's view of "Ireland provides a synecdochical glimpse into the cultural origins shared by all northern European nations, including, of course, England."[15] And Spenser's conviction that all northern regions were settled by people with northern "constitutions" makes *A View of the State of Ireland* an essay on the geohumoral foundations of Englishness as well as Irishness.[16]

In the wake of dismissing the Britons' noble Trojan lineage, Spenser follows Camden in attributing England's current state of civility not to its ancestry but to its status as a conquered nation. Indeed, it is Camden's primary thesis in

Britannia that the Britons had been tempered and civilized by Roman law and government. The Roman conquest, Camden asserts, "chased away all savage barbarisme from the Britans minds . . . and reduced the naturall inhabitants of the Iland unto the society of civill life . . ."[17] Here again Shuger is helpful in understanding the historiographic shift taking place: Camden's "narrative model . . . configures history as the gradual acquisition of civility – a civility, moreover, apparently dependent upon the forcible imposition of a more advanced culture."[18] And we might say that Spenser's *View* provides the next chapter in Camden's civilizing narrative, translating the English from colonized to colonizers, as they take up the task of civilizing the Irish. Just as the Romans brought civility to the Britons, or as the English gained civility in the Norman Conquest, it is Ireland's role to submit to the civilized government of England.[19] Where Shuger and I part ways, however, is in our different characterizations of the trajectory and cultural significance of this civilizing narrative. Shuger maintains that the old mythology of Brutish origins was construed as a decline from greatness – a story of slow degeneration that gets reversed by the progressive development of Camden's narrative model. I contend, instead, that the Trojan myth had enabled the Britons to claim a mystically preserved ethnological link to ancient Mediterranean civilizations – a link that proved resistant in the face of Britain's history of foreign invasions. In contrast, Camden's narrative did not simply imply cultural evolution – it inserted Britain into a classical framework wherein history moves cyclically, and a region's achieved civility necessarily gives way to degeneration. Consonant with the two central ways in which early moderns understood the transmission of culture, the Trojan mythology provided what Margaret Hodgen terms a " 'vertical' handing on of ideas and practices from father to son, along channels of genetically linked generations, or through the 'Conduit of Nature.' " In contrast, Camden's *Britannia* proved, I propose, "spatially or geographically oriented, involv[ing] the recognition that traits had been and could be carried 'laterally,' or 'transported' overland through the agency of moving, mingling peoples or their representatives."[20] As I suggested in the introduction, in discussing how in Juan Huarte's *The Examination of Men's Wits* (1594) the Egyptians could maintain and transmit – lineally – certain climatically determined traits after their exodus, geohumoralism accommodates the possibility that a population's shared humoral complexion will be influenced by lateral forces without excluding the potential for vertical inheritance.

With regard to the mythic Britons' constitution, even if Medieval writers ignored the obvious ethnological dilution that a history of repeated conquests signified, they were compelled to struggle with their belief that migration to a foreign climate affected a people's complexion. As Jean Bodin explains, transmigration will eventually alter the natural temperament of a people, though it may take several generations:

It is most certaine that if lawes and customes be not well maintained and kept, the people will soone returne to their naturall dispositions: and if they be transplanted into another countrey, they shall not be chaunged so soone, as plants which draw their nourishment from the earth: yet in the end they shall be altered, as we may see of the Gothes, which did invade Spaine, and high Languedoc; and the ancient Gaules which did people Germanie, about the blacke forrest and Francford, with their Collonies. *Caesar* saith, That in his time (which was some five hundred yeres after their passage) they had chaunged their manners and naturall disposition with that of Germany.[21]

As an immigrant population acclimates to the nature and culture of its new environment, transplantation effects a change in people's natural disposition and transforms their ethnicity; thus Gauls become German, or more radically, migrating Scythians turn Turk.[22] As Nathaniel Carpenter writes, in a similar vein, "the Gothes . . . long after their first invasion of Spaine, France, Italy and other territories of Europe, retained their own *disposition* and *nature*, altogether disagreeing with the nations amongst whom they lived . . . But in the process of time it came to passe, that putting off their harsh temper, they grew into one nation with the native Inhabitants."[23] As we observed in the introduction, Gerald of Wales maintained in the twelfth century that it was the effects of the warm Mediterranean climate that produced the early Britons' best virtues (as opposed to the northern inheritance of the Germanic English):

the English also, although placed in a distant climate [from Germany], still retain the exterior fairness of complexion and inward coldness of disposition, as inseparable from their original and natural character. The Britons, on the contrary, transplanted from the hot and parched regions of Dardania into these more temperate districts . . . still retain their brown complexion and that natural warmth of temper from which their confidence is derived. . . . from thence arose that courage, that nobleness of mind, that ancient dignity, that acuteness of understanding, and confidence of speech.[24]

Gerald's statement is provocative on several counts. For one, he makes quite clear that a warm, brownish, southern complexion denotes an array of innate virtues – virtues that set it far above the English people's paler skin and "inward coldness." Secondly, he acknowledges the fundamental importance of environmental influences, only to insist that the vertical, or lineal, transmission of traits can preserve these originary climatic effects. To underscore the significance of British nativity, Gerald maintains that the Britons' ancestors were "detained longer" in Greece and migrated later than other, less noble, tribes. Ultimately, however, the greatness of these Trojan-Britons depends less on temporal considerations than on a mystified and inexplicable resistance to complete subjugation.

Not unlike Gerald of Wales, Camden and his contemporaries located the roots of civility in the ancient Mediterranean world, but they shifted their emphasis away from inheritance to the horizontal forces of the civilizing process: for Camden, the Roman conquest – from its brutal violence to its implementation

of Roman law to its educational reforms to its installation of Britain's infras-
tructure – succeeded in transforming the native Britons utterly. Indeed, Camden
jokes, there was such mingling between the Britons and the Romans that if his
readers were still looking for a Trojan ancestry, they could find it in the after-
math of the Roman invasion.[25] In conquering Britain, the Romans had "completely made this country their own," thus abolishing native customs and, more
radically, annihilating the warlike and unruly character of the Britons, which
Camden himself praises.[26] Indeed, Camden observes, these barbarous traits are
what earned his ancestors the Romans' admiration upon conquest.[27]

Camden's view of Britain's subjugated past is consonant with Bodin's more
humorally oriented argument in *The Six Bookes of a Commonweale*, in which
all effective rulers must know the "diversitie of mens humors, and the meanes
how to discover the nature and disposition of the people" in order to "accommodat the publike weale to the nature of the place; and the ordinances of man
to the laws of nature."[28] Just as a physician applies remedies that contravene
the distempers of his patient, sovereign powers, who rule in less temperate regions, can institute laws that amend the particular imbalances of their country's
population. Hence, accommodating the laws to the people in the early modern
period does not mean that the government is directly "expressive of the indigenous character of a population," as Claire McEachern has suggested in *The
Poetics of English Nationhood*. It means, instead, that proper rule and leader-
ship can counter, reform, and temper the disordered bodies and temperaments
of a nation's population.[29]

Once their "civility" had been demystified, or debiologized, by the historiographic shifts that I have been describing, the English were compelled to confront not only their barbaric roots but also the alien origins of their subsequent
refinement. Put simply, as marginalized and belated northerners, the English in
the sixteenth century were in a constant struggle to alter, temper, counter, and
even recover what they presumed to be their "natural" complexion. If the origins of civility are located elsewhere – that is, in the south – then the horizontal
transmission of "civilizing" customs and traits will necessarily subject the native peoples to a dominant foreign culture and position them as submissive. As
such, the civilizing process in sixteenth-century England, whether conceived
as good government or the purging of humors, always threatened to exceed its
tempered goal and effect a lapse into effeminate degeneration.

It was not until English writers shifted their attention to England's Saxon
origins – and reconstructed a lineal transmission of traits that upheld a Tacitean
view of Anglo-Saxon purity – that the inhabitants of Britain were able to escape
the troubling implications of *Britannia*'s civilizing narrative. In the early seventeenth century, Camden (in *The Remains Concerning Britain* [1605]) together
with an antiquarian named Richard Verstegan, drew on Tacitus' philobarbaric
portrait of Germany to privilege England's Saxon roots. As I will suggest in

chapter 7, this historiographic turn had enormous repercussions not only for England's political future and national identity but also for the transmutation of the northerner's barbarous traits into the English subject's fixed, transmissible, and thus racialized "virtues."[30]

Without an appeal to a vertical transmission of traits, ethnic distinctions in the early modern period were necessarily plastic. Given the sheer number of variables in the external world (diet, environment, clothing) and the multiple cultural agents (government, travel, custom, performance, education, for example), people could intentionally or accidentally estrange themselves from their native kind. As John Sutton has argued, the physical world, the cultural environment, and "various technologies of the body" appeared to carry almost equal weight in producing the early modern "individual's current, fragile balance against imminent stagnation or excess."[31] But what further complicates our understanding of *English* ethnicity, in particular, is that the most prominent characteristic of Englishness proves to be its impressibility. Thus, within the already fluid variables of geohumoralism, the English are perceived to be exceedingly pliant and vulnerable.

As we noted in chapter 1, the classical discourse set the northerner's moist, easily moved complexion in opposition to the African's dry, hard, and fixed nature. But further exacerbating the English people's mutability was their status as islanders. Sara Warneke has demonstrated that Medieval and Renaissance writers very often attributed the Englishman's notoriously fickle and inconstant nature to the island's environs. In the twelfth century, Peter of Celle to Nicholas of St. Albans writes: "Your island is surrounded by water, and not unnaturally its inhabitants are affected by the nature of the element in which they live." Hundreds of years later in *A German Diet: or, the Ballance of Europe* (1653) James Howell maintained that "the sea tumbleth perpetually about...so their braines do fluctuat in their noddles, which makes [the British] so variable and unsteady." Such notions continued late into the seventeenth century; in 1676, Sir Thomas Baines comments that "The mutability of air in an island contributed to mutability of thought," making the English "a changing fluctuating people by nature, increased by diet, with the addition of rashness to it."[32] It was a general humoral commonplace that a man whose complexion is "moist and full of vapours" will "sodainly changeth his manners and his fashion of speech."[33] In this vein, the English writer Joseph Hall laments: "our [English] nature to bee like unto fire, which if there bee any infection in the roome, drawes it straight to it selfe."[34] For the early moderns, the English were inclined by their geographic circumstances to adopt, try on, or even absorb the shifting elements of the external world.

In *The Fyrst Boke of the Introduction of Knowledge* (1547), arguably England's earliest ethnography, the physician Andrew Boorde provides a visual and verbal portrait of the Englishman's "naturall dysposicion."[35]

Depicted wearing only a loin-cloth and hat, Boorde's Englishman holds a length of cloth in one hand, and in the other hand, shears (Fig. 3).[36] For Boorde the Englishman's love of fashion is a symptom of his general tendency to vacillate and waver – an inability to hold himself "styl." He proves rash, changeable, and faithless; he lacks fixed beliefs, allegiances, and loyalties. If he could be "wise" and "styl," there might be some merit in his forthrightness, but the unsteadiness of his disposition undermines his potential for virtue. Throughout the sixteenth and seventeenth centuries, English writers come back again and again to Boorde's portait, to decry the "constant...inconstancie of [their] attire" and nature.[37] As the following dialog in *The Fair Maid of the Inn* (1647) indicates, the early moderns understood that the nature of Boorde's Englishman was attributable to his native climate:

TAYLOR: Shall I be a moon-man?
FOROBOSCO: I am of opinion, the people of that world
             (If they be like the nature of that climate they live in)
             Do vary the fashion of their cloaths oftener than any
             Quick-silver'd nation in Europe.
TAYLOR: Not unlikely, but what should that be we call the man in the
             moon then?
FORO: Why 'tis nothing but an Englishman
             That stands there stark naked
             With a pair of sheers in one hand,
             And a great bundle of cloath in the other

                         . . .

             Cutting out of new fashions.[38]

Thus we can interpret England's supposed and well-known predilection for fashion as a humoral inclination produced by the region's unsteady climate. But more disturbingly for the sixteenth-century Englishman, this predilection also marked them as a people not only predisposed but also ready to imitate and absorb alien customs.

In *Palae-Albion or The History of Great Britanie* (1621), William Slatyer concludes that it is their "braine-sick humors" that send the "fantastique *English*-men" after the "far-fetcht and new-fangle fashions" of other countries.[39] John Deacon's *Tobacco Tortured* (1616) makes clear that however corrupt and contagious other nations may be, it is indiscretion and porousness that marks the English as "English":

our carelesse entercourse of trafficking with the contagious corruptions, and customes of forreine nations...from whence cometh it now to passe that so many of our English-mens minds are thus terriblie *Turkished* with *Mahometan* trumperies; thus ruefully *Romanized* with superstitious relickes; thus treacherously *Italianized* with sundry antichristian toyes; thus spitefully *Spanished* with superfluous pride; thus fearefully

Frenchized with filthy prostitutions; thus fantastically *Flanderized* with flaring net-works to catch English fooles; thus huffingly *Hollandized* with ruffian-like loome-workes, and other like Ladiefied fooleries; thus greedily *Germandized* with a most gluttenous manner of gormandizing; thus desperately *Danished* with a swine-like swilling and quaffing; thus sculkingly *Scotized* with Machiavillan projects; thus inconstantly *Englished* with every new fantasticall foolerie.[40]

In such prevalent satires of English "Apishness," the English nature is epito-mized, paradoxically, by its inability to project a fixed national identity. Hence, Thomas Dekker compares his countrymen's motley clothing to a

traitors bodie that hath beene hanged, drawne, and quartered, and is set up in severall places: his Codpeece is in *Denmarke*, the coller of his Duble and the belly in *France*: the wing and narrow sleeve in *Italy*; the short waste hangs over a *Dutch* Botchers stall; his huge sloppes speakes *Spanish*; *Polonia* gives him the Bootes.[41]

Susceptible to foreign influence, malleable, and inconstant, "Englishness" is always already about the forgetting of one's self. As Richard Helgerson's work has shown, "to be English was to be other," whether it was the otherness of the barbaric culture that they sought to reform or the otherness of the civility they embraced.[42]

Intriguingly, the early modern practice of characterizing the English as self-alienated corresponds with the Scottish geopolitical view of England as Britain's decadent "southern" region, corrupted by its long history of subjugation and foreign corruption. We can detect this pattern of thought in Hector Boece's *Scotorum Historiæ* (1526), which blames the loss of the Scottish people's native strength, virtue, and temperance on their interaction with "Inglismen":

For quhen oure nichtbouris, the Britonis, war maid effeminat be lang sleuth, and doung out of Britane be the Saxonis in Walis, we began to have alliance, be proximite of Romanis, with Inglismen; specially efter the exterminioun of Pichtis: and, be frequent and daily cumpany of thaim, we began to rute thair langage and superflew maneris in oure breistis; throw quhilk the virtew and temperance of our eldaris began to be of litel estimation amang us.[43]

In the same way that the Britons were made effeminate by yielding to the Sax-ons, Boece's Scotsmen lose their identities by intermingling with "Inglismen." As we shall see in chapters 5 and 7, the implications of Boece's historical narrative get played out in the early modern debates over the Anglo-Scottish union. In seeking to establish their own nation as unsullied by foreign in-vasion, Scottish writers claim that the repeated conquests of "southern" Britain weakened the Britons' capacity to resist not only subsequent invasions but also the effeminizing foreign luxuries that the conquerors brought with them.[44]

What we find when we turn to Boece's characterization of the elder Scots is a celebratory vision of the typical northern barbarian. Boece finds the ancient Scots' Scythian-like qualities most admirable, especially their capacity to endure cold and hard labor:

[The women] slepit on benkis, or bonchis of stra, bot ony cover; and lernit thair sonnis, fra thair first yeris, to eschew eis, and to sleip on the samin manner. Ilk moder wes nurice to her awin barne. It was ane suspition of adultre aganis ony woman, quhare hir milk failyeit. The wemen thocht thair barnis war not tender nor kindly to thaim, bot gif thay war nurist als weill with the milk of their breist, as thay war nurist afore with the blude of thair wambe. Attoure, they held that thair barnis war degenerat fra thair nature and kind, gif thay war nurist with uncouth milk. Thay war sa accustomit with ithand pine and laubouris, that thay curit nothir the fervent heites of the semer, nor yit the schil frostis in the winter.[45]

"Temperance and virtew" are the positive effects of this hard pastoral world, where the men, women, and children thrive in the face of harsh conditions and intemperate weather. Moreover, Boece suggests, it was the early Scots' strict maternal practices that warded off the usual disruptions in the transmission of admirable traits – such as the effeminating effects of ease and the dilution wrought by mingling – disruptions epitomized by the practice of wet-nursing. Strictly adhering to tribal and familial boundaries, the ancient Scottish women nursed their own children – a practice that early modern readers would have identified as recognizably Scottish. For Boece, breast-feeding not only carries the magical component of proving a child's legitimacy but it also helps ensure that the offspring will not "degenerat fra thair nature and kind," the certain consequence of imbibing foreign or "uncouth" milk.[46] Given that Boece has blamed his nation's decline on their mingling with the English, we should read in his description of breast-feeding a nostalgic portrait of ethnic purity.

I propose that Boece's idealization of Scotland's former barbarism and his characterization of England's decadence are national portraits that haunt early modern writings on the status of "Englishness." Keeping in mind Boece's positive valuation of his ancestors' northern temperament helps bring into focus the profound ambivalence that marks sixteenth-century English attitudes toward the acquisition of civility. Having been conquered so entirely by the Romans and then reconquered by the Saxons, the Danes, and the Normans, English writers betray a fear (*pace* Boece) that the only thing they have inherited from their earliest ancestors is the tendency to degenerate from their nature and kind.

It is worth noting here that even as late as the Jacobean period, English constructions of Scottish ethnicity continued to hearken back to Boece's portrait. Anthony Weldon's *A Perfect Description of the People and Country of Scotland* (1617) attributes "Scottishness" to the Scottish environs and to the savage mother's milk. But in his anti-Scots' view, Scottish ethnicity gets corrupted not by the English but by travel and the "civilizing" influences of more cosmopolitan France:

For the [Scottish] lords temporal and spiritual, [they are] temporizing gentlemen, if I were apt to speak of any, I could not speak much of them; only I must let you know they are not Scottishmen, for as soon as they fall from the breast of the beast of their mother, their careful sire posts them away for France, which as they pass, the sea sucks from them that which they have sucked from their rude dams; there they gather new flesh, new blood, new manners, and there they learn to put on their clothes, and then return into their countries to wear them out. There they learn to stand, to speak, and to discourse, and congee, to court women, and to compliment with men . . .[47]

As Weldon makes plain, Scottish civility is a vexed question for the English – a question I explore more fully in later chapters. We might say now, however, that Boece's barbarians are alive and well in Elizabethan Ireland; not only was it understood that the Scoto-Scythians descended from the Irish-Scythians, but English writers also held that the Irish remained as savage as their ancestors. We can, I propose, detect traces of Boece's valuation of English civility and Scythian barbarism at work in the writings of Camden and Spenser. And these Boecean vestiges suggest that condemnations of Irish intractability not only reveal early modern racial prejudices, but they also veil deeper anxieties about the malleability of the English. Camden, for example, makes a point of stressing that Rome forgot Ireland in its conquest of Britain, and as a result, the neglected Irish-Scythians failed to gain the "civility, learning, and elegance" that the Romans typically brought to "whom they conquered."[48] Hence, the Irish

are so stifly settled in observing of the old rites of their country, that not only they cannot be withdrawn from them, but are also able easily to draw the English unto the same (so prone is mans nature to entertain the worst) that one would not beleeve in how short a time some English among them degenerate and grow out of kinde.[49]

Boece had claimed that the "superflew maneris" of the English had brought about a decline in his admirably barbaric ancestors, thus equating degeneration with the spoliation of hyper-civility or decadence. In contrast, Camden inverts this narrative and suggests, more vaguely, that degeneration is a return either to the "old rites" or to "mans nature" at his "worst." This portrait of Irish barbarism is shaped, I believe, not only by Camden's desire to censure the Irish for their stubborn resistance but also by his troubled awareness of English tractability.

Speaking to the same subject, albeit with positive twist, Fynes Moryson suggests that the primary ethnological distinction between the English and Irish lies in their degree of malleability:

the English are naturally inclined to apply themselves to the manners and customs of any foreign nations with whom they live and converse, whereas the mere Irish by nature have singular and obstinate pertinacity in retaining their old manners and customs, so as they could never be drawn, by the laws, gentle government, and free conversation of the English, to any civility in manners or reformation in religion.[50]

Modern scholarship has detected racialist thinking in such Elizabethan constructions of the stubborn and intractable Irish; certainly such constructions
helped justify the Tudors' harsh measures of reform in Ireland.[51] But I want
to suggest here, and in the ensuing chapters, that the English also covet this
intractability, as a quality they locate nostalgically (and paradoxically) in their
own barbaric ancestors.

With regard to recent scholarly endeavors to understand early modern racialist notions, Spenser's *View* has gained canonical status.[52] Scholars have been
particularly intrigued by Spenser's thesis that the Old English, by living among
the Irish, have "degenerated," or "gone native," as some commentators have
put it. Though I do not have much to add to the rich work on the ethnological
tensions in *A View*, I do want to situate Spenser's ethnology among texts that
articulate similar ideas. How does Spenser's view of degeneration fit together
with what Boece, Bodin, and Camden say about it? We can see, I think, that
Spenser reverses Boece's narrative; the "civilized" English, rather than acting
as the corrupting force, are the ones who are altered by the Irish-Scythian barbarians. And not unlike Camden, Spenser indicates that the transformation of
the Old English may have more to do with the vulnerable effects of having been
"civilized" than with the contaminating influence of Irish barbarism. In his di-
alogue with Irenæus, Eudoxus wonders, "[I]s it possible that an Englishman,
brought up in such sweet civility as England affords, should find such likeing
in that barbarous rudenes, that he should forget his owne nature, and forgoe his
owne nation!"[53] In part what we have here is Spenser's articulation of Bodin's
thesis that if a people's counteractive and civilizing "lawes and customes be not
well maintained and kept," then barbarous "people will soone return to their
naturall dispositions."[54] But I am more interested in the implication that the
Englishman's "sweet civility" is what makes it all the more likely that he will
"forget his owne nature, and forgoe his owne nation." It is, of course, the un-
reformed and intractable Irish, not yet softened by "sweet civility," who refuse
to forget their nature.

Spenser recognizes that the ancient barbarians possessed qualities worthy of
admiration, and he grudgingly acknowledges these same traits in the stubborn
Irish-Scythians. Echoing Camden's praise of the ancient Britons, Spenser finds
the Irish-Scythian soldiers to be "very valiaunt, and hardie, for the most part
great indureres of colde, labour, hunger, and all hardnesse, very active and strong
of hand, very swift of foot."[55] This praise of the Irish-Scythians' capacity to
endure all "hardnesse" may remind us of Boece's veneration of the ancient
Scots.[56] It is, however, in another passage of *A View* where Spenser seems to
rework Boece's claim that the Scots' warrior qualities – and ethnological purity –
were maintained by the Scottish mothers' nursing their own sons. In a much-
noted passage, Irenæus describes how the Old English offspring have adopted
not just the speech but the manners and conditions of their Irish wet-nurses:

that young children be like apes, which will affect and imitate what they see done before
them, especially by their nurses, whom they love so well, they moreover drawe into
themselves, together with their sucke, even the nature and disposition of their nurses:
for the mind followeth much the temperature of the body.[57]

Whereas breast-feeding was identified with Scottish barbarism, the use of wet-
nurses in the sixteenth century would have been recognized as an elite English
custom. Read in light of Boece then, the failure of the Old English to eschew
"uncouth milk" not only points up their lack of rigor in maintaining tribal lines,
but it also reminds us that it is an ostensibly "civilized" *English* custom – wet-
nursing – that has led to this degeneration. The very malleability that enabled
English civility and that differentiated them from the hard Irish-Scythians is
also what makes the English so vulnerable to the indiscriminate absorption of
all things foreign and corrupt. Spenser's *View* implies, no doubt unintentionally,
that an Englishman *will* forget his own nature, for to do so is a symptom of
Englishness itself.[58]

Ethnological fashioning

Thus far I have been suggesting that in early modern England, the rise and
direction of geohumoralism followed changes in sixteenth-century English historiography – changes that led to questions regarding the nature and relative
civility of the English temperament. As we have noted, it was understood in this
period that a person's nature was determined not only by genealogy but also by
more immediate and manipulable influences, such as travel, diet, and education.
Part of what is fascinating about early modern ethnology is that very different
"technologies of the body," to use John Sutton's phrase, seem to have more or
less equal sway in effecting ethnic transformations. Hence, the implementation
of a law may counter the same humoral imbalance as a change in one's diet. The
primary distinction to be made, I propose, is whether the subject is fashioning
himself or being fashioned.

In this half of the chapter, I contend that the self-fashioning movement in
Elizabethan England – as represented in courtesy books, travel guides, educational handbooks, and dietaries – cannot be fully understood without attending
to the problem of regional identity. For the northerner, and the English in particular, to fashion oneself as a civilized, temperate gentleman meant countering
or refining one's innate disposition and inclinations. Thus, self-fashioning was
self-forgetting. But to help frame our discussion of Elizabethan English identities, it may help to recognize that at the root of what Norbert Elias has called the
"civilizing process" were the northern ethnological anxieties that I have been
outlining. What I mean is that Erasmus, whom Elias identifies as the originary
author in the reformation of Europe's "mental and emotional structure"[59] was

himself motivated to encourage temperamental and somatic transformations by his own ethnological subject-position as a Dutchman.

Sprinkled throughout Erasmus' writings are disparaging references to his own countrymen, whom he describes as fierce, gluttonous, dull-witted, "mean and uncultivated" barbarians – a "hungry race of people, born for the belly alone."[60] His own relationship to his national identity was troubled: he became an expatriate, forged a trans-national humanist identity, and sought the approval of Italian scholars; yet he also resented the Italians for their "pretentiousness and arrogance" and maintained hope that his own nation's disposition would improve.[61] In a private letter, Erasmus explicitly stated that his two life missions were "to civilize the Dutch by bringing them in contact with humanism and . . . to christianize the Italians."[62]

Dedicated to an heir of the Dutch royal family, Henry of Burgundy, the son of Adolph, Prince of Veere, *De civilitate morum puerilium* (1530) is premised on Erasmus' stated conviction that "[n]o one can choose his own parents or *nationality*, but each can mould his own talents and character for himself."[63] The close scrutiny and amusing detail with which Erasmus describes vulgar behavior in this text – he sees, Elias notes, "very exactly the exaggerated, forced nature of many courtly practices, and is not afraid to say so" – is consonant with his aim not just to establish decorum but to reshape a person's natural, and ethnic, inclinations. And the distinctive class consciousness that Elias and others have discovered in Erasmus – his capacity to "criticize 'rustic,' 'vulgar,' or 'coarse' qualities without accepting unconditionally . . . the behavior of great courtly lords" is, in part, attributable to the double vision that his own ethnic identity affords.[64] Since he imagines himself born of a naturally barbaric race, he also recognizes that, in the north at least, nurture rather than nature would produce a distinctive elite.

Bringing a regional framework to our reading of Erasmus helps us reconsider, I propose, how the importation of courtesy manuals in early modern England had ethnological implications. We should recall, for example, that when Thomas Hoby justifies his translation of *The Courtier* (1561), he not only seeks to refine the English language but he also concedes that the English people themselves have been "counted barbarous . . . time out of minde" in their "maners."[65] Indeed, the Italian manuals made it clear that one's success in cultivating a noble mind depended on the nature of the body. As Count Annibale Romei's *Courtiers Academie* declares, humans are:

of divers temperatures . . . and in their mindes different effects and affects are discovered: from whence it proceedeth in reason, that some are esteemed of noble race, and others of ignoble: some ingenious, others stupide: some prevaile with force of mind, and are truely worthy to command, and others be as it were lumpish sturdy, with whome servitude better befitteth.[66]

I am not disputing the view that Erasmus' work gave rise to an industry of courtesy books everywhere – books that focused on the internal social structures of individual regions – but I am proposing that the "civilizing process" had ethnological implications for those regions identified as "northern." In Elias' narrative, the whole of European society underwent a kind of maturation process, moving away from a warrior culture in which the "instincts, the emotions were vented more freely, more directly, more openly than later."[67] But in the north, where the native environment, it was presumed, continued to engender aggressive emotions and barbarous appetites, the evolution of civility had a more complicated narrative than merely temporal progression.

For the most part, scholars have conceived of the civilizing process in terms of class, without factoring in longstanding regional biases. I am suggesting that for early modern northern Europeans, and for the English in particular, class anxieties regarding the attainment of civility were necessarily entangled with concepts of ethnicity. It is worth reiterating that Erasmus reminds his readers that man cannot choose either his parents or his nationality, thus indicating not only that low status may be determined by birth *or* by birthplace but also that such deficiencies or flaws – rendered by either place or family – may be remedied by adopting new behaviors and bodily practices.

For the English, the loss of their primarily aristocratic myth of Trojan origins – of civilized, southern roots – threatened to level the entire nation to an ignoble sameness determined by their shared northern climate. As the ethnographic writings of Bodin, Huarte, Charron, and others made clear, laborers, soldiers, and rude mechanicals were presumed to thrive in the north, as opposed to the rulers and politicians who flourished in the temperate regions, and the priests and prophets that the south produced. In other words, in a ranked ordering of the world's triple regions, northerners were akin to the lowest of the three estates. The "dreams of racism," Benedict Anderson has argued, "actually have their origin in ideologies of *class*, rather than those of nation: above all in claims to divinity among rulers and to 'blue' or 'white' blood and 'breeding' among aristocracies," but what I am attending to here is the fluid interim between the formation of class ideologies and racialist claims: an interim when the British people's northern identity stood in contradistinction to noble aristocratic breeding.[68]

We can detect this distinctly northern tension between class and ethnicity in the humoral discourse of Levinus Lemnius, a Belgian physician who penned the popular *De Habitu et Constitutione* (Antwerp 1561), later translated into *The Touchstone of Complexions* (1576) by Thomas Newton. Establishing that "the diversity of spirits, and the differences of wittes and maners procedeth of the condition and nature of the Place, Ayre, Countrey and nourishment," Lemnius characterizes ethnic identity itself as a form of humoral intemperance.[69] As a "Zelander," whose son resides in London, Lemnius focuses primarily on the natural disposition of northern ethnicities – Hollanders, Flemyngs, Brabanders, Germans, and the English – and his general portrait of them echoes the classical texts: "they that dwell Northward and in cold regions, by reason of grosse bloud and thick Spirites, are seene to be bolde and full of venturous courage, rude, unmannerly, terrible, cruell, fierce" (fol. 13r). Confirming the ancient view that Thomas Walkington will later refute, Lemnius identifies "pure sanguine" men as having "the nature and Sense of bruite beastes (are commonly dotes and fooles, or at least, not greatly cumbred with much witte)" (fol. 96r). And while the Englishmen's sanguine complexion ensures that they are as physically fair and strong as the classical northern barbarians ("of stature comely and proportionable, and body lusty and wel complexioned"), Lemnius also notes that their "mynde and appetite" are continually ruled by "theyr high and hauty stomacks," a quality that lumps them with the Scots (fol. 18r).

And yet Lemnius is composing a handbook for humoral regulation, thus it is the implicit thesis of *De Habitu et Constitutione* that an individual can regulate his or her intemperance (however determined by location) with diet and custom. Moreover, Lemnius suggests, it is the barbarous northerner who is most needful of such correction:

For where the Spirites be grosse, thicke and cold, it happeneth the mynde to be over-clowded & (as the dymmed Sunne) not to shyne brighte out. And this is the reason that persons in this sort affected have duller Wyttes, and blunter capacities. For proofe whereof, we are to see & consider, such as are borne and bred neere to the Pole Articke & ycie Sea, who for the most part are very huge & stronge bodyed, but for witte and learning, meere doltes & Asseheads: albeit this Nacion through the greate care & singuler wyse-dome of the most noble Prince Erick Kynge of Sweden, is nowe trayned to more civill order, & have their mynds wyth goodly qualityes ryght vertuously adourned. (fol. 16r)

But we are also to understand that those with the greatest need for good government may also be most apt and humorally disposed to reformation, for it is the "rude wittes, not yet trained to any disciplyne and learning, [which] may like soft waxe, or as tractable and moyst clay, be fashioned, framed, and made applyable to learne any knowledge, any vertue, any civilitye" (fol. 4r). The sanguine-complected, for example, though innately foolish and beast-like, prove especially pliant and may be "broughte to much goodnes," with "use, exercise, and the framing of manners" (fols. 98f–99r). And the English, in particular, though somewhat slow-witted and not naturally given to the study of "artes or mysteries" are "right apt and inclynable" to learn (fol. 18r).

In recommending that his readers seek to change their regionally determined natures, Lemnius acknowledges that such interventions are what produce the behavioral and somatic distinctions between the upper and lower orders:

Not withstanding education, institution, and discipline, altereth the usuall nature, and ordynary conditions of every Region: for we see the common sort and multitude, in behaviour and manners grosse and unnurtured, whereas the Nobles and Gentlemen (altering theyr order & dyet, and digressing from the common fashion of their pezantly countreymen) frame themselves & theirs to a very commendable order, and civill behaviour. (fol. 16v)

Lemnius recognizes here that all men born in the north possess "behavior and manners grosse and unnurtured," or a "pezantly" nature. It is only by vigilant discipline in deportment and diet that the "Nobles and Gentlemen" are able to "digress" from the "ordinary" and crude influences of their home country. In the same way that Erasmus' northern perspective may have led him to question the natural origins of civility, Lemnius imagines that civil behavior can be cultivated. Moreover, such civility is cosmopolitan; it erases national boundaries and is opposed to the northerner's "usuall nature."

We can find an English example of the way region functions in the north as the first premise of humoral practices in Thomas Wright's *The Passions of the Minde in Generall* (1604). This treatise, which declares itself as a guide for discovering the humors and passions of others and for regulating one's own, opens with a preface that frames the text as an English handbook for ethnological refashioning. Trotting through what is now-familiar stuff, Wright acknowledges that the inhabitants of "these Northerne Climates," and notably the English, are accounted simple, uncivil, barbarous, unwary, and unwise due to the natural "constitution of the body."[70] Conversely, the southerners' "natural complexion and constitution of body" predisposes them to political "warinesse," understanding, and judgment – qualities that they perfect through education and experience.

But Wright's text is most significant, I contend, for its explicit articulation of the notion that the most potent remedy for the northerner's plain simplicity and rude behavior is the adoption of a southern temperament. Wright recognizes that for the northerner civility resides in others; thus, he encourages his countrymen to take a "little direction" from the darker, more "brazen" southerner – to cultivate their own version of southern "warinesse" – and to learn to "dissemble better his owne passions, and use himselfe therein more circumspectly, than we [currently] can doe" (pp. lix; lxii). In other words (following the counteractive logic of Galenic medicine), Wright suggests that the English contravene their "northern" excesses with southern qualities. Wright is aware that he is navigating dangerous waters, and he assures his readers that he is not encouraging men to be "craftie and deceitfull . . . [or] vitious," or "Italianate," but to attain, instead, a "prudent carriage" (pp. lxii–lxiii). Indeed, such advice – that the English should imitate their antipodal counterparts (variously identified by Wright as "brazen-faced" southerners, Spaniards, and Italians) – sounds a bit like a perverse celebration of Roger Ascham's Italianate Englishman.

Setting off a debate over travel that would expand into the next century, Roger Ascham had asserted in *The Scolemaster* that when the "plain" Englishman visits Italy, he returns monstrously transformed – becoming a "dull Asse, to understand either learnying or honestie: and yet shall he be as sutle as a Foxe, in breedying of mischief, in bringying in misorder, with a busie head, a discoursing tong, and a factious harte."[71] No longer simply English, but "Italianated," these travelers had forgotten their own country, deeming it "stale and rude" in their search for refinement abroad.[72] But as Ascham's opponents argued, travel to the continent was deemed necessary if one wished to "chase away such barbarousnesse and rudenesse as possesseth [the English and] establish a more humane and sociable carriage."[73] In his *Instructions for Forreine Travell* (1642), James Howell tells English travelers to

bring home the best . . . From the *Italian* he will borrow his *reservednesse*, not his *jealousie* and *humor of revenge*; From the *French* his *Horsemanship* and gallantnesse that way, with his *Confidence*, and nothing else: From the *Spaniard* his *Sobriety*, not his *lust*: From the *German* (clean Contrary) his *Continency*, not his *Excesse*, the other way: From the *Netherland* his *Industry*, and that's all. His heart must still remaine *English*, though I allow him some choice and change of *Habit* . . . If any Forrainer be to be imitated in his manner of *Discours* and *Comportement*, it is the *Italian*, who may be said to be a medium 'twixt the *Gravity* of the Spaniard, the *Heavinesse* of the *Dutch*, and *Levity* of our next Neighbours, for he seemes to allay the one, and quicken the other two; to serve as a *buoy* to the one, and a *ballast* to th'other.[74]

Depending on one's perspective, Italy represented either the birthplace or decay of western civilization, and exposure to Italian culture, combined with the physiological effects of warmer temperatures, held the promise or the threat of transformation. As late as the 1670s young Englishmen were still being sent to "bolder Climates to correct their Flegm."[75] And though Ascham condemns the educational tour, he does encourage his countrymen to read Castiglione (in translation) in an effort to improve their carriage as gentlemen.

Though scholars have read the admonition against travel in *The Scolemaster* primarily as an indictment of Italian corruption, we should also consider how Ascham's text registers an analogous concern with the impressibility and vulnerability of Englishness. Ascham's ambivalence regarding the education of English youth stems in part, I propose, from his understanding that they are perched precariously between domestic boorishness ("Mules and Horses") and utter dissipation into something neither English nor Italian ("Swyne and Asses").[76] Moreover, Ascham's interests involve the same temperamentally oriented issues that Wright and Lemnius raise – how to shape or ameliorate an "inclynable," "pliant" (Lemnius), or "unwary" (Wright) disposition. As Frank Whigham has argued in *Ambition and Privilege*, Ascham's description of England's excessive number of "quick wits" rests on a crucial "congruence between the quick wit and the Italianate Englishmen."[77] Not unlike Lemnius' "rude wits," who are "as tractable" and soft as wax or "moist clay," the quick wit is "apte to take." The downside, however, is that he is also "unapte to keepe."[78]

Invoking the stereotype so often applied to the English in the sixteenth century, Ascham observes that these quick wits, like the Italianated courtier, seek after whatever is "newfangle," thereby proving "unconstant," "light," and effeminately infirm "in purpose."[79] As Whigham notes, the parallel between the quick wit and the Italianate Englishman subtlety indicates that the true source of corruption lies not in Italy but in the English schools.[80] To push this even further, we could also say that the problem lies not so much in the educational system as in the excessively malleable nature of the typically "English" wit. The attainment of civility proves a risky business for the English, as Ascham makes abundantly clear. Since the pursuit of refinement often takes the form of adopting or experiencing the fashions and customs of the "Other," this, in turn, feeds the spreading cultural fear that the English people's further subjection to foreign cultures and habits will merely exacerbate their already impressionable natures.

These are, in fact, the frustrations that fuel William Rankins' *The English Ape* (1588) – a treatise that opens with the assertion that England's "natural manners" were, in fact, "created perfect" by its native climate, until apish desires for foreign fashions and customs brought about their current state of degeneration.[81] Acknowledging that attire and habit can transform the inner man, Rankins insists that it is the individual's willful, intrusive efforts to transform or fashion himself that produce the most monstrous results:

This continuall strife to frame a uniformity of inwarde condition to externall habite breedeth such intollerable inconvenience: that wee seeme rather the men, which nature hath marked for a prodigious spectacle of her contrary opinions, then a people, where pollitique proceedings, and peaceable governement swayeth with lawe, and equitie.[82]

Rankins' description of those who strive to align their inward condition with their adopted and strange "externall habite" may remind us in particular of that Elizabethan stereotype: the feigning melancholic – black-suited men, who sought to cultivate comparably black, and arguably alien, humors.[83] As I shall argue in the next chapter, the vogue of melancholia in England is a story that cannot be separated from the English people's conflicted perception of their native disposition, nor, more surprisingly, is it a story that can be separated from an emergent construction of racial differences.

3   An inside story of race: melancholy and ethnology

As I have been arguing, the early modern controversy over travel and foreign fashions – whether viewed as practices that would refine the northerner or ensure his corruption – reveals the Englishman's deep anxiety over his natural complexion. I would like to note further that when the transformation of the "English ape" or Italianated traveler was interpreted in specifically humoral terms, he was classified as a melancholic. Early modern writers may disagree over the authenticity of the traveler's melancholy, but we should see this quarrel as a part of the larger ethnological concern that any melancholic Englishman, whether feigning, infected, or struck with genuine sadness, is estranged from his native temperament and complexion.[1] As Shakespeare's Rosalind observes of the nominally French Jacques, who has gathered a lisp and strange suits from his journeys, his somber behavior shows him to be "out of love with [his] nativity" (*As You Like It*, 4. 1. 31). In describing the English malcontent's adopted melancholy, Thomas Lodge writes: "He hath been a longe Traveller, and seene manie countries, but as it is said of the toad, that he sucketh up the corrupt humors of the garden where hee keepeth: so this wretch from al those Provinces he hath visted, bringeth home nothing but the corruptions to disturbe the peace of his countrie, and destroy his owne bodie and soule..."[2]

Though scholars have long recognized that the Elizabethan vogue of melancholia began as a fashionable affectation of Italian dress, behavior, and affect, they have failed to consider this cultural phenomenon in ethnological terms.[3] In a strictly Galenic sense, the appeal of melancholia or black bile lies in its constancy and firmness – the very qualities that the English notoriously lacked.[4] But it was the legacy of Aristotle's *Problem* xxx, the seminal text on genial melancholy, together with Marsilio Ficino's reorientation of melancholic genius within both the pragmatics of humoral medicine and the transcendent framework of Neoplatonism that succeeded in imbuing melancholia with a power and agency that outstripped the other humors. I propose that England's profound and ambivalent interest in the cultivation of melancholy, once framed within the larger discourse of ethnographic humoralism, becomes a story of how the predominantly sanguine and phlegmatic English both censured and celebrated a humor initially perceived to be antithetical to their own. Perversely

Figure 4 "Melancholy," from John of Foxton, *Liber cosmographiae* (1408), Trinity College MS R.15.21.

anticipating the "love and theft" that Eric Lott finds in the blackface minstrelsy of the nineteenth century – "[u]nderwritten by envy as well as repulsion, sympathetic identification as well as fear" – the early modern English imitated and incorporated what was understood to be the affect and temper of southern blackness.[5] Indeed, melancholy in England was frequently cast as borrowed behavior, affected by class upstarts and political dissidents who longed to project an intellectual distinction and sophistication that would distinguish them from what Levinus Lemnius had identified as the northerner's "grosse" and "pezantly" nature.[6] The rub, for the English then, is that the northern validation of melancholy threatens to alienate them from their own "nativity."

In the continental writings of Bodin, Pierre Charron, and Juan Huarte, the regional origination of genial melancholy is unmistakable. Indeed, Bodin insists that any "judgment of history" should recognize that Aristotle's *Problem* xxx, the originary text to claim that all men who "become eminent in philosophy or politics or poetry or the arts are clearly of an atrabilious temperament," is most aptly applied to dark-skinned southerners.[7] Not only do these writers acknowledge a link between southerners, external blackness, and innate wisdom, they also explicitly exclude northerners from what Juliana Schiesari terms "the canon of melancholia."[8] From Huarte's Spanish perspective, for example, the excessively moist, cold northerners possess neither imagination, nor understanding. The Flemmish, Dutch, English, and French have wits "like those of drunkards . . . & this is occasioned by the much moisture, wherwith their braine is replenished, and the other parts of the bodie: the which is knowen by the whitenesse of the face."[9] Bodin contends that if "those corpulent and sanguin men towards the North" are struck with melancholy, they "do nothing but dance, laugh and leape in their fooleries."[10] Ironically, the English, who have in our day a reputation for "dry wit," were among those hampered by a great "abundance of blood and humor" and unable to "separate themselves from these earthly dregs."[11] The fleshiness that weighed northerners down on an implicit chain of being brings them closer to animals than angels. And since excess humors clouded the judgment, they were like beasts in not knowing, as Pierre Charron observes, "how to contein and governe themselves."[12]

For these continental writers, there is a reliable correspondence between the external "complexion" of one's skin and one's humoral complexion. Since Huarte's northerners are phlegmatic, they are white; Bodin's northerners are phlegmatic and sanguine, therefore white or ruddy. It makes sense then that the blackness of Ethiopians and Egyptians would be produced by an abundance of melancholy or black bile, which, as Bodin explains it, "subsides like lees to the bottom when the humors have been drawn out by the heat of the sun."[13] It is this same black bile that "sharpens the wits and divides man from man." As a result, southerners have been inclined to "seek the highest learning and the secrets of nature"; they are naturally prophets, astronomers, philosophers, and mathematicians.[14] Indeed, it is the notorious paradoxes of Aristotle's *Problem* XXX that underline Bodin's contention that southerners are either extraordinarily blessed or cursed, for their melancholic mind is "apter for great vertues" but also prone to "notorious vices of the minde...for greatest spirits are subject to greatest vertues and vices."[15]

As any student of melancholy knows, Marsilio Ficino's writings equated "the Aristotelian clinical category of melancholy with the Platonic poetics of 'divine frenzy,'" thus transforming black bile into a "positive virtue for men of letters."[16] In the history of melancholic discourse, however, Ficino's work may be more important for initiating the concept that melancholy is a humor to be cultivated. Ficino's *De Vita* is primarily a practical guidebook for scholars on how to fashion their bodies as instruments of contemplation, offering specific and detailed instructions on the diet, exercise, and meditative rituals – the technologies of the body that will best nurture the atrabilious condition. As Ficino sees it, melancholy and thought feed one another, for "[c]ontemplation itself...contracts one's nature like black bile."[17] Given the complexities of Aristotle's text and the instability of the humoral body, achieving and then regulating such melancholy proves to be a full-time job.

Continuing the difficulties of *Problem* XXX, while fostering a new tradition of abstruse melancholic discourse (which will eventually produce Robert Burton's tome, *The Anatomy of Melancholy* [1621]), Ficino makes careful distinctions between an ideal, subtle, moderately heated humor and other, less delicate, varieties, such as the "burning kind," which causes mania, and cold, dry soot, which "makes you dull and stupid" (p. 8). Excessive black bile must be avoided, he insists, for "even when it is moderated, and mixed with blood and bile, and its condition is as thin as its nature allows, its dry nature is easily inflamed because it is so strong and tough." But dryness in particular signifies the body's elect status: "Remember what Heraclitus said: Dry light = the wisest soul" (p. 10). If the ideal state of black bile is achieved, it has the capacity to move a student "to understand the highest things, since it is in accord with Saturn, the highest of planets" (p. 6).

In Bodin's view, the Ethiopians and Egyptians are most inclined to Ficino's idealized complexion, for if the southerners' "melancholy...has been well-tempered," he writes, they not only can "achieve remarkable strength of mind and body," but they are also open to the "knowledge of things divine."[18] In remarkably Ficinian terms, Bodin declares that

The heavenly light doth shine far more brighter in pure and cleane spirits [of the southerners], than in those which are poluted with base and earthly affections. And if it be so that the true purifying of the soule is by his heavenly light, and by the force of contemplation in the most perfect subject; without doubt they shall soonest attaine unto it which have their souls ravished up into heaven; the which we see happen unto melancholike men.[19]

Indeed, Bodin traces the origins of all wisdom to the southerners and their warm climate: "From these people letters, useful arts, virtues, training, philosophy, religion, and lastly *humanitas* itself flowed upon earth as from a fountain."[20] Though the Moors represented on the English stage would seem to possess few of these virtues, we can discern a faint Ficinian genealogy in their dramatic portraits: as we have seen, Aaron in *Titus Andronicus* attributes his appearance and his "cloudy melancholy" to Saturn's governing influence, and the Moor in *The Battell of Alcazar* (1594) claims that his nature is derived from that "fatall starre, what planet ere thou be."[21]

If we read Bodin's perspective back into Ficino, it is also possible to detect what will become a significant pattern in sixteenth-century geohumoralism: the northern appropriation of ancient Africa's melancholic darkness. As the translator of the *Corpus Hermeticum*, the basis of his Neoplatonist philosophy, Ficino would have known that the "Egyptians [were] particularly favored," for their warm climate and planetary aspects made them "exceptionally intelligent and wise."[22] When Ficino expresses doubts about his own identification with Saturn, his friend Giovanni Cavalcanti recalls that it was Saturn that gave him "the strength to travel through Greece and reach even the land of the Egyptians in order to bring back to us the wisdom of that ancient people."[23] But it is also a significant part of Ficino's achievement, as Schiesari has demonstrated, that he recreates melancholia as a "sign" of genius within, locating the darkness of black bile much more inside than outside.[24] Crucial to Ficino's appropriation of internal *atra bilis* is the obfuscation of more localized or environmental origins of melancholia:

So far it is enough to have shown that the priests of the Muses get melancholy either from the very beginning or as they study, because of *either heavenly, natural, or human causes*. Aristotle confirms this in his book of *Problems*. For all men, he says, who are distinguished in some faculty, are melancholiacs.[25]

Though Ficino may hint elsewhere that the Egyptians were the first priests and philosophers for either "heavenly" or "natural" reasons, here in *De Vita* he relies on the ambiguities of Aristotle to leave open the possibility that all melancholy may be traced to human will – that it can be cultivated by distinguished men anywhere in the world.[26] I am suggesting that we may interpret Ficino's careful production and monitoring of internal melancholia as displacing the Egyptian priest's readily visible and innate darkness without. In this reading, Ficinian melancholy, as a cultivated inscription within, relies on a disjunction between black bile and its more conventional physiognomic indicators.

However much Jean Bodin may praise the south's special melancholic powers, his humoral logic is determined by nationalist interests; indeed, across Europe, the substance of wisdom and the terms of melancholia were being rewritten to suit national biases. For Bodin, Ficinian *contemplativa vita* is faulted for its passivity and its removal from the business of government; it is suited solely for priests and prophets. Since he locates France in the middle temperate zone, he ultimately privileges a more muscular and active "prudence" as the best sort of wisdom – a wisdom he links to the French people's choleric complexions. And though the ancient origins of wisdom can be traced to Ethiopia and Egypt, Bodin also affirms that it is the extremes of Africa – its excessive heat and melancholic peoples – which have led to its degeneration.

Initially it is striking that Bodin willingly supports a history of wisdom that traces its origins to the hot climates of Africa, establishing an association between what we would term a "racialized" blackness and genial melancholy. Less surprising is his, Huarte's, and Charron's shared desire to challenge this history by rearranging classical geohumoral logic – a desire that paves the way, I believe, for racialist thinking. Whether they seek to appropriate melancholic wisdom or deny its elevated status, these continental writers struggle to establish their "temperate" home regions as superior, and to do so demanded the demotion of Africa's past. It would be overly hasty, however, to identify their discourse as racialist. More accurately, early modern geohumoralism is situated within the contradictions already present in the classical texts, setting, as we have seen, Hippocrates against Aristotle. Indeed it is both the fluidity and determinism of geohumoralism that compels European writers to denigrate African wisdom, for the decline of one culture implies the elevation of the other.

While Bodin maintains, rather simply, that French "prudence" is superior to melancholic contemplation, Juan Huarte in *The Examination of Men's Wits* (1594) makes the more complex argument that, when compared to the genuine genial melancholy of the Spanish, African melancholia is a form of madness. At first, Huarte concedes that those "men who inhabit very hot countries (as *Aegypt*) are more wittie and advised than those who are borne in cold regions," attributing the southerners' wiliness and appearance to the drying effects of their climate.[27] In Egypt, in particular,

the sunne yeeldeth a fervent heat: and therefore the inhabitants have their brain dried, and choler adust, the instrument of wilinesse and aptnesse: In which sense, *Aristotle* demandeth why the men of Aethiopia & Aegypt, have their feet crooked, & are commonly curlpated and flat nosed? to which probleme he answereth, that the much heat of the countrey rosteth the substance of these members, and wrieth them, as it draweth togither a peece of leather set by the fire; and for the same cause, their hair curleth, and themselves also are wily. (p. 188)

Though Aristotle informs Huarte's knowledge of the sun's drying effects, he has rejected the counteractive theory of temperatures in favor of Hippocrates' doctrine. Hence, Huarte's northerners are cold and moist, and his southerners are hot and dry. Rather than strengthening the Egyptians' faculty of "understanding," excessive internal heat ignites the imagination. And it is this heated imagination, Huarte maintains, that has produced their legacy of "wisdom":

Aegypt alone is the region which ingendereth in his inhabitants this differe[n]ce of imagination, wherthrough the Historiens never make an end of telling, how great enchaunters the Aegyptians are, and how readie for obtaining things, and finding remedies to their necessities... And *Plato* also sayd, that the Aegyptians exceeded all the men of the world in skill how to get their living; which abilitie appertaineth to the imagination. (p. 183)

Ultimately Huarte construes the Africans' extraordinary powers as a kind of frenzied busyness. Clearly valuing Ficino's more contemplative wisdom, he denigrates the southerners' pursuits of poetry, music, and preaching as heated *activities*. In the same vein, he casts their physic, mathematics, and astrology as mere "practices" associated with "all the engins & devises which artificers make" (p. 103).

Reconstructing the value of African melancholy enables Huarte to appropriate the exceptional qualities of *atra bilis* for his own countrymen, which he does by returning to the contradictions of Aristotle's *Problem* x x x. It turns out that Aristotle did not mean "that the cold blood... did better the understanding, but that which is lesse hote" (p. 57). Moreover, it is the variations in the temperature of black bile that affect the kind of "wisdom" it produces (p. 147). While excessive heat in the brain gives rise to those frenzied madmen and prophets found in the south (p. 45), a brain that "arrive[s] to that point of convenient heat" (p. 87) makes for men of great understanding – and this is, of course, "the ordinarie wit for Spaine" (p. 303). Thus the Spanish possess a melancholy made of delicate parts, conjoined with "reason" and "simplicity" (pp. 87; 147). And given their dry, moderately heated complexion, they excel in the *contemplative* studies of theology, "the *Theorick of Phisicke, logicke, natural and morall Philosophy*, and the praticke of the lawes" (p. 103).

In *Of Wisdome* (1612), Pierre Charron also affirms and then challenges the traditional argument that the "Southerne people of the world are drie, and moderate in the inward heat of the braine, by reason of their violent outward heat," and thus akin to dry, cool "melancholicke men... [who] are wise and ingenious."[28] Indeed, he concedes that

Speculative Sciences came from the South. *Cesar* and other ancients of those times called the Ægyptians ingenious, and subtile; *Moyses* is said to be instructed in their wisdome: and Philosophie came from thence into *Greece*. Greatnesse began rather with them, because of their spirit and subtiltie. (p. 165)

Like Bodin and Huarte, Charron maps the faculties of the mind onto the tripartite divisions of the world: understanding, which most consider "the first, most excellent and principall" faculty, thrives in the south, "in the second place is the imagination," which emerges in the middle regions, and the memory, which is "last," functions best among northern peoples (pp. 51, 48–9, 167).

It is, however, Charron's aim to consider the "great and almost infinite diversitie of opinions... those doubts and objections that have always crossed" the status of human understanding (p. 52).[29] Countering Bodin's thesis that southern understanding functions as pure and divine inspiration, Charron points out that some writers are of the opinion that

> It selfe either it understands not at all... or very darkly, imperfectly, and indirectly, by reflexion of the knowledge of things upon themselves, by which it perceiveth and knoweth that it understandeth. (p. 52)

Echoing Huarte, Charron identifies the imagination with a heated complexion, but unlike Huarte, he elevates this busy and unquiet faculty (p. 51) above "understanding" and locates it within his own "middle regions":

> The temperature of the imagination is hot, from whence it commeth that franticke men, and such as are sicke of burning maladies, are excellent in that that belongs to imagination, as *Poetry, Divination,* and that it hath greatest force in young men, and of middle yeeres (Poets and Prophets have flourished in this age) and in the middle parts betwixt North and South... Hereby it appeareth that the vivacitie, subtiltie, promptitude, and that which the common sort call wit, belongs to a hot imagination; soliditie, maturitie, veritie, to a drie understanding. The imagination is active and stirring, it is it that undertaketh all, and sets all the rest a worke: the understanding is dull and cloudie. (pp. 48–50)

Charron implies that Bodin's interpretation of Aristotle's *Problem* xxx is in error. The Egyptians' divine inspiration and their cool powers of understanding are but a dull reflection of the imaginative heat produced in France – a heat that derives its powers not from Ficino's technologies of the body but from its people's natural complexion.

White melancholy

Can we talk about race in *Hamlet*?   Peter Erickson[30]

England's profound interest in melancholy in the late sixteenth century puts even greater pressure on the same geohumoral logic that cast the English as barbaric, intemperate, pale-skinned northerners. For Huarte, Charron, and Bodin, rewriting melancholic discourse meant identifying the middle regions' form of "wisdom" as superior to southern melancholy. But for the English, rewriting melancholic discourse raises the more radical challenge of securing a position for the white *homo melancholicus.* Given the northerners' exclusion from genial melancholy in Renaissance ethnography, it should come as no surprise that the most unequivocally negative statements regarding melancholy are northern in origin. The English publication of *The Problemes of Aristotle* (1595), for example, whose title seems to announce itself as a translation of Aristotle's *Problems,* makes no mention of the paradoxical *Problem* xxx. Instead, the text poses the question, "Why is the melancholy complexion the worst of all complexions?"

And it answers: "Because it is the dregges of the bloud, which is an enmie of mirth, and farthest off from the beginning of mans life, and bringeth olde age and death, because it is dry and cold."[31] Similarly, Walkington's *The Optick Glasse* argues that those writers who have identified "melancholike men" as the "rarest wittes of all" have proven most "shallow" in their reasoning: "He that wishes this humor [melancholy] whereby he might become more witty, is as fond as *Democritus*, who put out both his eyes voluntarily to bee given more to contemplation."[32]

Timothie Bright, whose *Treatise of Melancholy* (1586) is the most extensive discussion of the humor by an English writer before Robert Burton's *Anatomy of Melancholy* (1621), is remarkably careful to draw a distinction between "natural" melancholy, which makes men pale, and the blackness of choler adust or unnatural melancholy. It is the natural, wan sort of melancholy, he maintains, that "profytheth moche to true judgment of wyt," while the blacker kind "annoyeth the wytte and jugment of man." What may surprise modern readers, however, is that "natural" melancholy manifests itself in those who are not naturally melancholic:

[Being] cold, drie, thick and hard of passage, in melancholick persons, procure[s] that leane, and spare bodie of the melancholicke: *except it be by former custome of diet, or naturally otherwise, which the force of melancholy hath not yet so farre altered.* Of this coldnes and drynes, riseth hardnes whereof the flesh of melancholy persons is: *except the melancholy rise of some disorder of diet, or passions, and hath not yet entred so farre upon the complexion.* Of colour they be black, according to the humour whereof they are nourished, and the skinne alwayes receaving the blacke vapors, which insensibly do passe from the inward parts, taketh die and staine therof: *saving that in the beginning it may come to passe otherwise, the body white, and bloud blacke*; nature for a time serving her selfe of that which is purest, and leaving the grossest in the vaines, till for want of better, in the end it be faine to take of the melancholicke, which before it disdained: then altereth it the colour, and fairenesse is turned into morphe.[33]

In other words, the white melancholic is not innately so but derives his humor from experience or practice, such as "custome," "diet," or "passions," while those predisposed to (unnatural) melancholy are "cold," "drie," "leane," and "black." Eventually, however, pale melancholics will take on the "die and staine therof" of the blackness within. If we read ethnological tensions in Bright's verbal gymnastics, we can detect some effort on his part to establish not only the legitimacy of "white" melancholy but also its superiority: "natural" melancholy does not simply profit the wit, it "disdaineth" blackness – for a time. Yet he must also concede that "natural" melancholy is secondary – the consequence of one's disordered diet or submission to "custom." The external whiteness of natural melancholy turns out to be merely a temporary and delayed state in the inevitable correspondence between black skin and black bile.

Further attesting to the importance melancholic discourse plays in the valorization of Englishness is the size and seeming exhaustiveness of Robert

Burton's *The Anatomy of Melancholy* (1621). Most obviously, by providing the definitive word on melancholy, Burton manages to "democratize" the humor so that it appears everywhere and in everyone. We should not, however, assume that Burton's prolixity negates a nationalist agenda. To the contrary, we should consider why traditional genial melancholy is practically non-existent in Burton's *Anatomy*. As Bridget Gellert Lyons has noted, "the favorable aspect of curiosity that the Florentine Neoplatonists elaborated upon, and that was stressed by Huarte, is never present when [Burton] is talking about [melancholy] directly."[34] Indeed, *The Anatomy* has a decidedly English perspective: it not only casts doubt on the conventional link between genial melancholy and southern climates, but it also seeks to validate the sanguine complexion. Arguably, the text's most direct link between melancholy and genius is Burton's own self-conscious commentary on the authorial production of the *Anatomy* itself. Burton writes the *Anatomy* in order to avoid melancholy, and in doing so, indulges in learned contemplations on natural, moral, and divine philosophy. As the author of his subject, Burton appropriates melancholy's elite genius.[35]

As the "Digression of the Ayre" illustrates, the relationship between national character and climate is an issue Burton must confront and bracket. Offering a jumbled survey of geohumoral tenets, he asks:

Whence proceed that variety of manners, and a distinct character (as it were) to several nations? Some are wise, subtile, witty; others dull, sad and heavy; some big, some little ... some soft, and some hardy, barbarous, civil, black, dun, white; is it from the air, from the soil, influence of the stars, or some other secret cause? ... How comes it to pass, that in the same site, in one latitude, to such as are *periœci* [neighbors], there should be such difference of soil, complexion, colour, metal, air, etc. The Spaniards are white, and so are Italians, whenas the inhabitants about *Caput Bonae Spei* [the Cape of Good Hope] are blackamoors, and yet both alike distant from the Equator.[36]

If we recall Wright's "brazen" Italians and Spaniards, or pay heed to Huarte's idealization of the Spaniard's "somewhat browne" complexion, then the "whiteness" that Burton discovers is all the more relative.[37] Considered on their own, Burton's questions have a disengaged, scientific air, and yet we should not assume that he is challenging older knowledge with empirical evidence. He has no doubt, for example, that the climate alters the "constitutions of ... bodies, and the temperature itself." What proves curious is his mistaken assertion that neither Aristotle nor Bodin attributed the transformation of "customs, manners, [and] wits" to environmental influences (II, p. 61).

Indeed, Burton must shape the writings of Bodin and Aristotle to suit his northern interests. In the chapter "Bad Air as a Cause of Melancholy," for example, he seems at first to affirm Bodin's views, citing the author "in his fifth book, *De repub. cap.* 1 and 5, of his Method of History," to "prove[ ] that hot countries are most troubled with melancholy" (I, p. 237). Yet he simply ignores

Bodin's subscription to Aristotelian counteraction. Making clear the ethnic distinctions between natural and unnatural melancholy implied by Bright, Burton contrasts the southerners' unnaturally heated complexions with those inhabitants of extremely "cold climes [who] are more subject to natural melancholy (not this artificial) which is cold and dry" (I, p. 239). Where Bodin had drawn a careful distinction between northern madness and the southerner's prophetic fury, Burton cites Bodin to claim that the melancholics "in Spain, Africa, and Asia Minor" are no different from "great numbers of mad men, insomuch, that they are compelled, in all cities of note, to build peculiar Hospitals for them" (I, pp. 237–8).

Burton's efforts to extricate melancholy from its Ficinian legacy go hand in hand with his elevation of a sanguine form of melancholy. Though Bridget Gellart Lyons has maintained that Burton, unlike other humoral writers, does not rank the humors or give "the definition of ideal temperaments," Burton does, in fact, assert that melancholy from blood is best.[38] In his chapter on the influence of the humors, Burton cites Laurentius to suggest that sanguine adust is the best kind of melancholy:

[sanguine adust] Aristotle meant, when he said melancholy men of all others are most witty, which causeth many times a divine ravishment, and a kind of *enthusiasmus*, which stirreth them up to be excellent philosophers, poets, prophets, etc. (I, p. 401)

By insisting that England is more temperate than Spain, Italy, and France, that regions cannot affect one's wits (though southern heat induces madness), and that genial melancholy is not derived from black bile, Burton's expansive work is premised on significant English challenges to conventional geohumoralism. We might even see his identification with Democritus, the laughing philosopher, as a northern counter to Ficino's celebration of the dry soul of Heraclitus, the weeping philosopher. Melancholy, Burton argues, is everywhere, but only the sanguine northerners have access to its positive powers.

Reading humoral discourse as a form of ethnology may even teach us something new about Renaissance England's most renowned case of melancholia – Shakespeare's Hamlet. When Hamlet makes his celebrated claim to "have that within which passeth show" (I. 2. 85), he has acknowledged on a fundamental level that his pale northern exterior fails to denote his internal blackness. It matters, ethnologically, that the Dane's "inwardness" stands in sharp contrast to Aaron the Moor's complexion, who was able to point to his physical appearance as the most conspicuous sign of his humor. Hamlet concedes that his own external signs of melancholy – his black clothing, his tears, the "shows of grief" (line 82) – are all plausible affectations. Not only are these the same pretensions that the feigning melancholic would adopt to counter a northern temperament, but they are also the behaviors (or "customes" as Bright would have it), that could give rise to actual melancholy. Hamlet, of course, distinguishes himself from those who merely put on the "trappings and the suits of woe" (line 86): he is genuinely mourning his father. Yet grief alone is not enough to generate a melancholy that "passeth show." Instead, Shakespeare indicates that the Dane's melancholy stems from a sorrow that has been compounded and intensified by an almost comic array of other melancholic origins, including travel, education, scholarly pursuits, philosophical interests, political inclinations, and possibly even the devil. All the external forces that might alter a man's complexion, from acts of the will to powers beyond his control, have conspired to transform Hamlet's interior self. In its representation of a melancholic *Dane*, Shakespeare's play tells the story of an extraordinary northerner – extraordinary because his inward melancholy has estranged him from his native, northern complexion.

As I have begun to suggest, the formation of the white melancholic required a rearrangement of geohumoralism that produced significant disjunctions between inner and outer complexions and between bodies and their environment. On the whole, the question of subjectivity in early modern scholarship has been a regionally blind one. Though increasingly sensitive to the complexities of gender and class, the history of the subject remains largely uninflected by the history of ethnicity. Yet Hamlet's distinction, his alienation and the romance of his "inwardness," rests on a now-obscured appropriation of southern melancholy – an appropriation that disrupts classical ethnological correspondences. Indeed, as I shall propose in the ensuing pages, the transformation of melancholy from a physical complexion to an undiscoverable mental state depended on severing the link between black skin and black bile and on reconceiving external blackness as an unnatural mystery that was no longer explicable within geohumoral discourse. Paradoxically, Hamlet's alienation from his native disposition helped pave the way for the eventual construction of essentialized racial differences.

The reinvention of blackness

Increasingly in the seventeenth century travel writers argued against the possibility that the blackness of Africans was produced by the heat of the southern sun. A representative passage from *Purchas His Pilgrimes* (1613) recites the commonplace objections:

> Some alledge the heat of this Torrid Region, proceeding from the direct beames of the Sunne [causes blackness]; And why then shoulde all the West Indies which stretch from the one Tropike to the other, have no other people ... why should Africa yeeld white people in Melinde?[39]

Though modern scholars have seen such questions as a small advance in the gathering of empirical knowledge, this position overlooks how and why geohumoral knowledge is being reworked in the period to transform blackness into a marvel. Indeed, most early modern writers, including Samuel Purchas, continued to subscribe to geohumoral theory, choosing to challenge only the traditional relationship between external heat and black skin. By the early seventeenth century, "blackness" had become a scientific mystery. And the earliest inquiries into this mystery were intended, I believe, to detach dark skin from the power and history of melancholia and to confirm its newly "discovered" status as an anomaly. The disruption of geohumoral discourse in *Hamlet* allowed for the construction of a mysterious inwardness – so that a seemingly modern (and universalized) subject was produced in the division between the white man's outward and inward complexions. The more obviously racialized flipside of this disruption is the growing contention that external blackness is unrelated to environmental factors. As such, blackness is denaturalized, and whiteness emerges as unrelated to any specific disposition or body type – representative, instead, of "humanity."

Sir Francis Bacon's inquiry into the mystery of blackness in *Sylva Sylvarum* (1627) is a telling example of how emerging racialist impulses put new pressures on classical ethnology. Bacon depends on the "science" of geohumoralism to explain variations in color, but he also reworks the classical doctrines so as to mark black skin as an aberration:

fire doth lick up the spirits and blood of the body, so as they exhale; so that it ever maketh men look pale and sallow; but the sun, which is a gentler heat, doth but draw the blood to the outward parts, and rather concocteth it than soaketh it; and therefore we see that all Aethiopes are fleshy and plump, and have great lips; all which betoken moisture retained, and not drawn out. We see also that the Negroes are bred in countries that have plenty of water, by rivers or otherwise; for Meroë, which was the metropolis of Aethiopia was upon a great lake; and Congo, where the Negroes are, is full of rivers. And the confines of the river Niger, where the Negroes also are, are well watered: and the region about Cape Verde is likewise moist, insomuch as it is pestilent through moisture; but the countries of the Abyssenes, and Barbary, and Peru, where they are tawny, and olivaster, and pale, are generally more sandy and dry. As for the Aethiopes, as they are plump and fleshy, so (it may be) they are sanguine and ruddy coloured, if their black skin would suffer it to be seen.[40]

Though Bacon concedes that the southern environment determines the Africans' physical appearance, it is water rather than heat that proves the determining force. Indeed, Bacon goes against the grain of traditional geohumoralism in a number of ways. First, he suggests that if a heat – such as fire – causes the exhalation of spirits and blood, it necessarily produces pale and sallow complexions, rather than blackness. Second, he maintains that the sun's heat is a gentler sort, for it only manages to draw blood to the outer parts without exhaling it. Thus, the Ethiopians, whom the classical writers had identified as excessively dry – their spirits and blood having been exhaled by external heat – prove, instead, to be moist. Bacon's empirical "evidence" is the anecdotal assertion that all Ethiopian bodies are fleshy and plump, sure signs of "moisture retained."

What Bacon implies, but does not state explicitly, is that the Ethiopians are black because their blood has been "concocted" in their "outward parts" only – thus creating, in a sense, a false layer of refined blood. In short, blackness no longer denotes humoral status but obscures it.[41] Though Bacon sets up a framework in which tawny, olive-colored, and pale complexions signify dryness, he stops short of declaring a correspondence between moisture and blackness. To assert, instead, that the Ethiopians must be sanguine despite their blackness, he inadvertently recalls an identification between moisture and lighter complexions. And by insisting that Ethiopian blackness alone is unrelated to humoral identity (as opposed to the paler tones that still denote their inward qualities), Bacon succeeds in estranging blackness from the realm of scientific inquiry. To understand Bacon's strange conclusion, we must recognize that he has no interest in discovering the cause of color differences; he aims instead to dissociate external blackness from its traditional humoral connotations. Severing the link between black skin and black bile in geohumoral discourse is, I believe, part of the same movement that transforms melancholy from a physical complexion to an indiscoverable, yet universally accessible mental state. Once black bile no longer manifests itself outwardly, black skin becomes a "scientific" mystery.

In *Pseudodoxia Epidemica* (1646) Sir Thomas Browne devotes three chapters to the mystery of "the Blackness of Negroes." For Browne (unlike George Best) the puzzle of blackness is not the transmission of color, which is "evidently maintained by generation," but how "this [black] complexion was first acquired."[42] Throughout his inquiry, Browne entertains a variety of possible explanations for blackness – from the ingestion of strange waters, to maternal imagination, to the use of paint – but he expresses grave doubts that the "fervour of the Sun, or intemperate heat of clime did solely occasion this [black] complexion" (p. 463). Despite the assumptions of many modern scholars, Browne's skepticism on this point does not translate to mean that he rejects climate theory. To the contrary, Browne reworks traditional ethnology when he contends that Africa is too full of rivers and moisture for Africans to be "more peculiarly scorched and torrified from the Sun, [which neccesitates the] addition of driness from the soil." It has been falsely "presumed," Browne contends, that "Negroes" reside in regions "void of Rivers and moisture" and in those places known to be dry and sandy, such as Libya, where "the people are not esteemed Negroes" (p. 465). But a quick look at Browne's sources points up the strain in his argument. Though he cites Leo Africanus on the dryness of Libya, he hearkens back to ancient Ptolemy for their "pale and Tawny" color, thus omitting Leo's description of the Libyans as "black."[43]

Though Browne appears intent on dissociating blackness from the drying and cooling effects of the sun, he finds it quite conceivable that the ingestion of water may have produced the African's physical traits:

It may be therefore considered, whether the inward use of certain waters or fountains of peculiar operations, might not at first produce the effect in question. For, of the like we have records in Aristotle, Strabo and Pliny, who hath made a collection hereof, as of two fountains in Bœotia, the one making Sheep white, the other black; of the water of Siberis which made Oxen black, and the like effect it had also upon men, dying not only the skin, but making their hairs black and curled. This was the conceit of Aristobulus; who received so little satisfaction from the other, or that it might be caused by heat, or any kind of fire, that he conceived it as reasonable to impute the effect unto water. (p. 466)

As this passage suggests, Browne makes some effort not only to disengage blackness from its former associations with dryness – and its implied connections to fixity, wisdom, and melancholia – but also to trace the "effect in question," as Bacon did, to the retention of moisture. But Browne's real interest lies in linking the origin of blackness to human intervention. And his motive for shifting in this direction is, I believe, rooted in a desire not only to cast blackness outside the bounds of nature but also to recast it as a sign of barbarous impressibility. Blackness is being reinvented to carry the former humoral connotations of extreme whiteness.

Invoking the longstanding and widely accepted theory of maternal imagination, best known as an explanation for offspring whose complexions did not match their parents', Browne hypothesizes that blackness originated in the "Power and Efficacy of Imagination." Hippocrates' tale of a white woman who had "conceived a Negro" by "an intent view of a Picture" is balanced by the tale from Heliodorus' romance:

And in the History of Heliodore of a Moorish Queen, who upon aspection of the Picture of Andromeda, conceived and brought forth a fair one. And thus perhaps might some say was the beginning of this complexion: induced first by Imagination, which having once impregnated the seed, found afterward concurrent co-operations, which were continued by Climes, whose constitution advantaged the first impression. (pp. 466–7)

As far as I am aware, Browne is the first writer to consider maternal imagination as the *originary* source of blackness, and in so doing, he recategorizes it as a marvel. Maternal impressions produced anomalies – hairy or beast-like people, "monsters," and strange birth marks – phenomena that were most often attributed to the wandering thoughts and inconstant appetites of conceiving or pregnant women.[44] Yet, as the Heliodorus narrative indicates, one could just as easily construe "whiteness" in the same terms.

That Browne's skepticism regarding climatic explanations of color may be more biased than empirical is made plain in his assertion that blackness, having been "induced first by Imagination," then "impregnated the seed," will thereafter be "continued by Climes" (p. 466). In other words, once the constitution of the body is impressed with blackness (through both the imagination and the seed), color is transmitted or continued by way of "co-operation" with the climate. And yet, at another point in his inquiry, Browne has asserted that the heat of the sun has no part in the communication of blackness, since "Negroes" are "dusky" at birth, even in their "abortions" (pp. 469–70). In allowing that the climate may "continue" blackness, Browne begs the question as to whether it still remains a viable explanation of its inception – as viable, at the very least, as maternal imagination.

While attributing blackness to the impressionable female mind seems to sever it from the geohumoral body, it still attaches dark skin to a "medical" theory that allows for the imaginative production of "whiteness" as well. More radical is Browne's hypothesis that blackness is the result of human artifice. Invoking the belief that non-European "Others" physically reshaped their bodies until nature eventually adopted their "perversions," Browne suggests that the original "cause and the like foundation of Tincture" may also stem from man's ingenuity. The "Macrocephali, or the people with long heads," the "Chineses little feet, [and] most Negroes great Lips and flat Noses" were initially produced when their "Symmetry" was "casually or purposely perverted," before descending "to their posterities, and that in durable deformities." In the same vein, there are "Artificial Negroes, or Gypsies [who] acquire their complexion by anointing their bodies with Bacon and fat substances and exposing them to the Sun" (p. 467). It seems plausible, Browne proposes, that the pigmentation of Africans is derived from the painted bodies of their ancestors.

Interest in the intersections between constructions of feminine beauty, impersonation, and the emergence of racial categories has led Kim F. Hall and others to take note of how "English discourses of blackness" play a significant role in the "rhetoric of women's fairness and value" through the "language of 'painting' and cosmetics."[45] Typically in these contexts, although blackness is equated with a lack of beauty, it is praised for its naturalness in order to critique white women for their use of cosmetics – a critique that ultimately aims to bolster the superiority of fair skin.[46] Abdella the Moor, for example, in Beaumont and Fletcher's *The Knight of Malta* (1647), declares that her "black Cheeke [cannot] put on a feigned blush, / To make [her] seeme more modest than [she is]," for the "ground-worke" of her complexion "will not beare adulterate red, / Nor artificiall white" (1. 1. 173–6).[47] Often noted for its indelible constancy, exemplified in the proverb, "to wash an Ethiop is to labor in vain," blackness could be deployed to point up the effeminate inconstancy of a white complexion, signified by the blush and the conventionally female practice of painting. Thus Browne's "discovery" of blackness-as-artifice not only works to establish whiteness as primary, but it also reverses the usual correspondences between fair skin, effeminacy, and cosmetics.

Showing further how racialization pervades the early modern discourses on beauty, Hall has helped us see that the denigration of blackness imbues female whiteness with ethical and aesthetic superiority. And yet, since it was understood that the ideal male complexion should be shades darker than the woman's "fair," establishing the superiority of whiteness on the basis of female appearance raises a host of problems for white masculinity.[48] As we have seen, the construction of northerners as youthful in vigor and appearance in early modern ethnology cannot be separated from the humoral corollary that their spirits are thick and their wits slow.[49] Moreover, as northerners, excluded from temperance, white English males could be effeminized by the red and white of their complexion, both internally and externally. Indeed, in *The Passions of the Minde in Generall* (1604), Thomas Wright seems torn between praising the northern males' blush as "a good commencement of Vertue, because it proceedeth from a judgement disliking of evil, which is an apt beginning of good" and urging them to attain a more masculine carriage by imitating the darker Italian and Spaniard.[50] The value of superficial appearance in early modern ethnology is always qualified by deeper humoral qualities, and darker skin, though opposed to beauty and physical strength, could denote spiritual, intellectual, or political power.

It is, however, within the framework of ethnographic discourse – even more than aesthetics – that we can see the ideological roots of Browne's speculation that blackness had its beginnings in human custom. In the classical texts, the identification between the Africans and blackness is neatly conveyed by the sense that "Aethiopian" purportedly means "scorched." But the recognized, and opposed, idiosyncrasy of northern barbarians in this classical framework, was their predilection for painting. Indeed, John White's famous drawings of the tattooed Picts were as much a response to such classical portraits as they were a reflection of the New World's painted Indians (Fig. 5).

Given that William Camden claimed that the "Brit" of Britannia means "to paint," we might consider how England's discovery of its barbaric history necessarily involved grappling with how to reconcile their ancestors' body painting with their national identity. Astonishingly, one hypothesis in circulation interpreted the ancient Welsh's body painting as evidence of their southern origins: once the northern climate began to lighten their skin, the argument went, the former southerners took up painting to recreate their progenitors' original color.[51] Whether intentionally or not, Browne's thesis does not simply establish whiteness as primary, it reinterprets the very motives for painting. What had been a longing to return to an original darkness has been transmuted into a monstrous desire to contaminate what is now conceived as natural and pure.

Not surprisingly, Browne's cosmetic theory of blackness is fully embraced by the quirky ethnographer John Bulwer in his *Anthropometamorphosis, or the Artificial Changeling* (1650). It is, however, surprising to find a barely veiled correspondence between an interpretation of blackness as artifice and the

Figure 5 "The true picture of one Picte," an engraving by Theodore de Bry of John White's illustration, from Thomas Hariot, *A Brief and True Report of the New Found Land of Virginia* (1590).

abiding ethnological anxieties represented earlier in the period by Andrew Boorde's shape-shifting and fashion-hungry Englishman.[52] Bulwer provides an inventory of every nation's supposed interventions in nature: circumcision, head-shaping, piercing, teeth sharpening, etc., and gives an account of how "nature" adopts human "artifice" in the transmission of traits. The main text of the 1650 edition concludes with an exposition on the origins of blackness, formulated by Bulwer's question: How is it that "some men . . . [did] first acquire, and still retain the glosse and tincture of Blacknesse?"[53] His conclusion is that they became "black by . . . artificial . . . denigration." The Moor's ancestors, it seems, had an "Apish desire . . . to change the complexion of their bodies into a new and more fashionable hue" (p. 254). Once they had satisfied their "affectation[] of painting," the color was "continued by [the climate, which transformed] the artificial into a natural impression" (p. 255). Hence, blackness had its origins in the effeminate (and what should strike us as a familiarly "English") desire to conform to changing fashions.

Indeed, Bulwer supplements his last words on the old "apish desire" for blackness with an appendix entitled "Exhibiting the Pedigree of the English Gallant." It is here that he reminds his readers of Andrew Boorde's portrait, made over one hundred years earlier:

And so markably uncertain and giddy-headed herein are we, that whereas all grave Nations are constant to their Habits, & may be described by them, they use to paint an *English-man* naked, with a pair of Sheers in his hand, to fit his own uncertain humour, and undetermined shape. (p. 262)

At first glance we may read Bulwer's appendix as one more addition to the knee-jerk condemnations of the English people's love of fashion, but his thesis is, in fact, more radical and fantastic. Rather than merely belated imitations of the advanced French and Italian cultures, fashion in England springs from the monstrous physical perversions of more barbarous nations. The Englishman's square-cap mimics the square-headed men of India, "sugar-loaf hats" resemble the Macrocephali's head, the pinking and slashing of doublets copy the barbarian's scarring practices, the cut of particular breeches is derived from the "Great Privy-memb'red Guineans" (p. 260), and so on. Though Bulwer acknowledges that the English people's predilection for fashion stems from their "uncertain humour, and undetermined shape," he also succeeds in presenting the English gallant as the most stable and "natural" body in the text. Set against the somatic alterations of scarring, piercing, dyeing, etc., the wearing of strange clothes becomes a "superficial" fault (p. 262). The appendix to *Anthropometamorphosis* reveals that a significant impetus behind early English ethnography is an abiding desire to stabilize and naturalize the English humoral body by projecting apishness and effeminacy onto Others.

As I explained in the introduction, the curse of Ham gained in popularity as an explanation of blackness throughout the seventeenth century, allowing for the justification of slavery and substantiating a link between blackness, sin, and sexual depravity. What I am suggesting here is that in the realm of natural philosophy, among scientists who rejected the curse of Ham as "perpetual promotion of ignorance,"[54] blackness was also being transformed into an unnatural aberration – a transformation that effectively enabled the reconstruction of whiteness. Browne and Bacon worked to loosen the former ties between skin color and humoral disposition, and it is this loosening that allowed for the restructuring of geohumoral theory. By the late seventeenth and eighteenth centuries, climate theory was still thriving, but it no longer rested on the ancient correspondences between the outer and inner complexion that had fixed the English at the margins of the world.[55]

Studies of the early formation of biological racialism have often identified Carl Linnaeus' classification of humans in *The System of Nature* (1758 edition) as a crucial shift in the history of science.[56] Linnaeus' work should be recognized as exemplifying "an increasingly vertical taxonomy," which replaced the "horizontal relations" of the Renaissance's more "reflexive system of signs, symbols, and correspondences."[57] But we can also still discern in Linnaeus the residual matter of early modern geohumoralism:

Homo sapiens, varying by education and situation, was composed of
1. Wild man: four-footed, mute, hairy.
2. American: copper-colored, choleric, erect. Paints self. Regulated by custom.
3. European: fair, sanguine, brawny. Covered with close vestments. Governed by laws.
4. Asiatic: sooty, melancholy, rigid. Covered with loose garments. Governed by opinions.
5. African: black, phlegmatic, relaxed. Anoints himself with grease. Governed by caprice.[58]

An implicit hierarchy of "races" is established quite obviously by color and cultural behavior (the lawful over the capricious), but it is also premised on the complex history of ethnological humoral significance that we have examined in this section. The sanguine complexion now denotes civility and applies to all Europeans: a unified group of "fair" people. Black Africans have become "phlegmatic," bearing all of that humor's attendant negative connotations – except whiteness. The internal characteristics that were once associated with the English climate – which the early modern English people had struggled to counter or reform – have not only been implanted in the African body, but they are now the natural justification of the inferiority and immutable biological otherness of blackness.

Part II

The English ethnographic theatre

4   *Tamburlaine* and the staging of white barbarity

In their invocation of early modern maps and classical geography, Christopher Marlowe's *Tamburlaine* plays, perhaps more than any other canonical drama of the Renaissance, draw our attention to the Elizabethan "metaphoric equivalence of *theatrum* and *mundus*."[1] By reducing expansive kingdoms to the space of a stage and offering a survey of other nations' customs and manners, the plays seem to participate in the production of ethnographic knowledge. And yet their perspective on this knowledge has puzzled critics; as Emily Bartels has noted in *Spectacles of Strangeness*:

> The play provides no stable comparative standard through which we can judge [Tamburlaine's] relative civility or barbarity and situates him instead within a dramatic landscape that "swarms" with figures whose nationalities (Persian, Turkish, Egyptian, Natolian, and so on) and whose "incivil outrages" are at least as incriminating as his.[2]

While it is hardly Marlovian to adhere to a stable standard of any kind, I do want to propose that our assumption that Elizabethan England was securely settled in a position of "civility" has influenced our perspective on Tamburlaine's barbarism. However persuaded we may be that Marlowe, as Stephen Greenblatt has maintained, always "broods upon and depicts" his "own countrymen," we have continued to filter our understanding of Tamburlaine's potential "Englishness" through the exotic alienness of his Scythian identity.[3] But to understand how Marlowe's ethnographic theatre may have played a dynamic role in the construction of English identity – just one to two years after the publication of William Camden's *Britannia* (1586) – demands that we also understand England's intimate though fraught affiliation with the Scythians.[4]

The Tamburlanian perspective

"Do you intend Tamburlaine to represent earthquakes and volcanoes?"
"O yes," said Will, laughing "and migrations of races and clearings of forests – and America and the steam-engine. Everything you can imagine!" George Eliot, *Middlemarch*[5]

Figure 6 Portrait of Tamburlaine, from Paolo Giovo, *Elogia virorum bellica virtute illustrium* (1575).

Well before Edmund Spenser's *A View of the Present State of Ireland* (*c*. 1596), it was held that the Scythians were among the earliest settlers of the British Isles. As Graham Parry has observed, "a chorus of chroniclers and historians, going back at least to Gildas in the sixth century, emphasized the etymological probability that 'Scoti' and 'Scythae' were linked."[6] But more than that, as I established in chapter 1, the early moderns understood the "Scythian" to be an ethnological type whose constitution and temperament were produced by the northern climate. We should recognize in Menaphon's portrait of Tamburlaine – "of stature tall," "large of limbs," "strongly knit," "pale of complexion," with a "knot of amber hair" (1: 2. 1. 7–23) – the same descriptors that Jean Bodin and others applied to all northern tribes, including the Irish, Scots, and Britons.[7] Indeed, Marlowe seems intent on presenting Tamburlaine in both particular and general terms. On the one hand, he dramatizes an historical personage born in Samarkand, Timur Khan (1336–1405), whose actions, I will argue, signified for the English a northern challenge to the classically inherited, Mediterranean-centered view of both the progress and the substance of "civility."[8] On the other hand, when he is described as a "Tartar" or the "Rogue of Volga," Tamburlaine's origins grow more obscure. However "eastern" Timur Khan may have been, Marlowe's Scythian clearly identifies himself with the frigid landscape of Hippocrates' *Airs, Waters, Places,* wooing Zenocrate with visions of "milk-white harts upon an ivory sled / ... amidst the frozen pools / And scale the icy mountains' lofty tops" (1. 2. 98–100) and declaring her "[b]righter than is the silver Rhodope, / Fairer than whitest snow on Scythian hills" (lines 88–9). These blindingly white conceptions of beauty, drawn in climatic and geographic images, establish Tamburlaine's perspective as insistently and peculiarly "northern."

Part of what I want to suggest in this chapter is that the most subversive elements of *Tamburlaine I and II* take on new resonances not only when we consider how the plays may be assessing the perceived inherent strengths of a northern warrior but also when we entertain the notion that an English audience may have had an ethnological interest in that assessment. Take for example Tamburlaine's rise from lowly shepherd to crowned ruler, an overreaching that violates, the play's critics tell us, what most Elizabethans accepted as divinely sanctioned social hierarchy.[9] And yet, if we understand Tamburlaine's "base-born," "peasant" status as determined by region as well as rank, his radical ascent threatens the same geographical structure that marginalizes the British as "pezantly" commoners.[10] With barbarism as the common ground, class and ethnic roots are intertwined in *Tamburlaine,* as when the Scythian declares that his "mean estate" will be elevated once he gains the admiration of distant nations (1. 2. 202–4). In the same way that the Persians characterize all "Tartars" as "base-born," "greedy-minded slaves," the commonness of Tamburlaine's birth is meant to epitomize the barbarity of his people as a whole (2. 2. 65–7). Censured more for presumptuousness than cruelty, Tamburlaine ruffles feathers for dismantling or ignoring an accepted order of things that classifies his complexion as barbarously inferior and "distempered" (1. 2. 62).

Noting that Tamburlaine "rebels against hierarchy, legitimacy, the whole established order of things," Greenblatt has observed that the Scythian's triumphs tease us with "a materialist alternative to the transcendental authority upon which all the 'legitimate' kings in the play base their power, but the suggestion is not realized."[11] *Tamburlaine I* in particular seems to swing between demystifying power structures – often with appeals to matter or brute force ("of what mould or mettle he be made") – and reinvoking some greater design ("what star or state soever govern him" [2. 6. 17–18]). I would like to suggest that the primary materialist cause of Tamburlaine's achievements is his distinctly northern constitution, and that this particular materialism is key to understanding the play's challenges to established hierarchies. Clearly Tamburlaine's physical nature matters in accounting for his success: we are told that "His arms and fingers [are] long and sinewy,/Betokening valour and excess of strength –/ In every part proportioned like the man/Should make the world subdued to Tamburlaine" (2. 1. 27–30). His best qualities, like all northerners, are corporeally oriented – for he possesses "martial flesh" (ii: 4. 1. 105) and a mind ("courageous and invincible" [1. 5. 73]) essentially directed toward conquest.[12] In the final scene of *Part II*, Marlowe brings on a physician not only to cast Tamburlaine's imminent death in the reductively materialist language of medicine but also to remind us of the importance of the hero's humoral composition. We learn that his "humidum and calor," the heat and moisture of a sanguine complexion, have been "extinguished" (5. 3. 86–9).[13] Though we may construe the physician's explanation as a general description of death – blood, "the cause of [all] life," has dried and cooled – his phrasing also suggests that a *Scythian*'s blood has particular worth (line 90). There are some, the physician informs us, who revere this combination of heat and moisture as "a substance more divine and pure" than just a "parcel of the elements" (lines 87–8) – a characterization that anticipates Thomas Walkington's nationalistic revaluation of sanguinity that I discussed in chapter 1.

Notoriously, Tamburlaine's principal appeal to "transcendental authority" emanates in his assertions that he is the scourge of God.[14] But rather than mystifying the materialist basis – or humoral composition – of his power, the Scythian's role as scourge is underwritten by his ethnological make-up. If we turn back to another text of the period that conflates scourges and Scythians, Spenser's *A View of the State of Ireland*, we can catch a glimpse of an incipient racialist notion that the northern barbaric invasions – and more literally the mingling of their blood with others – was providentially sanctioned. As David Glimp has observed, "Even though Irenæus feared the possibility that God would use the barbarous Irish to 'scourge' England, on looking back into Europe's ancient history he paints a much rosier picture" of such scourge-like behavior.[15] It was, Irenæus maintains, by the "singular providence of God, and a most admirable purpose of his wisedome" that "the Gothes, the Hunnes, and the Vandals: And lastly all the nations of Scythia" moved southward to where they "might receive Christianity, and to mingle nations so remote miraculously, to make as it were one blood and kindred of all people, and each to have knowledge of him."[16]

We should, I want to argue, view this providential interpretation of the barbaric invasions as an explicit example of northern revisionism. As historian Herwig Wolfram contends

The concept of a migration of peoples rather than the barbarian invasion ideology stood in opposition to both the ideas of catastrophe and of Renaissance set forth by the Italian historians...With the help of archaeology, linguistic studies and outright antiquarianism, [the German humanists] presented the image of healthy, strong, youthful migratory peoples...[Much later] French romanticism and German historicism in the nineteenth century were united in the belief that the invading Germans meant fresh blood for the Roman world.[17]

Actually, we need not look further than the early seventeenth century to find an articulation of the "racialist" idea that an infusion of northern barbarians was also an infusion of healthy "blood." In *The Anatomy of Melancholy* (1621), Robert Burton writes,

And sure, I think, it hath been ordered by God's especial providence, that in all ages there should be (as usually there is) once in six hundred years, a transmigration of nations, to amend and purify their blood ... and that there should be, as it were, an inundation of those northern Goths and Vandals, and many such-like people which came out of that continent of Scandia and Saramatia (as some suppose) and overran, as a deluge, most part of Europe and Africa, to alter for our good our complexions, which were much defaced with hereditary infirmities, which by our lust and intemperance we had contracted. A sound generation of strong and able men were sent amongst us, as those northern men usually are, innocuous, free from riot, and free from diseases ...[18]

Burton has adapted the classical cyclical view of history to suggest that the fall of southern civilizations can be traced to the physiological degenerative tendencies of those residing in Africa and parts of Europe. Astonishingly, the reinvigoration of those same nations (including England, it seems) derives from the pure, uncorrupted, physiological strengths of northern blood. Burton's acknowledgement of his own nation's "hereditary infirmities," made in the same breath that he praises the Goths and Vandals, should remind us of the inherent contradiction between Irenæus' hearty approval of the barbarians' influx and his fear that Ireland may prove to be England's scourge. As I argued in chapter 2, Englishness in the early modern period was identified, in turns, with the barbarousness associated with England's newly acknowledged ancestors and a perceived degeneracy brought about by the nation's repeatedly conquered and corrupted status.

When Burton makes the assertion that contemporary England would indeed benefit from the scourge of a northern invasion, it is, significantly, Tamburlaine's name he invokes:

We had need of some general visitor in our age, that should reform what is amiss ... [another] Tamerlane ... he should be as strong as ten thousand men, or an army of giants, go invisible, open gates and castle doors, have what treasure he would, transport himself in an instant to what place he desired, alter affections, cure all manner of diseases, that he might range over the world, and reform all distressed states and persons, as he would himself.[19]

We should see intimations of Burton's "Tamerlane" when Marlowe's hero famously correlates his desire for earthly power with ranging, moving, measuring, wandering, and climbing.[20] Pressed to explain the insatiability of his violence and ambition, Tamburlaine cites the war of elements within *all* men to claim that such endless, aspiring movement is the natural state of "Man." And yet, as Burton might counter, Tamburlaine has universalized northern propensities here, thus remaking (rather than simply demystifying) the natural order. Since it is Tamburlaine's physiological destiny, as a northern scourge, to range over the world, he sees it as the destiny of all men to do so (1: 2. 7. 12–29).

While it is unclear whether Marlowe would have been aware of the racialist notion of northern blood as Burton articulated it forty years later, he could easily have known that for some of his contemporaries Tamburlaine's conquests signified a northern historiographical challenge to the Italian historians' concept of the Renaissance. One potential source of Marlowe's play, Louis Le Roy's account of the Scythian shepherd in *Of Vicissitude, or the Variety of Things in the Universe* (1577), cites the Tamburlaine story to refute the geographic truisms of the conventional civilizing narrative – that barbarousness flows from the north and civilization emerges in the south. For Le Roy, Tamburlaine embodies the paradoxically barbaric origins of early modern cultural advancement, and his triumphs are identified as a radical disruption in the flow of history that succeeded in turning the tides of western civilization:

Since other epochs have been distinguished by some great warrior and by some great power manifest at each period of their development, it seems advisable to begin discussion of the wonders of this age with mention of the great and unconquerable Tamburlane who, from about the year of our Lord 1400, shattered the world with the terror of his name...[21]

Offering a broad historical perspective on the Scythian's rise, and the subsequent development of a "period," Le Roy reaches the fantastic conclusion that Tamburlaine, in effect, engendered the Renaissance. Once Greece had been "delivered from its fear of Bajazet who was held prisoner by Tamburlane," he explains, Greek scholars moved to Italy and began the "restoration of the wisdom of antiquity." Thus, it was "During Tamburlane's reign" that Europe saw "the re-establishment of the study of languages and of all other disciplines."[22] Without the Scythian's military discipline and cruelty, the early modern triumphs in the arts and sciences that ensued would never have been achieved. Though there is little in Marlowe's plays to suggest that the Renaissance is just around the corner, Le Roy's thesis does allow us to see how Tamburlaine's destruction of the order of things could potentially be interpreted by the English as a radically revisionist bid for the northerner's role in the progress of civilization. Rather than seeing themselves as passive inheritors of a Mediterranean-centered world, the English could, perhaps, be emboldened to shift that center northward.

This is, in fact, Samuel Daniel's thesis in *A Defence of Ryme* (1603), wherein he urges his countrymen to resist measuring their culture against ancient Greece and Rome and avoid assuming that "the superficiall figure of a region in a

Mappe" reveals "strait the fashion and place as it is."[23] Challenging the conventional argument that the *"Gothes, Vandales,* and *Longobards,* whose comming downe like an inundation overwhelmed, as they say, al the glory of learning in *Europe*," Daniel believes they should be cleared of this "imputation of ignorance." Moreover, it was the second wave of northern transmigrations – the "comming downe of *Tamburlaine* into *Europe*" – that corresponded (as in Le Roy) with the emergence of early modern learning.[24] In the course of relating the story of Emanuel Chrysolaras, Daniel observes that when *"Bajazeth* was taken prisoner by *Tamburlan,* and his country freed from danger, [this scholar Chrysolaras] stayed still at *Venice,* and there taught the Greeke tongue, discontinued before, in these parts the space of seaven hundred yeeres." Other scholars followed suit, thus "transporting Philosophie beaten by the Turke out of *Greece* into christendome. Hereupon came that mightie confluence of Learning in these parts…"[25] Since, as I have been arguing, Tamburlaine's conquests carried with them a way to reconceptualize accepted patterns of regionalized history, Daniel can draw on the Scythian's story to make an argument for the inherent, "barbaric" worth of his own native English language and culture.

Integral to reconceptualizing the northerner's role in history is the undoing of conventional ties between identity and geographic space – defying what Daniel calls "the superficiall figure of a region in a Mappe." As critics have noted, Tamburlaine aims to remap the world most pointedly when he proclaims to Zenocrate the necessity of wasting her native country, Egypt: "I will confute those blind geographers / That make a triple region in the world… Here at Damascus will I make the point / That shall begin the perpendicular – " (I: 4. 4. 74–81). The critical debate over these lines has focused on which kind of map Tamburlaine refers to – the Isidorian (TO) or the fifteenth-century Ptolemaic – since both can be construed as making "a triple region in the world."[26] If the "perpendicular" suggests the "T" of the medieval map, then the triple regions would mean the symbolic spaces of Asia, Europe, and Africa with Jerusalem at the center; if "perpendicular" denotes a longitudinal meridian, then "triple region" signifies the basic climatic zones of northern, *oikumene,* and southern. Proposing that the lines encourage us to imagine both maps simultaneously, John Gillies has argued that the "irony of the passage arises from Marlowe's awareness of the profound incongruity, the incommensurability, of the medieval and the Renaissance constructions of space."[27] Such ambiguity not only reminds us that history has always determined geographic meaning – which is the substance of Tamburlaine's threat – but also that the Scythian's motives for refashioning the world are Scythian in origin, for both maps – the Isidorian and the Ptolemaic – locate Scythia at the world's edge.[28] We might see further confutation of the triple regions in the very pairing of, and opposition between, Zenocrate and Tamburlaine – an Egyptian woman and a Scythian man – who conjure up the binary oppositions of Herodotan geography.[29] As Zenocrate's

spouse and Egypt's conqueror then, Tamburlaine destroys the antitheses associated with Scythia and Egypt – young and old, ignorant and wise – and by
reducing excluded regions to his own map and "Calling the provinces, cities
and towns / After [his] name and [hers]," he reorients the geographic future
around their union (1: 4. 4. 78–9).

Scythian theatre

Anacharsis beeing demaunded of a *Greeke*, whether they had not instrumentes of
Musicke, or Schooles of Poetrie in *Scythia*, answered, yes, and that without vice, as
though it were either impossible, or incredible, that no abuse should be learned where
such lesso[n]s are taught, & such schooles mainteined. Stephen Gosson, *The Schoole of
Abuse* (1579)[30]

Although I have been arguing that in their positioning of a Scythian, and specifically Tamburlaine, as a hero, the *Tamburlaine* plays offer up a northern revisionist perspective that may have tapped into English anxieties about their own
ethnic identity, I am not suggesting that Marlowe is unequivocal about the status
of English barbarism. Indeed, I want to complicate my argument by assessing
how *Tamburlaine I* and *II*, as works of English dramatic poetry and public theatre productions, are engaged in the question of how to fashion Englishness –
a question that stems from the culture's double vision of itself as either defi-
ciently or excessively "civilized." One half of this double vision is alluded to,
I believe, in the prologue to *Tamburlaine I*, which promises that the Scythian's
"high astounding terms" will supplant the customary "jigging veins of rhyming
mother wits / And such conceits as clownage keeps in pay" (lines 1–5). As
Richard Helgerson has shown us in *Forms of Nationhood*, many Elizabethan
poets equated rhyming with the native, "Gothic," barbarousness of the English
language.[31] Marlowe adopts these same associated values: the jigging rhymes
of other playwrights are what the native ("mother") wits produce for the rustic
and barbarous purposes of clowning. Obviously, Marlowe's mighty line is a
far cry from the quantitative meter that Spenser and others were considering as
the means to civilize English prosody. And it was, of course, on the rhyming
side of this debate that Samuel Daniel invoked Tamburlaine as a barbarian to
be admired. With tongue in cheek, Marlowe turns the poetic controversy inside
out by offering up a paradox – an eloquent barbarian – whose working words,
ironically, destroy civilizations as they civilize the English tongue.[32]

But to confuse the issue further, Marlowe's venue for elevating English poetry – the theatre – is, depending on your source, a place of profound barbarity
or a primary example of England's hypercivilized decline. Poets seeking distinction (including Marlowe, perhaps) together with theatre-insiders, such as
actors and playwrights, tended to worry more about the barbarity of the theatre
than the barbarity of their nation.[33] And many sought, as Helgerson has argued,

to "project themselves out of the base company of theatrical clowns and into the orbit of gentility."[34] The anti-theatricalists, however, were of a different mind. Most of the anti-theatrical texts, which were produced in the years leading up to the staging of *Tamburlaine* (1577–87), characterized the stage as a degenerative force – a force that had succeeded in corrupting the English people's original and admirably "barbaric" virtues.[35] In its exaltation of English dramatic poetry and barbarism, Marlowe's play, I want to argue, is responding to the same ethnological tensions that helped produce the period's controversy over the theatre.[36]

In what may be the most famous passage of the anti-theatrical writings, Stephen Gosson in *The Schoole of Abuse* (1579) pits theatricality – playing, dancing, piping – in opposition to the Scythian virtues of ancient England:

Consider with thy selfe (gentle Reader) the olde discipline of Englande, mark what we were before, & what we are now: Leave Rome a while, and cast thine eye backe to thy Predecessors, and tell mee howe woonderfully wee have beene chaunged, since wee were schooled with these abuses. Dion sayth, that english men could suffer watching and labor, hunger & thirst, and beare of al stormes hed and shoulders, they used slender weapons, went naked, and were good soldiours, they fed uppon rootes and barkes of trees, they would stand up to the chin many dayes in marishes without victualles: and they had a kind of sustenaunce in time of neede, of which if they had taken but the quantitie of a beane, or the weight of a pease, they did neyther gape after meate, nor long for the cuppe, a great while after. *The men in valure not yeelding to Scithia, the women in courage passing the Amazons.* The exercise of both was shootyng and darting, running & wrestling, and trying suche maisteries, as eyther consisted in swiftnesse of feete, agilitie of body, strength of armes, or Martiall discipline. But the exercise that is nowe among us, is banqueting, playing, pipyng, and dauncing, and all suche delightes as may win us to pleasure, or rocke us a sleepe.[37]

Adapting the classical portraits of northern barbarians, Gosson's highest praise for England's earliest inhabitants is that they resembled the Scythians in their physical strength and courageous minds. Able to thrive in their harsh environs, the ancient English had not yet been corrupted by poisonous "delightes" and effeminate idleness. Gosson makes the claim, in fact, that theatre is non-native – a foreign importation that has transformed his countrymen's virtues into vices: "We have robbed *Greece* of Gluttonie, *Italy* of wantonnesse, *Spaine* of pride, *Fraunce* of deceite, and *Dutchland* of quaffing. Compare *London* to *Rome*, & *England* to *Italy*, you shall find the Theaters of the one, the abuses of the other, to be rife among us."[38]

Gosson's nostalgic yearning for an "Englishness" in its pre-civilized state and his adherence to a narrative of degeneration are common denominators in the texts of John Northbrooke, William Rankins, and Philip Stubbes as well. Northbrooke for example, in *A Treatise wherein Dicing, Dauncing, Vaine Playes or Enterluds... are reproved* (1577) looks back to England's less degenerate past when the people engaged "in wrestling, running, and practice with the long bow."[39] William Rankins in *The Mirrour of Monsters* (1587) blames the players, or ministers of idleness, for "weaken[ing] the sences and members of men, that they shall never be able to profit their countrie or themselves."[40] Though Philip Stubbes' *The Anatomy of Abuses* (1583) finds the English to be innately "audacious, bold, puissant, and heroycal," he also fears that they have outstripped all other nations in their attachment to non-native "new fangles."[41] Unlike their hearty forefathers who "fead upon graine, corne, roots... lived longer... [and] were of better complection then we, and much stronger then we in everie respect," Stubbes' contemporaries have "altered [their] nature" and "distempered [their] bodies" with frivolous pursuits.[42] And where they were once "used to hardnesse," they are now "weker, tenderer, and ne[t]her."[43]

As these writings suggest, the barbarian, and the Scythian in particular, is idealized for his unyieldingly tough nature – that is, the hardness that Stubbes so admires. As it turns out, hardness is a predominant Scythian trait, and given that "bodily condition, subjective state, and psychological character" were "fully imbricated" in this period, there is little to distinguish somatic hardness from temperamental firmness, and *vice versa*.[44] That is to say, the Scythians' capacity to withstand harsh physical conditions meant they were literally thick-skinned *and* tough-minded.[45] Most often, however, Scythian hardness was represented as a resistance to what would move most people, as in the line from *Edward III* (1596) which marvels at the affective force "That... [could] rayse drops in a Tartar's eye. / And make a flyntheart Sythian [sic] pytiful" (2. 1. 72).[46] Thus, the anti-theatricalists, I propose, have construed the Scythians' emotional hardness as a positive quality that the English no longer possess. The danger of the theatre, they maintain, is that the actors' performances will "effeminate, & soften the hearts" of an already vulnerable and impressible nation.[47]

In a sense, the anti-theatricalists are expanding on (and inverting) a notion in ancient rhetoric wherein language development is what moved man from a state of natural barbarism to civilization. Adopted in the Renaissance and recited in most treatises on poetry, this argument held that poetic speech produced cultural refinement. As William Webbe puts it in *A Discourse of English Poetrie* (1586), it was "by the *force* of... measured and tuneful speaking" that people were "brought to civility and gentleness and right knowledge."[48] In effect, this civilizing "force" induces a kind of physical erosion – or a softening of barbaric traits. Sir Philip Sidney contends in *An Apology for Poetry* that even Indians and Irish-Scythians can be transformed "by having their hard dull wits softened and sharpened with the sweet delights of Poetry." Though initially resistant to the "fruits of knowledge," Sidney explains, the barbarian's natural temperament is gradually reshaped by poetry's "exercises of the mind." [49] There is a perceived correspondence, as the anti-theatricalists have implied, between the civilizing effects of rhetoric and the potentially softening influence of the popular theatre.

In his brilliant study of the history of acting, *The Player's Passion*, Joseph Roach has shown us how ancient beliefs about the powerful intersection between the use of language and one's corporeal state formed the theoretical foundation of early modern interpretations of the theatrical experience:

First, the actor possessed the power to act on his own body. Second, he possessed the power to act on the physical space around him. Finally, he was able to act on the bodies of the spectators who shared that space with him. In short, he possessed the power to act. His expressions could transform his physical identity, inwardly and outwardly and so thoroughly that at his best he was known as Proteus. His motions could transform the air through which he moved, animating it in waves of force rippling outward from a center in his soul. His passions, irradiating the bodies of spectators through their eyes and ears, could literally transfer the contents of his heart to theirs, altering their moral natures.[50]

Ideally, the altering of their moral natures would be for the better, as in Sidney's example in the *Apology*, where the "sweet violence" of tragedy so affects the tyrant Alexander Pheraeus that he withdraws "himself from hearkening to that which might mollify his hardened heart."[51] But, as Sidney's use of the word "mollify" confirms, the same theatrical force that Thomas Heywood celebrates (for its capacity to "new mold the harts of the spectators and fashion them to the shape of any noble and notable attempt") is what Gosson condemns.[52] And whether this penetrating power was construed as destructive or reformative depended to a large degree on whether the writer believed the English needed to be hardened or softened.

In turning back to *Tamburlaine*, the first point I want to make is that Marlowe has responded to the theatrical controversy with a clever joke. By putting his eloquent and spectacular Scythian on stage, Marlowe transmogrified Gosson's anti-theatrical ideal into an archetype of the popular theatre. In John Marston's *Histriomastix* (c. 1599) for example, the rebuke for underplaying one's role is to "Looke up and play the *Tamburlaine*..." Ben Jonson's Lorenzo Junior in *Every Man in His Humor* (1598) commends a performer for having "moulded himselfe so perfectly, observing everie tricke of their action...thou wouldst have sworne he might have been the Tamberlaine..."[53] Toward the end of this chapter, I will argue that the play acknowledges the shaping effects of Tamburlaine, as impersonated by an actor with irradiating energies, but first I want to examine how the plot centers on the ironic representation of an eloquent barbarian. Beyond the joke of a Scythian embodying theatricality, Marlowe insists (with a logic that undoes the classical meaning of *barbaros*) that Tamburlaine's power as a rhetorician is interimplicated with his ethnicity – in brief, his "hardness" ensures his resistance to the mollifying influence of rhetoric even as he persuades, imitates, and wields language as a weapon.

Setting the stage for Tamburlaine's paradoxical nature, the first two acts of *Tamburlaine I* invoke Gosson's criteria for a civilization-in-decline. Indeed, we are led to understand that the Persians have grown corrupt because they value words over swords. Their ineffectual king, Mycetes, has failed to exercise his soldiers, and they are now growing increasingly less "warlike," living "idle in the wallèd towns, / Wanting both pay and martial discipline" (1: 1. 1. 140; 146–7). Dependent on others for military advice, Mycetes places his trust in Meander, his war counselor, on the basis that he is "deeply read" in poetry (2. 2. 55). And when Mycetes selects Theridamas as the best man to face Tamburlaine, he chooses him for his rhetorical skills above all else: "thy words are swords, / And with thy looks thou conquerest all thy foes" (1. 1. 74–5). Tamburlaine, we presume, will easily defeat these effete Persians with brute force.

But, as it turns out, Marlowe has set up this simple binary of civilized rhetoricians versus barbaric warriors to frame the novelty of Tamburlaine's military strategy. As Theridamas' army approaches the Scythian camp, scouts bring in a report describing the Persians' large numbers and rich armor: "odds too great," Tamburlaine proclaims, "for us to stand against" (1. 2. 122). The Scythians then debate their plan of action:

TAMBURLAINE: Then shall we fight courageously with them,
              Or look you I should play the orator?
TECHELLES: No: cowards and faint-hearted runaways
              Look for orations when the foe is near.
              Our swords shall play the orators for us.
USUMCASANE: Come let us meet them at the mountain foot
              And with a sudden and an hot alarm
              Drive all their horses headlong down the hill.
TECHELLES: Come let us march.
TAMBURLAINE: Stay Techelles, ask a parley first.

(lines 128–37)

Voicing the expected response, Techelles dismisses oratory not only as an unmanly form of inspiration but as a weak substitute for violence. Likewise, Usumcasane is impatient for battle, begging to rush "headlong down the hill" to meet the enemy. Tamburlaine, however, ignores his soldiers' heated desires, choosing instead to stand his ground and play the rhetorician. If the enemy offers either "word" or "violence," Tamburlaine will fight, "five hundred men-at-arms to one," but he is more determined to defeat with eloquence (lines 142–3). When they meet face-to-face, Theridamas, the Persian "orator," speaks very few words, while Tamburlaine, the barbarian, surpasses Hermes, the gods' own prolocutor, in his "pathetical" "persuasions" (lines 210–11). It is, pointedly, Theridamas who softens or yields to the "strong enchantments" of Tamburlaine's speech, and when he declares himself "won with [Tamburlaine's] words and conquered with [his] looks," he transfers the very wording of his own fame to the barbarous Scythian (lines 224; 228).

While Theridamas capitulates rather easily, Tamburlaine must take a different tack with the Turks. Unlike the declining Persians, Bajazeth is invulnerable to persuasion; it is, instead, his "Turkish" pride that makes him susceptible to Tamburlaine's manipulations. Proclaiming himself the "high and highest monarch of the world," Bajazeth simply assumes that his title infuses his "Wills and commands" – his words – with a natural force (3. 1. 26–7). Tamburlaine, however, dismisses Bajazeth's words as arrogant, hollow, and typical of his nation: "Turks are full of brags / And menace more than they can well perform" (3. 3. 3–4). As it turns out, Tamburlaine's strategy is to mirror Bajazeth, matching his rhetoric but not his emotions. Their confrontation is a contest in bombast, as Emily Bartels has noted, but with the crucial distinction that Tamburlaine's outrageous threats and outlandish claims are produced only as comic reflections of the Turk's.[54] And though such *imitatio* could ignite the passions of some, Tamburlaine remains emotionally disengaged. We might even say he enacts a version of the schoolyard taunt "I'm rubber, you're glue":

BAJAZETH: I tell thee, villain, those that lead my horse
             Have to their names titles of dignity,
             And dar'st thou bluntly call me Bajazeth?
TAMBURLAINE: And know thou, Turk, that those which lead my horse
             Shall lead thee captive thorough Africa.
             And dar'st thou bluntly call me Tamburlaine?

                        (lines 128–37)

Back and forth they go. Bajazeth heaps praise on his own family; Tamburlaine glorifies Zenocrate. Bajazeth swears that "slaughtered carcasses / Shall serve for walls"; Tamburlaine retorts that his soldiers will "trampl[e]" the "bowels" of the "slaughtered foe" (lines 138–9; 149–50). But to understand the import of this scene, we must recognize that Bajazeth is more affected by the impertinence of Tamburlaine's words and behavior than he is by threats of violence. In simply having to "talk with one so base as Tamburlaine," he feels he has suffered a great indignity (lines 88–90). In contrast to this, when Bajazeth has been debased to the level of a caged animal, and the power relations are inverted, we are directed to note that nothing the Turk says seems to affect Tamburlaine. As such, we may even interpret Tamburlaine's systematic humiliation of Bajazeth – which literally lowers him to the rank of a footstool – as an elaborate premise for displaying his own imperviousness to an underling's insolence.[55] The more the Turk rants, the more impassive Tamburlaine becomes. Zenocrate voices our own wonder (and neatly echoes Bajazeth's former outrage): "how can you suffer these / Outrageous curses by these slaves of yours?" and the Scythian replies, "To let them see … / I glory in the curses of my foes" (4. 4. 26–9).

Of course the legendary example of Tamburlaine's "hardness" is his unfeeling response to the Virgins of Damascus. In a last-ditch effort to save Egypt from

Tamburlaine's sword, the governor stages a tragic and pitiable scene in the hopes that, like Sidney's tyrant, Tamburlaine can be mollified. Thus, we see the governor acting as the scene's director, measuring the affectivity of the Virgins' "unspotted prayers, /...blubbered cheeks and hearty humble moans," with the goal of "melt[ing]" the Scythian's "fury into some remorse" (5. 1. 20–2). The Virgins themselves acknowledge that their appeal is a "device" whose success depends on the effectiveness of their "words" and "looks" (lines 51–2) to penetrate their audience – that is, if their audience is made of penetrable stuff. The "device," they realize, will only "prove propitious," if they can "Convey events of mercy" through Tamburlaine's "eyes and ears" and ultimately move his "heart" (lines 52–4). Certainly the Virgins' supplication is pitiable, but in allowing us to see its behind-the-scene staging, Marlowe reminds us that Tamburlaine's position is comparable to that of a theatre-goer. But unlike the audiences censured by the anti-theatricalists, it looks as though Tamburlaine's heart cannot be softened, nor his mind effeminated.

In establishing Tamburlaine's Scythian "hardness," I have been postponing two questions. How are we to explain, in early modern ethnological terms, Tamburlaine's capacity to resist the degenerating effects of foreign customs and powerful rhetoric, when these are the very forces that supposedly softened England's barbaric ancestors? And secondly, hearkening back to chapter 1, how do we reconcile this assumption of Scythian hardness with the argument made by Levinus Lemnius and others that northern wits were, in fact, the most pliable? These are not simply my queries, but early modern puzzles, as illustrated by Jean Bodin's assertion that the relative softness and hardness of the Scythian was "open to question":

the southerners, weak by the consent of all, are yet hard; the northerners, indeed, are robust, but soft. In opposition to this, Hippocrates and almost all the other writers said that Scythians and mountaineers who resemble the type of the Scythians were hard, wild, and born to endure labor. Among these conflicting opinions of historians and philosophers, however, we shall judge correctly about history...if we grant that the northerners in a cold region patiently bear labor, but in a warm region dissolve in sweat and languish.[56]

Citing their sanguine complexion and fleshy bodies, Bodin comes to the conclusion that in their natural state Scythians are "robust" *and* "soft." It is, however, their cultural practices that inure them. Manual labor, continual warfare, and constant movement are what produce their characteristic hardness. But if they grow idle, ceasing to behave as Scythians, they turn soft.

These are the very terms that shape Thomas Proctor's discussion of "Englishness" and warfare in *Of the Knowledge and Conduct of Warres* (1578), (published nine years before the first production of *Tamburlaine*).[57] Devoting his preface to an assessment of his countrymen's martial status, Proctor begins

with an ethnological survey, employing geohumoralism to characterize variations in "the temperature & complexion of mens bodies." Thus, the Moor, the
Dutchman, and the Spaniard all differ from one another in their appearance,
temperament, and humors. As for the English, they are typical northern barbarians: fierce, strong, and warlike. Indeed, Proctor contends, it is their military
prowess alone that redeems them as a "race undegenerate." The problem is
that when the English are at peace, they are cursed by an innate "mutabilitie,
and variab'e chaunging of mynde, principallie shewed in [their inclination for]
delectable thinges."[58] And it is their changeable and imitative nature that lays
them open to the corrupting effects of such foreign "tryfles" as fashionable
attire and feasting.[59]

In what may strike us as a remarkable move, Proctor suggests that the English
should counter their vulnerability to idle habits by following the "arte and
practise" of great soldiers such as Tamburlaine.[60] It was, in Proctor's view, by
the "excellent discipline of warre" that Tamburlaine conquered the "greate Turke
[Bajazet] . . . in feawe yeares, arysinge from a poore Neteherde, to be Lorde over
the most mightie Prince in the worlde." Proctor finds Tamburlaine appealing for
several reasons, I believe. For one, his triumphs are interpreted as an eradication
of foreign decadence; at the same time, it is his military success that enables
him to rise above his own lowly origins. But more generally, and perhaps most
importantly, such active and unceasing discipline is celebrated by Proctor as
the cure-all for the effeminating "idlenes . . . [that will] sucketh the valure out of
noble myndes."[61] In a culture that fears not only its native barbarism but also
the subjugation and implicit softness inherent in adopting a classical model
of civility, "Tamburlaine" represents for Proctor the "undegenerate" state of
England's ethnic roots.

For Marlowe then, it makes sense that Tamburlaine's restlessness would
sustain the virtues of his natural complexion and fulfill his role as a northern
scourge, thus staving off the softness and degeneracy that idleness brings about.
The irony, of course, is that Marlowe has Tamburlaine conceive of triumph as
the cessation of movement:

> and never rest
> Until we reach the ripest fruit of all,
> That perfect bliss and sole felicity,
> The sweet fruition of an earthly crown.
> (2. 7. 26–9)

But in articulating the expansiveness of his "aspiring mind," which seeks
"knowledge infinite" (line 24), Tamburlaine also implies the precariousness
of his own strength – its utter dependence on activity. Though idleness will not
become a real threat to the Scythian until *Part II* (when he discovers the weak
decadence of his own sons), the inevitability of Tamburlaine's decline is hinted

at in the tension between restlessly "never rest[ing]" and reaching the "ripest fruit" or "sweet fruition." The lure of empire and its association with "fruition" (meaning not just consummation but generation as well) is that it promises to liberate Tamburlaine from his role as scourge. Rather than razing civilizations, he would rule them, and possibly even build them. Yielding to this lure, however, would also insert him in the classical civilizing narrative, where settlement gives way to stagnation, and ultimately corruption. The deflating note struck by Tamburlaine's "earthly crown," which critics have found so disappointing, is meant to resonate, I propose, with the physical deterioration that spoils the "ripest fruit."[62]

If the continuous military action of *Tamburlaine I* simply reinforces the hero's ascendancy, then it is fitting that the ultimate test of his invincible nature is a digression. Tamburlaine's soliloquy, his only moment of idleness and sustained introspection, is a "doubtful battle with [his] tempted thoughts" that proves more perilous than anything he faces in the field (1: 5. 2. 89). What provokes "thoughts effeminate and faint" (line 114) and "trouble[s his] senses" (line 95) (much more, he concedes, than the furious and pitiable rhetoric of his enemies) are Zenocrate's pleas for "Egypt's freedom and the Soldan's life" (line 90). The reasons why Zenocrate's sorrows penetrate and threaten to undo the otherwise invulnerable Scythian are varied and wide-ranging. In essence, Tamburlaine's soliloquy is an abstract meditation on the seductiveness and perils of yielding – to a woman, to beauty, to the exercise of sweet poetry, to civility – which culminates in a well-wrought and meta-poetic resistance to submission in any form.

As I suggested earlier, Tamburlaine relies on the ethnological significance of his union with Zenocrate to confute the triple regions of the world; their convergence combines a declining ancient civilization with a rising barbaric culture, and in so doing, it collapses the old world's tripartite divisions. But as a pairing of man and wife, Tamburlaine and Zenocrate's story also follows the conventional contours of a soldier whose hardened warlike disposition is jeopardized by uxoriousness. It is no accident that Tamburlaine compares Zenocrate to Flora who "Rain'st on the earth resolved pearl in showers," thus characterizing her as having the power not only to dissolve but also regenerate (line 79). As a woman then, Zenocrate both symbolizes and embodies the sweetest and most enervating enticements that civilization can offer: peace, fruition, and beauty. Though Tamburlaine's soliloquy seems to move without clear transitions over a range of unrelated topics – from the "sieg[ing]" effect of Zenocrate's sadness on his soul (line 92), to beauty, to poetic composition, to the "true nobility" of his *virtù* – all his thoughts are motivated, I contend, by the same twin desires: to possess the fruits of civilization without being mollified by them.

In his meditation on the poet's efforts to express beauty in words, Tamburlaine equates poetry with the "highest reaches of a human wit" (line 105), a phrase that takes us back, I believe, to the play's prologue and reinvokes the contemporary interest in the relationship between English poetry and civility. Intriguingly, in the very moment that he defines poetry with the language he had formerly applied to his own martial pursuits – as an endless labor driven by restlessness – he reverts back to Gosson's binary of masculine "discipline of arms and chivalry" versus the effeminacy of idle pursuits. Marlowe, I want to argue, in having his Scythian reflect on poetry, express himself in poetry, and then recoil from the "effeminate and faint" tenor of his own thoughts, has staged an aborted version of the civilizing process that Sir Philip Sidney described, in which Indians and Irish-Scythians become softened by the "sweet delights of Poetry" once they discover the "pleasure in the exercises of the mind." Where Sidney's barbarians are transformed, Marlowe's Scythian exemplifies his capacity, once again, to express himself eloquently yet remain untamed. Instead of conceding that Zenocrate's female beauty has affected him, he redefines it as a "beauty" that "beat[s] on," but does not alter, the warrior's "conceits" of "fame, of valour, and of victory" (lines 118–19). In the triumphant but notoriously abstruse closing lines of his soliloquy, Tamburlaine claims to have the capacity to conceive and subdue beauty, which means, I believe, that he has allowed beauty to penetrate his thoughts, but therein he poetically re-conceives it, and as such, emerges victorious over it:

> I thus conceiving and subduing both
> That which hath stooped the topmost of the gods,
> Even from the fiery-spangled veil of heaven,
> To feel the lovely warmth of shepherds' flames
> And march in cottages of strewed weeds,
> Shall give the world to note, for all my birth,
> That virtue solely is the sum of glory
> And fashions men with true nobility.
>
> (lines 120–7)

Although there may be a parallel between Tamburlaine's "conceiving and subduing," and the rhetorical power he has demonstrated throughout the play – that is, his ability to wield a shaping influence, yet resist subjection – I also believe that these lines defy paraphrase. I am more interested in commenting on what Harry Levin has described as Tamburlaine's "antithesis between virtue and nobility, [or] native capacities as against inherited advantages" – a sentiment that is "expressed ... so strongly," Levin adds, "that [Marlowe] approximated Machiavelli, and encouraged [some] critics ... to single out Tamburlaine as the 'incarnation of *virtù*.'"[63] I would like to explore briefly how reading "virtue" as "*virtù*" complements the play's ethnological interests as well.

When Levin identifies the old sense of nobility as "inherited advantages," he refers to the privileges of rank as well the more mystified sense of nobility as a transmissible essence. As I suggested in chapter 1, the aristocratic English could cite their Trojan lineage as support for such hereditary notions: the idea that generations of people were able to transmit particular qualities and preserve themselves from complete diffusion. Consider for example how Sidney appeals to the Trojan myth to situate the Britons outside the civilizing narrative that he has applied to the Irish-Scythians:

> In Wales, the true remnant of the ancient Britons, as there are good authorities to show the long time they had poets, which they called *bards*, so through all the conquests of Romans, Saxons, Danes, and Normans, some of whom did seek to ruin all memory of learning from among them, yet do their poets even to this day last.[64]

By claiming that the ancient Britons were poets well before they were conquered – that they had preserved elements of their ancient and revered culture – Sidney saves them from the effeminizing position of having to be "softened" in the way that barbarians must be. And significantly, he suggests, instead, that the Britons have an innate faculty to resist their invaders' penetrating attempts to "ruin all memory of [their] learning."

Given his barbarous roots, as Scythian and shepherd, Tamburlaine is unable to claim an inherited "nobility." But as a northerner, his innate and humorally based virtues are the manly strengths of a warrior – the very stuff of "*virtù*."[65] Tamburlaine's statement is radical not only because he has translated the class-inflected notion of "nobility" into the seemingly baser sense of willful power, but also because this "true nobility" is fashioned, or rather spawned, by the very qualities that Elizabethan culture identified as "northern." Conventionally, nobility, when fashioned, was the effect of disciplining one's body and manners through submission to an external set of rules sanctioned by an ideal (as in the work of *The Courtier*). But for the English, this civilizing process could also mean, as I asserted in chapter 1, the refinement or even the eradication of their natural complexion (what Lemnius called their "pezantly" nature). Conversely, according to Tamburlaine's logic, the men who are "fashioned" with "true nobility" are the fierce, intractable warriors who resist being "fashioned" at all.

Why sequels fail

Tamburlaine Part I, I am arguing, presents its hero's barbarism not only as an intrinsically worthy source of power but also as an ethnological trait, and it does so to challenge the Renaissance hierarchies of region and complexion that located northerners in a deterministically inferior position. Where *Tamburlaine Part I* views the world from a northern perspective, Marlowe's sequel takes up the problem of continuance – focusing on what the play's primary sources identify as the real tragedy of Tamburlaine's story – the failure of his "posterity or lineage."[66] Simply put, Tamburlaine's sons do not inherit their father's nature. In its turn toward the Scythian's sons, *Tamburlaine Part II* confronts the fact that early modern ethnology is *not* racialism – for ethnology neither delineates the boundaries of the body nor ensures the hereditary transmission of traits. More than an inert topic, ethnic inheritance so preoccupies Tamburlaine in *Part II* that his longing to see northern traits in his progeny supersedes even his thirst to conquer.[67] Indeed, it is in the play's representation of the Scythian's desire for such an inheritance that we can detect a nascent form of the same philobarbarism that eventually contributes to the construction of an English "race."

It is no accident that when we first encounter Tamburlaine in *Part II*, he is detailing all of the ways in which his sons are unlike him and that the most disturbing difference for him is that they are soft:

> ... methinks their looks are amorous,
> Not martial as the sons of Tamburlaine.
> Water and air being symbolized in one
> Argue their want of courage and of wit;
> Their hair as white as milk and soft as down,
> Which should be like the quills of porcupines,
> As black as jet, and hard as iron or steel,
> Bewrays they are too dainty for the wars.
> Their fingers made to quaver on a lute,
> Their arms to hang about a lady's neck,
> Their legs to dance and caper in the air,
> Would make me think them bastards not my sons ...
>
> (1. 4. 21–32)

In searching for signs of paternity, Tamburlaine looks less at physical appearance (his own hair is amber) than for evidence of a shared humoral disposition.[68] Entirely lacking in their father's heat, the boys are ruled by phlegm – symbolized by "water and air" and visible in the milky quality of their downy, white hair. Tamburlaine longs to see in them the hardness that he had achieved in the uncivilized north and sustained with martial activity. But they are predisposed instead to the civilized luxuries of dancing, playing, and courting. As if primed in the womb for the idleness of court culture, they have "fingers made to quaver" and "arms to hang about a lady's neck." As Marlowe allows, their weakness could be attributed to the dominance of their mother's seed (as Zenocrate admits, "they have their mother's looks" [line 35]) or to the cultural circumstances of their birth, but it certainly matters that they are succeeding to an already-conquered southern empire, for, unlike their father, they have endured nothing. As the most "effeminate" son Calyphus confesses, revealing his lack of a conquering spirit, his father has "won enough [of an Empire] for me to keep" (line 68).

The same ethnological fluidity that I traced in chapter 2 (wherein culture, nature, experience, and climate prove to be competing forces in the determination of identity) comes through plainly in Tamburlaine's description of his sons' effeminate nature. And much of Tamburlaine's subsequent energy in the play is devoted to discovering a counteractive agent that would redress their weaknesses and toughen them up. He tries education, training them in the "rudiments of war" with the hope that they will grow inured as they suffer "scorching heat and freezing cold, / Hunger and thirst" (3. 2. 54–8). When military exercises prove ineffective, he urges them to imitate his bravery, staging his own fearlessness as inspiration. In a strangely ritualistic move, Tamburlaine lances his arm to demonstrate his high threshold for pain. Here, I believe, his desire to transmit his sanguine nature takes a grotesquely comic turn when he urges them to "search [his] wound" with their fingers and "wash all [their] hands at once" in his blood (lines 126–7). But all of Tamburlaine's efforts fall short, for even the two younger sons, Amyras and Celebinus, who attempt to follow their "father's sword," can prove only "childish valorous" next to him on the battlefield (4. 1. 4; 17). Frustrated that he has failed to transmit his "incorporeal spirit" (line 113) and galled by Calyphus in particular, whose "folly, sloth, and damned idleness" he deems contagious (line 125), Tamburlaine (in an action original to Marlowe's play) murders his first-born. More than infanticide, killing Calyphus is a desperate attempt on Tamburlaine's part to abort a degenerative decline that cannot be arrested.[69] Invoking his birthplace, Samarcanda, "where [he] breathed first / And joyed the fire of this martial flesh" (lines 104–5), Tamburlaine frames the murder as an atoning tribute to his homeland.

Tamburlaine's inability to produce barbaric hardness in his sons is provocative on two counts. It indicates that although Scythian hardness must be cultivated and sustained by activity and labor, it also stems from an essential core disposition that cannot be taught or transferred laterally – a disposition that Tamburlaine's sons clearly lack. Moreover, these scenes suggest that while the barbarous can be civilized – thus eroding that core disposition – the civilized cannot retrieve the virtues of barbarism – they can only decline. Much in the same way that Spenser's construction of the Irish-Scythians – as essentially intractable – appears now to be an inchoate form of racialism, Tamburlaine's obsession with transmitting his own intractability can be interpreted as a nascent desire for the boundedness of race.

In an article entitled "Tamburlaine's 'Discipline to His Three Sonnes,'" T. M. Pearce suggested some fifty years ago that the Scythian's "condemnation of youths [as] 'too dainty for the wars'" conjured up the commonplace criticisms "by older Englishmen of the younger men from the mid-sixteenth century on to the 1580's."[70] Citing the anti-theatrical texts of Stephen Gosson and John Northbrooke and the educational writings of Roger Ascham and Thomas Elyot, Pearce contends that Tamburlaine's frustration with his effeminate progeny represented the very real cultural anxiety in Elizabethan England that the nation's youth were wallowing in an idleness that the English educational system seemed to exacerbate rather than remedy. What Pearce sees as a generation gap, however, I have argued is an ethnological crisis, wherein these writers are wrestling with the antipathy between their nation's supposedly native virtues and the otherness of "civility." Pearce focuses in particular on a proposal for an academy of educational reform made by Sir Humphrey Gilbert in the 1570s that would institute military training in combination with the standard academic fare offered at Cambridge and Oxford. Significantly Pearce quotes but does not comment on Gilbert's assertion that this plan was intended to bring "this seely, frosen, Island into such everlasting honnour [with] all the nations of the World..."[71] If we read Marlowe's sequel as participating in the cultural debates over Englishness – its perceived state of barbarism or degeneracy – the play conveys the dispiriting message that the few virtues this frozen isle engendered (military strength and youthful vigor) have long since been corrupted. But even more disturbingly, it implies that these hard qualities could only be cultivated in those not yet "civilized."

Yet neither Tamburlaine nor Marlowe gives up entirely on the possibility of transmitting the Scythian's spirit to his descendants. Just before he dies Tamburlaine makes one final bid to alter the nature of his sons:

> But sons, this subject, not of force enough
> To hold the fiery spirit it contains,
> Must part, imparting his impressions
> By equal portions into both your breasts;
> My flesh divided in your precious shapes
> Shall still retain my spirit, though I die,
> And live in all your seeds immortally.
>
> (5. 3. 168–74)

An informed viewer would know, of course, that Amyras and Celebinus lose their father's empire, thus Tamburlaine's confidence in a horizontal transfer of his spirit may be read as nothing more than a vain hope. Yet Tamburlaine also recalls the irradiating energies of theatrical performance as described by Joseph Roach and condemned by the period's anti-theatricalists. Indeed, Tamburlaine seems to echo Stephen Gosson's characterization of how the players' "outward spectacles" are "secretly conveyed" to the audience:

... as I have already discovered the corruption of playes by the corruption of their causes, The Efficient, the Matter, the Forme, the end, so will I conclude the effects [that] this poyson works among us. The divel is not ignorant how mightely these outward spectacles effeminate, & soften the hearts of men, vice is learned with beholding, sense is tickled, desire pricked, & those impressions of mind are secretly conveyed over to the gazers, which the players do counterfeit on the stage. As long as we know our selves to be flesh, beholding those examples in Theaters [that] are incident to flesh, wee are taught by other mens examples how to fall. And they that came honest to a play, may depart infected.[72]

Perhaps we are supposed to shift our attention away from Tamburlaine's hollow promise to his sons and focus instead on the actor's acknowledgement of his power to alter the natures of those in the audience.[73] It is an intriguing coincidence, nonetheless, that in having transformed Gosson's anti-theatrical Scythian into the embodiment of theatricality in *Part I*, Marlowe now seems to suggest that *Part II*'s targeted spectators are the idle and effeminate theatre-goers that Gosson and others denounced. If we cast the light just right, we might see Tamburlaine-the-actor as a theatrical scourge, using the energies of his performance and the example of his military prowess to harden and preserve the English people as (in Thomas Proctor's phrase) an "undegenerate race." But a shift in focus would remind us that in order to "transfer the contents of his heart to theirs," Tamburlaine must penetrate his audience – hence, the act of conveying undoes the hardness he wishes to convey. Marlowe, I believe, delighted in these very paradoxes.

Though Marlowe may have had little interest in resolving the ethnological crisis that occupied many of his contemporaries, his plays seemed to feed anxieties about the porousness of its theatrical audience. For several prominent poets and playwrights, performances of *Tamburlaine* took unfair advantage of the audience's susceptibility, overwhelming them with spectacle and rhetoric that made no pretense to moral reformation. Ben Jonson in *Timber*, for example, rails against "the *Tamerlanes* and *Tamer-Chams* of the late Age, which had nothing in them but *scenicall* strutting, and furious vociferation, to warrant them to the ignorant gapers." Joseph Hall emphasizes Tamburlaine's power (his "vaunt[ing]" voice and "Big-sounding sentences") to "ravish[ ] the gazing Scaffolders," and George Wither remarks on the Scythian's ability to "strike his hearers dead with admiration."[74] Implicit in these critiques is some recognition of the potential physiological influence of *Tamburlaine*. Although these writers dismiss the performance as strutting bombast, they also see something powerfully barbaric in the gapers, gazers, and admirers – a "something" that has been generated, or regenerated, by the sounds and sights of the players. There is no doubt that Marlowe's ethnographic theatre – in all of its exotic pageantry – incited wonder. But the more intense wonder may have been aroused by what it meant to be English.

5 Temperature and temperance in Ben Jonson's *The Masque of Blackness*

Ben Jonson's condemnation of the "ignorant gapers" who favored *Tamburlaine*'s "scenicall strutting, and furious vociferation" exhibits the antitheatrical prejudice that Jonas Barish discerned in him.[1] Yet Jonson's censure of the "loathed stage" also reflects disappointment, for he repeatedly expresses the hope that theatrical power can reform the audience's moral natures. To achieve such reformation, drama should appeal, Jonson believed, to an audience's "Understanding" over its coarser "senses."[2] But further complicating the playwright's theatrical philosophy and feeding his frustrations was the conviction that the "ignorant gapers" most in need of his corrections were especially resistant to such medicine.[3] I believe Jonson attributes this stubborn resistance (or lack of understanding) in part to England's position as a belated and marginalized region vis-à-vis the idealized temperance of classical Rome – a sentiment he articulates in the prologue to *The Alchemist*:

> Our scene is London, 'cause we would make known
> No country's mirth is better than our own.
> No clime breeds better matter for your whore,
> Bawd, squire, imposter, many persons more,
> Whose manners, now called humours, feed the stage,
> And which have still been subject for the rage
> Or spleen of comic writers. Though this pen
> Did never aim to grieve, but better men,
> Howe'er the age he lives in doth endure
> The vices that she breeds, above their cure.
> But when the wholesome remedies are sweet,
> And in their working, gain and profit meet,
> He hopes to find no spirit so much diseased,
> But will, with such fair correctives, be pleased;
>
> (lines 5–18)[4]

Though Jonson, more than any other literary writer of the period, is associated with the discourse of humoralism, there has long been a critical debate over what he means by "humour" – whether it should be defined in corporeal or psychological terms, or as an affectation.[5] In this prologue, the speaker indicates

Figure 7 A portrait of a daughter of Niger, *The Masque of Blackness* by Inigo Jones, from the Devonshire Collection, Chatsworth.

that what we would call "manners" have been newly designated as "humours."
Yet, he also states that it is the English "clime" that has bred such manners, thus
attributing social conduct to a natural and primary determinant of bodily humors.
In other words, even when Jonson turns to the psychological or behavioral sense
of "humor," the somatic meaning never fades entirely away.

While it is my chief aim in this chapter to offer an ethnological reading of
the geohumoralism at work in *The Masque of Blackness* (1604) – a text that has
become central to scholarly discussions of early modern "racialism" – I want
first to establish, in broad strokes, several crucial points about the humors in
Jonson's early comic satires.[6] There are significant, though not widely noted,
correspondences between Jonson's aims as a satirist in such plays as *Every Man
Out of His Humour* and *Cynthia's Revels* and his goals as a masque writer for the
Jacobean court – aims and goals that revolve around his belief that well-wrought
theatre could temper, in somatic and behavioral terms, a receptive audience.
Moreover, it is my contention that we cannot fully understand what Jonson
means by "humour" without also attending to the ethnological assumptions
that inform its use.

Most discussions of Jonson's humoralism turn to the Induction to *Every Man
Out of His Humour* (1600), where Asper defines "Humour" as "Moisture, and
fluxure" (lines 88–91) in the body, as well as applying "by *Metaphore*" to the
"disposition" of a man whose "affects, his spirits, and his powers, / In their
confluctions, all . . . runne one way" (lines 103–8).[7] Much has been made of the
term "metaphor" here, leading critics to conclude that the humors for Jonson are
not physiological but figurative. And yet this presumption forgets the somatic
nature of the "affects" and "spirits" in the pre-Cartesian body.[8] Jonson does,
however, go on to draw a distinction between the *affectation* of a humor and
one's innate, bodily-determined disposition when he has Cordatus condemn the
"Idiot" who claims an "apish, or phantasticke straine" as his own "Humour"
(lines 115–17). But on this point, two further qualifications are necessary. First,
the underlying threat (or promise) of affectation is the alteration of one's natural
self. "Wee so insist in imitating others," Jonson writes in the *Discoveries*, "as wee
cannot (when it is necessary) returne to our selves . . . [thus] mak[ing] the habit
to another nature."[9] Second, for Jonson, as for Elizabethan culture as a whole,
affectation is most often recognized as the infection of foreign customs and
behaviors. The "apes" that Asper aims to scourge "preferre all Countries before"
their "native" one.[10] As they are described in *Cynthia's Revels* (1601), "affected
humours" take the form of "spanish shrugs, french faces, smirks, irps."[11] And
even when these affectations have more domestic origins – as in Sordido's
dependence on almanacs – all the humor characters share a recognizably English
inclination for apish behavior – what Asper calls their "spongie natures."[12]

In his promises to "purge," "cure," "remedy," etc. his audience, Jonson relies on a long tradition of associations between the satirist and the physician,

and between theatre and medicine – associations that further underscore the persistent corporeality of the plays' humoral references.[13] And yet, as I already noted, Jonson is persuaded that the spongy natures (line 145) he aims to correct (the ones Asper identifies as "fooles, so sicke in taste, / That they contemne all phisicke of the minde" [lines 131–2]) are least likely to be the "attentive auditors, / Such as will joyne their profit with their pleasure" (lines 201–2).[14] To resolve this very paradox – that his satire will only reach "good men, and vertuous spirits, that lothe their vices" – Jonson concludes both *Cynthia's Revels* and *Every Man Out of His Humour* with "rudimentary" masques.[15] By invoking the authority and quasi-magical presence of the queen, Jonson is able to elevate the interventionist power of his comedies beyond that of mere scourge. As Helen M. Ostovich maintains, the sight of the queen at the end of *Every Man Out* has the capacity to civilize, tame, and purge the characters in the play. But more importantly, the royal authority of the masque produces "a similar catharsis . . . in the audience."[16]

When Jonson began composing masques for James I, he hoped, I believe, that the royal venue and audience would help ensure the success of his "phisicke of the minde." As Stephen Orgel has demonstrated in *The Illusion of Power*, Stuart masques were complex expressions of the king's will that had to do "with wit and understanding, with the ability to control natural forces through intellect, with comprehending the laws of nature, and most of all, with our own virtue and self-knowledge."[17] For Jonson, the masque functioned as a panegyric and a representation of Jacobean political ideology, but it also enabled him to collaborate with the king in the control of natural forces. Thus, Jonson's first endeavor at the genre, *The Masque of Blackness* (1604), celebrates King James' presumed capacity to civilize his subjects as he effects a peaceful union of England and Scotland – the chief political issue on the table at the beginning of his reign. But more significantly, I contend, *The Masque of Blackness* stages a mythopoetic solution to the English fear that uniting with its northern neighbor would move England further from the origins of civilization and the civility of temperance. Indeed, Jonson dramatizes the possibility that James I's rule will temper the humoral imbalances that the northern climate breeds. And, as I shall demonstrate, blackness – both symbolically and humorally – plays an astonishingly positive role in this masque's vision of Britannia's past and future.

Blanching an Ethiop and blackening the Britons

When James I came to the English throne in 1603, the question of union engrossed all of his subjects – opponents and supporters, Scottish and English. In the first four years of the Stuart reign not only did the union controversy influence people's perspectives on practically every current issue but most of the pressing concerns directly involved the legal, economic, and social ramifications of James I's vision of Great Britain.[18] The objections to a union took various forms; English parliamentarians feared a usurpation of English law, while Scots dreaded a loss of independence and neglect by their king. Moreover, mutual prejudice engendered and exacerbated resistance on both sides; the English, in particular, identified the Scots as northern barbarians: excessively warlike, ignorant, incontinent, and "grabbing 'everything they could lay their hands on.' "[19] The Scots, in other words, were perceived to be extreme versions of the English. In James I's idealized view, however, the formation of Great Britain would resurrect an ancient empire, and the wisdom of his government would bring civility to even the basest of subjects. Underestimating English prejudices, union advocates urged parliament to celebrate the merging of England and Scotland as a "restitution," rather than an "alteration," and James I compared the "Union of two ancient and famous Kingdomes" to the reunion of the Houses of Lancaster and York within his own lineal descent.[20] Jonson began his long affiliation with the Jacobean court by celebrating and elaborating on the king's vision in complex and often cryptic ways.

The familiar language of unionist ideology in *The Masque of Blackness* has not escaped notice.[21] Certain passages echo King James' rhetoric from his opening speech to Parliament in 1603. The king's idealization of the united kingdom as "one Island, compassed with one Sea" and of the "marriage" of Scotland and England as "fastened and bound up by the wedding Ring of *Astrea*"[22] appears in Jonson's praise of "Britannia" as a "world divided from the world" not unlike a diamond set in the world's ring.[23] What remains unclear in the scholarship, however, is the exact role that blackness plays in the masque's representation of union. Martin Butler contends, for example, that the Ethiopians' quest for whiteness "was clearly an analogue to the dilemmas of national and individual identity which Union posed." Yet he does "not wish to imply that the distinction between British whiteness and their blackness is a one-to-one allegory of the English/Scots divide." Although the Ethiopians are "received as aliens at Whitehall," Butler adds, "the king's magic proved them to have the pale skins of aristocratic ladies underneath ... thereby demonstrating his sovereign power to incorporate alien nations and do the proverbially impossible."[24]

It is, however, the very implausibility of transforming the Ethiopians from black to white that has led several scholars to dismiss *The Masque of Blackness* as a spectacular failure. Balking at the outrageousness of Jonson's praise that the king can "blanch an Ethiop, and revive a corse," quite a few critics have found the masque to be "distressingly extravagant" – an instance of an ambitious poet's shamefully "gross flattery."[25] Orgel contends that we would "be doing Jonson some injustice if we identify [this light] simply with King James ... If we force it into visual or literal terms ... we are in danger of arriving at some such ludicrous formula as 'Negroes become white in the presence of the king.' "²⁶ To do Jonson justice we should recognize that *The Masque of Blackness* is somewhat equivocal about whether it is the English sun or James I whose "beams" are able to lighten the Ethiopian nymphs:

> Ruled by a sun that to this height doth grace it,
> Whose beams shine day and night, and are of force
> To blanch an Ethiop, and revive a corse.
>
> (lines 223–5)²⁷

Though I will return later to the masque's oblique reference to England's climate and its whitening effects, I want first to consider how Jonson's praise of King James becomes much more grounded in Anglo-Scottish politics when we pursue the etymological history of the curious, and deliberately chosen, word "blanch." "Blanching," it turns out, is a Scottish legal term that denotes the king's ability to transform a subject's debt to the crown into a ceremonial display of allegiance. Early modern Scottish law allows the king to "blacken" or "black-ward" a Scotsman into military duty, and thereupon, it is within the king's power to convert that "blackened" state to "blanch," or to transfer an obligation of military tenure to a nominal fee or payment of honor.²⁸ Moreover, this conversion of debt – from ward to blanch – is akin to a civilizing process. For, according to the *OED*, the blanched subject may remunerate the king with "a white rose, a pair of gloves, pair of spurs, [which are] paid in acknowledgment of superiority," affirming the subject's position as a courtier. Rather than "gross flattery," the word circumscribes royal sovereignty to the realm of potentially real action.

In the *Trew Law of Free Monarchies* (1598, published 1603), King James cites his ability to "blanch" as a specific example of the far reaches of his power. "Blanching," he indicates, helps to justify his absolutist conviction that the kings of Scotland are "the authors and makers of the Lawes, and not the Lawes of the kings":

> the whole subjects being but [the king's] vassals, and from him holding all their lands as their over-lord, who according to good services done unto him, chaungeth their holdings from tacke to few, *from ward to blanch*, erecteth new Baronies, and uniteth olde.²⁹

In spite of James I's assertion that

> All the Lawe of Scotland for Tenures, Wards and Liveries, Seigniories and Lands, are drawn out of the Chauncerie of England, and for matters of equitie and in many things else, differs from [English law] but in certaine termes,

the English, no doubt, would have viewed this display of royal power as singularly Scottish and troubling.³⁰ Notably it is the king's refrain throughout the beginning of his reign that a union of England and Scotland would effect a *revival* of ancient Britain rather than an eradication of Scottish law.³¹ By employing this Scottish legal term "blanch" as a pun in his masque, Jonson playfully supports James I's belief that his authority precedes and is sanctioned by the ancient unity of Scottish and English law.

"To revive a corse" also takes on new meaning within a legal context, for the phrase suggests that James I's intention to resuscitate the ancient dignity of Britannia is enhanced by his ability to bring a *body* of laws to life. Once again, we can turn to James I's own writing to find an equation between the Scottish king's authority to "ward" and "blanch," and the power to give life itself:

> And as ye see it manifest, that the King is over-Lord of the whole land: so is he Master over every person that inhabiteth the same, having power over the life and death of every one of them: For although a just Prince will not take the life of any of his subjects without a cleare law; yet the same lawes whereby he taketh them, are made by himselfe, or his predecessors: and so the power flowes always from him selfe.[32]

When framed by the king's own interpretation of his power, Jonson's play on the words "blanch" and "corpse" suggests that the "real point" of the masque may be more than the external metamorphosis of Ethiopians from black to white.[33]

The Scottish and legal valences of "blanch" complicate the masque in a couple of ways. First, "blanch" underscores the identification between the Ethiopian nymphs and James I's Scottish subjects that the critic Martin Butler had resisted making. Second, the word encourages us to associate King James' quasi-magical force with the implementation of law. This association is further intensified by Jonson's subsequent descriptions of the sun's ruling powers: "His light sciential is, and past mere nature, / Can salve the rude defects of every creature . . . / This sun is temperate, and refines / All things on which his radiance shines" (lines 226–7; 234–5). In characterizing James I's power as "sciential," Jonson invokes the contemporary debates on wisdom and government, which equate "scientia" with the active prudence of a sage ruler.[34] Moreover, these lines explicitly analogize climatic influence and the civilizing effects of good government in a way that should recall the geohumoralism that Jean Bodin outlined in *The Six Bookes of a Commonweale*. Both the sun and the king, it seems, are able to temper, refine, and "salve the rude defects of every creature."

Indeed, I want to suggest that this climate/government analogy appeals, yet again, to King James' political writings, which are quite obviously indebted to the following argument in Bodin:

> a wise governour of any Commonweale must know [his subjects'] humours, before he attempt any thing in the alteration of the state and lawes. For one of the greatest, and it may be the chiefest foundation of a Commonweale, is to accommodat the estate to the humor of the citizens; and the lawes and ordinances to the nature of the place, persons, and time.[35]

Echoing Bodin, King James writes in *Basilikon Doron*:

And that yee may the readier with wisedome and Justice governe your subjects, by knowing what vices they are naturallie most inclined to, as a good Physician, who must first know what peccant humours his Patient naturallie is most subject unto, before he can begin his cure ... for the better reformation of all these abuses among your estates, it will be a great helpe unto you, to be well acquainted with the nature and humours of all your Subjects.[36]

We should emphasize here that King James does not simply adopt Bodin's geohumoralism as a general philosophy, he does so with regard to the specific question as to how he should subdue the Scottish Highlanders – the most northern, and the most notoriously uncivilized, inhabitants of Scotland.

As King James himself had exclaimed, it was understood that the Highlanders were lascivious, intemperate barbarians – suspected of cannibalism and known for living detestable and godless lives.[37] In other words, the Highlander is the stereotypical northern brute. We may recall Bodin's assertions that the farther one moves north:

the farther one is from human culture, that is, from the nature of men, the nearer he approaches to the likeness of beasts, which, since they are lacking in reason, are unable to restrain their wrath and appetites. So it happens that the northerners are carried by impulse into acts of cruelty.[38]

To temper the incivility and rude defects of the Highlander Scots, King James recognizes that he must consider their nature and humours.[39] Thus, he plays the role of physician by applying laws that counter his subjects' humoral imbalance. It is not surprising then that Jonson, who has also aspired to play the physician, would allude to his new king's capacity to temper the humors that the northern climate breeds.

I am, in part, suggesting that the conventional argument about this masque – that it enacts a "world of self-evident truths, such as that whiteness is better than blackness or good better than evil" overlooks entirely its implicit appeals to early modern ethnology, which maintained that white northern complexions were in humoral terms as intemperate and barbaric as the burnt complexions of Ethiopia.[40] I am not disputing the fact that *The Masque of Blackness* plays out the familiar commonplace that white is fair and black is foul – a sentiment that goes unquestioned for the most part in early modern western aesthetics.[41] I am, instead, resituating the masque within the geohumoral canon of historiography, medical texts, and political philosophy that regularly placed the pale Britons on the periphery of a wide spectrum of complexions. We should keep in mind, for example, that when Niger's daughters move northward in their search for a place where the sun, which has "heat[ed] / Their bloods" and darkened their skin, "doth never rise or set" (lines 165–6), their progress charts a direct correspondence between coloration and environment that occurs not only in Ethiopia but throughout the world. Their travels take them from "Aethiopia," the "blackest nation of the world" (lines 15–16) through "Black Mauretania," "Swarth Lusitania," and "Rich Aquitania," to their arrival in Britannia, also known as "Albion" or the "white land" (lines 173–80).[42] That Spain is marked as "swarth" points up the instability of "whiteness" as the dominant complexion of European identity: the Spanish physician Juan Huarte in *The Examination of Men's Wits* (1594), for example, praises the "somewhat browne" skin of his own countrymen as a sign of their humoral temperance.[43] When the Ethiopian sisters return whitened in *The Masque of Beauty* (1608), Jonson acknowledges that such beauty is an achievement "to whose having, every clime laid claim; / Each land and nation urgèd as the aim... / Now made peculiar to this place alone" (lines 321–4). In its effort to establish the temperance of the British isles – as "*A world divided from the world*" – and to fashion whiteness as the dominant complexion, *The Masque of Blackness* is compelled to confront Britain's marginalized northern position in the "triple world" (lines 218; 211).[44]

Not surprisingly the threat of union exacerbates England's anxieties about its northern status. Traditionally, the English had projected onto Scotland the intemperate characteristics associated with extremely northern complexions – slow wits, ferocity, and barbarism. In an effort to conceive of themselves as more *temperate*, the English persistently characterized Scotland as "a baryn and a waste countrey" inhabited by unruly peoples.[45] Yet the fragile distinction between barbaric Scotland and civilized England was jeopardized by the implications of a perfect union. The anti-union tract "A Discourse of Naturalisation" expresses England's concerns in environmental terms: with the formation of Great Britain, "All the Poor People of that [Scottish] Realm... will draw nearer the Sonn, and flocking hither in such Multitudes, that death and dearth is very probable to ensue."[46] That is to say, not only will the Scots want to be closer to their king, but they will also view the union as an opportunity to live in a more temperate clime. Jonson inverts this concept when he has the Ethiopians drawn northward to Britannia's sun. Though opposed in every other way, northerners and southerners shared, it seems, the experience of climatic extremes. As Edmund Spenser writes in *A View*:

all those Northerne nations, having beene used to be annoyed with much colde and darkenesse, are wont therefore to have the fire and the sunne in great veneration; like as contrarywise the Moores and Egyptians, which are much offended and grieved with extreame heat of the sunne, doe every morning, when the sunne ariseth, fall to cursing and banning of him as their plague.[47]

Moreover, the English reference to Scottish multitudes invokes the commonplace in geohumoral discourse that northern regions were the populous "Storehouse of Mankind" that resemble "swarmes of Bees" as they move southward.[48] Thus, James I's speech to Parliament in 1607 attempts to dissuade his audience of the notion that "if the Union were effected" then "England will then bee overwhelmed by the swarming of the Scots...[who] would raigne and rule all."[49] Indeed, King James frames his rhetoric to address the particular regional biases feeding England's dread of union: "Some thinke that I will draw the Scottish Nation hither, talking idly of transporting of Trees out of barren ground into a better, and of leane cattell out of bad pasture into a more fertile soile."[50] When Francis Bacon repudiates English objections to Scotland's impoverished status, he conjures up the very basis of England's fear: the Scots are, he writes, "*Alteri Nos*, Other our selves...they are a People ingenious; in Labour industrious; in Courage valiant; in Body hard, active, comely."[51] But Bacon inadvertently identifies the root of the problem, as the English objectors saw it: the formation of Great Britain would join them to a country whose environment produced the very qualities that they were striving to amend or deny in themselves.

Black paint and Britannia

However persuasive this chapter has been thus far in linking the Aethiopian nymphs to the Scots, we must also acknowledge that the shocking effect of the ladies' painted blackness may have blinded the court audience to Jonson's more enigmatic messages. Certainly ambassador Dudley Carleton's notorious reaction to the masque's performance suggests as much. Describing in detail the costumes that Queen Anne and her ladies wore, he writes:

Their Apparell was rich, but too light and Curtizan-like for such great ones. Instead of Vizzards, their Faces, and Arms up to the Elbows, were painted black, which was Disguise sufficient, for they were hard to be known; *but it became them nothing so well as their red and white, and you cannot imagine a more ugly Sight, then a Troop of lean-cheek'd Moors.*[52]

Though I will return to the matter of Carleton's color prejudice later in this chapter, I want to observe for now that his revulsion is focused in particular on the use of black paint, as opposed to "Vizzards" or "red and white" cosmetics.[53] Critics have made much of Carleton's distaste, often concluding as Hardin Aasand does, that his "aversion...derives from the obvious incongruity of the pageant: a fair English queen is adorned in the exotic yet corruptible guise of a Nigerian princess."[54] Unable to reconcile the queen's "blackness" with the requisite laudatory tone of a court performance, scholars have decided that the masque is compromised. In the preamble to the printed text, Jonson attributes to Queen Anne the proposal that he make the ladies "blackamores at first," prompting several commentators to suggest that this collaboration with the queen restricted the poet's artistic scope.[55] Aasand states, for example, that "Jonson must compromise his own poetic prerogative to orchestrate a work that is not wholly his own design," and Ann Cline Kelly asserts that "Jonson's task of praising the Queen as black was almost an insuperable one, given the

Figure 8 "The true picture of a yonge dowgter of the Pictes," an engraving by Theodore de Bry of John White's illustration, from Thomas Hariot, *A Brief and True Report of the New Found Land of Virginia* (1590).

ethnocentric prejudice intrinsic in the English language."[56] And yet there is also evidence that Jonson's use of black paint is purposeful, significant, and consistent with the analogous relationship I have drawn between the Ethiopians and the Scots.

Whether by geographical proximity or acknowledged kinship, the Scots had long been associated with the Picts, those ancient barbarians whose name denoted their practice of painting their bodies.[57] By 1604, the learned community was quite prepared to identify body paint with the Picts after Theodore de Bry published engravings of John White's illustrations in the 1590 edition of Thomas Hariot's *A Brief and True Report of the New Found Land of Virginia* (1590) (Fig. 8).

Jonson cleverly links painting with northern identity when he has Niger contrast the natural "blackness" of his daughters with those "painted beauties other empires sprung" (line 133) who, it turns out, reign only in Britannia (lines 213–14). In part, the use of paint is meant, I believe, to conjure up images of Scotland's barbaric past. Thus, the king's blanching will civilize the Pictish Scots by literally erasing their savage practices. But more complexly, the ladies' painting signifies the formation of Britain and metonymizes its proposed name. To glorify Britannia, Jonson has drawn much of the masque's language and imagery from his former teacher's text of the same name: William Camden's *Britannia* (1586).[58] Fittingly, Jonson's most explicit textual debt to Camden is the historian's discovery of Britannia's etymological significance: "unto the word *Brith*, [was] added *Tania*: which…betokenth in Greek, a region"; furthermore, Britannia shares this "termination" with those three countries "lying all in this west part of the world, namely, *Mauritania*, *Lusitania*, and *Aquitania*."[59] As we have already noted, *The Masque of Blackness* lists these same lands "Whose termination, of the Greek / Sounds -*tania*…Black Mauretania first, and secondly / Swarth Lusitania; next…Rich Aquitania" (lines 164–75). As for the prefix, Camden explains "that word *Brith*, among the Britans, implieth that which the Britans were indeed, to wit, *painted*, *depainted*, *died*, and *coloured*."[60] Just as "the Aethiopians" derive their name from "their black hue," he writes, the etymology of "Britannia" can be traced to the nature of the island's inhabitants. Citing Pomponius Mela, Cornelius Tacitus, Herodian, Pliny, Solinus, among others, Camden suggests that most nations acquire their name from the "nature, conditions, and inclination" of their people.[61] Given that the union controversy took a keen interest in determining the proper "Style" for a *unified* Britain, we should note that Camden not only links the Britons to the Picts by way of painting, but he also contends that they are kin: "the Picts… were verie naturall Britans themselves, even the right progenie of the most ancient Britans."[62] Jonson's reliance on Camden suggests, yet again, that the British people are the primary targets of King James' "sciential light." While the Ethiopians seek to transform their complexion from black to white, the

Britons, whose barbarism is epitomized in the practice of painting, also need the blanching, civilizing presence of a "temperate sun."

Most of Camden's classical references make no distinction between men and women in the practice of painting (and John White had portrayed Picts of both sexes). However it may have been Pliny's quotation in particular that caught Jonson's eye: *"There groweth an herbe in Gaule like unto Plantaine, named Glastum, that is, Woad, with the juice whereof, the women of Britaine, as well maried wives, as their young daughters anoint and die their bodies all over; resembling by that tincture the colour of Aethiopians."*[63] By making women the focus of the masque's promised physical transformation, Jonson seems to translate British barbarism into the more frivolous problem of female vanity.[64] To draw on Jodi Mikalachki's thesis that the "savagery of ancient British women consistently thwarted early modern attempts" to construct a masculine and civil national history, Jonson represses the warrior implications of the Britons' painting by presenting it as a harmless argument in "great beauty's war" (lines 126–7).[65] Also repressed is Hippocrates' assertion that pale skin and spongy humors made the northern Scythians the most effeminate of all races.[66]

Of course, it is the English historians who regularly identified the Scots with the Scythians; the Scots had their own ideas. Striving to outdo the elitism of the British race, the Scots claimed to be descendants of the Egyptians. Scottish myths held that Gathelus, a Greek Lord, had met and married Scotia, an Egyptian, and together they settled in Scotland.[67] Camden speaks for most English writers when he calls the story a complete fabrication: "Scotish writers falsely devised *Scota* the Ægyptian Pharaoes daughter to be the Foundresse of their nation."[68] Edmund Spenser writes that the Scots

build and enlarge many forged histories of their owne antiquity, which they deliver to fooles, and make them believe for true; as for example, That first of one Gathelus the sonne' of Cecrops or Argos, who having married the King of Egypt his daughter, thence sailed with her into Spaine, and there inhabited.[69]

However, those that attest to Scotland's Egyptian lineage also claim that the ancient Scots "used at the first the rites and maners of the Aegyptians from whence they came, and in all their private affaires they used not to write with common letters, as other nations did; but rather with . . . this hieroglyphical maner of writing."[70] We are invited to discern this more southern genealogy in *The Masque of Blackness* when the daughters of Niger each present to the court "a mute hieroglyphic expressing their mixed qualities" (lines 238–9).[71] Jonson also implies (in his characteristically erudite way) that the proper origin of these southern ancestors should be Ethiopian rather than Egyptian, for "Egyptians are said first to have brought [hieroglyphic writing] from the Ethiopians" (lines 241–2). This translation of wisdom would have been recognized by many early moderns as the first step in a natural progress of civilization which moves not simply westward but *northward*. As Louis Le Roy explains in *Of the Interchangeable Course of Things* (1594):

antiquitie hath given the first praise of Letters to the Ethiopians, attributing the invention to them, which they communicated with the Egiptians their neighbors; where they have bin augmented: from thence they came to the Libians, Babylonians, and Chaldeans; consequently to the Greeks; then to the Romains; the Arabians, Italians, Frenchmen, Almains, Englishmen, Spaniards, and Polonians.[72]

Thus in the Scottish mythography, the Scoto-Egyptian ancestors have circumvented the slow translation of civilization. If we take seriously the implicit connection between Scotland and ancient Africa, the Scots' status as stereotypical northerners becomes much less certain in Jonson's poetic framework.

To adopt Orgel's language, the "real point" of *The Masque of Blackness* may not be the deferred transformation of the Ethiopians' skin, but the presentation of a genealogy of people who transmitted southern wisdom and culture to a region that eventually granted them external whiteness. Taken literally, the possibility that the early moderns could imagine an ancient Britain inhabited by dark Africans (who not only brought knowledge with them but who also blended in with the indigenously white inhabitants) may sound as "ludicrous" as a king's ability to "blanch" an Ethiop. Yet consider the remarkably similar narrative put forth by John Twynne, an antiquarian much admired by William Camden. According to T. D. Kendrick, Twynne finds evidence to suggest that the ancient colonizers of Wales were dark Phoenicians:

in Wales women actually preserve a Phoenician form of dress. The Phoenicians, of course, introduced the famous magic of the East. They were folk of cunning and corrupt manners, and of a physique weakened by luxurious life, and they were originally a swarthy folk; but those who settled in Britain became pale as a result of our climate, and they therefore took to painting themselves with woad.[73]

While Twynne equates the Phoenicians' knowledge, mystery, and wisdom with "cunning" and corruption, thus casting the importation of southern learning in negative terms, his speculations are founded in the same geohumoral tenets held by Gerald of Wales and Juan Huarte: though descendants will conform to a new environment, they also maintain and transmit qualities derived from their ancestors' environment. Astonishingly, Twynne not only indicates that over time Britain's northern climate will turn "swarthy folk" white, but he also suggests that the very practice of painting betrays a southern derivation. Twynne's speculation brings us back, in a perverse way, to the seeming confusion in Jonson's humoralism between natural and cultural traits – or between "apish" and genuine humors. In Twynne's story, the Welsh affected darkness to retrieve their lost complexion. That the Scots may have been dark-skinned at one point may be more believable to some English writers than the possibility that they ever possessed the wisdom associated with blackness. As Spenser writes:

whether it be a smack of any learned judgment, to say, that Scota is like an Egyptian word, let the learned judge. But . . . Scota rather comes of the Greek . . . that is, darknes, which hath not let him see the light of the truth.[74]

For Spenser, the only "darknes" the barbarous Scots have retained is ignorance.

The subtle flood

In *The Masque of Blackness*, Jonson hints that the blackness the Ethiopian nymphs wish to shed denotes much more than an argument in "great beauty's war." In an explicit appeal to climate theory, Niger establishes that the southern sun has "formed" his "dames" and given them their "scorched" appearance (lines 113; 150). Anticipating Shakespeare's Cleopatra ("Think on me, / That am with Phoebus' amorous pinches black" [1. 5. 27–8]), Niger explains the sun has "draw[n] / Signs of his fervent'st love" in "their firm hues" (lines 117–18). Jonson's use of the word "draw" corresponds with Bodin's geohumoral explanation of the sun's influence: "southerners abound in black bile, which subsides like lees to the bottom when the humors have been *drawn out* by the heat of the sun."[75] As we saw in chapter 3, the neoplatonic tradition maintained that black bile predisposed men to religious contemplation, and conversely, "contemplation itself . . . with a kind of rigorous gathering up . . . contracts one's nature like black bile."[76] It is "black bile," Bodin claims, that gives "southern people . . . continued zeal for contemplation" and their harmony with "nature and the power of religion and the celestial bodies."[77] By alluding to the physiological process that supposedly produced black skin and black bile, Jonson portrays the Ethiopians' complexion not only in terms of the western aesthetics of "great beauty's war," but also as a temperament associated with the inner qualities of wisdom, civility, piety, constancy, and a contemplative nature. From Niger's perspective, his daughters' blackness denotes their "near[ness to] divinity" and their freedom "from passion and decay" (lines 128–9). The distinctive characteristic of the Ethiopians' "blackness" is its admirable changelessness: "No cares, no age can change, or there display / The fearful tincture of abhorrèd grey, / Since Death herself (herself being pale and blue) / Can never alter their most faithful hue" (lines 122–5).[78] "Faithful," I propose, refers simultaneously to the southerners' capacity for divine contemplation and the fixity of their blackness: for black bile "provokes the soul so that it might gather itself into one piece, stay in one piece, and be contemplated."[79] Even as Jonson equates physical blackness with a lack of beauty, his imagery acknowledges the virtuous link between "blackness" and wisdom, constancy, and piety.

What I want to suggest is that the deferred transformation of the Ethiopians' skin – from black to white – is only one half of the masque's imagined exchange: Britannia promises external whiteness, but gains the internal qualities of a black complexion. This "blackness" is incorporated, I contend, in a number of ways, for Britain not only receives the Ethiopians' hieroglyphs, it absorbs their humoral qualities into its land and water – the very humoral qualities that should remedy the northerner's spongy nature and dull wits. In the masque, rivers, oceans, and land signify on macrocosmic and microcosmic levels, conforming with the commonplace notion that the continuous circulation of the waters of the earth is maintained through channels corresponding to the veins and canals of the human body. As Sir Walter Ralegh writes in *The History of the World* (1614),

> blood, which disperseth it selfe by the branches of veines through all the bodie, may be resembled to those waters, which are carried by brookes and rivers over all the earth; his breath to the aire; his naturall heate to the inclosed warmth, which the Earth hath in it selfe, which stirred up by the heate of the Sunne, assisteth Nature in the speedier procreation of those varieties, which the Earth bringeth forth.[80]

Hence, Jonson presents Niger and his daughters in an effluent form. Macrocosmically the river embodies the fertility of moisture and heat in Ethiopia, but in microcosmic terms, the water also symbolizes the humors of the Ethiopian people.[81] While it was presumed that the transformation of the southerners' skin color would take years (hence Jonson's delay of the ladies' visual metamorphosis), the "stage action" that corresponds to the "real point" of the masque – the incorporation of southern wisdom – is enacted through an elaborate dance that imitates the flowing movement of southern waters into northern land.

It is in this dance that the ladies present "their fans, in one of which were inscribed their mixed names, in the other a mute hieroglyphic expressing their mixed qualities" (lines 237–9). The emphasis on "mixed names" and "mixed qualities" underscores the interchange between the south and the north, while also hearkening back to the beginning of the Ethiopians' journey northward. Jonson opens the masque with a description of the river Niger's course across Ethiopia to the western coast, where Oceanus questions Niger's wish to "mix" his "fresh billow with" the Ocean's "brackish stream" (line 96). Niger explains that it is possible for his water to flow into the Ocean, while maintaining its integrity:

> ... 'tis not strange at all
> That, since the immortal souls of creatures mortal
> Mix with their bodies, yet reserve forever
> A power of separation, I should sever
> My fresh streams from thy brackish, like things fixed,
> Though with thy powerful saltness thus far mixed.
> *Virtue, though chained to earth, will still live free,*
> *And hell itself must yield to industry.*
>
> (lines 100–7)

This claim – that the stream of Niger's river will reserve its singularity as it travels through the ocean – articulates a point of tension in the relationship between corporeal and spiritual matters. Although the environment influences a body's humoral complexion, which affects the passions, determines behavior, and engenders particular vices, Niger insists that some part of a mortal's instilled "virtue" remains unaffected by these circumstances. As Timothie Bright in *A Treatise of Melancholy* contends, the body's humors may affect the spirits, and the spirits communicate with the soul, but the soul exists separately from the body. However, while housed in the body, the soul is

neither in such perfection, nor yet so freely, as she doth separated, and the knot loosed betwixt her and the body, being withdrawn, by actions exercised with corporall instrument, of baser sort.[82]

In spite of this, Jonson's Niger sees a certain freedom in the relationship between body and soul: although virtue is chained to the earth (and the soul housed in the body), it still exists in its purest form, allowing for the possibility that with proper governance or "industry," one can ameliorate vice. Furthermore, Niger is assured that certain rooted qualities of his purer stream will be transmitted in their flow northward. Niger's understanding of the "power of separation," combined with the masque's references to geohumoral theory, suggests what Michael Ryan has described as a genealogical "transmission over time of some uncorrupted natural substance from [an] ancestor to its progeny."[83]

The nature of that uncorrupted substance is alluded to, I believe, when Jonson calls the Ethiopian nymphs "Daughters of the subtle flood." "Subtlety" describes, of course, the fluidity of water, but in geohumoral terms it implies the *refinement* brought about by heated concoction.[84] "Subtle" humors are those which have achieved a thin, rarefied state, and the subtle qualities of Ficinian/Aristotelian *atra bilis* or black bile are what produce genius in a person's body. Bright explains the process

Sometime it falleth out, that melancholie men are founde verie wittie, and quickly discerne: either because the humour of melancholy with some heate is so made subtile, that as from the driest woode riseth the clearest flame, and from the lyes of wine is distilled a strong & burning aqua vitæ, in like sort their spirits, both from the drinesse of the matter, and straining of the grosse substance from which they passe, receaving a purenesse, are instrumentes of such sharpnesse.[85]

In other words, the physical quality of the humor connotes the "subtlety" of the wit it effects. As we noted in chapter 3, Pierre Charron identifies subtlety with southern wisdom:

Speculative Sciences came from the South. *Cesar* and other ancients of those times called the Ægyptians ingenious, and subtile; *Moyses* is said to be instructed in their wisdome:

and Philosophie came from thence into *Greece*. Greatnesse began rather with them, because of their spirit and subtiltie.[86]

Rather than censuring southern "subtiltie" as mere artifice and craft to bolster the Britons' unrefined humors and phlegmatic complexion (as William Harrison does in *The Description of Britaine*), *The Masque of Blackness* celebrates the transmission of this southern quality: Jonson's Britannia calls the "subtle flood" (line 289) ashore and invites the daughters to "Indent the land with those pure traces / They flow with in their native graces" (lines 230–1). While the satirical Jonson criticized his contemporaries' affectation of melancholia and other foreign humors, *The Masque of Blackness* presents the imagined possibility that the Britons have inherited, from ancient African influences, the revered subtlety of inward blackness – a subtlety that would have tempered their spongy natures and slow wits.[87]

It is the masque's emphasis on Ethiopia's classical status as the origin of all human life and civilization that infuses the purity of this "subtle flood" with significance. In the notes Jonson directs his audience to "Read Diodorus Siculus, III. It is a conjecture of the old ethnics that they which dwell under the south were the first begotten of the earth."[88] Diodorus' history not only establishes the Ethiopians as "first of all men" but as the first priests, who "by reason of their piety towards the deity, manifestly enjoy the favour of the gods."[89] Moreover, it is Diodorus who affirms that "the larger part of the customs of the Egyptians are, they hold, Ethiopian, the colonists still preserving their ancient manners."[90] Significantly, Diodorus attributes Ethiopia's eminence to its southern climate. That the wise Ethiopians, he writes, were

the first to be generated by the earth, is clear to all; since, inasmuch as it was the warmth of the sun which, at the generation of the universe, dried up the earth when it was still wet and impregnated it with life, it is reasonable to suppose that the region which was nearest to the sun was the first to bring forth living creatures.[91]

Like Diodorus' revered Africans, Jonson's Ethiopians are recognized as "the first formed dames of earth" and the sun as the "most formal cause." Moreover, Jonson generalizes Diodorus' notion that the climate matters in the origins of things: "All rivers are said to be the sons of the Ocean, for, as the ancients thought, out of the vapors exhaled by the heat of the sun, rivers and fountains were begotten ... Oceanus is celebrated *as father and source of gods and things, because nothing is born or decays without moisture*."[92] Niger and his daughters flow from the world's originary fountain of wisdom to indent the land and mix with the water of Britannia.[93]

The mingling and confluence of flowing water is an early modern trope for the mingling of peoples in a nation's genealogy; as Samuel Daniel writes, the Danes and Normans had been to Anglo-Saxons "but as rivers to the Ocean, that changed it not, but changed into it."[94] Likewise, in his opening speech to Parliament in 1603, James I compares the union of England and Scotland to the mixing of rivers in the ocean, insisting that the differences and conflicts between the two nations will lose their distinction when they are part of a larger whole:

For even as little brookes lose their names by their running and fall into great Rivers, and the very name and memorie of great Rivers swallowed up in the Ocean: so by the conjunction of divers little Kingdomes in one, are all these private differences and questions swallowed up.[95]

Niger's insistence that his stream will maintain a power of separation proves to be a panegyrical qualification of James I's parliamentary address. *The Masque of Blackness* suggests that in "the conjunction of divers little Kingdomes," an exchange of "differences" will actually produce a more temperate nation. By representing Britannia as an ancient union of southern wisdom and northern "beauty," *The Masque of Blackness* "revives" the island's ancient history and establishes the land and its people as "temperate."

"Wee are all one countreymen now"

Having pursued the complex signification of blackness in this masque, I would like now to return to Dudley Carleton's profoundly negative reaction to its performance:

The presentation of the mask at the first drawing of the traverse was very fair and their apparel rich, but too light and courtesanlike. Their black faces and hands, which were painted and bare up the elbows, was a very loathsome sight and I am sorry that strangers should see our court so strangely attired. The Spanish and Venetian ambassadors were both there and most of the French about the town.[96]

For several critics, Carleton's censure and repugnance indicates that Jonson's first masque was a failure. Indeed, if the masque's primary aim is to celebrate the beauty and dignity of the queen and her ladies, a "courtesanlike" and "loathsome" effect would appear to miss the mark. However, as a glorification of the Anglo-Scottish union, before a politically mixed and anxious court audience, *The Masque of Blackness* was bound to ruffle some feathers. I would like to entertain the possibility that Carleton's response attests more to its effectiveness as a political statement than to its failure as a panegyric.

   In his correspondence with John Chamberlain, Carleton stresses that the impending union was the court's central concern at the time. He notes that "the commissioners for the union are summoned by proclamation to meet" in November 1604, two months before the masque's performance.[97] The

proceedings then continued through December with further discussion anticipated for the following year.[98] In one letter Carleton observes that *The Masque of
Blackness* was performed on Twelfth Night, 1605 during the expectant interval
between the commissioners' meeting and the February session of Parliament.[99]
Carleton's active interest in the proceedings stems from his hostility toward the
union itself.[100] In fact, his personal aversion to the Jacobean court predates the
masque's performance. Upon Queen Anne's arrival at court in 1603, Carleton
had assessed, with some disdain, the appearance of the queen's Scotchwomen,
whom he found merely "passable for their faces and fashions"; as for the queen
herself, "she hath done [her favor] some wrong, for in all this journey she hath
worn no mask."[101]

In both of his written responses to *The Masque of Blackness*, Carleton is
acutely aware of how the foreign ambassadors perceive the new court. Not only
is he "sorry that strangers should see our court so strangely attired," but he also
observes tension among the visitors:

> The *Spanish* and *Venetian* Ambassador were both present, and *sate by the King in State*;
> at which Monsieur *Beaumont* quarrells so extreamly, that he saith *the whole Court is
> Spanish*.[102]

The French ambassador De Beaumont viewed the union as detrimental to a
French-Scottish alliance and his characterization of the court as "Spanish"
speaks to King James' refusal at this time to "make any decision as to the
precedence between France and Spain."[103] This nonpartisanship evidently fed
the social jockeying among the ambassadors – a rivalry played out in their
fervent bids for personal invitations to masque performances. Carleton himself expresses an active antipathy toward Beaumont, perhaps because of the
ambassador's pro-Scottish sentiments.[104] At the same time, he may have found
himself sympathizing with Beaumont's protestations, since they both object to
the Anglo-Scottish union. Indeed, Carleton's comments suggest that he, too,
is concerned that the "whole court" is, if not Spanish, then "strangely attired"
and foreign. Sensitive to court politics, Carleton's decidedly anti-union and
anti-Scottish position would not make him sympathetic to Jonson's clever use
of blackness in a pro-union production.

Of course, Jonson himself may have harbored deep prejudices toward the
Scots. He was jailed for his possible involvement in the anti-Scottish portions
of *Eastward Ho*. One passage that was cut from the play's second printing
wishes that the "industrious Scots" would migrate to Virginia: "I would a hundred thousand of 'hem were there, for wee are all one Countreymen now, yee
know; and wee shoulde finde ten times more comfort of them there, then we
do heere."[105] This snide attitude toward being "all one Countreymen" stems
from the environmentally based anxiety that England cannot afford to yield its
space and provisions to the marauding Scots. Indeed, Jonson's feelings may

have been that refining a Scot was as impossible as washing an Ethiop white. But in its denigration of outer blackness and appropriation of internal blackness, *The Masque of Blackness* captures British identity in transition. And by deliberately fashioning "whiteness" as the shared and temperate complexion of all the inhabitants of Britannia, Jonson succeeds in forecasting the eventual construction of racialism.

6   Othello's jealousy

Central to the plot of one of Ben Jonson's humor plays, *Every Man in His Humour* (1601), is a stereotypical portrait of marriage and unruly passions: the jealous husband and his innocent wife. Having played a role in Jonson's production, William Shakespeare retold his own version of this familiar tale in *Othello*, but with a tragic and racialized twist.[1] I remind readers of the domestic, comic, and humoral origins of Shakespeare's tragedy to remind us further that early modern English audiences were quite familiar with the jealous man and his city wife as stock comic characters. And these predictably jealous husbands of Elizabethan and Jacobean drama – primarily Italian and English merchants and shopkeepers – were derived from the cuckolded old men and merchants of the *fabliaux*.[2] Yet for critics of Shakespeare's tragedy, Othello's jealousy has traditionally been viewed as an extravagant and barbaric passion – the emotional eruption of a racial stereotype.[3] Indeed, whenever we see or read *Othello*, we are already influenced by its legacy – which has forever identified Moors with jealousy. This is not to say that *Othello* is the only text in the period to characterize Moors as jealous or intemperate. We need only look to Shakespeare's primary source, Giraldi Cinthio's tale, to find that his heroine, Disdemona, believes that "Moors are so hot by nature that any little thing moves [them] to anger and revenge."[4] And it is in another acknowledged source of the play, John Pory's 1600 translation of Leo Africanus' *The History and Description of Africa*, where we find the statement that Moors were the most jealous nation in the world.[5]

Yet the roots of Othello's jealousy are intertwined: the Moor's passionate fury may affirm an inchoate racial stereotype, but it has its prior origins in England's obsession with an Italianate and urban form of dramatic jealousy. To comprehend fully why and precisely how the spectacle of Othello's jealousy would matter to a Jacobean audience, we first need to explore the culture's profound interest in this passion as a symptom of hypercivility rather than barbarism.[6] In neglecting to historicize emotion, we have misconstrued the contours and ethnological valences of early modern jealousy in its most popular English form.[7] Jealousy in the early seventeenth century, though linked to sexual heat and to melancholy, was understood primarily as a state of paranoid suspicion born out

Figure 9 A Moor, woodcut from Cesare Vecellio, *De gli habiti antichi, et moderni* (1590).

of a corrupt inwardness that the English typically associated with Italians and, surprisingly enough, with neo-Stoic control.[8] It is my argument that, from a defensive English perspective, Italians came to represent over-disciplined interventionists, whose willful self-regulation produced pathological inwardness rather than temperance. Indeed, I will contend that as a hypercivilized Italian, Iago's strangely detached jealousy would have been more familiar to an English audience than Othello's violent metamorphosis.[9]

While the *commedia dell'arte* and *fabliaux* had established jealousy as a comic vice, the English city comedies deviated from these earlier representations by focusing less on the transgressions of the rival and wife and more on the nuances and paradoxes of the husband's passion.[10] Consider the psychological and physiological torment of Ben Jonson's Thorello in *Every Man in His Humour*:

> [jealousy] begins
> Solely to work upon the fantasy,
> Filling her seat with such pestiferous air,
> As soon corrupts the judgement; and from thence,
> Sends like contagion to the memory:
> Still each of other catching the infection,
> Which, as a searching vapour, spreads itself,
> Confusedly through every sensive part,
> Till not a thought or motion in the mind
> Be free from the black poison of suspect.
> Ah, but what error is it to know this,
> And want the free election of the soul
> In such extremes? Well, I will once more strive,
> Even in despite of hell, myself to be
> And shake this fever off that thus shakes me.
>   (1. 4. 211–25)[11]

In this self-anatomy of the somatic effects of jealousy, Thorello's wife and her supposed lover have taken a backseat to the jealous subject's internal disintegration. Not unlike melancholy, Thorello's jealousy alienates him from the world by heightening and distorting his powers of perception: "the black poison of suspect" clouds Thorello's vision and divides him from himself.[12] This self-division (the "I" that strives to be "myself" again), produces a recognizably modern and sympathetic interiority amidst the Galenic language.[13] Jealousy clouds the judgment and rules the senses but also intensifies the mind's capacity for self-scrutiny.

Jonson's representation of Thorello's self-conscious inwardness is a distinctly English and early modern perspective on male jealousy. Nicholas Breton in "Pasquils Mistresse" (1600) characterizes jealousy in much the same way: "While darke suspicion makes the day a night . . . / An inward poyson, that hath throughly vain'd / The haplesse wit, that workes for wils behoue. . ."[14] But this new breed of jealous suffering surfaces amidst more familiar jealousy plots and themes reproduced on the English stage. Like their continental forerunners, the Jacobean city comedies were acutely interested in the humiliating effects of male jealousy. Since cuckoldry was taken proverbially to be a given, patriarchal culture, at home and abroad, remained fascinated with the paradox that men could be emasculated by the intemperance of jealousy but also effeminated when they felt nothing – as in the wittol's disgrace.[15] Moreover, like the *fabliaux*, English city comedies tended to associate jealousy with the middling ranks.[16] Indeed jealous passions usually struck those who were aspiring beyond their proper social station. The perception of merchants, for example, as class aspirants whose economic power blurred the aristocratic social order, cast them as anxiously liminal – as outsiders and insiders.[17] The citizen's desire to transcend his social position signified a covetous nature, cursing him with an inability to trust not just his wife but the entire world. This is all to say that English representations of the jealous husband, like their continental predecessors, expressed the culture's persistent anxieties about rank and gender. But my interest lies elsewhere. I contend that the English playwrights' peculiar interest in anatomizing the experience of jealousy points to something more geographically specific than the fear of masculine shame or the threat of a rising middle class. In this chapter I argue that that "something" is the revaluation of a distinctly *English* temperament.[18]

Civil monsters

What is jealousy but distrust? (Robert Burton *The Anatomy of Melancholy*)[19]

As I argued in part i, the English people's resistance to the unflattering implications of classical geohumoralism involved a revisionary approach to the discourse itself. For obvious nationalistic reasons, English ethnography often incorporated a cyclical view of history, casting the south and the middle regions as degenerated and the north as rising in power. Since Africa and Rome have both declined in greatness, the argument goes, then the formerly admirable temperaments of their peoples have also grown corrupted. William Harrison's *The Description of Britaine* (1587) suggests that the southerners' natural "gifts" of blackness, wisdom, and civility do "often degenerate into meere subtiltie, instabilitie, unfaithfulnesse, & crueltie."[20] In turn, the English people's notorious simplicity – a northern trait – is reinterpreted by Harrison as an admirable "vertue to deale uprightlie with singlenesse of mind, sincerelie and plainlie, without anie such suspicious fetches in all our dealings, as they commonlie practise in their affaires."[21] Thomas Wright, too, suggests that despite the English people's inability to cloak or even control their emotions, their complexion may "sheweth a better ground, whereupon Vertue may build."[22]

From an English perspective, it was the Italian, more than any "Other," whose natural complexion had degenerated most severely.[23] As Levinus Lemnius explains it, the Italians are of a most "speciall constitution," but their brooding and capacity to hold a grudge overturns their good complexion.[24] In the same vein, William Thomas in *A Historie of Italie* (1549) makes the contradictory argument, as Sara Warneke has observed, that "Italian nobility surpassed the nobility of other nations in temperance, modesty and virtue, so their fleshly appetites, unnatural heats and vicious habits passed all terms of reason and honesty."[25] Unlike the English to the north or the Moors to the south, the Italians' temperate climate was understood to give them a greater measure of control in their pursuit of temperance. In revising a discourse that privileges the Mediterranean, it makes sense that the English would question Italian "temperance." Thus, English critiques of the hypercivilized Italian emerge out of their own fear that the northern achievement of temperance is an impossibility.

In his important study *Bodies and Selves in Early Modern England*, Michael Schoenfeldt has argued that in the early seventeenth century the "Neostoic privileging" of humoral "self-discipline . . . produced the parameters of individual subjectivity."[26] However, Schoenfeldt's emphasis on self-regulation overlooks a distinctively English anxiety that their own northern climate produced bodies that were shaped and influenced by forces beyond the individual's control. Moreover, many viewed the intentional cultivation of an interior self as a detrimental and unnatural estrangement from the outer world. William Harrison's elevation of English plain sincerity over and above "inward Italian or French craft and subtiltie" is not an unusual sentiment.[27]

Indeed, there is a tendency among northern texts to demonize neo-Stoicism as unnatural. Lemnius maintains that the temperate man is "most farre from sulleyne sterne severity and from Stoycall indolencye: for who will not judge them voyde of all humanitye, and without any sence of mans nature?"[28] In *A Treatise of the Passions and Faculties of the Soule of Man* (1640), Edward Reynolds sees the emotional control associated with Stoicism as an inward state of corruption:

Those imputations therefore which *Tully* and *Seneca*, and other Stoicall Philosophers make against Passions, are but light and emptie, when they call them diseases and perturbations of the Mind; which requireth in all its actions both health and serenitie, a strong and a cleare judgement; both which properties, they say, are impaired by the distempers of Passion: For it is absurd to thinke, that all manner of rest is either healthfull or cleare; or on the other side, all motion diseased and troublesome: for what water more sweet than that of a Spring, or what more thick or lothsome, than that which standeth in a puddle, corrupting it selfe?[29]

It is my conjecture that the English vilification of neo-Stoicism is not unrelated to the English inclination to associate Italians with a corrupted inwardness.

We would be mistaken to conclude that the Elizabethan and Jacobean playwrights' censure of Italianate suspicion is purely moralistic, for it is founded in a set of ethnological assumptions that also identified the Englishman's more northern complexion as simple, uncivil, barbarous, unwary, and unwise. As we saw in chapter 2, Thomas Wright, in the preface to his 1604 edition of *The Passions of the Minde in Generall* (published the same year as the staging of *Othello*), acknowledges that northerners are innately credulous and sincere – traits engendered by the natural constitution of the English people's bodies.[30] While much of Wright's text provides a fairly traditional examination of early modern psychology, the preface frames the experience of passions as a topic of ethnology.

Presenting his book as an English manual tailored "for the good of [his] Countrie," it is Wright's explicit hope that his countrymen will learn how to discern the shrouded and often cryptic emotions of the non-English – primarily Italians and Spaniards. But more importantly, Wright wishes to teach the English how to "behave [them]selves when such passions extraordinarily possesse" them. Lamenting that his fellow citizens "for the most part reveale and disclose themselves very familiarly and easily," Wright expresses grudging admiration for the Mediterranean who can "dissemble better his owne passions, and use himselfe therein more circumspectly, than we can doe." Beneficiaries of a temperate climate and central location, Italians and Spaniards possess a "natural complexion and constitution of body" that predisposes them to political "wariness," understanding, and judgment. Wright's Italians and Spaniards have an innate capacity to misrepresent themselves and manipulate the emotions of others:

the Spaniard and Italian demurreth much, and selleth his secrets and his friendship by drammes, you shall converse very long with him, before you shall know what is in him: he will shew a countenance of friendship, although he intendeth revenge: he can trayne his purposes afarre off, to undermine where hee pleaseth: hee will praise where he spiteth, and disprayse where he loveth for further project: hee can observe his times better than we for his plots, and marke fitter occasions to effectuate his intent: he can winne ground in a mans affection by some small conversation, and after prevaile in what he list, when he hath got the advantage.[31]

For Wright, a little dose of Italian wariness would help the English avoid political missteps. Wright's Englishman is at a disadvantage, humorally and politically, but his Italian is admired for the control he seems to exercise over himself and others – he "effectuates his intent[s]" and achieves his "purposes." He has an impenetrable inwardness that the Englishman lacks. Like other writers of the period, Wright sees his countrymen caught in an ethnological bind: the English people's notoriously imitative nature is understood not only as a symptom of humoral inconstancy but also, paradoxically, as the means by which they might gird their impressionable complexions.

English ambivalence toward Italianate behavior is what shapes the representation of jealousy in Jacobean drama. Though the Moor has became synonymous with this passion, English culture tended to associate Italians with excessive jealousy. *Westward Ho* (1607), for example, describes Italians as so "Sun-burnt... that your great Lady there thinkes her husband loues her not if hee bee not Jealous" (3. 3. 82–4).[32] *The Blazon of Jealousie* (1615) maintains that "at this day the Italian is counted the man that is most subject to this vice, the sallow complectioned fellow, with a blacke beard, being hee that is most prone, as well to suspect, as to be suspected about Womens matters."[33] James Howell recommends that English travelers should borrow "From the *Italian*... his *reservednesse*, [but] not his *jealousie* and *humor of revenge*."[34] Living in the country of machiavels, spies, and politicians, Italians were understood to reside in a culture of distrust. Thus, jealousy is the household manifestation of a more general state of Italianate suspicion – the pathological downfall of the otherwise subtle machiavel.

In Nicolas Coeffeteau's *A Table of Humane Passions* (1621), it is suspicion alone that determines the jealous man's perspective:

If the party beloved hath any joy, it then presupposeth a rivall; if she be pensive, they are suspitions of contempt: if shee speakes to another it is Infidelity; if she have wit, they apprehend practices; if shee be advised, they imagine subtilties; if she be plaine, they call it simplicity; if shee bee well spoken, it is affectednesse; if she be courteous, it is with a designe. So as *Jealousie* is like unto those counterfeit glasses, which never represent the true proportions of the face.[35]

Similarly, in the English tract *Tell-Trothes New-Yeares Gift* (1593), the fictive narrator Robin Goodfellow insists that jealous husbands "eate uppe their owne harts through suspition of disloyalty."[36] As *The Blazon of Jealousie* explains, "Jealousie, in a manner, is no other thing than a kinde of suspicious Care, or a carefull kinde of Suspition."[37] And it is, I want to argue, the jealous individual's inability to trust appearances or to resist suspicious thoughts that proves most fascinating to the early modern English dramatists.[38] Primarily a form of distrust, Italianate jealousy is construed by English writers to be an internal corruption and an appropriate scourge of those who appear in every other way to be invulnerable.

In George Chapman's *The Widow's Tears* (*c.* 1605) produced around the same time as *Othello*, jealousy and political subtlety are linked together as effects of the Italian climate[39]:

CYNTHIA: Brother, I fear me in your travel you have drunk too much of
            that Italian air, that hath infected the whole mass of your
            ingenuous nature, dried up in you all sap of generous
            disposition, poison'd the very essence of your soul, and so
            polluted your senses that whatsoever enters there takes from
            them contagion, and is to your fancy represented as foul and
            tainted, which in itself perhaps is spotless.
THARSALIO: No, sister, it hath refin'd my senses, and made me see with
            clear eyes, and to judge of objects as they truly are, not as
            they seem, and through their mask to discern the true face of
            things.[40] (lines 128–37)

Echoing the travel guides of the period, Cynthia maintains that Italy has transformed her brother-in-law's natural complexion.[41] Not only has it dried up the "sap of generous disposition" – the moist humors of blood and phlegm that make people more impressionable and forgiving – but it has also poisoned the soul and polluted the senses. Whatever impressions Tharsalio now receives from the external world, his fancy or imagination presents those images and sensations to his understanding in a "foul and tainted" form. Yet Tharsalio's rebuttal captures the ambivalence surrounding jealous passions: he construes his new suspicions as a clear-sighted awakening. By distrusting innocent appearances, Tharsalio believes he has shed his former naïveté and gained insight into the "true face of things."[42] To hearken back to Coeffeteau, Tharsalio has put on the "counterfeit glasses" of jealousy.

In 1604, the quintessential jealous man, as I have been describing him, has very little in common with Othello, but instead, looks an awful lot like Iago. Yet to see the pathology of Iago's hypercivilized state of suspicion as a recognizable and clichéd form of early modern jealousy may initially strike readers not only as a reductive take on his "motiveless malignity" but also a misconstruction of sexual jealousy – which takes its modern contours in part from our familiarity with Othello's fury.[43] But it is anachronistic to assume that Shakespeare's audiences would have dismissed Iago's jealousy in their anticipation of Othello's more spectacular emotions. As I shall demonstrate, the early modern association between Moors and heated passions, so definitively linked in Leo Africanus, has a less than tidy history.

The jealous Moor

Modern conjectures about the nature and origins of the Moor's jealousy have depended in part on a narrow understanding of early modern climate theory – the notion that the "geography of Africa, especially the intense heat, explained both the extremes of lust and jealousy."[44] Of course, we can easily find corroboration for the unproblematized view that hot climates produced heated passions, particularly in texts that postdate *Othello*. In *The Anatomy of Melancholy* (1621), for example:

Bodine, *cap. 5 Meth. hist.*, ascribes a great cause to the country or clime, and discourseth largely there of this subject, saying, that southern men are more hot, lascivious, and jealous than such as live in the north; they can hardly contain themselves in those hotter climes, but are most subject to prodigious lust. Leo Afer telleth incredible things almost of the lust and jealousy of his countrymen of Africa, especially such as live about Carthage, and so doth every geographer of them in Asia, Turkey, Spaniards, Italians.[45]

In 1604, however, jealousy was understood to have a much more vexed relationship to regional identity than Burton allows – a vexed relationship that Shakespeare's *Othello* explicitly highlights.

In a passage that critics either dismiss or ignore, Desdemona directly challenges modern assumptions about southern climates and heated passions. When Emilia asks Desdemona if Othello is naturally jealous, Desdemona insists that "the sun where [Othello] was born / Drew all [jealous] humors from him" (3. 4. 30–1). As we saw in the introduction, Desdemona appeals to conventional ethnology: in the Aristotelian theory of counteraction, the sun was thought to draw out the body's heat and moisture. As I argued in chapter 1, within the schematic logic of this strain of geohumoralism, the African would be less inclined to sexual excess than his northern counterparts. There is no question, of course, that Othello becomes jealous over the course of the play, and it is, I want to suggest, the seeming inadequacy of Desdemona's appraisal that attests to drama's up-to-the-minute revision of early modern ethnology. Indeed, *Othello* stands at a crossroads in the history of ethnological ideas when an emergent racial discourse clashed with the still-dominant classical and medieval geohumoralism. To comprehend the tensions between these competing discourses, we need to look directly at the sixteenth-century sources that Robert Burton cites in his dissection of southern jealousy – Leo Africanus and Jean Bodin.

The earlier text, Leo Africanus' *The History and Description of Africa* was written at the beginning of the sixteenth century, translated into Italian in 1524, and published in Ramusio's anthology of travel texts in 1550. Bringing an Islamic perspective on Africa to western culture, Leo's description of choleric, passionate, and jealous Moors inverted the classical notion of a cool, dry southern temperament. Leo's first-hand narrative has been praised by modern scholars for correcting the Plinian notions of a monstrous Africa. Yet for many early modern writers and readers, Leo did not displace Pliny or the western classical perception of Africa: he augmented these accounts.[46] As Othello's own travel narrative suggests, the English imagined an Africa of "Anthropophagi, and men whose heads / Do grow beneath their shoulders" (1. 3. 143–4) at the same time that they maintained modern trade relations with North Africa. The English translation of *The History and Description of Africa* (1600) amends Leo's most radical challenge to the classical western perspective – his insistence that Ethiopia is not a part of Africa. Indeed, the translator John Pory includes a survey of all those parts of Africa left "undescribed by Leo" and reinserts Ethiopia and its classical history back onto the early modern African map.

John Pory's English translation of Leo Africanus also indicates that the text was recognized in the early modern period for going against the grain of classical accounts of the African's innate temperament. Pory's rough translation of Leo's portrait of African virtues reads: "Most honest people they are, and destitute of all fraud and guile; not onely imbracing all simplicitie and truth, but also practising the same throughout the whole course of their lives," to which Pory adds "albeit certaine Latine authors, which have written of the same regions, are farre otherwise of opinion."[47] What Pory controverts here is the opinion in the classical texts that the Ethiopians and Egyptians, due in part to their climate, were notably wise and cunning – an opinion that even Pliny embraced. As we saw in part 1, since the heat in Africa draws out the body's heat and moisture, Africans were perceived as cool, dry, melancholy, fixed in their natures but crafty in their politics.

Unlike the classical northern African, who was subtle and wise, Leo's Moors are not only passionate – they are guileless and simple.[48] He characterizes the inhabitants of Barbary as mean-witted, ignorant of natural philosophy, abounding with choler, and unchaste. And the Negroes lead a beastly kinde of life "utterly destitute of the use of reason, of dexteritie of wit, and of all artes. Yea, they so behave themselves, as if they had continually lived in a forest among wilde beasts. They have great swarmes of harlots among them."[49] His characterization of the black man's beastliness is aimed explicitly at their classical legacy of wisdom and political acumen: in a sense, Pliny's monstrosities are incorporated in the excessive passions of Leo's Africans.[50] It is intriguing to note that Leo's *History* derives much of its knowledge of Africa from Arabic historians, who subscribe to their own non-western theories of climatic difference.[51]

On the reception of Leo's history, modern scholars remain confused regarding two significant points: (1) exactly when his influence began and (2) exactly what that influence consisted of. Literary critics have been distracted by the 1600 publication of Pory's English translation, which may have been the first edition Shakespeare knew. However we must acknowledge the widespread popularity of Ramusio's 1550 publication. In other words, Leo's work was available in a popular printed source *before* the earliest English travel narratives. When early modern authors cite a textual origin for their characterization of "Negroes" as jealous and lascivious, it is Leo Africanus who is named.[52]

It is in Jean Bodin's discussion of jealousy that we can discern more explicitly how Leo Africanus' characterization of the Africans' temperament clashed with the prevailing assumptions. Since Bodin subscribes to the Aristotelian theory of counteraction he cannot impute the Moors' supposed jealousy to internal heat or blood. He opts instead to justify Leo's description of Moorish jealousy by attributing this passion to their extraordinary intellectual power. Bodin's Africans are subject to extremes: they are "infected with great diseases of the bodie, and notorious vices of the minde: and contrariwise there are no people that have their bodies better disposed to live long, and their minds apt for great vertues." It is this "greater spirit" – this bias toward extremes – which drives the African to attain a kind of magnificence but also to seek greater pleasures and commit greater sins:

the southerners, who have more wisdom and reasoning power, have *through their special gift* brought it to pass that they might sin more freely for the sake of pleasure. Because self-control was difficult, particularly when plunging into lust, they gave themselves over to horrible excesses. Promiscuous coition of men and animals took place, wherefore the regions of Africa produce for us so many monsters. Hence is derived that unbelievable jealousy of the southerners and of the Carthaginians referred to in Leo.[53]

Bodin's Africans, a composite of Leo's history and classical climate theory, are provoked not by a physical burning or innately heated passions, but by what begins as a product of their "special gift" and quickly devolves into monstrous desire – more monstrous because it emerges from a cool, dry complexion. Bodin's struggle to harmonize these competing sets of knowledge not only indicates that the link between jealousy and hot climates may have been more tenuous than we have presumed, but it also underscores the ruptures in early modern ethnology that will lead eventually to the construction of less permeable categories of difference: the more familiar racial stereotypes that over-wrote the old humoral knowledge.

In light of Bodin's strained effort to locate the natural origins of the Africans' sexual excess, Othello's claim to be not "easily jealous, but being wrought, / Perplexed in the extreme" (5. 2. 354–5) begins to sound like *more than* a desperate man's rationalization of his behavior. Othello articulates an *experience* of passion that distinguishes the African from the Englishman more radically perhaps than his outsider status or even his skin color. As I suggested in chapter 3, "racialism" in its earliest and most rudimentary form detached people's complexions from their traditional humoral significance. By attributing excessive sexual passions to cool, dry southerners, Bodin helped initiate this detachment, and Shakespeare's *Othello* dramatized it. Bodin maintains that "southerners are not easily angered, but when once angered they can with difficulty be softened."[54] And Bodin's follower, Giovanni Botero reiterates this sentiment: "the Southerne man is not easily provoked; nor once in passion, is easily to be reconciled" whereas the northern man is easily provoked and easily pacified.[55] As incredible as it may sound, the Moor's violent metamorphosis – his transformation from an extraordinarily calm state to passionate rage – severs external blackness from its longstanding (though now obscured) geohumoral associations with dispassion and constancy. And it is the legacy of Shakespeare's play that this portrait of "Moorish behavior" established many of the strains of modern racial discourse.

Motiveless jealousy

There is no question that Iago's professions of jealousy fail to correspond with our modern sense of what emotionally sincere expressions look and sound like. Indeed, it was Iago's lack of "emotional sincerity" that led Bernard Spivack to trace his villainy to the medieval vice figure.[56] Certainly, Iago's exultant articulation of his hatred marks him as a descendant of the old vices, but it is also true that early modern ethnology helped produce the estranged and seemingly arbitrary intensity of Iago's emotionality.

Iago is the epitome of the Italianate Italian.[57] He fascinates us as the play's most self-reflective character – displaying his thoughts in soliloquies and influencing the audience with his commentary – yet we cannot get a handle on his motives or feelings. We recognize him as a Machiavel who delights in his duplicity, and his inwardness marks him as the supersubtle Venetian.[58] When Iago describes himself, we are taken back to Wright's politic Italian, whose deportment and invulnerability stood in admonitory contrast to the Englishman's naïvely sincere and blushing complexion:[59]

> For when my outward action doth demonstrate
> The native act and figure of my heart
> In complement extern, 'tis not long after
> But I will wear my heart upon my sleeve
> For daws to peck at. I am not what I am.
>
> (1. 1. 61–5)

Janet Adelman identifies Iago as the "play's spokesman for the idea of the *inside*, the hidden away," and the play consistently associates hidden interiors with the monstrous or the unnatural.[60] Iago, I propose, is not only the spokesman for the "inside," but he also embodies a self-cultivated inwardness. The detachment that Iago describes between his inner and outer selves – the "I am" and the "what I am" – is condemned in the play as the unnatural and monstrous effect of Iago's will.

Iago voices his subscription to neo-Stoic self-discipline when he describes the body as a garden. In his speech to Roderigo he insists that all human passions are inborn and the sole property of the will:

Virtue? A fig! 'Tis in ourselves that we are thus or thus. Our bodies are our gardens, to the which our wills are gardeners; so that if we will plant nettles or sow lettuce, set hyssop and weed up thyme, supply it with one gender of herbs or distract it with many, either to have it sterile with idleness or manured with industry, why, the power and corrigible authority of this lies in our wills. If the beam of our lives had not one scale of reason to peise another of sensuality, the blood and baseness of our natures would conduct us to most preposterous conclusions. But we have reason to cool our raging motions, our carnal stings, our unbitted lusts; whereof I take this that you call love to be a sect or scion. (1. 3. 316–27)

Cooling or tempering one's "raging motions" with reason is, of course, an admirable goal. Thomas Wright would find merit in this strain of Iago's neo-Stoic argument. But where Iago's conception of the body falters is in its enclosed self-sufficiency. In imagining the body as a contained garden, which can be weeded or planted, manured or made sterile by the individual's will alone, Iago succeeds in disconnecting man's interior self from the outside world. The "raging motions," "carnal stings," and "unbitted lusts" that may heat the blood are not characterized as physiological or emotional responses to other people; they are, instead, eruptions from within.

While this speech may reveal Iago's fantasy of willful self-control, he would never be mistaken for a model of temperance.[61] It is, of course, Iago's internalized, and bizarrely disengaged, motions of jealousy, hate, and envy that drive his plotting and the play forward. But we should understand, at the same time, how Iago's garden analogy recasts the politic Machiavel's overweening self-mastery into a stagnant and corrupting inwardness. While Iago may believe that his deceit gives him the power to govern his own emotions, he proves instead that an emotional mask prevents the reciprocal flow of affections. Because Iago's passions are never expressed or purged, they fester and breed – monstrously and inhumanly. The closest he comes to affective communion is his manipulation and perversion of other people's passions.

As a pathology of distrust then, Iago's jealousy is a symptom of his cultivated inwardness. When Emilia characterizes jealous souls as never "jealous for the cause, / But jealous for they're jealous" (3. 4. 155–6), she is describing Italianate jealousy. Neither the heat of the sun nor doubts about Emilia's infidelity produce Iago's passion: his "[jealousy] is a monster / Begot upon itself, born on itself" (3. 4. 1156–7). In fact, it is the autochthonous and detached nature of Iago's jealousy that leads so many critics to dismiss it. In his soliloquies, Iago explicitly and repeatedly names jealousy as the primary catalyst for his actions, but since his accusations of adultery are so implausible that even *he* must struggle to believe them, modern readers have presumed that "jealousy" cannot be one of Iago's genuine motives.[62] But in his first confessional statement, Iago insists

> . . . I hate the Moor,
> And it is thought abroad that 'twixt my sheets
> He has done my office. I know not if't be true,
> But I, for mere suspicion in that kind,
> Will do as if for surety.
>
> (1. 3. 368–72)

Iago assumes that others think he is a cuckold and this thought gives way to suspicion. Indeed, we know he behaves as a jealous husband, out of our earshot and in his own home, for Emilia later presumes that some "scurvy fellow" must have "turned [Iago's] wit the seamy side without" to make him "suspect [her] with the Moor" (4. 2. 150–1). Actual knowledge of adultery matters little to the jealous soul once the seeds of suspicion have been planted. In the same way that Thorello witnesses the black poison of suspect spread through the houses of his brain, Iago watches himself embrace suspicion even where all signs point to honesty and fidelity. Jealous passions are less a motive than a lens through which Iago sees the world.[63]

When Iago describes Othello's jealousy as "unbookish," he implicitly contrasts the Moor's unfamiliarity with jealousy with the Italianate experience – which is exceedingly well-versed and self-conscious in its affect. For Iago the paranoia of jealousy is always already a cliché, and it is with an almost clinical fascination that he observes the manifestation of his own passions.

Like Thorello, Iago is caught in the paralyzing grips of jealous suspicion, but unlike his comic counterpart, he purposely nourishes these obsessions. And it is Iago's self-manipulation – his willful weeding and pruning – that produces a jealousy that strikes us as apathetic. Consider, for example, his sudden and impulsive declaration of love for Desdemona:

> ... Now I do love her too,
> Not out of absolute lust – though peradventure
> I stand accountant for as great a sin –
> But partly led to diet my revenge,
> For that I do suspect the lusty Moor
> Hath leapt into my seat, the thought whereof
> Doth, like a poisonous mineral, gnaw my inwards.
>
> (2. 1. 278–84)

In the same way that he takes advantages of others' weaknesses, he embraces his own feelings for Desdemona as an effective spur to his suspicious jealousy. He does not feel lust, or any other passion that might be elicited by Desdemona's actual person; he only acknowledges this transitory eruption of "love" for its use-value – "to diet [his] revenge" and suspicion. Similarly, when Michael Cassio crosses his mind, Iago capriciously adds him to his list of rivals: "For I fear Cassio with my nightcap, too – " (line 294). Hate and love grow confusedly and without cause in Iago's garden, only to become food for his self-devouring suspicion. The black poison of suspect gnaws Iago's innards and detaches him from himself and the external world.[64]

Suspicion both distorts and augments the jealous man's powers of observation. On the one hand, the jealous Italian cannot see a situation without imagining base motives or the possibility of betrayal; on the other hand, he scrupulously detects and marks the slightest details that may attest to inward corruption. Cassio's courtly handholding is "an index and obscure prologue to the history of lust and foul thoughts" (2. 1. 249). Desdemona's disinclination to love "her own clime, complexion, and degree" (3. 3. 235) denotes "Foul disproportions, and thoughts unnatural" within (line 238). When we consider how profoundly tormented Iago may be by his jealous, counterfeit vision, his initial attempts to poison Othello may strike us not only as depraved but tragically (and even sympathetically) self-revelatory: "As I confess it is my nature's plague / To spy into abuses, and oft my jealousy / Shapes faults that are not" (3. 3. 151–3). In warning Othello that jealousy is the "green-eyed monster which doth mock / The meat it feeds on" (lines 170–1), Iago reminds us that jealous suspicions are eating away at his own entrails, driving him to poison everything in his path. Iago's hypercivilized and overregulated body implicitly attests to a natural virtue in the English people's easy susceptibility to external forces. For the northerners' innate vulnerability not only foils the cultivation of a self-poisoning inwardness, but it also ensures the natural ebb and flow of passions.

Of one not easily jealous

Critics continue to debate whether Shakespeare's Moor is easily made jealous or not: older scholarship quibbled over how quickly Othello yields to his "barbaric nature," while modern readings of the play reframe the question, evaluating instead how readily Othello falls prey to racial stereotypes. Since no one seriously disputes the associations between savagery, blackness, and jealousy, scholars make the assumption that Othello's initial "civility" has been fostered by his interaction with western culture.[65] When Othello loses control, readers conclude that the Moor has either surrendered to the beast within or he has cracked under the strain of colonization or hybridity – thus, in the latter reading, the cumulative pressure of being a black man in a white man's world makes Othello particularly vulnerable to Iago's hateful rhetoric. But when framed by early modern ethnology, Othello's initially calm deportment, or civility, is a natural effect of his cool and dry complexion. As Botero and Bodin described him, the dark southerner's innate humoral constancy inclines him either to great virtue or great vice. Indeed, Desdemona will exclaim she should not "know him / Were he in favor as in humour altered" (3. 4. 120–1).

Othello and his malevolent predecessor, Aaron in *Titus Andronicus*, epitomize the two possible extremes of the southerner's fixed complexion. As with Aaron's "cloudy melancholy," Othello's external blackness signifies black bile within – but unlike Aaron, whose lack of inwardness made him a transparent vice figure – the continuity between Othello's inner and outer self has endowed him with a "clear spirit" and a profound integrity. At the start of the play, Othello's most admirable and ethnologically distinctive quality is his unhybrid and undivided constitution. As I shall argue, Iago's manipulation of Othello does not awaken the Moor's repressed passions or provoke his innate savagery: it utterly transforms the Moor's humors.

The play's first two acts are filled with tests of Othello's temperament, and he responds to each incitement with admirable composure. He shows neither anger, nor even displeasure when Iago reports that Brabantio intends to dispute his marriage. With unshaken confidence, and a nod to his undivided nature, he expresses assurance that his "parts," "title," and "perfect soul / shall manifest [him] rightly" (1. 2. 31). When Brabantio and his men threaten violence, Othello calmly instructs them to put their weapons away, declaring that such provocations will have no effect on his "cue to fight" (line 84). Even when drawn from his marriage bed by Cassio and Roderigo's scuffle, Othello shows only a glimmer of impatience. He warns his officers that his anger may soon rise: "Now, by heaven, / My blood begins my safer guides to rule, / And passion, having my best judgement collied, / Essays to lead the way" (2. 3. 187–90). What is extraordinary about Othello's statement is that its anatomizing description illustrates his long fuse; Othello's judgment triumphs in the very act of self-narration. The Moor is not devoid of passion, but he does not act on impulse.

Iago himself describes Othello's temperament on the battlefield as imperturbable when he pretends to wonder whether it is possible for the Moor to be angry:

> . . . I have seen the cannon
> When it hath blown his ranks into the air,
> And, like the devil, from his very arm
> Puffed his own brother; and is he angry?
> Something of moment then. . .
> There's matter in't indeed, if he be angry.
> (3. 4. 130–5)

When Othello does express rage, it astonishes those who know him well. Truly mystified by Othello's uncharacteristic display of passion, Lodovico wonders

> . . . Is this the nature
> Whom passion could not shake, whose solid virtue
> The shot of accident nor dart of chance
> Could neither graze nor pierce?
> (4. 1. 262–5)

Othello's naturally dry and fixed complexion has given him a kind of solid impermeability. Humorally cold and arid, he cannot be incited easily, and his immunity to the vicissitudes of passion leads him to seek out hardships and "hardness" (1. 3. 230). Since he does not succumb to the mere "shot[s]" and "dart[s]" of provocation that might affect the English or the Italian, he has attained a revered position in Venetian culture.

Invoking the paradoxes of Bodin's ethnography, the play sustains a conflict between an emerging racial stereotype of African sexuality and an older geohumoral discourse. While Iago and Roderigo characterize Othello as a lascivious beast, the Moor draws attention to his distinct lack of ardor when he requests that Desdemona accompany him to Cyprus:

> . . . not
> To please the palate of my appetite,
> Nor to comply with heat – the young affects
> In me defunct – and proper satisfaction,
> But to be free and bounteous to her mind.
> (1. 3. 260–4)

Modern notions of sexual repression, combined with the legacy of racial stereotyping, have led twentieth-century readers to misconstrue Othello's cooled appetite as deviant.[66] But if, in fact, the sun has drawn all humors from him, his age has exacerbated an already dispassionate complexion.[67] Whereas the younger and more sanguine Desdemona may speak of a love that will "increase / Even as our days do grow" (2. 1. 191–2), perhaps referring to the consummation of their marriage, Othello feels utterly content with a simple embrace: "If it were now to die, / 'Twere now to be most happy" (186–7).[68] In a passage that is often misread or poorly annotated, Iago claims that Desdemona's "appetite shall play the god / With [Othello's] weak function" (2. 3. 321–2). In general, "function" translates to mean performance or activity, and in Shakespeare's *A Midsummer Night's Dream*, "function" implies the activity of a physical organ.[69] Yet most editions of *Othello* insist on glossing "function" as intellectual capacity, such as "faculties" (Norton) or "thought" (Signet) or "mental faculties" (Riverside). Tellingly and circularly, the *Oxford English Dictionary* identifies this line in *Othello* as the first recorded use of this word as "intellectual and moral powers." Our assumptions about early modern racialism have precluded us from recognizing that Iago's reference to the strength of Desdemona's "appetite" corresponds more logically with a reading that reaffirms Othello's claim to a physiologically "defunct" status.[70]

When Desdemona describes her love for Othello, she emphasizes the Moor's undivided nature:

> . . . My heart's subdued
> Even to the very quality of my lord.
> I saw Othello's visage in his mind,
> And to his honours and his valiant parts
> Did I my soul and fortunes consecrate.
>
> (1. 3. 249–53)

As if to illustrate the lack of distinction between Othello's internal and external parts, Desdemona's speech intermingles references to both. She has subdued her heart, her inner core, to Othello's "quality" – a word that may connote his inward nature or his military occupation.[71] His honors and her fortunes, her soul and his "valiant parts" blend together in their consecration. To see Othello's visage in his mind does not simply translate to mean that Desdemona sees Othello's countenance as he perceives it but that Othello's visage and mind are interchangeable. The constancy of his external blackness denotes the constancy of his internal disposition.

But, being wrought, perplexed to the extreme

When Iago first warns him of the "green-eyed monster," Othello responds by denouncing the (dramatically) conventional behavior of jealous husbands. Mocking the jealousy of a Corvino or Thorello or Leontes, Othello insists that

> ...'Tis not to make me jealous
> To say my wife is fair, feeds well, loves company,
> Is free of speech, sings, plays, and dances well.
> Where virtue is, these are more virtuous
>
> (3. 3. 187–90)

Unlike the innately suspicious Iago, it is Othello's impulse to trust Desdemona's loving and frank spirit – not to construe it as a "prologue" to "lust and foul thoughts." Othello makes a legitimate point: the jealous husbands of city comedies, more often than not, *do* misread their wives' mirth and warmth as signs of cuckoldry. Most repugnant to Othello, however, is the inconstancy of jealous emotions:

> Think'st thou I'd make a life of jealousy,
> To follow still the changes of the moon
> With fresh suspicions? No, to be once in doubt
> Is once to be resolved...
>
> (lines 181–4)

It should strike us as significant that Othello's initial response to the possibility of Desdemona's infidelity is not one of the passions that might precede or accompany jealousy, such as rage, hatred, melancholy, or love. Instead, his first thought is to censure the vacillating condition of suspicious men. Embedded in Othello's denunciation of jealousy is a repudiation of northern and medial temperaments: he dismisses the Iagos of the world, who actively cultivate their suspicions, as well as the English, who fittingly bear the nickname "moon men" for their changeable natures.[72] Remarkably, before his passions have been stirred, Othello finds the loss of fixedness more disconcerting than the loss of Desdemona.

As Bodin and Botero suggest, the southerners' constant complexion determines them as either full of vice or devoted to virtue. In his poem *Microcosmos*, Sir John Davies of Hereford combines these ethnological assumptions with an emergent, and more familiar, racial discourse:

> Southward men are cruel, moody, mad
> Hot, black, lean leapers, lustful, used to vaunt
> Yet wise in action, sober, fearful, sad
> If good, most good, if bad, exceeding bad.[73]

While Davies has already reconciled the incipient stereotype of African lust to a naturally heated temperament, he also delineates the classical genial melancholic in the descriptors "wise," "sober," "fearful," and "sad." What interests me most, however, is that Davies, like Bodin and Botero, characterizes the southern complexion in extremes, as "most good" or "exceeding bad." And if we recall Bodin's schema, the African's extreme nature cannot be attributed to inward heat or unruly passions. It attests, instead, to a cold, dry, intellectual power devoted wholly to either vice or virtue.

Othello possesses a fixed and undivided nature, which has proven "most good" in its inclinations. Moreover, in the ethnological homologies that inform Shakespeare's play, Othello's impolitic sincerity pairs him with Wright's Englishmen – in opposition to Iago's cunning nature. Yet the bases for this seeming similarity are radically different. The northerner is physiologically predisposed not only to reveal himself but to trust others; his lack of inwardness manifests itself in his mutable, impressionable nature and blushing complexion. Othello's lack of wariness, conversely, is the effect of an integrated self. It is his solid and fixed virtue that precludes him from seeing others as dishonest or disaffected.

How, then, is Othello "wrought"? This is the question, in fact, that energizes Iago's scheming powers and comprises much of the play's narrative. The play not only distinguishes itself from the city comedy plot by transforming jealousy into an exotically tragic passion, but its dramatization of the propagation of jealousy – Iago's poisoning of Othello – sets it apart as well. While the stock characters Corvino, Justiniano, and Thorello make their entrances already stricken, *Othello* tells the story of a jealous husband, Iago, who incites jealousy in a contented husband, Othello. But to understand Iago's transformation of Othello, we need to relinquish our twentieth-century suppositions about emotion. Modern individuals often imagine that they possess their emotions; a person's feelings are conceived to be part of their overall character or personality. We are quick to assume that if a man becomes jealous, he already has an inclination toward jealousy. While these presumptions often apply to early modern subjects as well, Renaissance affective culture also maintained the more peculiar notion that one person could infect another with an utterly foreign passion – an emotion completely antithetical to the victim's own natural disposition or inclinations.

The infectious and manipulative nature of early modern passions is neatly illustrated in John Ford's play *The Queene* (performed 1621). Clearly influenced by *Othello*, the plot of *The Queene* is master-minded by an Iago-like character named Muretto, who exults to the audience that he has by his persuasive words turned the King of Aragon into a jealous husband. Muretto, it turns out, is a kind of doctor, who has learned through careful study how to affect the passions of others by way of his artful performances. But the real wonder of the king's metamorphosis is that he had, up to this point, always hated his wife. Before the court in a final staged spectacle, Muretto transforms the king's emotions yet again, this time converting his jealousy into love. In Muretto's strange and anatomizing view, jealousy functions as an intermediary between hate and love, as well as the means by which one man can transform the temperament of another.[74]

If we take Othello at his word that he, unlike Iago, or Corvino, or Leontes, is not easily jealous, then what allows Iago to act on him in the way that Muretto preys on the King of Aragon?[75] While an easily jealous husband could find suspicion in Desdemona's beauty alone, Iago recognizes Othello to be of a "constant, loving, noble nature" (2. 1. 276) whose innate assurance makes him easily "led by th'nose / As asses are" (1. 3. 383–4). How does Iago transform Othello's innate lack of wariness into enraged suspicion? How does he inflame the passions of a man who has proven immune to most provocations?

Turning again to Wright's *The Passions of the Minde* reminds us that the passions were most often conceived as disruptive physiological forces that could rise up and perturb the mind. As in Iago's garden, the mind – reason and the "will" – must work to curb these "raging motions." It is, however, possible for this interchange to run in reverse. The mind could also stir the passions, or more colloquially, one might be moved from the top down.[76] Recognizing that Othello is unaffected by the incitements that would rile others, Iago aims first to poison Othello's mind with incommensurable conceits. Those conceits will then simmer, before burning the Moor's blood and *producing* heated passions.

Assessing his prey, Iago makes an important ethnological assertion, on par with Desdemona's characterization of her husband's humoral complexion: "These Moors are changeable in their wills" (1. 3. 339–40).[77] Although critics have accommodated this statement to the inchoate racial stereotype that all Africans are emotionally volatile, we should emphasize that Iago does not simply say that "These Moors are changeable" – he identifies the "will" as the locus of their instability. On this point commentators have defined Iago's use of "will" as "desire," crudely translating the statement to mean "These Moors are easily made lustful."[78] Yet this reading ignores that all of Iago's previous references to "will" in this speech pertain to the "will" of the rational soul.[79]

As we have already seen, Iago insists that his own intellectual will has the power to cool, control, and restrain all the "carnal stings" that may plague him. And for Iago, love is merely "lust of the blood" let loose by "permission" of this will. Even though he twists the knowledge of moral philosophy to his own ends, Iago still invokes a definition of the "will" far removed from mere base desires. "Will" functions, instead, on a higher ground as "reason's appetite," aiming to follow the wit, but always vulnerable to the passions. Virtue is the will's "natural proclivity." As Wright maintains

that these affections which reside in the will, differ much in nature and quality from those that inhabit the inferiour parts of the soule, because, these being bredde and borne in the highest part of the soule, are immateriall, spirituall, independent of any corporall subject; but those of the sensitive appetite, are materiall, corporal, and depending upon some bodily instruments...[80]

For the English, it is an overly active sensitive appetite – their material and corporal vulnerabilities – which make them easily incited and easily assuaged. The northerners' generous humors move the passions, which may mislead the will, but these same humors are tractable and readily give way to a reasserted will. But in one "not easily" moved, the metamorphosis is more radical. If corrupted reason perverts the will, and the redirected "will" stirs the passions, then regaining one's equanimity is nearly impossible.

The dangerous conceit that poisons Othello's mind is that he has been deceived either by Iago or Desdemona. If he trusts Iago, then he must distrust Desdemona; if he trusts Desdemona, then he must distrust Iago. Echoing Troilus' self-division when he witnesses Cressida's betrayal, Othello finds himself caught in the suspense of suspicion: " I think my wife be honest, and think she is not. / I think that thou [Iago] art just, and think thou art not" (3. 3. 389–90). And it is, in fact, Othello's lack of familiarity with Italianate jealousy that compels him to choose Iago over Desdemona. When Iago instructs Othello on how to proceed as a jealous husband, he identifies Desdemona's supposed dishonesty as an ethnological trait:

> Look to your wife. Observe her well with Cassio.
> Wear your eyes thus: not jealous, nor secure.
> I would not have your free and noble nature
> Out of self-bounty be abused. Look to't.
> I know our country disposition well.
> In Venice they do let God see the pranks
> They dare not show their husbands; their best conscience
> Is not to leav't undone, but keep't unknown.
>
> (3. 3. 201–8)

As a jealous husband, it is Iago's fear that all Venetian women are innately false. But he could just as easily say that it is his country's disposition for men to see infidelity where none exists. Although Othello knows enough about the snares of jealousy to mock those men who suspect their fair wives for loving company and feeding well, he does not recognize that jealousy itself motivates Iago's ethnological claims about Italian women.

When Othello objects that Desdemona "had eyes and chose me," Iago plants the notion that Desdemona does not see Othello's visage in his mind, but instead loved the very "looks" she also seemed to fear (line 211). If Desdemona is the stereotypical Venetian woman, as Iago suggests, then it would be in her nature not just to hide her inward self but to be enamored of appearances alone. However virtuous Othello's blackness may be in its integrity and fixity, European aesthetics equated fairness and beauty. Thus, for Desdemona to reject the physically fair "proposed matches / Of her own clime, complexion, and degree" and choose Othello for his appearance alone becomes further proof that she hides a "will most rank, / Foul disproportions, thoughts unnatural." The question up for debate is Desdemona's ethnic identity: Othello is inclined to believe that Desdemona is honest, but given Iago's logic, an honest Venetian woman capable of loving beyond appearances would be an example of nature "erring from itself" (line 232).

Following each dart of his poison, Iago assesses whether he has succeeded in rousing Othello's passions. "I see this hath a little dashed your spirits," he says. "Not a jot, not a jot," Othello responds. Then a few lines later, "But I do see you're moved," Iago insists, and Othello reiterates his denial. Then again, "My lord, I see you're moved," and Othello: "No, not much moved" (3. 3. 218–29). A conventional interpretation of this back and forth exchange would maintain that Othello is already "wrought" – and that his denials barely mask a raging tempest within. But as Iago explains it, the "wak[ing]" of Othello's "wrath" will unfold in stages:

> The Moor already changes with my poison.
> Dangerous conceits are in their natures poisons,
> Which at the first are scarce found to distaste,
> But, with a little act upon the blood,
> Burn like the mines of sulphur.
>
> (3. 3. 329–33)

In contrast to the blood that threatens fleetingly to rule Othello's "safer guides" or darken his "judgment," dangerous thoughts or conceits barely trouble the blood "at the first." Yet the more Othello allows suspicion to infiltrate his mind, the more these conceits corrupt the will and "act upon the blood."[81]

Once Othello is "wrought," he is transformed utterly. Unlike the Italianate jealous husband, who remains suspended between love and hate, Othello is "perplexed to the extreme":

OTHELLO: O, blood, blood, blood!
IAGO: Patience, I say. Your mind may change.
OTHELLO: Never Iago. Like to the Pontic Sea,
     Whose icy current and compulsive course
     Ne'er knows retiring ebb, but keeps due on
     To the Propontic and the Hellespont,
     Even so my bloody thoughts with violent pace
     Shall ne'er look back, ne'er ebb to humble love,
     'Till that a capable and wide revenge
     Swallow them up.

> (3. 3. 454–63)

Othello insists, in the very moment he changes, that his metamorphosis is irreversible. He is driven compulsively, I would argue, less by a desire for truth or reliable evidence and more by a corporeal inability to live in a state of irresolution. Twice he affirms that his passions cannot ebb until he reaches the preposterous conclusion of revenge. Ironically, and counterintuitively for modern readers, Othello is undone by his attachment to constancy rather than by barbarous mutability. For unlike the protean Englishman, whose passions ebb and flow with ease, Othello's sole passionate transformation is complete and irrevocable: "to be once in a doubt / Is once to be resolved."

In comparing his inner turmoil to the macrocosmic movement of water, Othello returns us to the homologies of climate theory. His geographical references are not arbitrary, for the Black, or Pontic, sea was reputed to lack an ebb and flow.[82] Seneca, following his discussion of how the southern sun pulls moisture from the land, noted that it is the

northern regions [that] abound in water. (For this reason the swift current of the Pontus runs constantly towards the lower sea and does not ebb and flow in alternating tides the way other seas do, but always has a torrent descending in one direction.)[83]

The movement of Othello's bloody thoughts plays on the inverse relationship between internal and external temperatures. Like the cold, black, motionless sea in the north, Othello's natural complexion had been fixed and dispassionate. But once the waters of the Pontic leave their icy origin and move south, they gather heat until their current reaches the warm Aegean. From north to south, from cool to hot, from mind to body – these analogical shiftings constitute the complete inversion of Othello's former self. Once wholly good, now exceeding bad.

With the onset of his epilepsy, a symptom of overheated melancholy, Othello's passions forge a wedge between himself and the external world.[84] And it is Iago's poison of suspicion that constitutes Othello's newly created inwardness. But unlike Iago's disciplined interiority, which is equally estranging but also insidiously empowering, the Moor's turn inward disables him – his solid virtue and undivided self are shattered. Once eloquent and unhesitating in his self-narration, his fragmentation is now externalized by barbarous and inarticulate phrases: "Lie with her? Lie on her?... Noses, ears, and lips!" His self-division does, however, give him Iago's poisoned vision; Othello now sees Desdemona's corporeal inwardness as insulated and rank:

> But there where I have garnered up my heart,
> Where either I must live or bear no life,
> The fountain from the which my current runs
> Or else dries up – to be discarded thence,
> Or keep it as a cistern for foul toads
> To knot and gender in!
>
> (4. 2. 59–64)

Initially, as paired opposites, Othello's naturally cold, dry complexion had perfectly complemented Desdemona's sanguinity. When he trusted her, Othello had imagined that Desdemona's internal warmth and moisture gave him life, nourishing and keeping the affections that had been defunct in him. But now, in place of a flowing fountain, Othello pictures an interior space that has either dried and then discarded his heart (perhaps depriving it of "generous sap") or perverted it into yet another enclosed space – putrid and foul in its stagnation.[85] Indeed, Othello's image of a cistern full of spontaneously generating toads takes us back to Iago's garden, where Iago gendered and engendered his own solipsistic territory.[86] Poisoned by suspicion and driven now by base bloody passions, Othello has become hybrid – alienated from his Moorish complexion by an Italianate doubleness. And his murder of Desdemona, I want to argue, anticipates his self-murder in its design to eradicate the duplicity and inconstancy that he now feels.

En route to Desdemona's bed, Othello announces his intentions: "Strumpet, I come. . . / Thy bed, lust-stained, shall with lust's blood be spotted" (5. 1. 35–7). When we next see Othello, he has entered the bedchamber in mid-speech, arguably continuing his thoughts on the nature of Desdemona's blood:

> It is the cause, it is the cause, my soul.
> Let me not name it to you, you chaste stars.
> It is the cause. Yet I'll not shed her blood
>
> (5. 2. 1–3)

If we read these two speeches as one sequence, then the "cause" that Othello will not name is "blood." The perfect revenge for Desdemona's infidelity would be to shed the very blood that incited her wantonness. But when faced with the prospect, Othello is troubled by blood's multivalence.[87] Sanguinity – its vibrancy and warmth – also gives Desdemona her "Promethean heat." Her virtue is constituted by the warmth and moisture of blood: indeed, Othello loved her for being spirited, frank, open, and generous. Ironically, it is Othello's feverish heat that not only blinds him to blood's virtues but also compels him to destroy in Desdemona the same "bloody passion[s]" that Iago ignited in him. To shed Desdemona's blood or scar her alabaster skin would be to realign her appearance with the monstrous inner self that Othello now believes she is hiding. Unless he puts out Desdemona's light, he fears her snowy whiteness will betray more men.

As Adelman has argued, Othello is "so self-divided" by the end of the play, "he can take arms against himself, Christian against Turk, literalizing self-division by splitting himself graphically down the middle."[88] Othello's division takes multiple forms in his final speech. He represents himself in both past and present terms: the soldier that did Venice some service and the man he is now. As one who was not easily jealous, and then "Perplexed in the extreme" (5. 2. 355). As one who had been "unused to the melting mood," and then "drop[ping] tears as fast as the Arabian trees / Their medicinable gum" (lines 358–60). Rather than focusing on Desdemona's virtue or Iago's treachery, Othello's parting words lament the loss of his constant and dispassionate temperament – the African complexion that had been delineated in the ancient ethnography. As he moves closer to suicide, Othello represents his self-division in a mini-drama that reenacts Iago's poisoning of him at the same time that it destroys the inwardness which that poison produced. The malignant Turk who beats the Venetian and "traduce[s] the state" (line 363) stands in for Iago (the two are verbally linked in a span of seven lines by the epithet "dog" [lines 364, 371]). Iago's hidden and malignant Turkishness – his deceit and treachery – is what has traduced the Venetian state and subdued Othello.[89] Iago has proven himself to be the enemy within Venice and within Othello. By equating his self-murder with the smiting of this Turkish dog, Othello's final act is intended to abolish inwardness itself.

Othello reversed the familiar paradigms of the domestic comedy. Rather than witnessing a husband already struck with the Italian plague and remedied by comic closure, as in Every Man in His Humor or The Merry Wives of Windsor, the Jacobean audience saw the tragic consequences of an African infected by jealous passions. In the same way that classical and medieval ethnography schematized northern complexions in terms of southern ones, Othello's portrait of the Moor is an antipodal representation of the Englishman's temperament. In other words, the play's generic inversion is rooted in the homologies of early modern ethnology. When Desdemona claims that the sun where Othello was born drew all jealous humors from him, some portion of Shakespeare's audience could have inferred the other half of this doctrine: the cooler air in England generates excessive blood and humors. When framed by the tripartite structure of geohumoral theory, the contrast between medial (or Italian) and southern (or Moorish) temperaments in Othello necessarily points to the third party in the classical schema – the northerner – and for a Jacobean audience, the English.

As we observed, the northerner was understood to experience heated passions easily, but he felt them only fleetingly. On the experience of jealousy in particular, Bodin claims that the "people of the North are . . . little subject to jealousie" in spite of their humoral excesses.[90] And The Blazon of Jealousie (1615) maintains that northerners tend not to take the "foule blot of Unchastite . . . so deep at the heart . . ."[91] Although described as both rash and irresolute, the Englishmen are never ruled by any particular passion for long. These ethnologically distinctive qualities are neatly dramatized in Thomas Dekker and John Webster's portrayal of a jealous Englishman in Northward Ho, a city comedy performed one year after the first production of Shakespeare's Othello. When the jealous Mayberry confronts his wife with suspicions of her infidelity, she denies his accusations. Strikingly, her claims of innocence are sufficient to alleviate Mayberry's doubts. He takes her word upon faith and calmly proclaims that his "streame of jelozy / Ebs back againe" (1. 3. 127–8).[92] As a model of Englishness, however, Mayberry's jealousy and its sudden dissipation takes on new significance. Indeed, Thomas Wright had drawn on the same meterological language in his description of those men ruled by inconstancy:

[The passions] toss and turmoile our miserable souls, as tempests & waves the Ocean sea, the which never standeth quiet, but either in ebbing or flowing... now they be flowing with concupiscences and desires, and presently ebbing with desperation and sadnesse.[93]

Yet in contrast to Wright's censorious words, the flowing and ebbing of Mayberry's passions serve to redeem his complexion. To feel no jealousy would place Mayberry in the shameful position of caring little for unchastity; but to feel jealousy fleetingly before gaining his equanimity suggests a more virtuous model of English feeling. Like Jonson's Thorello, Mayberry has no control over the onset or effects of his jealous passions, nor does he affect its quick evaporation.[94] Instead, it is Mayberry's innate inconstancy – and his apparent susceptibility to persuasive words or external forces – that brings about his change of heart and reinstates his capacity to trust. The Englishman's protean, vulnerable, and threateningly effeminate emotional nature proves, in this instance, to be an admirable virtue.

"Whiter skin of hers than snow": Desdemona and the English

It has been my argument throughout this chapter that passionate experiences enacted on the early modern stage were always already framed by an ethnological knowledge that proves to be neither intuitive for the modern reader nor simple in its implications. While the stereotypical association between hot climates and hot tempers becomes solidified in the seventeenth century, Shakespeare's *Othello* plays out the tensions between classical, homological, and fluid notions of difference and an emergent system of more familiar racial distinctions. Desdemona quite plainly gives voice to the older knowledge. She loves Othello for the virtues of his natural complexion: his integrity, his constancy, his lack of jealous passions. And her love for the Moor represents an English admiration and desire for those very qualities that the northern complexion lacks. Within a framework of homologies, Othello and Desdemona are a perfect match. Her generosity, warmth, and fruitful nature complement his cool, hard, dispassionate constancy.

Conversely, Iago articulates a nascent racialism. His slander of Othello, which is unrelated to the Moor's natural complexion, proves prescriptive rather than descriptive. Constituted by suspicion and a pathological inwardness, Iago is incapable of trusting a system of knowledge premised on the correspondences between external complexions and inward temperaments. To acknowledge the power of external forces, or more simply, the possibility of honest exchange between two people, would undermine Iago's sense of self-created autonomy. But the force of Iago's hostility toward Othello outweighs our impulse to condemn him. Iago succeeds in dislodging the geohumoral homologies that not only established blackness as a sign of wisdom and constancy but also placed England on the margins. Desdemona's classical knowledge gives way to a racialized construction of Moors as passionate, lascivious, volatile, jealous savages.

Yet Desdemona's representation of the older ethnographic knowledge extends beyond her appraisal of Othello's temperament. Not only does she love those qualities in Othello that racialism erases, but her love for Othello also brings about her downfall, suggesting that the play proffers a kind of object-lesson in letting go of the classical humoral system that still dominated early modern ethnography. At the same time, we love in Desdemona what are stereotypically northern qualities (the very qualities that make her a remarkable exception to her "country's disposition"): her sincerity, her openhearted nature, her generosity, her inclination to feed well, her love of company – her sanguine warmth. In other words, the play aims to validate the northern complexion while forgetting its origins in a tripartite geohumoral system. As we saw in Wright, the English sought out the constancy associated with blackness and the wariness of Italianate inwardness in their effort to counter those qualities of their natural complexion that were construed as excessively effeminate: impressionability, inconstancy, naïveté. *Othello* answers back that the incorporation of blackness – whether it be the black poison of suspicion or the blackness of melancholy – necessarily destroys the inherent virtues of a white complexion.

Returning to Wright's preface, we can begin to see how racialism emerges in part out of the validation of the English people's inconstant humors and changeable complexion. Although devoted to rectifying the English people's mutability and lack of inwardness, Wright also entertains, momentarily, the more essentializing notion that the northern complexion may be predisposed to virtue:

The very blushing also of our people, sheweth a better ground, whereupon Vertue may build, than certaine brazen faces, who never change themselves, although they committe, yea, and be deprehended [sic] in enormious crimes.[95]

Yet this celebration of English "whiteness" is brief. For when we turn to the body of his text, Wright identifies the blush as a sign of subordination, common to women, children and servants. Rather than constituting a stable ground "whereupon Vertue may build," "whiteness" remains for Wright the most apparent signifier of an intemperate and effeminate complexion.

Shakespeare's play, I contend, makes the essentialist move that gleamed only faintly for Wright. *Othello* implies that the English people's notorious weaknesses – their "unwariness" and inconstancy – may foster a more fertile ground for virtue than the southerner's complexion. Where Wright urges the English people to temper their natural complexions by imitating the darker southerners, Shakespeare's dissection of medial and southern temperaments suggests that English "intemperance" and its signifier, "whiteness," have their own essential worth – distinct and removed from the climatological homologies that had traditionally marginalized them. The struggle now is for us to see these tensions in Shakespeare's play. For as whiteness gained normative status, it whitewashed the contradictions of its own construction – blinding us to the English vulnerabilities that gave rise not only to *Othello* but racialism itself.

Cymbeline: *Othello* revisited

In the romance *Cymbeline*, Shakespeare turns the *Othello* plot northward. Once again, jealous passions originate with the Italian, but this time Iago's heir, Giacomo, poisons Posthumus – a British "erring barbarian." Is Posthumus more easily jealous than Othello? We might compare their incitements to jealousy: Giacomo's description of Innogen's mole versus Iago's report of Cassio's dream, or the "evidence" of the handkerchief versus the bracelet. But as I have argued, most of *Othello* is devoted to the challenge of implanting jealousy in the Moor; Posthumus, on the other hand, is persuaded of Innogen's adultery in a single scene. Exiled in Rome, he orders his wife's murder without even confronting her. Not only is Posthumus infected by a "false Italian" (3. 2. 4), but he is also corrupted by the "spongy" southern air; embracing jealousy and forgetting Britain are the same motions. While in Italy, Posthumus equates Innogen (who symbolizes Britain throughout the romance) with all women and identifies all women with vice. But once he returns to British soil, Posthumus makes a complete *volte-face*, lamenting that he has murdered a wife "much better than" himself "For wrying but a little" (5. 1. 4–5). As if to illustrate that the ebbing of jealousy has ethnological significance, Posthumus chooses this moment to "disrobe... / Of these Italian weeds and suit [himself] / As does a Briton peasant" (lines 22–4).

It is, however, Giacomo's transformation that invokes the northern half of Desdemona's ethnological knowledge. Driven by the same suspicious villainy that Iago embodied, Giacomo finds himself physiologically transformed by the British climate. At first, Giacomo's politic "Italian brain" has a great advantage in "duller Britain" (5. 6. 196–7). Granted, he must reconcile himself to Innogen's chastity, but he can easily dupe a nation of "credulous fool[s]" and ruin her reputation (line 210). Yet on his second visit north, the air of "duller Britain" begins to take effect:

> The heaviness and guilt within my bosom
> Takes off my manhood. I have belied a lady
> The princess of this country, and the air on't
> Revengingly enfeebles me; or could this carl,
> A very drudge of nature's, have subdued me
> In my profession?
>
> (5. 2. 1–6)

Unlike the Italian climate, which dries up the body's "generous sap," or the African air, which draws out all of the body's humors, the British climate has the capacity to regenerate a seeming miscreant. Britain does not simply weaken Giacomo physically, it produces a "heaviness and guilt within [his] bosom" that enervates his Italianate malevolency. In the play's closing scene, Giacomo declares that external forces (the British environment and Posthumus' strength) have succeeded in transforming his inward self: "I am down again, / But now my heavy conscience sinks my knee / As then your force did" (5. 6. 413–15). In stark contrast to Iago's impenetrable and hardened silence at the end of *Othello*, Iago's descendant offers to pay for his villainy with his life – a gesture that inspires forgiveness in the entire British court. Reformed by the northern air, Giacomo has grown a distinctly British "conscience."

The metamorphoses of Posthumus and Giacomo, whose identities are more or less "Briton" or "Italian" depending on their immediate locale, underscore the astounding instability of early modern ethnic distinctions. As I shall argue in the next chapter, however, the fluidity of ethnology in this play applies only to "others" and not, it turns out, to the English themselves. As in *Othello*, *Cymbeline* anticipates the essentialism of modern racial categories at the same time that it keeps the older geohumoral knowledge in play. While Posthumus' inconstancy and impressionability signify his northern, therefore marginalized, humoral status, I will argue that he represents early modern Scotland – still barbaric in nature, but poised to receive the civilizing embrace of England in the proposed Jacobean union project. The distinctly *English* temperament is valorized, instead, in Innogen's long-lost brothers, Guiderius and Arviragus. Perfectly in tune with their rugged environment, Guiderius and Arviragus portray the English people as unconquerable, innately civil, and resistant to the degenerative forces that have presumably plagued other nations. As a romance about the politics of historiography, *Cymbeline* prophesies a vision of Englishness that will develop into the racialized myth of Anglo-Saxon exceptionality – a myth that continues to shape the writing of British history to this day.

7   *Cymbeline*'s angels

As I indicated at the close of the last chapter, by staging a version of the *Othello* plot, *Cymbeline* helps us see how the tragedy's representation of Italianate manipulation and Moorish jealousy implicitly delineates the northerner's temperament. But *Cymbeline* does not simply represent northern vulnerability and tractability as potential virtues – though that is, I will contend, a central thrust of Posthumus' plot trajectory – it also reinterprets the effects of the British environment itself. At odds with its reputation for producing barbarous behavior, the air in Shakespeare's Britain, we discover, has a newfound capacity to regenerate what should be a lost cause: the monstrously hypercivilized Italian. At the end of this chapter, I will return to *Cymbeline*'s reworking of *Othello* and the ethnological significance of Giacomo's transformation in Britain, but for now I want to entertain how the play, in its neat (though not necessarily intentional) invocation of Jonson's *Masque of Blackness* and Marlowe's *Tamburlaine*, also brings together many of the ethnological arguments that I have been pursuing. Like *The Masque of Blackness, Cymbeline* is deeply engaged in the political issues of the Anglo-Scottish union, and it draws on the symbolic dimensions of the masque genre to personate – and question – King James' vision of a unified Britain. We can, for example, as Leah Marcus and others have done, discern in the marriage of Posthumus and Innogen a national fantasy on England's part to incorporate Scotland.[1] As too with Jonson's masque, *Cymbeline* plays out how the union controversy put pressure on the question as to whether, and to what degree, the British islanders – be they Irish, Welsh, Scottish, or English – are ethnically diverse.

Though I will also return to the play's investment in Anglo-Scottish politics, I would like to begin my reading of *Cymbeline* with how it resurrects some of the ethnological concerns of Marlowe's *Tamburlaine*. *Tamburlaine*, on the heels of William Camden's first edition of *Britannia* (1586), produced a hero whose admirably barbaric qualities corresponded with the northerner's unrefined traits. Characterizing the civilizing process as effeminate submission, *Tamburlaine* spoke to early modern England's philobarbaric fear that the acquisition of civility had eradicated their rugged "English" virtues. Probably

Figure 10 "The Arryval of the First Anceters [sic] of Englishmen out of *Germanie* into *Britaine*" from Richard Verstegan, *A Restitution of Decayed Intelligence* (1605).

staged in the year following Philemon Holland's English translation of Camden's *Britain* (1610), *Cymbeline* makes a nice counterpoint to the chaos generated in Marlowe's ethnographic theatre. Clearly indebted to Camden's historiography, most prominently in its seeming celebration of ancient Britain's capitulation to Roman rule, *Cymbeline* reassesses what the civilizing narrative means to early modern British identity.[2] Given that Camden's narrative was hardly new in 1610, it should not surprise us that Shakespeare's romance does not merely affirm the salutary influence of the Roman conquest of Britain, but seeks instead to resolve for the English *Britannia*'s more troubling implications. As I have suggested, the anxiety that civility (acquired through submission) always carried with it the seeds of future degeneration is part of the legacy of Camden's historical perspective. And since the union debates often pitted Scottish characterizations of England as a decayed nation against England's demands for Scotland's complete acquiescence, the early Jacobean period was saturated with this very anxiety.[3]

As a romance about historiography, *Cymbeline* interrogates the logic of temporal progression or national development by commingling, anachronistically, progenitors and descendants.[4] As I shall argue, this mingle-mangle dramatizes the cyclical but downward spiral of Camden's narrative – the inevitability of decline.[5] But beyond this, it is my contention that *Cymbeline* ultimately answers the uneasy temporality of Camden's history with the romance of "race" – an answer that Camden himself provided in his quirky and anonymously published *Remains Concerning Britain* (1605). Embedded in *Cymbeline*'s strange prophecies and patchwork of sources is a familiarity with Camden's *Remains* and with an emergent representation of English roots that defies the passage of time: the racial myth of Anglo-Saxon origins. Generated by the ethnological tensions and historiography of the early seventeenth century, *Cymbeline* spins out an English historical fantasy in which the Scots and early Britons must submit to Roman rule (thus providing a historical precedent for submitting to Anglo-British rule in the proposed union), while the English emerge as a superior and naturally civilized race, unaffected by Britain's ancient history of mingled genealogies and military defeats.

Saxon roots

Though "Long considered a collection of miscellaneous material that could not be fitted into the *Britannia*," William Camden's *Remains Concerning Britain* (1605) "has recently been re-evaluated," as Graham Parry has observed, "and shown to be a separately planned work from the beginning, more popular in intent, written in English for an English audience, and more patriotically coloured than the larger work."[6] The "patriotism" of the *Remains* is reflected primarily in Camden's shift in interest away from the Romanization of those early Britons to the English people's Anglo-Saxon lineage:

After the Scottishmen, the Angles, Englishmen or Saxons, by Gods wonderfull providence were transplanted hither out of Germanie . . . This warlike, victorious, stiffe, stowt, and rigorous Nation, after it had as it were taken roote heere about one hundred and sixtie yeares, and spread his branches farre and wide, being mellowed and mollified by the mildenes of the soyle and sweete aire, was prepared in fulnes of time for the first spirituall blessing of God.[7]

This celebration of England's Saxon lineage contrasts sharply with earlier editions of *Britannia*, which "were not," as Parry notes, "enthusiastic about the Saxons, who were not so agreeable to Camden's imagination as the British or the Romans, being a harsh and alien race."[8] We should be alerted here to the racial significance of Camden's transfer of allegiance (which I explore in more detail below), for in much the same way that Robert Burton in *The Anatomy of Melancholy* (1621) reinterprets the Gothic invasions as a divinely sanctioned transmigration of robust peoples, Camden has reframed the Saxon invasion as a providential "transplantation" of hearty Englishmen in Britain.[9] Moreover, he stresses, the Saxon "conquest was more absolute here over the Britaines, than either of the Francs in Fraunce over the Gaules, or the Gothes & Lombards in Italie over the Romans, or of the Gothes, Vandales, and Moores over the ancient Spaniards in Spaine."[10] It is significant too that in his final revisions to *Britannia* in 1607, Camden amended his earlier discussion of the "English-Saxons" to accommodate his newfound attachment to this "harsh and alien race," thus supporting the supposition that the *Remains* is not simply "miscellaneous material that could not be fitted into" the larger work.[11]

In part, Camden's enthusiasm for the Anglo-Saxons can be ascribed to his expanding knowledge of Germanic languages; however, purely academic interests fail to account for the fervency of his Tacitean praise.[12] It seems likely that his embrace of England's Anglo-Saxon roots was influenced by Richard Verstegan's almost fanatical endorsement of the Germanic races in *A Restitution of Decayed Intelligence*, a text also published in 1605 and recognized by modern scholars as seminal in the construction of English "racialism."[13] Part of what I wish to argue about Camden's and Verstegan's fascination with Anglo-Saxonism is that they make an effort to fix a line of biological inheritance for the English – an effort that is distinct from the study of Anglo-Saxon language roots and which precedes, to a large degree, the common lawyers' imminent engagement in establishing the pre-Norman origins of English law.[14]

As Hugh MacDougall has maintained, what ultimately differentiated the myth of Anglo-Saxonism from Geoffrey of Monmouth's Trojan origins was its "racial element."[15] Verstegan, for example, spends a good deal of energy establishing the Germans' exclusivity. As their descendants, the English-Saxons are praised for having preserved an undiluted genealogy, thus setting them apart from all the other mingled populations of Britain. Not only had they never been conquered, Verstegan argues, but the Saxons, unlike the polyandrous Britons, remained chaste in marriage.[16] Just as Tacitus had located heroic virtue in the barbaric vigor and ruggedness of the Germanic races, Verstegan makes the paradoxical contention that the English-Saxons' "incivillitie appeereth to have bin such that it might have given great example of civillitie, to all the rest of the barbarous nations of the world besyde."[17] As for the argument that the "te[m]perature of the ayr of any regio[n], doth make the inhabitants more or lesse learned or ingenious," he finds that the civilizations of Africa, Greece, and Rome – those warm, southern regions – have long since declined into barbarism. It is the Germans "now a dayes [who] flowrish in all learning and cunning."[18]

Though Verstegan rejects the paradigms of ancient climate theory, he has also (no doubt inadvertently) forecast the north's downfall by appealing to the Polybian logic of degeneration implicitly at work in the *translatio* of empire: since the south has decayed, the north has emerged as the center of civilization, and so on.[19] In striking contrast, Camden has opted to rework the conventional tenets of climate theory when he declares that it was the "mildenes of the [British] soyle and sweete aire" which "mellowed and mollified" the "warlike, victorious, stiffe, stowt, and rigorous [Saxon] Nation." By making this assertion Camden has extricated the English from the difficulties of *Britannia*'s civilizing narrative: rather than gaining civility through submission to a conquering foreign power, the Saxons were softened, "mellowed and mollified" by their adopted environment. Indeed, Camden implies that what makes the English *English* (and not German) is this perfect accommodation between the inheritance of hearty Saxon qualities and the civilizing effects of the British environment. While civility gained by conquest and intermingling inevitably affixes nations to a degenerative cycle, Camden has imagined, ingeniously, that English ethnic identity and civility are sustained by a continual transaction between external, environmental forces and internal, innate traits.

Mollis aer

For those Shakespeareans who have connected *Cymbeline* to the Anglo-Scottish union, Posthumus' prophecy seems to present a united Britain as the fulfillment of Merlin's prediction in Geoffrey of Monmouth that "the *British Empire* after the *Saxons* and *Normans*, shall return againe to her auncient *Stocke* and *Name*."[20] To pursue this reading, however, critics must gloss over the prophecy's two-pronged structure, which deliberately separates the revival of Britain's "old stock" from the union implied by the embrace of Posthumus:

Whenas a lion's whelp shall, to himself unknown, without seeking find, and be embraced by a piece of tender air, and when from a stately cedar shall be lopped branches which, being dead many years, shall after revive, be jointed to the old stock, and freshly grow: then shall Posthumus end his miseries, Britain be fortunate and flourish in peace and plenty. (5. 6. 436)

If, as several persuasive commentaries have proposed, Posthumus (the "lion's whelp") represents Scotland, joined to England in his marriage to Innogen, then we need to ask why the prophecy, and the play as a whole, is so invested in separating Posthumus' murky and mingled roots from the genealogical branches of Arviragus and Guiderius (whose own identities have been obscured by a "search so slow / That could not trace them" [1. 1. 65–6]).[21]

The search for Britain's "lopped branches" moves us away from Geoffrey of Monmouth's mythography, I propose, in the soothsayer's belabored interpretation of Posthumus' prophecy. As Mikalachki has observed, Philharmonous' etymological derivation of "tender air" seems to echo Camden's antiquarian language studies.[22] But even more strikingly, it translates the prophecy in such a way that it recalls the phrasing of Camden's assertion in the *Remains* that the English branches are predominantly Saxon in origin:

> The piece of tender air, [Cymbeline's] virtuous daughter,
> Which we call '*mollis aer*'; and '*mollis aer*'
> We term it '*mulier*': which '*mulier*' I divine
> Is this most constant wife, who even now,
>
> . . .
>
> Unknown to you [Posthumus], unsought, were clipped about
> With this most tender air.
>
> . . .
>
> The lofty cedar, royal Cymbeline,
> Personates thee, and thy lopped branches point
> Thy two sons forth, who, by Belarius stol'n
> For many years thought dead, are now revived,
> To the majestic cedar joined, whose issue
> Promises Britain peace and plenty.
>
>   (5. 6. 446–58)

In its references to a tree, its branches, and the effects of the air, this passage resonates with the *Remains*' natural imagery.[23] But the most compelling link between the two texts is Camden's use of the word "mollified" and Shakespeare's "*mollis aer.*" Before it gathers its analogical meaning of "*mulier*" or Innogen (Posthumus' "constant wife"), "*mollis aer*" is equivalent to Camden's mollifying air. There is, however, an important distinction between the *Remains*' account of England's Saxon roots and Shakespeare's prophecy: although Posthumus is the one to be "clipped about," he is not, as we have already observed, joined to the cedar or its "lopped branches." In other words, the prophecy may echo Camden in its recognition of England's Saxon roots (a point I demonstrate more fully below), but it also revises its source by characterizing the Scots, and not the Saxons, as the people to be mollified.[24]

Traditionally, *Cymbeline* criticism has maintained that these "lopped branches" represent the exiled Britons of Geoffrey of Monmouth's mythography; however, as John Curran has argued, this interpretation overlooks how the play's philobarbaric celebration of Arviragus and Guiderius' primitivism owes more to Camden's revisionary historiography than to "an antiquated Galfridian concern for royalty."[25] Brilliantly, Curran demonstrates that the princes' aliases,

Polydore and Cadwal, point up the fictional status of Geoffrey's tales. "Polydore" recalls, of course, the historian Polydore Vergil, best known for his challenges to Geoffrey's *Histories of the Kings of Britain*, and "Cadwal" may hint at the noted problem that Geoffrey's Cadwallader appeared to be a distorted version of Bede's Cadwalla.[26]

Indeed, these false names do suggest that the Trojan myths overshadow a truer, or less glamorized, genealogy. But to push Curran's conclusions a bit further, we need to question whether Arviragus and Guiderius should be identified as "Britons" at all. Though Curran recognizes that the play glorifies the brothers' untamed nature as heroically virtuous, he forgets that the barbaric Britons of Camden's *Britannia* (unlike Arviragus and Guiderius) were conquered and "civilized" by the Romans. As we shall see, *Cymbeline*'s naturally civilized and racially pure brothers actually function as superior foils to the play's Romanized and mingled Britons. And by locating these princes in the rugged mountains of Wales (which should be, as Mikalachki notes, the "last preserve and final retreat of pure Britishness"), Shakespeare succeeds in supplanting Welsh/Briton/Trojan claims to a distinctive ethnic identity.[27] As Garrett Sullivan has astutely observed, there are no Welshmen in *Cymbeline*'s Wales.[28]

In the same way that Camden's Anglo-Saxons transcend the temporality of his own civilizing narrative, Guiderius and Arviragus reside in a world removed from *British* historiography.[29] While the play's other narrative threads suggest that the mingling, conquest, and transmigration of Britain's early history have led to various forms of degeneration, the princes' timeless, pastoral scenes stage an atemporal interplay between Britain's natural environment and the brothers' extraordinary temperaments – an interplay that should remind us of Camden's "mollified" Saxons.[30] Indeed, Arviragus and Guiderius possess an inherent and paradoxically rough civility that belies their savage surroundings and excels courtly breeding. Belarius repeatedly marvels at their innate virtues:

> O thou goddess,
> Thou divine Nature, how thyself thou blazon'st
> In these two princely boys! They are as gentle
> As zephyrs blowing below the violet,
> Not wagging his sweet head; and yet as rough,
> Their royal blood enchafed, as the rud'st wind
> That by the top doth take the mountain pine
> And make them stoop to th' vale. 'Tis wonder
> That an invisible instinct should frame them
> To royalty unlearned, honour untaught,
> Civility not seen from other, valour
> That wildly grows in them, but yields a crop
> As if it had been sowed.
>
> (4. 2. 170–82)

The boys share more than an analogous relationship with the rude and gentle winds: this correspondence denotes the mutuality between their nature and the nature of the place. Unlike those with continental courtly manners, which signify artifice or portend degeneracy, the princes possess an innately wild civility that is "untaught," "unlearned" and resistant to decay. They are paradoxically hardy and gentle, civil and barbaric. Moreover, these mixed qualities are fashioned from within and without: both internal valor and Britain's harsh climate "enchafes" their blood; an invisible "instinct," simultaneously savage and royal, "frames" them. The entangled imagery of wild growth, husbandry, intrinsic heat, and external conditions points to a harmonious convergence between the princes' natures and the natural elements that belies the passage of time.

And while the determinants of the brothers' admirable qualities exist outside the temporal world, their status as warriors is celebrated by a peculiar and time-specific allusion to a battle in Holinshed's *Historie of Scotland* that occurs almost a thousand years after Cymbeline's reign, during a period in which (as the English chronicles tell us) the Scottish and Welsh Kings had sworn allegiance to England.[31] With this one swift reference, the play shifts its history forward to the era of Anglo-Saxon rule and frames Arviragus and Guiderius as anachronistic figures in Roman Britain. When Posthumus recounts the illustrious deeds of Arviragus and Guiderius, an attendant lord responds, "This was strange chance: / A narrow lane, an old man, and two boys" (5. 5. 51–2). The phrase refers to a farmer and his two sons who were working in a field adjacent to a battle between the Scots and the Danes. When they see the Scots fleeing in fear, they place "themselves overthwart the lane, beat them backe whome they met fleeing" (S, 155).

Since the play is so concerned with developmental stages in history (most notably in its contrast between ancient Rome and early modern Italy), we are compelled, I believe, to attend to the temporality of this allusion as well. Just as Arviragus and Guiderius enter the play's course of events by way of the battle-field (and the Anglo-Saxons entered English history as indomitable conquerors), Holinshed exclaims that Hay and his sons deserve "immortall fame and commendation" for their bravery (S, 155). And in the same way that England's discovery of its Saxon roots reestablishes the English as innately brave, Guiderius and Arviragus do not simply aid the Britons in battle, they transform the fleeing cowards into courageous "lions."[32] In this same scene, a British captain arrives for no other apparent purpose than to announce "'Tis thought the old man, and his sons, were angels" (5. 5. 85). It may strike us as a throwaway line until we consider how a commonplace glorification of English-Saxon roots rests on the similarity between "Angles" and "Angels." Fast upon his praise of England's Saxon origins in the *Remains*, Camden recounts the Venerable Bede's story of how Bishop Gregory recognized the "*Angleshmen . . . for they have Angelike faces, and seeme meete to be made coheires with the Angells in heaven.*"[33] If we read *Cymbeline* alongside the *Remains*, the play suggests that genealogy, environment, and providence have come together to produce a race of Anglo "Angels" who will resist the cycle of degeneration implicit in the translation of empires.

Claiming British history

It has been my argument thus far that Camden solves the problems raised by *Britannia*'s civilizing narrative with a precocious appeal to racialism. Northern fears regarding both the fluid nature of ethnicity and the cycle of degeneration (implicit in a civility gained by submission) nourish Camden's and Verstegan's antiquarian turn to Tacitus and Anglo-Saxonism. Thus, in detecting this racial appeal in *Cymbeline*, I have begun my reading of Shakespeare's play with what I believe is a climactic (and climatic) solution to many of its critical puzzles. Scholars have long wrestled, for example, with the play's conclusion: although Britain is triumphant in battle, it voluntarily submits to Roman rule. This submission has been interpreted as either the western translation of Empire or ancient Britain's yielding to the civilizing process, and sometimes, paradoxically, as both. As Heather James puts it, the play seems "deliberately vague about whether the transference is a matter of Rome's expansion or her eclipse by Britain."[34]

Confronting the problem of Britain's submissiveness head-on, Jodi Mikalachki has characterized the final embrace between Rome and Britain as triumphantly masculine because it eradicates the effeminate savagery of Britain's pre-Roman past. As Tacitus notoriously observed, the early Britons made no distinction in the sex of their rulers, and as we have already seen, Caesar characterized Britain as a matrilineal society. The monstrous rule of women – from Hippocrates' *Air, Waters, Places* to Tamora of *Titus Andronicus* – appears to have been a perceived trait of northern intemperance. To secure an elevated historical position for *Cymbeline*'s Britons, Mikalachki (*pace* Camden of *Britannia*) must trade in the hard effeminacy of their ancient history for the soft, and certainly questionable, "masculinity" of their submission to Rome.

But northern resistance to this sort of historical trade-off – between native female dominance and submission to a masculine foreign power – is what helped produce early modern Anglo-Saxonism. Thus, Verstegan begins *A Restitution of Decayed Intelligence* by distancing the English not only from the polyandry of the Britons but also from Caesar's conquest of Britain:

[Historians] wrytheth that *Ceasar* in his comentaries saith, that the Englishmen of his tyme had but one woman to serve for ten or twelve men, whereas in deed *Ceasar* never said so, or could so say, for that hee never knew or hard [heard] of the name of Englishmen, seeing their coming into *Britaine* was almost 500. yeares after [Caesar's] death.[35]

As descendants of the Saxons, the English had not yet arrived in Britain when Caesar invaded. And since Verstegan's Saxons have never been conquered and maintain proper decorum in their sexual relations, their racial purity makes Britain's earlier history of submission irrelevant – to the English.

Our general uneasiness with Britain's continuing tribute to Rome stems primarily from the specter of a degenerate future that the conventional civilizing narrative always entails. As Heather James argues, "*Cymbeline* stages the possibility of Britain's failure to fulfill the prophetic union: the emergent nation may instead leap headlong from its rugged origins to 'spongy' or effeminate ends."[36] And, in a similar vein, Peter Parolin maintains that "Britain's future becomes bound up with Rome at the same time that *Cymbeline*'s Italian anachronism continually reminds audiences that imperial Rome degenerated into contemporary Italy."[37] What Parolin and James recognize is that the play does not simply dramatize the civilizing narrative by embracing (as Mikalachki has suggested) Britain's "subordinate status in the Roman empire."[38] Instead, it interrogates both the benefits and drawbacks of acquiring civility by way of subordination. We need to keep in mind that Camden's initial idealization of Roman Britain in *Britannia* was not Elizabethan culture's monolithic view. Holinshed's *Historie of England*, for example, delineates the corruptions of Roman civilization, exemplifying the Tacitean perspective expressed in *Agricola*, wherein the Romans led the ignorant Britons to "accustome themselves to fine fare and delicate pleasures, the readie provokers of vices...which amongst the unskilfull was called humanitie or courtesie" (*E*, 48).

As many critics have noted, Britain's vulnerability to Italian corruption is represented most pointedly in the anachronistic plot that triangulates Posthumus, Giacomo, and Innogen, in what I have described as a northern version of *Othello*. And visually, it is Giacomo's violation of Innogen's bedchamber that epitomizes what Parolin has characterized as Britain's "fears of the Italian within."[39] The cultural scripts played out in the princess' bedchamber suggest that Giacomo's presence merely fulfills an inevitable historical cycle that had been set in motion the moment Caesar conquered the island. Not only does Giacomo compare himself to Tarquin (established by his instigation of the wager), which alludes to "Rome's transition from monarchy to a republican form of government," but on the wall of Innogen's room is a tapestry of Cleopatra on her barge – an image that can be linked to Roman degeneration if not also to the decline of Roman republicanism.[40] In other words, Britain is acquainted with, if not already enlisted in, the cyclical movement of the civilizing process well before Giacomo's arrival.

If *Cymbeline* does indeed displace England's Briton lineage with an appeal to Anglo-Saxon origins, we are left to ask why most of the play is concerned with the non-English: characters who represent both ancient Britons and early modern Scoto-Britons, playing their scripted roles in the civilizing narrative. To answer this question, I return to my central assertion that *Cymbeline* is a romance about historiography. As I will demonstrate, the play self-consciously stages, with its temporal shifts and symbolic personages, the political implications of historical precedents and patterns. And it is, I contend, the ethnological tensions provoked by King James' union project that gave rise to the historiographical awareness that *Cymbeline* displays. As D. R. Woolf has observed, King James' proposal for union shaped the direction of early Jacobean history, for writers of every stripe were struggling to adjudicate the "conflicting and hostile accounts of English and Scottish historians."[41] This struggle, however, failed to produce a harmonious British history and engendered instead a more critical view of the competing narratives. Therefore, before we turn back to *Cymbeline* and its staging of British historiography, we need to review the historical precedents and patterns that mattered most in the Anglo-Scottish controversy.

At the heart of the union debate was the question of Scotland's submission to England, and how it squared with the historical precedent of Britain's submission to Rome. England could not fathom a union unless it had assurance that its laws, institutions, and governmental power would dominate. Scotland, in turn, refused to assent to a union that positioned its people as subordinate; as Scottish advocate John Russell proclaims, "The said unioun to be mutuall and reciproque, not the translatioun of the estait of ane kingdome in ane uther, not of Scotland as subalterne to Ingland...the ane to command, the uther to obey – thairby ancienne Scotland to loss hir beautie for evir!"[42] It was, in fact, a long-held tradition for the Scots to insist that they, unlike the English, had always remained "unsullied by either conquest or feudal submission."[43]

Ironically, Scottish claims to independence were blurred by the Scots' competing assertion that all inhabitants of Britain were ethnologically indistinguishable, a viewpoint expressed by the pre-Jacobean unionist and Scottish historian John Major in *A History of Greater Britain* (1521):

all men born in Britain are Britons, seeing that on any other reasoning Britons could not be distinguished from other races; since it is possible to pass from England to Wales, and from Scotland by way of England to Wales, dryshod, there would otherwise be no distinction of races...I reckon both Scots and Picts to be alike Britons.[44]

Further obscuring efforts to disentangle Britain's ethnological origins was the conviction among most late sixteenth-century historians that Britain's prehistory was, as Edmund Bolton put it, a "vast Blanck upon the Times of our

Country, from the Creation of the World till the coming of Julius Caesar."[45] Hence, for revisionists, determining the identity of the Britons came to focus in particular on the Roman conquest.

Geoffrey of Monmouth had, of course, insisted that upon the Romans' arrival, Caesar recognized the Britons as his Trojan kin. To honor this noble ancestry, Geoffrey interprets Britain's downfall, paradoxically, as evidence of his people's admirable courage. Underscoring how the Britons twice drove Caesar away, he finds them praiseworthy "even in defeat," for they "withstood him whom no nation of the earth had been able to withstand."[46] Slanting this same story in a different direction, the Scottish historians intervened with the assertion that the Britons had only succeeded in defeating Caesar "at first because the Scots and Picts were helping them," and it was only after they had forfeited the aid of their northern allies that the Britons were easily subdued.[47] As Holinshed laments, the Scots sought to attribute "what notable feat soever was atchived by the old Britains against the Romans" to the Scots and the Picts (*E*, 41). Moreover, they did so while maintaining their claims to a history of independence.[48]

After King James' accession, advocates of the Scottish union cite Caesar's conquest not only as the island's punishment for the inhabitants' ancient disunity but also as evidence that Britain's integrity had depended primarily on the Scots and the Picts. It was, as one Scottish author contends, "by the perpetuall discords of the Brittons, Scotish, and Pights, [that] the Romans maid there conquest of the iland."[49] In a similar vein, Scottish union commissioner Sir Thomas Craig contends that the "dissensions of the island paved the way for Caesar's invasion." Moreover, Craig asserts, Caesar's triumph over the *southern* Britons led to their degeneracy and subsequent losses of liberty, for "by abandoning themselves to luxury, [the Britons] relapsed into cowardice, and so opened the island first to the Saxons and then to the Danes, who encountered little resistance from the effeminate and luxury-loving natives."[50] By selectively inserting themselves into British history, the Scots could lay claim to the Britons' ancient valor (which Camden and Geoffrey of Monmouth had both praised) yet direct the ensuing tales of degeneration away from themselves and onto the Anglo-Britons.

We can only speculate as to why Camden and Verstegan would turn to England's Saxon origins in 1605 – at the height of the union controversy. While most union advocates relied on the assimilative effect of depicting Britain's future as a revival of its mythically unified past, the historians attesting to English-Saxon roots aimed, I believe, to extricate the English people from a history of Briton savagery, Roman domination, and Scottish kinship. Certainly there was a growing sense among English scholars that the history of the Britons should simply be dismissed. According to Henry Spelman, an antiquarian scholar whose interest in the union most likely reflected Camden's views, the formation of a unified Britain threatened to obfuscate the *English* people's glory with barbarous memories of the Britons:

[I]f the honorable name of England be buried in the resurrection of Albion or Britannia, we shall change the goulden beames of the sonne for a cloudy day, and drownde the glory of a nation triumphant through all the worlde to restore the memory of an obscure and barberouse people, of whome no mention almoste is made in any notable history author but is either to their owne disgrace or at least to grace the trophyes and victoryes of their conquerors the Romans, Pictes, and Saxones.[51]

As it turns out, Camden's revaluation of England's Saxon heritage in the *Remains* is directly related to his representation of Scottish origins. The Saxons, he argues, conquered "as farre as Orkeney. Which cannot be doubted of, when their English tongue reacheth so farre along the East coast, unto the farthest parts of Scotland, and the people thereof are called by the Highland-men, which are the true Scots, by no other name then Saxons, by which they also call us the English."[52] Camden's assertions accomplish two seemingly conflicting, but politically compatible, objectives: he embraces the Scots as "English" while also declaring that the true Scots are none other than the notoriously barbarous Highlanders. Hence, those southern Scotsmen who resist submitting to England should recognize that the civilized inhabitants of Scotland have already been conquered – by the Anglo-Saxons.

When Camden revises *Britannia* in 1607, he develops this Scottish-Saxon link to support his now-acknowledged political motive: an Anglo-Saxon genealogy will ensure, he implies, a peaceful (and Anglo-dominated) union:

[T]hey beare now the name of Scotish-men, yet are they nothing lesse than Scots, but descended from the very same Germane originall that we English men are. And this, neither can they chuse but confesse, nor we but acknowledge, being as they are, termed by those abovesaid, High-land men, *Sassones*, as well as we; and using as they doe the same language with us, to wit, the English-Saxon, different onely in Dialect, a most assured argument of one and the same originall. In which regard, so farre am I from working any discredit unto them, that I have rather respectively loved them alwaies, as of the same bloud and stocke, yea and honoured them too, even when the Kingdomes were divided: but now much more, since it hath pleased our almightie, and most mercifull God, that wee growe united in one bodie, under one most Sacred head of the Empire, to the joy, happinesse, welfare, and safetie, of both Nations, which I heartily wish and pray for.[53]

The antiquarian turn to Saxon origins in the early seventeenth century is neither accidental nor innocent, for, as Roger A. Mason has argued, the rise of Anglo-Saxonism simultaneously "reinforced the irrelevance of the Scottish past and the Englishness of Britain."[54] Or to rephrase this insight more accurately with regard to *Cymbeline*, the rise of Anglo-Saxonism reinforced the Scottishness of Britain's ancient past and the Englishness of its future. Once the Saxons displaced the Britons as the progenitors of English history, all of Britain's early activity – the valiant acts, the barbarous rebellions, the female savagery, and the ignoble submissions – could be ascribed to the clamoring and resistant Scots.

Entangled ethnicities

As Jodi Mikalachki's reading of *Cymbeline* has shown us, the play's use of its historical sources is self-consciously engaged in the project of national construction. Noting that Cymbeline's queen "has no direct source in Holinshed's reign of Kymbeline," Mikalachki contends that the play may be confronting and exorcizing a larger problem, or pattern, in Britain's early history – the phenomenon of savage female leaders – exemplified most notoriously by Voadicia, or Boadicea, "who appears in Holinshed's narrative of Roman Britain roughly sixty years after the events depicted in Shakespeare's play."[55] In the spirit of Mikalachki's attention to *Cymbeline*'s historiographical sophistication, I propose that we explore further how the romance deploys those portions of Holinshed's *Chronicles* that correspond more directly to the time period of Shakespeare's play.[56] The first thing that registers with scholars who turn to Holinshed's English *Chronicles* is the incongruity that the historical Cymbeline paid peaceful tribute to the Romans throughout his reign. Without much speculation as to why, critics such as Emrys Jones observe that Shakespeare seems to have superimposed the documented rebellions of Guiderius and Arviragus onto their father's reign.[57] Indeed, it is this sort of chronological confusion, together with the play's more notorious anachronisms, that has led some commentators to treat *Cymbeline*'s historical strands as "merely ornamentation."[58]

We should note, however, that just following his brief summary of Cymbeline's reign, Holinshed acknowledges that there is a discrepancy between the British histories and what the Roman writers have written of this same period. According to the Roman historians, the Britons had refused to pay tribute not only under the supposedly peaceful rule of Cymbeline's father, Theomantius, but during Cymbeline's reign as well.[59] Though it seems, as the Romans report, that Augustus Caesar endeavored to quell the Britons' defiance, he was distracted by rebellions in other countries. And among those rebelling were the Pannonians and Dalmatians, whose resistance Shakespeare's Cymbeline cites as an important model for his own actions – "a precedent / Which not to read would show the Britons cold" (3. 1. 72–3). Granted, if we look to Holinshed's description of Cymbeline's reign to find the *plot* of Shakespeare's play, it's not there; what we do find, however, is evidence of the play's historiography. In the span of three paragraphs, Holinshed reveals that there are conflicting narratives about this period in Britain's history, and that those disagreements pertain to the historian's nationality – Roman versus Briton. Moreover, the debate over Cymbeline's reign revolves around the status, as an historical precedent, of Caesar's conquest of Britain: did Cymbeline revive the Britons' ancient valor (*pace* Geoffrey), or did he peacefully submit to Roman rule (*pace* Camden)?

The intertextual, or international, weaving of historical narratives becomes more complex in the *Chronicles'* accounts of Guiderius and Arviragus (where Emrys Jones suggested we look), for it is also here that Holinshed complains that the Scottish historians continually take credit for whatever "notable feat... atchived by the old Britains against the Romans" (*E*, 41).[60] Indeed, *Cymbeline's* indebtedness to Holinshed cannot be fully understood unless we consider how the Scottish *Chronicles* function as a rival source for the historiographical tensions in the play. Though literary scholars recognize that Shakespeare flipped the pages of his Holinshed to the Scottish *Chronicles* when he made reference to Hay and his sons, no one has seriously entertained the possibility that *Cymbeline's* central plot may be an amalgamation of Scottish, English, and Roman histories.[61] Or more accurately, that the play may be staging competing and irreconcilable perspectives on Britain's early history.

When we read the Scottish chronicles alongside the English chronicles it becomes clear why Holinshed acknowledges that there are "diverse opinions and variable reports of writers touching the partile conquest of this Iland by the Romans" (*E*, 35). Though the Scots and the English both agree, for example, that Guiderius led the Britons in a rebellion against Rome, they differ on whether or not the Scots played a role in the conflict. The English chroniclers will admit only that Guiderius was "a man of stout courage" who died in battle (*E*, 33), whereas the Scottish historians contend that Guiderius' southern Britons were helpless without the Scots: indeed, it seems, the Roman army immediately "vanquished Guiderius in battell, so that he was constreined to send to Caratake king of Scots for aid against the common enemies of both nations" (*S*, 45).

As for Arviragus' reign, during which the Britons reinstated their tributary relationship with Rome, the English chroniclers begin on the defensive, arguing that accounts of the period constitute a historiographical problem; indeed, it is difficult to determine, Holinshed suggests, when exactly Arviragus ruled. But once we survey the English and Scottish chronicles together, the primary issue of contention is the status and ethnicity of Arviragus' wife. The English version proposes, tentatively, that it was Arviragus' marriage to Genissa, daughter of emperor Claudius, that reestablished Britain's peaceful relations with Rome (*E*, 36). When Arviragus later rebels on account of "pride," it is his Roman wife's "good mediation" that helps restore Britain to its properly submissive position. And yet, the English chroniclers hasten to add, historians simply cannot agree on whether or not "this supposed marriage betwixt Arviragus and the daughter of Claudius is but a feined tale" (*E*, 36). To confuse matters further, the English version claims, the Scottish chroniclers have mistaken Arviragus for Prasutugus, the man who married Voadicea or Boadicea, erroneously fusing the legend of the female British warrior with Arviragus' more nebulous story (*E*, 42).

In the Scottish chronicles, Arviragus' tale can be read as a fierce defense of Scoto-Briton identity – an identity directly threatened by Britain's continued submission to Rome. The Scottish historians not only maintain that Arviragus married the Roman Genissa, but they also assert that it was this very action that brought about Britain's noble rebellion. Arviragus, it turns out, already had a Scottish wife, Voada, the sister of King Caratake, and this second marriage to a Roman was an "act manie of the Britans disallowed; the more in deed, because he had faire issue alreadie by Voada" (*S*, 46). As the Scottish chroniclers tell it, the rebellion against Rome was not insubordination on Arviragus' part, but a populist movement *against* him for having spurned his Scottish queen. The betrayed Britons willingly join forces with the Scots and Picts to defend the honor of the abandoned Voada.[62] From the Scottish perspective, then, British defiance against Rome is not simply an exercise in bravado, it is an action that unifies the disparate peoples of Britain in the face of a faithless king and a foreign invader.

Voada is a ghostly presence in the English chronicles, implied only in the assertion that the Scottish historians have confused Arviragus with Boadicea's husband (*E*, 42); indeed, this is as close as the English historians come to giving a name to Arviragus' Scottish wife.[63] But it is, I contend, Voada's erasure from the English *Chronicles* that attests to her importance. Voada represents a history of mingled ethnic identities: the rebellious Britons have not only intermarried with the Scots, but they repeatedly appealed to their northern neighbors for aid when battling the Romans. We may presume that, for the English, the Scots' Arviragus violated decorum less for marrying two women than for having a rebellious Scottish wife who generated the shared sympathy of Britons, Picts, and Scots. The Britons' loyalty to their Scottish queen over and above their "Briton" ruler underscores a messy ethnological history that the English chroniclers have chosen to ignore. Rather than affirming a history that binds the Britons to a female Scot and her Pictish rebels, the English historians place their emphasis on the peaceful civility of Roman rule.

By now I would imagine that readers can see intimations of *Cymbeline*'s nameless queen in the source material, both as a presence in the Scottish *Chronicles* and an absence in the English account. Given that the Scottish historians (according to the English view) mistook Voada for Boadicea, we might even say that Mikalachki's argument has already connected the queen to Voada. And yet, the implied reason why the English chroniclers erased Voada from Arviragus' history is that her presence would confuse British nationalism with Scottish and Pictish rebellion. *Cymbeline*'s queen, I want to argue, is meant to embody this very confusion. Notoriously delivering the play's most patriotic speech, which invokes the legend of Caesar to instigate Britain's rebellion, the queen and her "nationalism" make sense only in light of the ethnological tensions of British history and Jacobean politics:

> Remember, sir, my liege,
> The kings your ancestors, together with
> The natural bravery of your isle, which stands
> As Neptune's park, ribbed and paled in
> With rocks unscalable and roaring waters,
> With sands that will not bear your enemies' boats
> But suck them up to th' topmast. A kind of conquest
> Caesar made here, but made not here his brag
> Of 'came, and saw, and overcame'. With shame –
> The first that ever touched him – he was carried
> From off our coast, twice beaten; and his shipping,
> Poor ignorant baubles, on our terrible seas
> Like eggshells moved upon their surges, cracked
> As easily 'gainst our rocks; for joy whereof
> The famed Cassibelan, who was once at point –
> O giglot fortune! – to master Caesar's sword,
> Made Lud's town with rejoicing fires bright,
> And Britons strut with courage.
>
>   (3. 1. 16–33)

As critics have noted, we are challenged to reconcile the queen's villainy with the speech's rousing patriotism. It is, in fact, this discrepancy between rejecting the speaker and empathizing with her sentiments that has led Mikalachki and others to ask whether the play critiques "nationalism" itself.[64] By act five, we know that the queen's defiance is condemned, for she (recalling Voada) has put Cymbeline between a rock and a hard place: to stand up for British identity means submitting to his wife and to reject uxoriousness means submitting to Rome.

   Given that many of the period's historians and politicians were asking the question, "What is my nation?" we should recognize that the queen's nationalism is not wrong-headed in spirit but cheering (in the context of the play) for the wrong tribe. Her chauvinistic speech conflates, I believe, the old British myths with Scottish historiography. As John Curran has shown, the queen's historical perspective is reminiscent of Geoffrey of Monmouth's account of the Britons – a "self-made, exaggerated, and self-aggrandizing view of history" – that is to say, it resembles Geoffrey's myths under the harshest revisionary light.[65] And like Geoffrey, she emphasizes the Britons' courage and warlike temperament – so much so that she glosses over the fact that Caesar won. Yet the queen is also marked as an interloper, as an anonymous second wife and step-dame, and her "patriotism" is necessarily tainted by her outsider status. Walking a fine line between self-alienated and "self-aggrandized," she begins her oration in the second person (praising "your" island) before shifting to the inclusive "our." Her rhetoric subtly conveys a usurpation of the Britons' mythic past and echoes, for the English, those meddling Scottish historians and union advocates. In much the same way that the Scots would claim British triumphs, but not their losses, her feelings of ethnic kinship are selective.

Since, as I have been arguing, the play has a sophisticated sense of historical dissension, the queen's appropriation of British history is not, as we might expect, directly refuted. Indeed, there is no effort in the play to disentangle the Britons from their association with the queen and Cloten. And if the Scottish and British histories are hopelessly entangled, then it is the queen's blindness to the Britons' eventual defeat that has the most profound political resonance for a Jacobean audience. When we frame the queen's speech with Cloten's boast that the Britons "will nothing pay for wearing [their] own noses" (3. 1. 13–14) – a hollow bid for ethnological purity that invites ridicule – then the impossible insularity of her nationalism ("ribbed and paled in / With rocks unscalable") becomes a mocking indictment of the British Isle's mingled stock.

Though the queen, like the Scots, may omit her ancestors' subjugation from history, she and her son Cloten do not behave as though they are unsullied by foreign influence. Indeed, they seem to represent particular northern stereotypes of southern corruption: she is a scheming Machiavel and he recalls Roger Ascham's "English ape."[66] As such, they reside in multiple temporal registers, representing, simultaneously, Britain's barbaric origins, an early modern historiographical perspective on those origins, and the degenerative consequences of a submission that they have refused to acknowledge.[67] I should interject here that to discern an entire cycle of the "civilizing narrative" within a single character is an interpretative approach that jibes with the structure of the play. *Cymbeline*, I submit, is an amalgamation of individual characters' trajectories that resist our reading for "plot" but beg instead for typological interpretations. That the play signifies most complexly on the characterological level is hinted at in the number of individuals who deliver soliloquies – Posthumus, Innogen, Giacomo, Belarius, Cloten, Pisanio, the queen, the second lord. This is not to say, of course, that any of these figures possesses a deep interiority. Quite the contrary. It is to observe that these characters symbolize or comment on competing narratives of nationhood and ethnicity.

In light of these caveats, I want to suggest that the representation of Cloten as an "English ape" is not a static reiteration of the Ascham figure but an ethnological and historical reframing of that stereotype. Rather than equating apishness with *Englishness*, Shakespeare suggests that Cloten is both the alpha and omega of *Britain*'s civilizing narrative. On the one hand he identifies with the barbaric valor of his ancestors (not unlike the Scot who boasts of the vigor of his uncorrupted stock), while on the other hand, he shows himself to be a degenerate slave to continental customs (not unlike the Scot mocked by the English for his ties with France). Given that the play idealizes Guiderius and Arviragus for the harmonious ebb and flow they achieve between their internal qualities and the rugged British climate, we are also invited to attend to Cloten's physiological intemperance – which is manifested as a distinct lack of harmony between self and environment. When we first encounter Cloten, a lord is joking about how much he reeks, "Where air comes out, air comes in. There's none abroad so wholesome as that you vent" (1. 2. 2–4) – a jest that the second lord continues a few scenes later. Without pushing the point too far, Cloten's excessive sweating not only hints at his imbalanced constitution (seemingly exacerbated by the adoption of foreign practices) but also underscores his natural inferiority to the "rustic mountaineer[s]" (4. 2. 102) who cut off his head. Indeed, it is in response to their killing of Cloten that Belarius declares Arviragus and Guiderius paradoxically "gentle" and "rough," civil and rude. Thus, the "English ape," or rather "British ape," is supplanted by an Englishness that resists degeneration.

While the brothers supplant Cloten's "model of degeneration" with ease, it is a primary question of the play whether or not Posthumus has the capacity to supersede Cloten, his recognized "foil and double."[68] The connection between these two characters extends beyond Cloten's adoption of Posthumus' clothes and Innogen's mistaken identification of the headless corpse; they are, I maintain, ethnologically linked. If Cloten stands in for the more barbaric Scoto-Britons who misrepresent their past, then Posthumus is his early modern counterpart – the Scot who is poised but not yet prepared to receive England's embrace in union.[69] It is for this reason that Posthumus also fulfills the role of "English ape" during his exile on the continent; as a Scoto-Briton, he is temperamentally vulnerable to Giacomo's manipulations.[70] Indeed, Posthumus' plot trajectory is the play's most complete interrogation of the civilizing process. Initially an outsider to the British court, he is educated, scrutinized, exiled, tested, and finally embraced. Yet, even with Cymbeline's acceptance and Innogen's *mollis aer*, it remains questionable to the very last scene as to whether Posthumus – as a Scoto-Briton – has gained, or even has the potential for, *English* temperance and civility.

People such that mend upon the world

As we observed in the Anglo-Scottish debates, England refused to embrace Scotland unless she renounced her claim to an inherent independence and adopted a submissive position in the union. In the ethnological logic of Shakespeare's romance, Scottish claims to independence will be rendered null and void once they fully acknowledge *all* (and not just the glory) of Britain's early history as their own. It is therefore part of Posthumus' journey that he fully accept his own British identity. The play introduces him as a man of mysterious origins when the court gentlemen observe that they cannot "delve him to the root" (1. 1. 28). And his obscure ancestry recalls the Scots' status in *Britannia*, where Camden finds only Britons and Anglo-Saxons in Britain's early history and insists that the Scots are not readily identifiable as a separate branch. Thus, the unveiling of Posthumus' genealogy is established in the very first scene as an implicit but central narrative in the play. As such, when Posthumus doffs his early modern Italian weeds and assumes the apparel of a Briton peasant, it is a climactic and revelatory moment in his journey.

Though Posthumus must struggle to reject degenerate Italian influences, there is no question that he is a fully Romanized Briton.[71] Roman in name, and connected to Aeneas in the masque-like sequence in which the ghosts of his family plead with Jupiter to save his "valiant race," Posthumus is the progeny of Camden's vision of ancient Britain. For, as Camden jests in the *Britannia*, any historian who still seeks to trace the Britons to the Trojans can find a more direct line through the intermingling of Britons and Romans during the latter's occupation.[72] But in contrast to Cloten and the queen, Posthumus readily acknowledges his Romanized past and even articulates a revisionist's view of history when he assesses the Britons' status as warriors:

> Our countrymen
> Are men more ordered than when Julius Caesar
> Smiled at their lack of skill but found their courage
> Worthy his frowning at. Their discipline,
> Now mingled with their courage, will make known
> To their approvers they are people such
> That mend upon the world.
>
> (2. 4. 20–6)[73]

Rather than merely celebrating his ancestors' "natural bravery," Posthumus emphasizes the civilizing effects of the Roman conquest. The order and discipline that now tempers the Britons' natural courage indicates, he posits, that they are a race of people who have progressed, and who will continue to improve over time.

Though, as I discuss below, there remain disturbing correspondences between Posthumus and Cloten, we are repeatedly invited (by Innogen's love and the courtiers' admiration, for example) to recognize him as the more genuinely refined Scot. If we take him to be an exemplar of the civilizing process, we can attribute Posthumus' "order," as he does, to time and Roman influence. Or we can point to his early education in the British court: as one of the courtiers notes, Cymbeline "Breeds [Posthumus], and makes him of his bedchamber; / Puts to him all the learnings that his time / Could make him the receiver of, which he took, / As we do air" (1. 1. 42–5). Yet the play, as I have been arguing, has a more complicated view of the civilizing process; indeed, the courtier's reference to "air" should remind us of Shakespeare's distinction between acquired civility and civility "untaught" – that which Arviragus and Guiderius exhibit as naturally as breathing.

Once exiled in Italy and exposed to its spongy air, Posthumus shows himself to be little better than Cloten. Indeed, he proves the stereotypical northern traveler: having boasted and quarreled as a young man about Innogen's superior beauty, he now foolishly engages in Giacomo's wager to verify her faithfulness. Posthumus' remarkably quick transformation from loyal Briton to jealous husband is intended to demonstrate not only the "false Italian's" poisonous influence but more pointedly, the Briton's "too ready hearing" (3. 2. 6). We are meant to contrast Othello's temperament (whose metamorphosis took more time and labor, multiple instances of "proof," and face-to-face confrontations with the accused) with Posthumus'. The Briton, after only minutes of conversation with Giacomo, takes to heart a story, which Filario finds "not strong enough to be believed" (2. 4. 131), and swears "to tear [Innogen] limb-meal" (2. 4. 147). But what makes the northerner's jealousy even more reprehensible is that while Othello doubts Desdemona in part because she is Italian, Posthumus' suspicion of Innogen necessitates that he forget Britain (1. 6. 114).[74] And within the context of *Cymbeline*'s interest in how Britain's past informs its present, Posthumus' susceptibility to such forgetful degeneration is implicitly connected to his ancestors' subjugation to Rome.[75]

Once struck with jealousy, Posthumus comes to the impassioned conclusion that if Innogen is unfaithful, then all vices must be generated by women, gendered female, and located, if the subject is male, in the "woman's part." Beyond the conspicuous irony that his misplaced suspicions have cast *him* as the mutable one (while Innogen remains "Fidele"), we are also given to understand in his next scene that it is the "woman's part" that releases him from jealousy's degrading hold. In contrast to Othello's inflexibility, Posthumus has a complete change of heart when he proposes that all married men should forgive their wives for "wrying but a little." I do not mean to imply that his *volte-face* redeems him as a hero, for it is troubling, to say the least, that Innogen must be presumed dead for Posthumus to behave sympathetically. However, I do want to point out that Posthumus' emotional transformation – his softening toward his wife – corresponds with his return to British air and his immediate decision to exchange his Italian finery for the clothes of a Briton peasant. Though mutability may be the Briton's curse, especially when exposed to the corrupting influences of spongy Italy, mutability is also what allows him to reclaim his identity as a Briton.

Our disappointment with Posthumus supports my thesis that he is not scripted to play a hero but to learn, instead, a more submissive role. As a Romanized, and more recently Italianated, Scoto-Briton, Posthumus' state of civility is suspect to the very end. When he strikes the disguised Innogen, for example, we are encouraged to contrast his boorishness with the more noble instincts of Arviragus and Guiderius – who discern virtue in Fidele from the start. Thus, to eradicate his barbaric traits, Posthumus must "be embraced by a piece of tender air." Just as England demanded that Scotland take the "woman's part" in the Anglo-Scottish union, Britain's prosperity depends on Posthumus' submission to the mollifying embrace of his wife.

To put a finer point on it, the prophecy does not state definitively that Posthumus will be "clipped about" or embraced – only that when it occurs, Britain will thrive. The embrace that matters for the immediate moment is Britain's reunion with Rome, which stands as a historical precedent for Scotland's submission to England. But we can puzzle still further over why Britain chooses to submit despite its martial victory. We might see Shakespeare's conclusion as a negotiation between the conflicting perspectives in Holinshed's *Chronicles*: to have Cymbeline rebel upholds the Roman history and to have him willingly pay tribute bears out the English version. But it is also, I want to suggest, the anachronistic presence of Arviragus and Guiderius that makes possible this paradoxical ending. It is only with the help of the "Saxons" that the Britons are able to win the war. And while the Britons yielded to Rome, the Anglo-Saxons (who represent a later period) can still claim to be (*pace* Camden and Verstegan) unsullied by conquest or submission.

Foreshadowing Posthumus' embrace by a "piece of tender air" is Giacomo's transformation from villain to ally – a transformation he attributes to the British climate. Since he embodies Italy's decline, Giacomo, as we have noted, haunts the Britons' submission to Rome and the future of the British empire. And as the stereotypical foreign villain, his metamorphosis may strike the reader not only as beyond belief (even for a romance) but also as superfluous in a play most concerned with the fate of Britain. However, I would like to entertain, by way of a conclusion, how Giacomo's regeneration aims to undo the conventional associations between place and climatic effects, and, as such, dislocates Britain from the world's margins.

On his first visit to Britain, as Giacomo explains to the court, he found that his "Italian brain / Gan in your duller Britain operate / Most vilely: for my vantage, excellent" (5. 6. 196–8). If he employs the same counteractive logic of Aristotelian climate theory that his predecessor Aaron invokes in *Titus Andronicus*, then we might interpret these lines in the following physiological terms: Britain's northern climate has heated Giacomo's relatively cool, dry brain and exacerbated his villainous and politic qualities ("southerners," Bodin writes, "become more energetic in a cold region").[76] And yet, on his subsequent trip to Britain, Giacomo's experience exceeds the logic of geohumoralism: not only does he feel enfeebled by the climate but also unmanned by the "heaviness and guilt within [his] bosom" (5. 2. 1). In the play's final scene, he identifies this same heaviness as his "conscience" and offers his life for Posthumus' forgiveness. The staging of Giacomo's reformation thus endows Britain with uniquely restorative powers. And if the British air can regenerate the epitome of southern decadence, then (we are to infer) it most certainly has the capacity to sustain the supposed vigor, civility, and greatness of the English race that it helped to create.

Notes

1. Unless otherwise stated, all quotations from Shakespeare follow *The Norton Shakespeare*, gen. ed. Stephen Greenblatt (New York: Norton & Company, 1997).
2. See Jack D'Amico's *The Moor in English Renaissance Drama* (Tampa: University of South Florida Press, 1991), for example, which suggests that Desdemona is blinded by her love for Othello when she "revers[es] the traditional idea that the sun produced a hot, jealous disposition" (p. 191).
3. Virginia Mason Vaughan writes that Othello's jealousy contradicts Desdemona's assertion and "confirms Renaissance stereotypes about Moorish behavior – the sun was believed to create passionate furies, not dry them up." *Othello: A Contextual History* (Cambridge: Cambridge University Press, 1984), p. 68.
4. Discussions of the influence of environmental theory in the early modern period include Joshua Scodel, *Excess and the Mean in Early Modern English Literature* (Princeton: Princeton University Press, 2002), pp. 79–110; Ivan Hannaford, *Race: The History of an Idea in the West* (Baltimore: Johns Hopkins University Press, 1996); Seymour Phillips, "The Outer World of the European Middle Ages," *Implicit Understandings: Observing, Reporting, and Reflecting on the Encounters Between Europeans and Other Peoples in the Early Modern Era*, ed. Stuart B. Schwartz (Cambridge: Cambridge University Press, 1994), pp. 45–56; Andrew Wear, "Making Sense of Health and the Environment in Early Modern England," *Health and Healing in Early Modern England*, ed. Andrew Wear (Aldershot: Ashgate, 1998), section 4, pp. 119–47; A. J. Hoenselaars, *Images of Englishmen and Foreigners in the Drama of Shakespeare and His Contemporaries: A Study of Stage Characters and National Identity in English Renaissance Drama, 1558–1642* (London and Toronto: Associated University Press, 1992), pp. 18–19; John Wands, "The Theory of Climate in the English Renaissance and *Mundus Alter et Idem*," *Acta Conventus Neo-Latini Sanctandreani* (1982), *Medieval and Renaissance Texts and Studies* 38 (1986): 519–29; John Block Friedman, *The Monstrous Races in Medieval Art and Thought* (Cambridge, Mass.: Harvard University Press, 1981), pp. 35–8 and 51–6; Waldemar Zacharasiewicz, *Die Klimatheorie in Der Englischen Literatur Und Literaturkritik* (Stuttgart: Wilhelm Braumuller, 1977); Clarence J. Glacken, *Traces on the Rhodian Shore: Nature and Culture in Western Thought from Ancient Times to the End of the Eighteenth Century* (Berkeley: University of California Press, 1967); Margaret T. Hodgen, *Early Anthropology in the Sixteenth and Seventeenth Centuries* (Philadelphia: University of Pennsylvania Press, 1964), pp. 276–90; J. W. Johnson,

"Of Differing Ages and Climes," *Journal of the History of Ideas* 21 (1960): 465–80; Samuel Kliger, *The Goths in England: A Study in Seventeenth and Eighteenth Century Thought* (Cambridge, Mass.: Harvard University Press, 1952); Marian J. Tooley, "Bodin and the Mediaeval Theory of Climate," *Speculum* 28 (1953): 64–83; Z. S. Fink, *The Classical Republicans: An Essay in the Recovery of a Pattern of Thought in Seventeenth-Century England* (Evanston: Northwestern University Press, 1945); Leonard F. Dean, "Bodin's *Methodus* in England before 1625," *Studies in Philology* 39 (1942): 160–6; Z. S. Fink, "Milton and the Theory of Climatic Influence," *Modern Language Quarterly* 2 (1941): 67–80.

Karen Ordahl Kupperman has produced important work on the cultural influence of climate theory in the New World: *Seventeenth-Century New England* (Charlottesville: University Press of Virginia, 1984), pp. 3–37; "Fear of Hot Climates in the Anglo-American Colonial Experience," *William and Mary Quarterly* 41 (1984): 213–40; "The Puzzle of the American Climate in the Early Colonial Period," *American Historical Review* 87 (1982): 1262–89. Other American studies include Joyce E. Chaplin, "Natural Philosophy and Early Racial Idiom in North America: Comparing English and Indian Bodies," *William and Mary Quarterly* 54 (1997): 229–52; John Canup, *Out of the Wilderness: The Emergence of an American Identity in Colonial New England* (Middletown, Conn.: Wesleyan University Press, 1990); Jim Egan, *Authorizing Experience: Refigurations of the Body Politic in Seventeenth-Century New England Writing* (Princeton: Princeton University Press, 1999); Janet Moore Lindman and Michele Lise Tarter, eds., *A Center of Wonders: The Body in Early America* (Ithaca: Cornell University Press, 2001); Joyce E. Chaplin, *Subject Matter: Technology, the Body, and Science on the Anglo-American Frontier, 1500–1676* (Cambridge, Mass.: Harvard University Press, 2001).

5. The most current work on the subject is Michael C. Schoenfeldt's *Bodies and Selves in Early Modern England: Physiology and Inwardness in Spenser, Shakespeare, Herbert, and Milton* (Cambridge: Cambridge University Press, 1999); Gail Kern Paster, "The Body and its Passions," *Shakespeare Studies* 29 (2001): 44–51; Paster, "The Unbearable Coldness of Female Being: Women's Imperfection and the Humoral Economy," *English Literary Renaissance* 28 (1998): 416–40; Paster, "Nervous Tension: Networks of Blood and Spirit in the Early Modern Body," *The Body in Parts: Fantasies of Corporeality in Early Modern Europe*, ed. David Hillman and Carla Mazzio (London and New York: Routledge, 1997), pp. 107–25; Paster, *The Body Embarrassed: Drama and the Disciplines of Shame in Early Modern England* (Ithaca: Cornell University Press, 1993). See also *Reading the Early Modern Passions: Essays on the Cultural History of Emotion*, ed. Mary Floyd-Wilson, Gail Kern Paster, and Katherine Rowe (Philadelphia: University of Pennsylvania Press, forthcoming).

For more information on early modern physiology and humoralism, see Nancy G. Siraisi, *Medieval and Early Renaissance Medicine: An Introduction to Knowledge and Practice* (Chicago: University of Chicago Press, 1990); Stanley W. Jackson, *Melancholia and Depression: From Hippocratic Times to Modern Times* (New Haven: Yale University Press, 1986), pp. 3–25; Lester S. King, "The Transformation of Galenism," *Medicine in Seventeenth-Century England*, ed. Allen G. Debus (Berkeley: University of California Press, 1974), pp. 7–31; Raymond

Klibansky, Erwin Panofsky, and Fritz Saxl, *Saturn and Melancholy: Studies in the History of Natural Philosophy, Religion, and Art* (New York: Basic Books, 1964); Lynn Thorndike, *"De Complexionibus," Isis* 49 (1958): 398–408; J. B. Bamborough, *The Little World of Man* (London: Longmans, 1952).

For classic studies on the humors in relation to early modern drama, see Ruth Leila Anderson, *Elizabethan Psychology and Shakespeare's Plays* (New York: Russell and Russell, reissued 1966); John W. Draper, *The Humors and Shakespeare's Characters* (Durham, NC: Duke University Press, 1945); Lily B. Campbell, *Shakespeare's Tragic Heroes: Slaves of Passion* (New York: Barnes and Noble, reprinted 1952).

6. See Mary Floyd-Wilson, "Temperature, Temperance, and Racial Difference in Ben Jonson's *The Masque of Blackness*," *English Literary Renaissance* 28 (Spring 1998): 183–209. Humoralism and climate theory will continue to play a crucial role in the ongoing construction of racial categories in the seventeenth and eighteenth centuries. See Roxann Wheeler, *The Complexion of Race: Categories of Difference in Eighteenth-Century British Culture* (Philadelphia: University of Pennsylvania Press, 2000).

7. *Batman upon Bartholome, his booke De Proprietatibus rerum, newly corrected, enlarged, and ammended*, compiled by Steven Batman and translated by John Trevisa (London, 1582): fol. 223v.

8. *Airs, Waters, Places* in *Hippocratic Writings*, ed. G. E. R. Lloyd, trans. J. Chadwick and W. N. Mann (New York: Penguin, 1983). See my discussion of Hippocrates in chapter 1.

9. Schoenfeldt observes in *Bodies and Selves* that Galenic humoralism "appears at once deeply materialist and incorrigibly determinist" but "in actual practice it was possible to manipulate the humoral fluids and their concomitant behaviors through diet and evacuation" (p. 2). Once framed by the external forces of the environment, however, humoralism appears more intractable.

10. For surveys of classical environmental theory, see Richard F. Thomas, *Lands and Peoples in Roman Poetry: The Ethnographical Tradition* (Cambridge: Cambridge Philosophical Society, 1982) and Frederick Sargent II, *Hippocratic Heritage: A History of Ideas About Weather and Human Health* (New York: Pergamon Press, 1982).

11. In *Shakespeare and the Geography of Difference* (Cambridge: Cambridge University Press, 1994), John Gillies discusses how early modern writers persistently adapted ancient geographical frames to new discoveries (pp. 159–82). Renaissance mapmakers tried to "reconcile the new with the ancient, before rejecting" what would appear "to be the irreconcilable elements of an ancient theory" (p. 165). For medieval variations of the tripartite paradigm in mapping, see Friedman, *The Monstrous Races*, pp. 37–58. In the mid sixteenth century, Jean Bodin bases his geohumoralism on a tripartite structuring of the early modern world, which not only subdivides the temperate world into northern, middle, and southern regions but also incorporates the New World; see *Method for the Easy Comprehension of History* (1566), trans. Beatrice Reynolds (New York: Columbia University Press, 1945), p. 87.

12. In his study of the ethnology of Herodotus, Francois Hartog contends that the rhetoric of inversion shaped the classical historian's descriptions of non-Greek peoples. It is Herodotus' familiarity with Egyptian culture that determines his portrayal of the

lesser-known Scythians: the northern tribe's customs and nature are inferred by simply inverting the details of the Egyptian account; see Hartog, *The Mirror of Herodotus: The Representation of the Other in the Writing of History*, trans. Janet Lloyd (Berkeley: University of California Press, 1988). For a literary exploration of this paradigm, see John Michael Archer, *Old Worlds: Egypt, Southwest Asia, India, and Russia in Early Modern English Writing* (Stanford: Stanford University Press, 2001), pp. 106–11.

13. See Gillies, *Shakespeare and the Geography of Difference*, esp. pp. 37–9 and Stephen Greenblatt, *Marvelous Possessions: The Wonder of the New World* (Chicago: University of Chicago Press, 1991), pp. 122–8.

14. I use the term "Briton" here to refer to residents of the British Isles; as we shall see, however, the identity of the ancient Britons, and their kinship with the Scots, Irish, Welsh, and English, is a point of contention in early modern ethnography.

15. See Zacharasiewicz, *Die Klimatheorie, passim*.

16. Jean Bodin, *The Six Bookes of a Commonweale* (1606), trans. Richard Knolles, ed. Kenneth Douglas McRae (Cambridge, Mass.: Harvard University Press, 1962), pp. 545 and 547. In *Early Anthropology*, Hodgen notes that Bodin is extremely popular in England, citing his influence on Heylyn, Carpenter, Holinshed, Sidney, Nash, Bolton, Hobbes, Wheare, and Hakewill (pp. 283–5). See also Dean, "Bodin's *Methodus*."

17. Literary studies of early modern racialism include Eldred D. Jones, *Othello's Countrymen: The African in English Renaissance Drama* (London: Oxford University Press, 1965) and *The Elizabethan Image of Africa* (Charlottesville: University Press of Virginia, 1971); G. K. Hunter, *Dramatic Identities and Cultural Tradition: Studies in Shakespeare and his Contemporaries* (New York: Barnes and Noble Books, 1978), pp. 31–59; Elliot H. Tokson, *The Popular Image of the Black Man in English Renaissance Drama, 1550–1688* (Boston: G. K. Hall, 1982); Anthony Barthelemy, *Black Face, Maligned Race: The Representation of Blacks in English Drama from Shakespeare to Southerne* (Baton Rouge: Louisiana State University Press, 1987); Ania Loomba, *Gender, Race, Renaissance Drama* (Manchester: Manchester University Press, 1989); D'Amico, *The Moor in English Renaissance Drama*; *Women, 'Race,' and Writing in the Early Modern Period*, ed. Margo Hendricks and Patricia Parker (London and New York: Routledge, 1994); Gillies, *Shakespeare and the Geography of Difference*; Kim F. Hall, *Things of Darkness: Economies of Race and Gender in Early Modern England* (Ithaca: Cornell University Press, 1995); *Race, Ethnicity, and Power in the Renaissance*, ed. Joyce Green MacDonald (Madison: Fairleigh Dickinson University Press, 1996); Michael Neill, " 'Mulattos,' 'Blacks,' and 'Indian Moors': *Othello* and Early Modern Constructions of Human Difference," *Shakespeare Quarterly* 49 (1998): 362–74; Geraldo U. de Sousa, *Shakespeare's Cross-Cultural Encounters* (New York: St. Martin's Press, 1999); Arthur L. Little, Jr., *Shakespeare Jungle Fever: National Imperial Re-Visions of Race, Rape, and Sacrifice* (Stanford: Stanford University Press, 2000); Imtiaz H. Habib, *Shakespeare and Race: Postcolonial Praxis in the Early Modern Period* (Lanham, Md.: University Press of America, 2000); Dympna Callaghan, *Shakespeare Without Women: Representing Gender and Race on the Renaissance Stage* (London and New York: Routledge, 2000). See also the following special issues: "Constructing Race: Differentiating Peoples in the Early Modern World," *The William and Mary Quarterly* 54 (1997); "Race and Shakespeare Studies," *Shakespeare Studies*

26 (1998); "Race and Ethnicity in the Middle Ages," *The Journal of Medieval and Early Modern Studies* 31.1 (2001).

18. The environment in classical and early modern humoralism encompasses not only "air," but all six Galenic "non-naturals": air, exercise and rest, sleep and waking, food and drink, repletion and excretion, and the "accidents of the soul," or passions. The non-naturals were often presented as a "series of headings under which recommendations for regimen could be compiled." Siraisi, *Medieval and Early Renaissance Medicine*, p. 101.

19. The relationship between environmental influences and "Englishness" has received attention primarily among American historians. Initiating work in this area is Kupperman, who has argued that English colonialists feared the American climate in part because leaving England might mean leaving their "Englishness also." "Fear of Hot Climates," p. 215. In *Authorizing Experience*, Jim Egan observes that the early modern English believed in "an indissoluble bond between place and person . . . between bodies and their native soil" (p. 16). Colonial writers often claimed that New England suited their bodies better than the old world, producing, as Egan contends, an Englishness located in the body rather than the place (p. 24). What Egan and others neglect to realize is the significant resistance in England to embracing a bond between their northern, marginalized environment and their emergent national identity – a resistance that enabled the colonial writers to claim that North America is more healthful or less corrupting than their native soil.

20. See Richard Helgerson's *Forms of Nationhood: The Elizabethan Writing of England* (Chicago: University of Chicago Press, 1992), which traces England's struggle to purge its language of its perceived barbarity and form a national identity through poetry. Jodi Mikalachki's *The Legacy of Boadicea: Gender and Nation in Early Modern England* (London and New York: Routledge, 1998) finds a similar struggle in England's historiographic projects as early modern writers confront an originary history of female savagery. Debora Shuger's essay, "Irishmen, Aristocrats, and Other White Barbarians," *Renaissance Quarterly* 50 (1997): 494–525, provides a lucid discussion of the classical ethnographic paradigms of barbarism and civility as they were applied to the English in William Camden's *Britannia*, and then to the Irish in Edmund Spenser's and John Davies' tracts. She argues that the fashioning of a warrior aristocracy was rooted in a heroic form of northern barbarism. These studies share with my project an interest in the relationship between barbarism and the emergence of "Englishness" in the early modern period. Also on English identity, see Claire McEachern, *The Poetics of English Nationhood, 1590–1612* (Cambridge: Cambridge University Press, 1996).

21. William Harrison, *The Description of Britaine*, in Raphael Holinshed's *The First and Second Volumes of Chronicles* (London, 1587), p. 114. Here Harrison's geohumoralism contradicts Desdemona's knowledge ("our braines are not made hot and warmed"); however, elsewhere, in the *Description of England*, Harrison maintains that the "situation of our region, lieng neere unto the north, dooth cause the heate of our stomaches to be of somewhat greater force . . . than the inhabitants of the hotter regions . . . bicause their internall heat is not so strong as ours, which is kept in by the coldnesse of aire" (p. 165).

22. Studies of "whiteness" in the early modern period include Francesca T. Royster, "White-limed Walls: Whiteness and Gothic Extremism in Shakespeare's *Titus*

Andronicus," *Shakespeare Quarterly* 51 (2000): 432–55; Kim F. Hall's " 'These bastard signs of fair': Literary Whiteness in Shakespeare's Sonnets," *Post-Colonial Shakespeares,* ed. Ania Loomba and Martin Orkin (London: Routledge, 1998): 64–83; Mary Floyd-Wilson, "Temperature, Temperance, and Racial Difference"; Barbara Bowen, "Aemilia Lanyer and the Invention of White Womanhood," *Maids and Mistresses, Cousins and Queens: Women's Alliances in Early Modern England,* ed. Susan Frye and Karen Robertson (Oxford: Oxford University Press, 1998); Peter Erickson, "Profiles in Whiteness," *Stanford Humanities Review* 3 (1993): 98–111 and "Seeing White," *Transition* 67 (1996): 166–85; Gary Taylor, "Buying White," *Writing Race Across the Atlantic World, 1492–1763,* ed. Philip Beidler and Gary L. Taylor (New York: Palgrave, forthcoming).

23. For other important perspectives on the development of racialism in the period, see the recent work of Valerie Traub, "Mapping the Global Body," *Early Modern Visual Culture: Representation, Race, and Empire in Renaissance England,* ed. Peter Erickson and Clark Hulse (Philadelphia: University of Pennsylvania Press, 2000), pp. 44–97; Ania Loomba, " 'Delicious traffick': Racial and Religious Difference on Early Modern Stages," *Shakespeare and Race,* ed. Catherine M. S. Alexander and Stanley Wells (Cambridge: Cambridge University Press, 2000), pp. 203–24; Nabil Matur, *Turks, Moors, and Englishmen in the Age of Discovery* (New York: Columbia University Press, 1999). One possible strand that deserves further investigation is the shaping influence that the Spanish "purity of blood" laws may have had on English constructions of racial difference. See Jerome Friedman, "Jewish Conversion, the Spanish Pure Blood Laws and Reformation: A Revisionist View of Racial and Religious Antisemitism," *Sixteenth Century Journal* 18 (1987): 3–30.

24. Most scholars understand climate theory to be solely an explanation of black skin as an effect of the sun's burning heat, as it is portrayed in the refutations of sixteenth-century travel writers and the mid-seventeenth-century scientific inquiries of Sir Thomas Browne, John Bulwer, and Robert Boyle. For scientific inquiries into the "problem" of blackness, see Sir Thomas Browne, "A Digression Concerning Blackness," *Pseudodoxia Epidemica* (1646), *The Works of Sir Thomas Browne,* ed. Geoffrey Keynes, vol. II (Chicago: University of Chicago Press, 1964); John Bulwer, *Anthropometamorphosis: Man Transform'd; or, the Artificial Changeling* (London, 1650), pp. 253–5; Robert Boyle, *Experiments and Considerations Touching Colours* (London, 1664), pp. 151–67. On the debate over climate theory and blackness, see Hall, *Things of Darkness,* pp. 94–7; James Walvin, *The Black Presence: A Documentary History of the Negro in England, 1555–1860* (New York: Schocken Books, 1971), pp. 32–47; Joseph R. Washington, *Anti-Blackness in English Religion: 1500–1700* (New York: E. Mellen Press, 1984), pp. 70–101.

25. Winthrop Jordan, *White Over Black: American Attitudes Toward the Negro, 1550–1812* (Chapel Hill: University of North Carolina Press, 1968).

26. Jordan, *White Over Black,* p. 20. Jordan argues further that the "impact of the Negro's color was the more powerful upon Englishmen ... because England's principal contact with Africans came in West Africa ... where men were not merely dark but almost literally black" (p. 6).

27. What has received less attention, however, are the alternative environmental theories that travel writers invoke to explain variations in color. Jordan cites Richard Hakluyt and Peter Martyr as his two main sources that the Indians' coloration

cast doubt on climatic theories, yet both of these travel accounts also suggest that determinants such as humidity or topography would produce inconsistencies between the latitude and the inhabitant's complexion. To contend, as Jordan does, that these writers are simply blinded by the "tenacity of the old logic" (*White Over Black*, p. 14) is to underrate the complexity of geohumoralism and to overestimate the teleological drive of scientific racialism. Scholars have noted that the travel literature varies widely in its descriptions of the Indians' color: H. C. Porter, *The Inconstant Savage: England and the North American Indian, 1500–1660* (London: Duckworth, 1979), p. 226 and Alden T. Vaughan, *Roots of American Racism: Essays on the Colonial Experience* (New York: Oxford University Press, 1995), pp. 3–33.

28. Jordan's thesis that blackness produced a sense of shock in English travelers is widespread among scholars; see for example, *The French Encounter with Africans: White Response to Blacks, 1530–1880* (Bloomington: Indiana University Press, 1980), in which William B. Cohen argues that "The Africans' color drew much attention because of the shock that Europeans experienced in seeing people of dark skin... It has been argued that negative feelings for the color black are a primeval human impulse..." (p. 13). More recently, Alden T. Vaughan and Virginia Mason Vaughan have endorsed Jordan's position: "after centuries of relative ethnic isolation English men and women were jolted by sudden exposure, in print and in person, to peoples remarkably different from themselves." "Before *Othello*: Elizabethan Representations of Sub-Saharan Africans," *William and Mary Quarterly* 54 (1997): 29. The Vaughans add in a footnote that "*Some* English people were already familiar with black pigmentation, of course, because a small number of the English were of African descent. Presumably, they were quite thoroughly integrated into English society, so that the post-1550 English face-to-face encounter of whites with blacks was a relative rather than an absolute" (p. 29, n. 29). I aim to qualify this position even further by demonstrating how the construction of white, northern complexions was already dependent upon an imagined, yet "scientific," construction of black complexions, available well before the mid-sixteenth-century encounters.

Recognizing that the early modern English had a complex understanding of color difference undermines the quasi-psychological thesis that white people necessarily experience a traumatic "jolt" at the sight of blackness. See the introduction to Theodore W. Allen's *The Invention of the White Race*, vol. 1 (London and New York: Verso, 1994), which astutely recognizes that Jordan located the causes of white prejudice against blackness "outside of time... in instinct (or, at most, the unconscious). There, in an atavistic domain of aversion to black, of guilt as blackness, of blackward projection of guilt; there, in the pits of identity crisis, in the realm of dreams and symbols, Jordan said, was prefigured time out of mind the 'unthinking decision' that produced racial slavery in Anglo-America" (p. 9). Allen also notes that work by Nicholas P. Canny and P. E. H. Hair has "explicitly challenged Jordan on this question" (p. 7). Literary studies of racialism, however, remain under the shadow of Jordan's ahistorical explication of prejudice. See Hall's acknowledgement in *Things of Darkness* that her study "complements Winthrop Jordan's landmark contribution..." (p. 2).

29. For a cogent survey of the theoretical and critical scholarship regarding colonial encounters, see the introduction to *Amazons, Savages, and Machiavels: Travel*

and Colonial Writing in English, 1550–1630: An Anthology, ed. Andrew Hadfield (Oxford: Oxford University Press, 2001), pp. 1–15.

30. Although there may have been "color prejudice" in antiquity, the origin of blackness is not treated as a mystery until the early modern period. On the existence of ancient color prejudice, see Christian Delacampagne, "Racism and the West: From Praxis to Logos," *Anatomy of Racism*, ed. David Theo Goldberg (Minneapolis: University of Minnesota Press, 1990), pp. 83–8; for an opposing view, see Frank M. Snowden, Jr., *Before Color Prejudice: The Ancient View of Blacks* (Cambridge, Mass.: Harvard University Press, 1983). I find the question of ancient "color prejudice" to be a misguided one since it focuses on blackness to the exclusion of classical views of northern peculiarities. See chapter 1 for a fuller discussion of classical ethnological thought.

31. In *Black Athena: The Afroasiatic Roots of Classical Civilization* (New Brunswick: Rutgers University Press, 1987), Martin Bernal contends that the "Egyptians were 'blackened' in the 15th century, when they were very much admired. There also appears to have been a relation between blackness and Egyptian wisdom. Many medieval and Renaissance paintings portray one of the *magi* – presumably an Egyptian – as a Black" (p. 242). See also volume 11 of *The Image of the Black in Western Art*, ed. Jean Devisse and Michel Mollat (New York: W. Morrow, 1976–89), which discusses the popular representation of the wise black man in Italian Renaissance Art (p. 164). For the tradition of Egypt in the Renaissance, see Wayne Shumaker, *The Occult Sciences in the Renaissance: A Study in Intellectual Patterns* (Berkeley: University of California Press, 1972); Don Cameron Allen *Mysteriously Meant: The Rediscovery of Pagan Symbolism and Allegorical Interpretation in the Renaissance* (Baltimore: Johns Hopkins University Press, 1970); Erik Iversen, *The Myth of Egypt and its Hieroglyphs in European Tradition* (Copenhagen: GEC GAD, 1961).

32. Karl H. Dannenfeldt, "Egypt and Egyptian Antiquities in the Renaissance," *Studies in the Renaissance* 6 (1959): 10.

33. Jordan acknowledges that in English discourse the "terms Moor and Negro [were] used almost interchangeably" (*White Over Black*, p. 5), but he insists that the phrase "black Moor" was coined to draw a distinction between Negroes and the lighter Moors of North Africa. In fact, the first recorded use of "blake More" in English contradicts Jordan's assertion: the "black More" of Andrew Boorde's *The Fyrst Boke of the Introduction of Knowledge* (1547), ed. F. J. Furnivall (London: Early English Text Society, 1870), was "born in Barbary." In *A History of Greater Britain* (1521) (Edinburgh: Edinburgh University Press, 1892), John Major notes that men who "are born blackish . . . we call white Moors" (p. 90). Barthelemy has demonstrated that John Pory's English translation of Leo Africanus' *History and Description of Africa* follows the Italian version in its "darken[ing] the people of Northern Africa," providing further evidence that most English assumed Africans of any name were black (*Black Face*, pp. 12–16). See Robert Ralston Cawley's *The Voyagers and Elizabethan Drama* (London: Oxford University Press, 1938) for evidence that English authors often made little distinction between northern and western Africans on the basis of skin color.

34. This account is included in Richard Eden and Richard Willes' *The History of Travayle in the West and East Indies, and other countreys lying either way . . .* (London, 1577). I am quoting the version in Richard Hakluyt, *The Principal*

Navigations, Voyages, Traffiques, and Discoveries (1600), 8 vols. (London: J. M. Dent, 1927) IV, p. 57. The Vaughans observe that the running heads of Hakluyt attribute this anonymous description to Gainsh. "Before *Othello*," p. 25, n. 17. Since Jordan relies almost exclusively on this text in his assertion that the "Englishmen recognized that Africans south of the Sahara were not at all the same people as the much more familiar Moors" (*White Over Black*, p. 5) it is rather astonishing to discover that Gainsh's account directly contradicts his thesis.

35. See Christopher L. Miller, *Blank Darkness: Africanist Discourse in French* (Chicago: University of Chicago Press, 1985), who also contends that in the European imagination "Africa has been made to bear a double burden, of monstrousness *and* nobility" (p. 5).

36. Harrison, *Description of Britaine*, p. 114.

37. Jordan, *White Over Black*, p. 6. Hakluyt, *The Principal Navigations*, IV, p. 65.

38. It is a commonplace fear that northerners will "grow weak and languish, the more they goe towards the South . . . [they become] molten with sweat, and languished with heat." Jean Bodin, *The Six Bookes of a Commonweale*, pp. 549 and 551.

39. George Best, *A true discourse of the three Voyages of discoverie*, in Hakluyt, *The Principal Navigations*, V, pp. 180–1. Published in 1578 after Best's third voyage with Martin Frobisher, and later reprinted in the 1600 edition of Hakluyt.

40. For representative approaches to Best, see Tokson, *Popular Image of the Black Man*, p. 13; Michael Neill, "Unproper Beds: Race, Adultery, and the Hideous in *Othello*," *Shakespeare Quarterly* 40 (1989): 409; Karen Newman, *Fashioning Femininity and English Renaissance Drama* (Chicago: University of Chicago Press, 1991), pp. 78–80; Arthur Little, " 'An essence that's not seen': The Primal Scene of Racism in *Othello*," *Shakespeare Quarterly* 44 (1993): 307; Lynda E. Boose, " 'The Getting of a Lawful Race': Racial Discourse in Early Modern England and the Unrepresentable Black Woman," *Women, "Race," and Writing*, ed. Hendricks and Parker, pp. 43–4.

41. See Sara Warneke's *Images of the Educational Traveller in Early Modern England* (Leiden: E. J. Brill, 1995), especially chapter 3, for early modern anxieties concerning travel and climatic effects. In the mid seventeenth century, propaganda tracts encouraging further settlement in the new world made extravagant promises: "No country yields a more propitious ayre for our temper, than New-England, as experience hath made manifest, by all relations: manie of our people that have found themselves always weake and sickly at home, have become strong and healthy there perhaps by the dryness of the ayre and constant temper of it which seldome varies suddenly from cold to heate as it doth with us: so that Rhumes are very rare among our English here." "The Planter's Plea," [1630], quoted in Wear, "Making Sense of Health," section 4, p. 127. Given the high mortality rate of the early settlers, these rather outrageous claims indicate how ideologically malleable climate theory could be.

42. D'Amico, *The Moor in English Renaissance Drama*, p. 27.

43. Hakluyt, *The Principal Navigations*, V, pp. 174 and 172.

44. *Ibid.*, V, p. 179. Africa "is rather the moderate, temperate, and delectable habitation, where none of these troublesome things [clothes] are required, but that we may live naked and bare, as nature bringeth us foorth."

45. *Ibid.*, V, p. 187.

46. By detaching climatic discourse from humoralism, scholars have followed Best in assuming that the hereditary transmission of ethnic traits was incompatible with an environmental theory of somatic differences. For a pointed example of this presumption, see Boose, "The Getting of a Lawful Race," pp. 43–4. See also Virginia Mason Vaughan's conclusion that the "quasi-scientific suggestion that blackness was nature's defense against intense tropical sun was quickly but not universally discredited when black men and women in northern climes produced equally black children." *Othello: A Contextual History*, p. 53. She goes on to cite George Best as her textual support for this generalization. As the seventeenth-century physician Sir Thomas Browne makes clear in *Pseudodoxia Epidemica* (1646), the mystery of blackness was not a question of transmission, but origin. As I discuss in chapter 3, Browne focuses his inquiry on how "this complexion was first acquired," since "it is evidently maintained by generation" (p. 469).

47. The baby's nurse invokes geohumoralism when she refers to the "fair-faced breeders of [the Goth's] clime" (*Titus Andronicus*, 4. 2. 68–9).

48. Juan Huarte, *The Examination of Men's Wits* (1594), trans. Richard Carew (Gainesville, Fla.: Scholars' Facsimiles & Reprints, 1959). *The Examination of Men's Wits* was published first in Spanish, and then translated into English in 1594. The English version was "imprinted six times in four editions by 1616." "Introduction," by Carmen Rogers, *The Examination of Men's Wits*, p. x. Hereafter cited parenthetically in the text.

49. The degree of moisture and heat in parents of all complexions contributed to the appearance and wit of their offspring, as Huarte explains: "if the father be wise in the works of the imagination, and by means of his much heat & drinesse, take to wife a woman cold and moist in the third degree, the sonne born of such an accouplement, shalbe most untoward, if he be formed of his fathers seed, for that he made abode in a belly so cold and moist, & was maintained by a bloud so distemperat" (*The Examination of Men's Wits*, p. 318).

Work on early modern distinctions between the sexes has shown the medical discourse to be complex and inconsistent. For notable discussions of the one-sex model, see Thomas Laqueur, *Making Sex: Body and Gender from the Greeks to Freud* (Cambridge, Mass.: Harvard University Press, 1990) and Stephen Greenblatt, *Shakespearean Negotiations: The Circulation of Social Energy in Renaissance England* (Berkeley: University of California Press, 1988), pp. 66–93. Challenges to this model include Patricia Parker, "Gender Ideology, Gender Change: The Case of Marie Germain," *Critical Inquiry* 19 (1993): 348–9; Paster, *The Body Embarrassed* and "The Unbearable Coldness of Female Being"; Janet Adelman, "Making Defect Perfection: Shakespeare and the One-Sex Model," *Enacting Gender on the English Renaissance Stage*, ed. Viviana Comensoli and Anne Russell (Urbana: University of Illinois Press), pp. 23–52.

50. Best maintains that when Noah's son Ham violated his father's commandment and "craftily went about thereby to dis-inherit the off-spring of his other two brethren," God decreed that his posterity "should bee so blacke and lothsome, that it might remaine a spectacle of disobedience to all the worlde." Hakluyt, *The Principal Navigations*, v, p. 182. In the Genesis story there is no mention of blackness: Ham sees Noah naked in his tent, and Noah curses Ham's son Canaan to be a servant of servants unto his brothers. Jordan as well as others have proposed that the association

with blackness was derived from "approximately contemporaneous Talmudic and Midrashic sources" that "contained such suggestions as that 'Ham was smitten in his skin,' [and] that Noah told Ham 'your seed will be ugly and dark-skinned.'" *White Over Black*, pp. 18–19. Yet this conjecture appears to be dependent upon crucial mistranslations of the Hebrew. See David H. Aaron's "Early Rabbinic Exegesis on Noah's Son Ham and the So-Called 'Hamitic Myth,'" *Journal of the American Academy of Religion* 63 (1996): 721–59, which provides a critical analysis of the inherited distortions in translation supporting this mythic tradition. My thanks to Benjamin Braude for this citation.

51. See Benjamin Braude's essay, "The Sons of Noah and the Construction of Ethnic and Geographical Identities in the Medieval and Early Modern Periods," *William and Mary Quarterly* 54 (1997): 135–9. He notes that there is some "question as to how [Best's] view was initially received in England. The first edition of Hakluyt's *Principall Navigations* (1589) ... its concluding index ... conveys a neutral and almost respectful attitude [toward the inhabitants of Africa]" (p. 135). See also n. 25 in the Vaughans' "Before *Othello*" in the same volume of the *William and Mary Quarterly*, p. 27. Best's specific interpretation of Ham's curse did not, it seems, garner any followers among his contemporaries.

52. Jordan, *White Over Black*, p. 19.

53. *Ibid.*, p. 18.

54. Braude persuasively argues that the Noachic genealogies have "indeed been deeply rooted symbols through which Otherness and Selfness have been regularly expressed, [but] contrary to conventional assumptions, the racial identities the sons have borne have been remarkably unstable." "The Sons of Noah," p. 142. In his study *The Legend of Noah*, Don Cameron Allen insists that "Renaissance historians were quite aware that not all of Ham's descendants were black; moreover, they were far more eager to discover the scientific explanation of the Negroid type than to accept miracles." *The Legend of Noah: Renaissance Rationalism in Art, Science, and Letters* (Urbana: University of Illinois Press, 1949), p. 119.

55. T. D. Kendrick, *British Antiquity* (London: Methuen, 1950), p. 70.

56. Denys Hay, *Europe: The Emergence of an Idea* (Edinburgh University Press, 1957), p. 44.

57. The Carthaginian origin of the Irish "appears in the P. R. O. MS" of Spenser's *View*; see *The Works of Edmund Spenser: A Variorum Edition*, ed. Edwin Greenlaw, Charles Grosvenor Osgood, Frederick Morgan Padelford, and Ray Heffner (Baltimore: Johns Hopkins University Press, 1932–49), x, p. 320. On the Scots' Egyptian origins, see Andrew Hadfield, "Briton and Scythian: Tudor Representations of Irish Origins," *Irish Historical Studies* 28 (1993): 390–408; Marjorie Drexler, "Fluid Prejudice: Scottish Origin Myths in the Later Middle Age," *People, Politics and Community in the Later Middle Ages*, ed. Joel Rosenthal and Colin Richmond (Gloucester: Alan Sutton, 1987), pp. 60–76; William Matthews, "The Egyptians in Scotland: the Political History of a Myth," *Viator: Medieval and Renaissance Studies* 1 (1970): 289–306. Kendrick cites John Twynne's *De Rebus Albionicis Britannicis atque Anglicis* (1590), *British Antiquity*, p. 107.

58. A selection of studies that consider the religious and iconographic symbolism of blackness in the early modern period include volume II of *The Image of the Black in Western Art*; Washington, *Anti-Blackness in English Religion*; Paul H. D. Kaplan,

The Rise of the Black Magus in Western Art (Ann Arbor: University of Michigan Research Press, 1985); Carolyn Prager, " 'If I be Devil': English Renaissance Response to the Proverbial and Ecumenical Ethiopian," *Journal of Medieval and Renaissance Studies* 17 (1987): 257–79; Peter Erickson, "Representations of Blacks and Blackness in the Renaissance," *Criticism* 35 (1993): 499–527.

59. Emily C. Bartels, "*Othello* and Africa: Postcolonialism Reconsidered," *The William and Mary Quarterly* 54 (1997): 48. See also Ania Loomba's response to Bartels in " 'Local-Manufacture Made-in-India Othello Fellows': Issues of Race, Hybridity and Location in Post-Colonial Shakespeares," *Post-Colonial Shakespeares*, ed. Ania Loomba and Martin Orkin (London and New York: Routledge, 1998). For another perspective on Britain's early imperial impulses, see David Armitage, *The Ideological Origins of the British Empire* (Cambridge: Cambridge University Press, 2000).

60. Thomas Cogan, "To the Reader," *The Haven of Helthe* (London, 1584), ¶¶2r–¶¶3v; Thomas Wright, *The Passions of the Minde in Generall* (1604), ed. Thomas O. Sloan (Urbana: University of Illinois Press, 1971), pp. lxii–lxiii. For a brief discussion of the regional perspective applied to imported medical handbooks, see Vivian Nutton, " 'A Diet for Barbarians': Introducing Renaissance Medicine to Tudor England," *Natural Particulars: Nature and the Disciplines in Renaissance Europe*, ed. Anthony Grafton and Nancy Siraisi (Cambridge, Mass.: MIT Press, 1999), p. 280. See Thomas Elyot's explanations of how color is determined by inward and outward causes: "Colour of outwarde causes. Of colde or heate, as englyshe me[n] be white, Morie[n]s be black" (fol. 13v). His reference to these extreme complexions takes for granted the natural and parallel processes that produce "black" and "white." As a popular household text, published well before the mid-sixteenth-century surge in English travel and travel literature, *The Castel of Helthe* hints at an unquestioned acceptance of geohumoralism's relevance for Moors and Englishmen alike. *The Castel of Helthe* (London, 1534), ed. Samuel A. Tannenbaum (Delmar, New York: Scholars' Facsimiles & Reprints, 1937). See Louis B. Wright's *Middle-Class Culture in Elizabethan England* (Chapel Hill: University of North Carolina Press, 1935) on the widespread popularity of health handbooks during this period (p. 582).

61. Paster, for example, refers to the "ideal heat of the sanguine man" ("The Unbearable Coldness," p. 422).

62. On the ideological implications of humoralism, see Paster's *The Body Embarrassed, passim*. Regarding gender, see Paster, "The Unbearable Coldness." Regarding class, see Paster, "Nervous Tension."

63. Lloyd A. Thompson, *Romans and Blacks* (Norman: Oklahoma University Press, 1989), pp. 105–6.

64. Paster, "The Unbearable Coldness," p. 437.

65. On "*crasis*," see Siraisi, *Medieval and Early Renaissance Medicine*, p. 101.

66. Ian Maclean, *The Renaissance Notion of Woman* (Cambridge: Cambridge University Press, 1983), p. 34.

67. Huarte, for example, observes it is an "ill token, to have the flesh tender" – a characteristic he ascribes to women and to northerners (*The Examination of Men's Wits*, pp. 80 and 116).

68. Quoted in Charles Taylor, *Sources of the Self: The Making of Modern Identity* (Cambridge, Mass.: Harvard University Press, 1989), p. 200.

69. Harrison, *Description of Britaine*, p. 115.
70. Anderson in *Elizabethan Psychology* notes that the phlegmatic are "slothful, given to bodily pleasures, sleepy, idle, dull of wit, heavy, and slow" (p. 34). On the effeminacy of phlegmatics, see Paster, "The Unbearable Coldness."
71. Quoted in Mario Praz, *The Flaming Heart* (Gloucester, Mass.: Peter Smith, 1966), p. 91.
72. I am quoting Fink's paraphrase of Milton's sentiments, "Milton and the Theory of Climatic Influence," p. 76.
73. On the influence of Roger Ascham and the early modern Englishman's concerns about travel, see Warneke, *Images of the Educational Traveller*; on the Englishman's "spungy brain," see p. 132. Representing the opposing view, Sir Thomas Palmer (1606) contended that travel will "chase away such barbarousnesse and rudenesse as possesseth them [and] establish a more humane and sociable carriage" (quoted in *Images of the Educational Traveller*, p. 243), and a fellow observer noted how England's sons should be sent into "bolder Climates to correct their Flegm" (p. 244).
74. Hall, *Things of Darkness*, pp. 3–4. Hall acknowledges Peter Fryer's *Staying Power: The History of Black People in Britain* (London: Pluto Press, 1984) as her main source for this position.
75. Religious conflicts and interests in the period necessarily inform and produce what constitutes ethnic identity. As we shall see, the English people's notoriously changeable complexion is inextricably tied to England's shifting religious allegiances in the sixteenth century, much in the same way that the Irish people's stubborn nature is epitomized by their adherence to Catholicism. While *English Ethnicity* primarily attends to the secular implications of ethnology, I contend that there is fruitful work to be done on the ways in which geohumoral tenets shaped northern reformist theology – work I intend to take up in a later project.
76. See Mikalachki's discussion of the problems of England's historiographical discovery of its past: "the lack of any native records of antiquity . . . forced them to search for textual evidence of native origins in the records of their Roman conquerors . . . [and] when they examined these records, they found a race of barbarians more like the American "savages" and "wild Irish" of their budding colonial ventures than the civilized and powerful people of ancient Rome." *The Legacy of Boadicea*, p. 3.
77. Giraldus Cambrensis, *The Historical Works of Giraldus Cambrensis* (London: George Bell, 1881), p. 500. On the "racialism" of the Trojan myth, see Hugh A. MacDougall, *Racial Myth in English History: Trojans, Teutons, and Anglo-Saxons* (Montreal: Harvest House, Ltd., 1982), pp. 7–50.
78. See Kendrick's *British Antiquity* for a discussion of the skeptical attitude towards Geoffrey's genealogy, pp. 4–6; 89–98; see also MacDougall, *Racial Myth*, pp. 12, 18 and 21.
79. Helgerson, *Forms of Nationhood*, p. 35.
80. For a discussion of "vertical" and "horizontal" transmissions of culture, see Hodgen, *Early Anthropology*, pp. 265–7.
81. Edmund Spenser, *A View of the Present State of Ireland*, ed. Andrew Hadfield and Willy Maley (Oxford: Blackwell, 1977), p. 74.
82. Richard Verstegan, *A Restitution of Decayed Intelligence* (1605) (Ilkley: Scolar Press, 1976), p. v.

83. *Ibid.*, pp. 43 and 49.
84. *Ibid.*, pp. 51–2.
85. Kendrick notes that sixteenth-century Englishmen had been extremely "unwilling to acknowledge the barbaric Saxons as their ancestors." *British Antiquity*, p. 38. On the growing popularity of England's Saxon origins, see MacDougall, *Racial Myth*.
86. For a general approach to the theatre and its association with mutability, see Jonas Barish, *The Antitheatrical Prejudice* (Berkeley: University of California Press, 1981). Laura Levine's *Men in Women's Clothing: Anti-Theatricality and Effeminization, 1579–1642* (Cambridge: Cambridge University Press, 1994) offers a sharp analysis of the gendered "self" and its vulnerabilities in early modern attacks on the theatre. For an historicized account of early modern performance theory and its foundation in ancient physiological doctrine, see Joseph R. Roach, *The Player's Passion: Studies in the Science of Acting* (Ann Arbor: University of Michigan Press, 1993).
87. Wright, *The Passions of the Minde*, pp. 136–7.
88. *Ibid.*, p. lxii.
89. Barish, *Antitheatrical Prejudice*, pp. 102–3.

PART I CLIMATIC CULTURE: THE TRANSMISSIONS AND
TRANSMUTATIONS OF ETHNOGRAPHIC KNOWLEDGE

1. Richard Helgerson, *Forms of Nationhood: The Elizabethan Writing of England* (Chicago: University of Chicago Press, 1992), p. 243.
2. Ivan Hannaford, *Race: The History of an Idea in the West* (Baltimore: Johns Hopkins University Press, 1996), p. 28.
3. Mikhail Bakhtin, *Rabelais and His World*, trans. Helene Iswolsky (Bloomington: Indiana University Press, 1984), p. 355.

1 THE GHOST OF HIPPOCRATES: GEOHUMORAL HISTORY IN THE WEST

1. For an example of this commonplace, see Ian Smith, "Barbarian Errors: Performing Race in Early Modern England," *Shakespeare Quarterly* 49 (1998): 179–80.
2. On the popularity of Hippocrates in the early modern period, see Waldemar Zacharasiewicz, *Die Klimatheorie in der Englischen Literatur und Literaturkritik* (Stuttgart: Wilhelm Braumuller, 1977), p. 664.
3. Hippocrates, *Airs, Waters, Places*, in *Hippocratic Writings*, ed. G. E. R. Lloyd, trans. J. Chadwick and W. N. Mann (New York: Penguin, 1983), p. 161. Parenthetical citations refer to this text. On Hippocrates' climate theory, see John Block Friedman's *The Monstrous Races in Medieval Art and Thought* (Cambridge, Mass.: Harvard University Press, 1981), p. 51 and Ivan Hannaford, *Race: The History of an Idea in the West* (Baltimore: Johns Hopkins University Press, 1996), pp. 28–30.
4. Richard F. Thomas, *Lands and Peoples in Roman Poetry: The Ethnographical Tradition* (Cambridge: Cambridge Philological Society, 1982), p. 1. On this paradigm, see Francois Hartog, *The Mirror of Herodotus: The Representation of the Other in the Writing of History*, trans. Janet Lloyd (Berkeley: University of California Press, 1988). Also on Herodotus, see Hannaford, *Race*, p. 26.
5. Hippocrates, *Hippocratic Writings*, p. 163.

6. Ancient writers regularly maintained that the cold northern regions matched Africa for its peculiarities and monstrosities. In his survey of ancient and medieval ethnological writing, Friedman notes that Amazons, horned men, cannibals, men with backward turned feet, noseless men, and others were all located in the north; see *Monstrous Races*, pp. 9–18.

7. Hippocrates, *Hippocratic Writings*, p. 164.

8. On the "scythian disease," see Ann Rosalind Jones and Peter Stallybrass, "Dismantling Irena: The Sexualizing of Ireland in Early Modern England," *Nationalism and Sexualities*, ed. Andrew Parker *et al.* (New York: Routledge, 1992), p. 162.

9. On the historiographical and national significance of the barbaric women in British history, see Jodi Mikalachki's *The Legacy of Boadicea: Gender and Nation in Early Modern England* (London and New York: Routledge, 1998).

10. As Ann Rosalind Jones and Peter Stallybrass have argued with regard to Edmund Spenser's *A View of the State of Ireland*, the absence of Hippocrates' name can be as significant as its presence. It is their thesis that invoking the effeminacy of Hippocrates' Scythians in his portrait of the Irish would have undermined Spenser's argument that Ireland needed to be mollified by English forces ("Dismantling Irena," p. 163). Debora Shuger, however, maintains that "little can be inferred from [Spenser's] silence" on the Scythians' effeminacy because there is no evidence that he read Hippocrates. "Irishmen, Aristocrats, and Other White Barbarians," *Renaissance Quarterly* 50 (1997): 499, n. 16. There is, however, evidence that Spenser read Jean Bodin, and Bodin, as we shall see, makes much of the Hippocratic Scythian disease in his *Methodus* and *Six Bookes of the Commonweale*. W. L. Renwick acknowledges in the *Variorum Spenser* that "Spenser . . . was applying the latest methods as laid down by Jean Bodin . . ." *A View of the Present State of Ireland*, ed. W. L. Renwick, *The Works of Edmund Spenser: A Variorum Edition*, ed. Edwin Greenlaw, Charles Grosvenor Osgood, Frederick Morgan Padelford, and Ray Heffner (Baltimore: Johns Hopkins University Press, 1932–49), X, p. 308.

11. On the critical reception of Thomas Walkington, see John A. Popplestone and Marion White McPherson's introduction to the facsimile edition of *The Optick Glasse of Humors* (1631) (Delmar, New York: Scholars' Facsimiles & Reprints, 1981).

12. Walkington, *The Optick Glasse*, p 18. As the *Oxford English Dictionary* defines it, *crasis* is the "blending or combination of elements, 'humours,' or qualities, in the animal body." See Nancy G. Siraisi, *Medieval and Early Renaissance Medicine: An Introduction to Knowledge and Practice* (Chicago: University of Chicago Press, 1990), which explains that the "term 'complexio' was, from the twelfth century, the Latin commonly used for the Greek *crasis*, or temperament, that is to say, the balance of the qualities of hot, wet, cold, and dry resulting from the mixture of the elements in the human body" (p. 101).

13. Michael C. Schoenfeldt, *Bodies and Selves in Early Modern England: Physiology and Inwardness in Spenser, Shakespeare, Herbert, and Milton* (Cambridge: Cambridge University Press, 1999), p. 9.

14. Walkington, *The Optick Glasse*, pp. 24–5. Parenthetical citations are to this text.

15. On the significance of the spirits in the early modern period, see John Sutton's *Philosophy and Memory Traces: Descartes and Connectionism* (Cambridge: Cambridge University Press, 1998), pp. 31–49.

16. On changing conceptions of the Scythian throughout western history, see James William Johnson's "The Scythian: His Rise and Fall," *Journal of the History of Ideas* 20 (1959): 250–7.

17. In the classical texts, the association between Britain and Scythia was not uncommon, as the following verse by Florus suggests: "I don't want to be a Caesar, / Walk among the Britons . . . / And endure the Scythian winters." Johnson, "The Scythian," p. 253.

18. Aristotle, *Problemata* in *The Works of Aristotle*, trans. E. S. Forster, vol. VII (Oxford: Clarendon Press, 1927), 910b. (The *Problemata*, or in the English translation, *Problems*, had long been attributed to Aristotle (in the sixteenth century, for example), but now scholars attribute it to an unknown author whom they identify as Pseudo-Aristotle. So even though the *Problems* are not genuine Aristotle, they are included in the collected works of Aristotle. Hereafter, I will refer to this work, simply, as "Aristotle, *Problems*.")

19. Vitruvius, *On Architecture*, ed. and trans. Frank Granger (London: William Heinemann, 1931), pp. 11–13.

20. *Ibid.*, p. 13.

21. *Ibid.*, p. 17. Aristotle also notes the "dryness" of Africans: "Why are the Ethiopians and the Egyptians bandy-legged? Is it because the bodies of living creatures become distorted by heat, like logs of wood when they become dry? The condition of their hair supports this theory; for it is curlier than that of other nations, and curliness is as it were crookedness of the hair." Aristotle, *Problems*, 909a.

22. See the introduction for a discussion of the sunburn theory of blackness.

23. On coloration and densification, see Aristotle, *Problems*, 966b.

24. Pliny, *Natural History*, trans. H. Rackham, vol. I (Cambridge, Mass.: Harvard University Press, 1938), p. 321.

25. Aristotle, *The Politics*, ed. Stephen Everson, trans. Jonathan Barnes (Cambridge: Cambridge University Press, 1988), p. 165.

26. Pliny, *Natural History*, pp. 321–3.

27. On the ancient barbarian, see Anthony Pagden, *The Fall of Natural Man: The American Indian and the Origins of Comparative Ethnology* (Cambridge: Cambridge University Press, 1982), pp. 1–26 and Edith Hall, *Inventing the Barbarian: Greek Self-Definition Through Tragedy* (Oxford: Clarendon Press, 1989). See also John Gillies, *Shakespeare and the Geography of Difference* (Cambridge: Cambridge University Press, 1994) on the import of classical notions of barbarism in the early modern period, pp. 8–11.

28. Pliny, *Natural History*, p. 323.

29. Aristotle, *Problems*, 909a.

30. *Ibid.*, 910a.

31. Frank M. Snowden, Jr., *Before Color Prejudice: The Ancient View of Blacks* (Cambridge, Mass.: Harvard University Press, 1983).

32. Gillies, *Shakespeare and the Geography of Difference*, p. 9.

33. Ranulph Higden, *Polychronicon*, trans. John Trevisa, vol. I (London: Longman, 1865), pp. 51–3.

34. On Higden's role in the invention of Europe, see Denys Hay, *Europe: The Emergence of an Idea* (Edinburgh: Edinburgh University Press, 1957), p. 43.

35. Jean Paul Tilman observes that the place of Albert's birth is "uncertain"; however, "Lauingen in Swabia (now in southern West Germany), located on the Danube near the city of Ulm, is considered" likely. *Albert the Great (Albertus Magnus), The Nature of Places (De Natura Locorum)*, trans. and ed. Jean Paul Tilman, *An Appraisal of the Geographical Works of Albertus Magnus and His Contributions to Geographical Thought*, Michigan Geographical Publication 4 (1971): 14. Parenthetical citations are to this text.

36. Clarence J. Glacken, *Traces on the Rhodian Shore: Nature and Culture in Western Thought from Ancient Times to the End of the Eighteenth Century* (Berkeley: University of California Press, 1967), p. 270.

37. J. P. V. D. Balsdon, *Romans and Aliens* (London: Duckworth, 1979), p. 69 and n. 77, p. 271. In arguing a similar point in *Romans and Blacks* (Norman: University of Oklahoma Press, 1989), Lloyd A. Thompson misreads Vitruvius, claiming that the Latin writer stereotyped the "southern barbarian" as sensual (p. 102 and p. 209, n. 64), though his only evidence is a passage in Vitruvius that makes no mention of southern "sensuality."

38. Caius Julius Solinus, *The Excellent and Pleasant Worke: Collectanea Rerum Memorabilium of Caius Julius Solinus* (1587) trans. Arthur Golding (Gainesville, Fla.: Scholars' Facsimiles & Reprints, 1955), P3v.

39. Strabo quoted in Andrew Hadfield, "Briton and Scythian: Tudor Representations of Irish Origins," *Irish Historical Studies* 28 (1993): 401.

40. Julius Caesar, *Seven Commentaries on the Gallic War*, trans. Carolyn Hammond (Oxford: Oxford University Press, 1996), p. 96.

41. J. W. Johnson, "Of Differing Ages and Climes," *Journal of the History of Ideas* 21 (1960): 474.

42. *Ibid.*

43. Herodotus, *The Persian Wars*, trans. George Rawlinson (New York: Modern Library, 1942), p. 374.

44. *Ibid.*, p. 148.

45. For the iconographic associations between Venus and the sanguine complexion, see Raymond Klibansky, Erwin Panofsky, and Fritz Saxl, *Saturn and Melancholy: Studies in the History of Natural Philosophy, Religion, and Art* (New York: Basic Books, 1964), p. 397. Lawrence Babb notes that "[e]rotic love, since it is a species of desire, is a warm and moist (or sanguine) passion." *The Elizabethan Malady: A Study of Melancholia in English Literature from 1580 to 1642* (East Lansing: Michigan State College Press, 1951), p. 129.

46. Zacharasiewicz, *Die Klimatheorie*, p. 664.

47. Bodin composed *Methodus* in 1565, and thirteen Latin editions appeared between 1566 and 1650. Parenthetical citations are to the English translation by Beatrice Reynolds, *Method for the Easy Comprehension of History* (New York: Columbia University Press, 1945). Richard Knolles translated *The Six Bookes of a Commonweale* into English in 1606; citations are to the facsimile edition, ed. Kenneth Douglas McRae (Cambridge, Mass.: Harvard University Press, 1962).

   Bodin's popularity among English writers prompted Gabriel Harvey to observe that "you cannot stepp into a schollar's studye . . . but (ten to one) you shall litely find open . . . Bodin *de Republica*." Quoted in Margaret T. Hodgen's *Early Anthropology in the Sixteenth and Seventeenth Centuries* (Philadelphia: University of Philadelphia Press, 1964), p. 283. Hannaford acknowledges that Bodin's "new divisions of mankind" were translated into "the scientific classifiers of the eighteenth century," and "[h]is division of historical time into stages permitted his important conclusion that in the history of the world the North was at the beginning of its ascendancy." *Race*, p. 158.

48. Pierre Charron, *Of Wisdome*, trans. Samson Lennard (London, 1612), p. 164.

49. *Ibid.*, p. 167.

50. Babb, *The Elizabethan Malady*, p. 9.

51. Klibansky *et al.*, *Saturn and Melancholy*, pp. 61–2.

52. *Ibid.*, pp. 61–3. Levinus Lemnius in *The Touchstone of Complexions*, trans. Thomas Newton (London, 1581) writes "(as Galene saith) 'sharpnes & finenes of wit cometh of Choler, Consta[n]cy and ste[a]dfastnes of Melancholy, & Phlegm to the framying and disposing of the manners . . .' " (fol. 96r).

53. William Harrison, *The Description of Britaine* in Raphael Holinshed's *The First and Second Volumes of Chronicles* (London, 1587), p. 115.

54. See Harrison's appeal to the Aristotelian theory of counteraction in *The Description of England*, in Holinshed, *First and Second Volumes*, p. 165.

55. On gender distinctions in humoralism, see Gail Kern Paster, "The Unbearable Coldness of Female Being: Women's Imperfection and the Humoral Economy," *English Literary Renaissance* 28 (1998): 416–40.

56. For a brief survey of the traditional associations made between female/flesh and male/spirit, see Phyllis Rackin's "Historical Difference / Sexual Difference," in "Privileging Gender in Early Modern England," ed. Jean R. Brink, *Sixteenth-Century Essays and Studies* 23 (1993): 48–50.

57. I am quoting Peter Erickson, "The Moment of Race in Renaissance Studies," *Shakespeare Studies* 26 (1998): 33. On the ways in which the studies of race and sex necessarily intersect, see Londa Schiebinger, "The Anatomy of Difference: Race and Sex in Eighteenth-Century Science," *Eighteenth-Century Studies* 23 (1990): 387–405. On the social implications of the early modern humoral body, see Gail Kern Paster's *The Body Embarrassed: Drama and the Disciplines of Shame in Early Modern England* (Ithaca: Cornell University Press, 1993).

58. I am quoting Jyotsna Singh, "Othello's Identity, Postcolonial Theory, and Contemporary Rewritings of *Othello*" in *Women, "Race," and Writing in the Early Modern Period*, ed. Margo Hendricks and Patricia Parker (London and New York: Routledge, 1994), which critiques discussions of early modern racialism, for "in trying to chart the complexities of the relation between race and gender oppressions, [they] implicitly *collapse* categories of difference by assuming a common history of marginalization" (p. 291).

59. Juan Huarte, *The Examination of Men's Wits* (1594), trans. Richard Carew (Gainesville, Fla.: Scholars' Facsimiles & Reprints, 1959), p. 22.

60. Shuger, "Irishmen," p. 498. Shuger refers to Le Roy's statement: "The Ethiopians being neeere unto the Sun which burneth them with his beames, are blacke . . . On the contrary they which inhabite the cold ycie countries, have their skinne white and soft . . . both the one and the other being naturally cruell by reason of their cessive [sic] cold and heat . . . For the extreme Northern or Southern people are not ciuil by nature, nor gouerned by discipline" (p. 498).

61. For a reading of the Venetians in *The Merchant of Venice* as "English," see G. K. Hunter, *Dramatic Identities and Cultural Tradition: Studies in Shakespeare and His Contemporaries* (New York: Barnes and Noble, 1978), pp. 3–30.

62. I am quoting Flavius Vegetius Renatus, *The foure bookes of Flauius Vegetius Renatus*, trans. John Sadler (London, 1572), sig. A1v.

63. Anthony Barthelemy, *Black Face, Maligned Race: The Representation of Blacks in English Drama from Shakespeare to Southerne* (Baton Rouge: Louisiana State University Press, 1987), p. 149.

64. Elliot H. Tokson, *The Popular Image of the Black Man in English Drama, 1550–1688* (Boston: G.K. Hall, 1982), p. 57.

65. Smith, "Barbarian Errors," pp. 179–80.

66. Smith is not alone in his characterization of Aaron. Barthelemy insists that "Aaron ...exhibit[s] lecherousness..." (*Black Face*, p. 91). In *Gender, Race, Renaissance Drama* (Manchester: Manchester University Press, 1989) Ania Loomba contends that "Aaron is... easily reconciled to the stereotype of... lust" (p. 46). Conversely, Jack D'Amico's *The Moor in English Renaissance Drama* (Tampa: University of South Florida Press, 1991) notes that "[a]lthough the stereotype may identify Aaron with lust, his will to destroy seems divorced from passion" (p. 142). Tokson acknowledges that Aaron is more interested in revenge than love (*Popular Image of the Black Man*, p. 97). Consider too Jean Brink's argument that Tamora the Goth's inordinate lust must lead us to conclude that her "hue" is darker than the Roman Lavinia: "No sooner has Saturnius committed himself to the fair, 'lily-like' Lavinia, than he expresses his preference for Tamora: 'A goodly lady, trust me, of the hue / That I would choose, were I to choose anew' (I. i. 264–5). Tamora's 'hue' or complexion is never explicitly identified as dark, and a surviving contemporary illustration depicts her as white, but Saturnius' preference for her 'hue' over that of the pale Lavinia allows us to infer that [she]... may be 'colored ill.' Her erotic involvement with the black Moor Aaron, who holds her 'fett'red in amorous chains' (II. i. 15), further associates her with dark passions." Jean R. Brink, "Domesticating the Dark Lady," in *Privileging Gender in Early Modern England*, ed. Brink, p. 99. Not only is Tamora never identified as "dark," but she is repeatedly described as pale. Brink appears unable to imagine that the virtuous woman (Lavinia) may be less pale than the play's sexually charged villain. On the Goths' extreme "whiteness," see Francesca T. Royster, "White-limed Walls: Whiteness and Gothic Extremism in Shakespeare's *Titus Andronicus*," *Shakespeare Quarterly* 51 (2000): 432–55.

67. Emphasis added.

68. Thomas Dekker, *Lust's Dominion*, ed. Fredson Bowers, *The Dramatic Works of Thomas Dekker*, vol. IV (Cambridge: Cambridge University Press, 1968).

69. *A description and historicall declaration of the golden Kingdome of Guinea*, in Samuel Purchas' *Hakluytus Posthumus or Purchas His Pilgrimes* (1625), 20 vols. (New York: AMS Press, 1965), VII, p. 275. This text seems to have been influenced by Leo Africanus' *History and Description of Africa*, which played a significant role in transforming the cultural perception of the African's temperature and temperament, as I argue in chapter 6. Not only does *A description... of Guinea* contain repeated references to African jealousy – a notable point in Leo Africanus' *History*, but it also echoes his description of persons speaking angrily in the streets (Purchas, *Hakluytus Posthumus*, VII, p. 267); see Leo Africanus, *The History and Description*

of Africa (1600), trans. John Pory, 3 vols. (London: The Hakluyt Society, 1896), I, p. 185.

70. A description... of Guinea, Hakluytus Posthumus, VII, p. 270. See also VII, pp. 251 and 257–8.

71. I am quoting Alden T. Vaughan and Virginia Mason Vaughan's "Before Othello: Elizabethan Representations of Sub-Saharan Africans" (1997), a collation of the pejorative descriptions of Africans that circulated in this period. William and Mary Quarterly 54 (1997): 21.

72. Emily Bartels, "Othello and Africa: Postcolonialism Reconsidered," William and Mary Quarterly 54 (1997): 53.

73. Lynda E. Boose, "'The Getting of a Lawful Race,' Racial Discourse in Early Modern England and the Unrepresentable Black Woman," Women, "Race," and Writing, ed. Hendricks and Parker, p. 36. David Beers Quinn in The Elizabethans and the Irish (Ithaca: Cornell University Press, 1966) first advanced the argument that the Irish provided the English colonists with the "standard of savage or outlandish" behavior when they recorded their encounters with African and New World peoples (p. 26).

74. Gainsh quoted in the Vaughans' "Before Othello," William and Mary Quarterly, p. 25. Sir John Davies, A Discovery of the True Causes Why Ireland Was Never Entirely Subdued (1612), ed. James P. Myers, Jr. (Washington, DC: Catholic University of America Press, 1988), p. 171.

75. Linschoten quoted in the Vaughans' "Before Othello," p. 34. Tellingly, the Vaughans concede that Linschoten "wrote quite favorably about the Congolese and other sub-Saharan Africans," yet they only quote his negative comments. Campion is excerpted in Strangers to That Land: British Perceptions of Ireland from the Reformation to the Famine, ed. Andrew Hadfield and John McVeagh (Gerrards Cross, Buckinghamshire: Colin Smythe Limited, 1994), p. 38.

76. Campion quoted in Strangers to That Land, p. 60.

77. See Jennifer L. Morgan, "'Some Could Suckle Over Their Shoulder': Male Travelers, Female Bodies, and the Gendering of Racial Ideology, 1500–1700," William and Mary Quarterly 54 (1997): 167–92.

78. Bodin, Six Bookes, p. 557.

79. See my discussion of Bodin and jealousy in chapter 6.

80. The historical relationship between melancholy and venery is complicated. While Klibansky's Saturn and Melancholy indicates that medieval natural melancholics (cold and dry) were associated with a lack of carnality (see p. 117), Aristotle's Problems, XXX notoriously connected melancholia to sexual desire. Among early modern writers, the distinction seems to rest on whether the writer refers to cold melancholy, or choler adust – heated melancholy. Consider, for example, Jacques Ferrand's statement in On Lovesickness (1623), ed. Donald A. Beecher and Massimo Ciavolella (Syracuse: Syracuse University Press, 1990): "But the melancholy humor, hot and dry through the adustion of yellow bile, blood, or natural melancholy, is the principal cause of erotic melancholy or erotic mania, for which reason Aristotle in his Problems says that 'melancholiacs are subject to incessant sexual desire.' This would appear absurd if you understand this text to mean melancholy from an abundance of natural melancholy, that is by nature cold and dry and therefore contradictory to this disease" (p. 250).

81. Giovanni Botero, *Relations of the Most Famous Kingdomes and Common-wealths thorowout the World*, trans. R. I. (London, 1630), p. 10.
82. *Ibid.* Botero also questions Hippocrates, asking why he suggested that all "Northern Nations were unapt for generation . . . whereas the conjectures of heat and moisture, argued in their hot and fervent breathings, proceeding from the stomacke . . . are not so effectually verified in any people, as in the inhabitants of the North" (p. 10).
83. Botero, *Relations*, p. 14. See also Bodin, *Method*, p. 102.

2 BRITISH ETHNOLOGY

1. Thomas Heywood, *The Rape of Lucrece* (1638), first published 1608 (Cambridge: Chadwyck-Healey English Verse Drama Full-Text Database, 1994), lines 1609–13.
2. George Wither, *Abuses, Stript, and Whipt*, book 11, "Satyre 1" (London, 1613), p. 157.
3. On the appeal of the Brutish myths, see T. D. Kendrick, *British Antiquity* (London: Methuen, 1950), p. 38. On the shift from the Trojan genealogy to Saxon origins, see Hugh A. MacDougall, *Racial Myth in English History: Trojans, Teutons, and Anglo-Saxons* (Montreal: Harvest House, 1982).
4. A phrase adapted from John Sutton, *Philosophy and Memory Traces: Descartes to Connectionism* (Cambridge: Cambridge University Press, 1998), p. 40.
5. See Margaret T. Hodgen, *Early Anthropology in the Sixteenth and Seventeenth Centuries* (Philadelphia: University of Pennsylvania Press, 1964), p. 257.
6. Juan Huarte, *The Examination of Men's Wits* (1594), trans. Richard Carew (Gainesville, Fla.: Scholars' Facsimiles & Reprints, 1959), p. 240.
7. As R. F. Jones, *The Triumph of the English Language* (Stanford: Stanford University Press, 1953), Richard Helgerson, *Forms of Nationhood: The Elizabethan Writing of England* (Chicago: University of Chicago Press, 1992), and Jodi Mikalachki, *The Legacy of Boadicea: Gender and Nation in Early Modern England* (London and New York: Routledge, 1998) have demonstrated, sixteenth-century writers were engaged in a complex struggle with their nation's savage past – a struggle that manifested itself prominently in the ongoing projects to purge England's language, laws, and history of residual barbarism. What has not been examined, however, is the effect that these shifts in historiography had on the British people's conception of their somatically based temperament.
8. Leonard F. Dean, "Bodin's *Methodus* in England before 1625," *Studies in Philology* 39 (1942): 162.
9. Though Edmund Spenser composed *A View of the Present State of Ireland* before 1598, it was not published until 1633. See the introduction to *A View of the State of Ireland*, ed. Andrew Hadfield and Willy Maley (Oxford: Blackwell, 1997), p. xi.
10. Debora Shuger, "Irishmen, Aristocrats, and Other White Barbarians," *Renaissance Quarterly* 50 (1997): 496.
11. *Ibid.* Of course, Polydore Vergil's *Anglica Historia* (1534) had already rejected the Trojan legends and Arthurian tales to suggest that Britain had been settled by tribes "from northern Gaul moving across the Channel, a movement of barbarians that did not invest the beginnings of the British nation with any dignity or glamour." Graham Parry's *The Trophies of Time: English Antiquarians of the Seventeenth Century* (Oxford: Oxford University Press, 1995), pp. 27–8. As Arthur B. Ferguson observes, the "truly primitive character of [Britain's] early inhabitants dawned

upon Tudor intellectuals rather slowly." *Clio Unbound: Perception of the Social and Cultural Past in Renaissance England* (Durham: Duke University Press, 1979), p. 109. Sometime before 1550 the English antiquarian John Twynne had already acknowledged that the Britons were barbarians – savage in appearance and customs – but it was not until Camden's *Britannia* that historical attention shifted away from the Trojan legends to focus on the Britons' more immediate geographic origins (*Clio Unbound*, pp. 109–11). Moreover, the publication of John White's pictures of Indians, Britons, and Picts in Thomas Hariot's *A Brief and True Report of the New Found Land of Virginia* (1590) helped drive home the primitive nature of Britain's early inhabitants (p. 380). See Kendrick, *British Antiquity*; Stuart Piggott, *Ruins in a Landscape: Essays in Antiquarianism* (Edinburgh: Edinburgh University Press, 1976); Piggott, *Ancient Britons and the Antiquarian Imagination* (London: Thames and Hudson, 1989).

12. Parry, *Trophies of Time*, pp. 31–2.
13. Spenser, *A View*, pp. 44, 50–1. See Maryclaire Moroney, "Apocalypse, Ethnography, and Empire in John Derricke's *Image of Irelande* (1581) and Spenser's *View of the Present State of Ireland* (1596)," *English Literary Renaissance* 29 (1999): 371.
14. Spenser, *A View*, p. 50.
15. Shuger, "Irishmen," p. 503.
16. For a discussion of climate theory and the Irish "race" in Spenser's *View*, see Jean Feerick, "Spenser, Race, and Ire-Land," *English Literary Renaissance* 32 (2002): 85–117.
17. William Camden, *Britain*, trans. Philemon Holland (London, 1610), 1, p. 63.
18. Shuger, "Irishmen," p. 497.
19. See Nicholas Canny, "The Ideology of English Colonialization: From Ireland to America," *William and Mary Quarterly* 30 (1973): 575–98.
20. Hodgen, *Early Anthropology*, p. 257.
21. Jean Bodin, *The Six Bookes of a Commonweale* (1606), trans. Richard Knolles, ed. Kenneth Douglas McRae (Cambridge, Mass.: Harvard University Press, 1962), p. 566.
22. Bodin identifies the Turks as originally northerners, who had moved south and converted (*Six Bookes*, p. A145). Roger Ascham in *Toxophilus* (1545) notes that "After them the Turkes having an other name, but yet the same people, borne in Scythia . . ." *English Works*, ed. William Aldis Wright (Cambridge: Cambridge University Press, 1904), p. 48.
23. Quoted in Hodgen, *Early Anthropology*, p. 288.
24. Gerald of Wales, *Description of Wales*, trans. Sir Richard Colt Hoare, *The Historical Works of Giraldus Cambrensis*, ed. Thomas Wright (London: George Bell and Sons, 1881), p. 500.
25. Camden, *Britain*, p. 88.
26. I am quoting Parry, *Trophies of Time*, p. 36.
27. Parry notes "Camden was able to offer the admiration that the Romans expressed for the hardy, vigorous martial spirit of the British, and to suggest that these were the true native virtues of the race." (*Trophies of Time*, pp. 28–9).
28. Bodin, *Six Bookes*, p. 545.
29. Claire McEachern, *The Poetics of English Nationhood, 1590–1612* (Cambridge: Cambridge University Press, 1996), p. 11. McEachern discusses in particular a

quotation from Robert Doleman's *Conference About the Next Succession to the Crown* (1594), which states that "the particular formes are left unto every nation and countrey to chuse that forme of government which they shall like best, and think most fit for the natures and conditions of their people" (p. 9). Consider too the following verse lines by Fulke Greville: "Therefore ought monarckes to be providente / In weighing thinges, which though they triviall seeme, / Yet are of consequence in governemente, / As difference of dyet, custome, clyme; / Since high rais'd *Athens*, and *Pireum* port, / Had manners, and askt lawes of divers sort." Quoted in Waldemar Zacharasiewicz, *Die Klimatheorie in der Englischen Literatur und Literaturkritik* (Stuttgart: Wilhelm Braumuller, 1977), p. 195. On the complex exchanges between "medical and political institutions and their discourses," see Jonathan Gil Harris, *Foreign Bodies and the Body Politic: Discourses in Social Pathology in Early Modern England* (Cambridge: Cambridge University Press, 1998), pp. 19ff. Harris traces a shift in political languages from "Galenic notions of proportion, hierarchy, and humoral balance, to a new emphasis on the body politic's boundaries as the sites of potential corruption and contamination" – a shift that may have parallels to the movement I am tracing in this period from a fluid ethnological discourse to emergent notions of more bounded racial categories.

30. For considerations of English ethnicity in later periods, see Linda Colley, *Britons: Forging the Nation, 1707–1837* (New Haven: Yale University Press, 1992); Colin Kidd, *British Identities Before Nationalism: Ethnicity and Nationhood in the Atlantic World, 1600–1800* (Cambridge: Cambridge University Press, 1999).

31. Sutton, *Philosophy and Memory Traces*, pp. 39–40.

32. The preceding quotations on British mutability are taken from Sara Warneke's "A Taste for Newfangledness: The Destructive Potential of Novelty in Early Modern England," *Sixteenth-Century Journal* 26 (1995): 886. See also Warneke, *Images of the Educational Traveller in Early Modern England* (Leiden: E. J. Brill, 1995), which provides numerous examples to support the contention that the "English traveller's susceptibility revolved around . . . his very nationality, his 'Englishness' " (pp. 74 and *passim*).

33. Huarte, *The Examination of Men's Wits*, p. 60.

34. Joseph Hall, *Quo vadis? A Just Censure of Travell as it is commonly undertaken by the Gentlemen of our Nation* (London, 1617), p. 85. On Hall's deep familiarity with, and ambivalence toward, climate theory, see John Wands, "The Theory of Climate in the English Renaissance and *Mundus Alter et Idem*," *Acta Conventus Neo-Latini Sanctandreani* (1982), *Medieval and Renaissance Texts and Studies* 38 (1986): 519–29.

35. Andrew Boorde, *The Fyrst Boke of the Introduction of Knowledge* (1547), ed. F. J. Furnivall (London: Early English Text Society, 1870), p. 116.

36. Accompanying the woodcut is the following poem:

> I am an English man, and naked I stand here,
> Musying in my mynde what rayment I shal were;
> For now I wyll were thys, and now I wyl were that;
> Now I wyl were I cannot tel what.
> All new fashyons be plesaunt to me;
> I wyl have them, whether I thryve or thee.
> . . .
> What do I care, yf all the worlde me fayle?

I wyll get a garment, shall reche to my tayle;
Than I am a minion, for I were the new gyse.
The next yere after this I trust to be wyse,
Not only in wearing my gorgious aray,
For I wyl go to learnying a hoole somers day;
I wyll learne Latyne, Hebrew, Greeke and Frenche,
And I wyl learne Douche, sittying on my benche.
I do feare no man; all men feryth me;
I overcome my adversaries by land and by see;
I had no peere, yf to my selfe I were trew;
Because I am not so, dyvers times I do rew.
Yet I lake nothying, I have all thynge at wyll;
Yf I were wyse, and wold holde my self styl,
And medel wyth no matters not to me partayning,
But ever to be trew to God and [to] my kynge.
But I have suche matters rolling in my pate,
That I wyl speake and do, I cannot tell what;
No man shall let me, but I wyl have my mynde,
And to father, mother, and freende, I wyll be unkynde;
I wyll folow myne owne mynde and myn old trade;
Who shal let me, the devyls nayles unpared?
Yet above al thinges, new fashions I love well,
And to were them, my thryft I wyll sell.
In all this worlde, I shall have but a time;
Holde the cuppe, good felow, here is thyne and myne!

                                                                    (pp. 116–17)

37. William Harrison, *The Description of England* in Raphael Holinshed's *The First and Second Volumes of Chronicles* (London, 1587), p. 172. See Warneke, *Images of the Educational Traveller*, pp. 87–8.
38. Francis Beaumont and John Fletcher, *The Fair Maid of the Inn* in *Beaumont and Fletcher*, ed. A. R. Waller, vol. 9 (Cambridge: Cambridge University Press, 1910), p. 197. See also Robert Codrington, "A Discourse upon some Innovations of Habits and Dressings," published with Francis Hawkins' *Youths Behavior, or Decency in Conversation Amongst Men* (London, 1663), which cites Boorde's portrait as exemplifying the English people's "giddy humour . . . be from the changeable complexion of the Climate, or the peculiar influence of some phantastical Planet" (p. 54).
39. William Slatyer, *The History of Great Britanie* (1621), p. 9 and the second (unnumbered) page of "To the Reader."
40. John Deacon, *Tobacco Tortured* (London, 1616), p. 10.
41. Thomas Dekker, *The Seven Deadly Sinnes of London* (London, 1606) in *The Non-Dramatic Works of Thomas Dekker*, ed. Alexander Grossart, 4 vols. (London and Ayksburg: Hazell, Watson, and Viney, Ltd., 1884), II, pp. 59–60.
42. Helgerson, *Forms of Nationhood*, p. 243.
43. Quotations are from the sixteenth-century Scots translation. Hector Boece, *The History and Chronicles of Scotland* (1540), 2 vols., trans. John Bellenden (Edinburgh, 1821), I, pp. lix–lx.
44. Sir Thomas Craig, *De Unione Regnorum Britanniæ Tractatus* (1606) (Edinburgh: Scottish History Society, 1909), pp. 414–15.

45. Boece, *The History and Chronicles of Scotland*, pp. lvi–lvii.
46. In his discussion of the distinctions between Bellenden's translation and the English version in Holinshed's *Chronicles*, A. R. Braunmuller points out that "[William] Harrison omits Boece's claim that where the mother's milk 'fails' . . . the failure signals the mother's adultery. Further, Boece and Bellenden claim, milk from any woman other than the biological mother made the child so nursed 'degenerate from their nature and kind' [rather than as Harrison has it, "degenerate and grow out of kind"] – that is, wet-nursing made the child non-natural and from a genealogical or dynastic point of view invalid, a failed heir." "Introduction," *Macbeth*, ed. A. R. Braunmuller (Cambridge: Cambridge University Press, 1997), p. 38. It may also be possible to infer from Boece that the Scottish women have communicated through their milk a kind of Amazonian vigor to their sons. Much in the same way that the parents' natural complexions gave shape to their child's initial disposition, it was understood that milk, whether a nurse's or the mother's, could transmit "moral and ethical qualities." Gail Kern Paster, *The Body Embarrassed: Drama and the Disciplines of Shame in Early Modern England* (Ithaca: Cornell University Press, 1993), p. 200. As Kathryn Schwarz has observed, early modern texts are sprinkled with "[s]tories of children who gain martial valor through being nursed by Spartan women . . . recalling Volumnia's claim to Coriolanus: 'Thy valiantness was mine, thou suck'st it from me.' " "Missing the Breast: Desire, Disease, and the Singular Effect of Amazons," *The Body in Parts: Fantasies of Corporeality in Early Modern Europe*, ed. David Hillman and Carla Mazzio (London and New York: Routledge, 1997), pp. 152–3.
47. Sir Anthony Weldon, "A Perfect Description of the People and Country of Scotland" (1617; from the edition printed in London, 1659) in *Macbeth: Texts and Contexts*, ed. William C. Carroll (New York: Bedford / St. Martin's Press Inc., 1999), p. 295.
48. Moroney, "Apocalypse, Ethnography, and Empire," p. 364.
49. Quoted in Hodgen, *Early Anthropology*, p. 366.
50. Quoted in Dympna Callaghan's *Shakespeare Without Women: Representing Gender and Race on the Renaissance Stage* (London and New York: Routledge, 2000), p. 125.
51. Ann Rosalind Jones and Peter Stallybrass argue that "to justify the expense of such repression, as well as to justify its moral necessity, [Spenser and others] insisted upon the absolute difference between English and Irish." "Dismantling Irena: The Sexualizing of Ireland in Early Modern England," *Nationalism and Sexualities*, ed. Andrew Parker *et al.* (New York: Routledge, 1992), p. 158. Jean Feerick casts this argument in humoral terms: "by arguing for the potential *reform* of the 'unruly' Irish, the New English not only justified their presence on Irish soil . . . but effectively established an image of the Irish as essentially *irreformable*, as having a predisposition toward barbarity and humoral excess that could be countered only through constant force" ("Spenser, Race, and Ire-Land," pp. 95–6).
52. On the question of whether Spenser's *View* expresses proto-racialist views, see Shuger, "Irishmen," Jones and Stallybrass, "Dismantling Irena," and Moroney, "Apocalypse, Ethnography." See also Andrew Hadfield, *Spenser's Irish Experience: Wilde Fruit and Savage Soyl* (Oxford: Clarendon Press, 1997), Willy Maley, *Salvaging Spenser: Colonialism, Culture and Identity* (New York: St. Martin's

Press Inc., 1997); *Representing Ireland: Literature and the Origins of Conflict 1534–1660*, ed. Brendan Bradshaw, Andrew Hadfield, and Willy Maley (Cambridge: Cambridge University Press, 1993).

53. Spenser, *A View*, p. 54. As Jones and Stallybrass note, "If the so-called wild Irish were imagined in terms of a supposedly resolute virility, the fantasy of the degenerate masculinity was displaced from the barbarian onto the Catholic Anglo-Irish, or the Old English, as Spenser called them ... The denial that the Irish are transformable is set in odd juxtaposition to the total permeability of English civility by the 'wild Irish.'" "Dismantling Irena," p. 163.

54. Bodin, *Six Bookes*, p. 566.

55. Spenser, *A View*, p. 74.

56. In the notes to *A View*, Ware suggests that Spenser may have known Bellenden's Boece, who "speaks of the mantles of the ancient Scots." *The Works of Edmund Spenser: A Variorum Edition*, edited by Edwin Greenlaw, Charles Grosvenor Osgood, Frederick Morgan Padelford, and Ray Heffner (Baltimore: Johns Hopkins University Press, 1932–49), x, p. 330. For a provocative discussion of the multiple forms of Irishness, Englishness, and Scottishness in *A View*, see Willy Maley, "The British Problem in Three Tracts on Ireland by Spenser, Bacon, and Milton," *British Consciousness and Identity: The Making of Britain, 1533–1707*, ed. Brendan Bradshaw and Peter Roberts (Cambridge: Cambridge University Press, 1998), pp. 162–72.

57. Spenser, *A View*, p. 71.

58. On the degeneration of the English colonizers, see Nicholas Canny, "The Permissive Frontier: Social Control in English Settlements in Ireland and Virginia, 1550–1650," *Westward Enterprise: English Activities in Ireland, the Atlantic and America 1480–1650*, ed. K. R. Andrews, N. P. Canny, and P. E. H. Hair (Detroit: Wayne State University Press, 1979), pp. 17–44. See also Michael Neill, "Broken English and Broken Irish: Nation, Language, and the Optic of Power in Shakespeare's Histories," *Shakespeare Quarterly* 45 (1994), who likens degeneration to "going native" (p. 9). Neill also observes that Spenser blames degeneration not only on the nature of the country but on the fact that the "English, like all fallen mortals, are fatally susceptible to the lure of license and disorder" (p. 10). On the "*topos*" of degeneration of the Old English, see Patricia Coughlan, " 'Some secret scourge which shall by her come unto England': Ireland and Incivility in Spenser," *Spenser and Ireland: An Interdisciplinary Perspective* (Cork: Cork University Press, 1989), p. 49.

59. Norbert Elias, *The Civilizing Process: The Development of Manners*, trans. Edmund Jephcott (New York: Urizen Books, 1978), p. 56.

60. Ari Wesseling, "Are the Dutch Uncivilized?: Erasmus on the Batavians and his National Identity," *Erasmus of Rotterdam Society Yearbook* 13 (1993), pp. 71, 74.

61. *Ibid.*, pp. 70, 74.

62. *Ibid.*, p. 88.

63. Desiderius Erasmus, "On Good Manners For Boys," trans. Brian McGregor, ed. J. K. Sowards, *Collected Works of Erasmus* (Toronto: University of Toronto Press, 1985), x x v, p. 289. Emphasis added.

64. Elias, *The Civilizing Process*, p. 77.

65. Quoted in R. F. Jones' *The Triumph of the English Language*, p. 18.

66. Quoted in Steven Shapin's *A Social History of Truth: Civility and Science in Seventeenth-Century England* (Chicago: University of Chicago Press, 1994), pp. 75–6.

67. Elias, *The Civilizing Process*, p. 200.

68. Benedict Anderson, *Imagined Communities: Reflections on the Origin and Spread of Nationalism*, rev. edn. (London: Verso, 1991), p. 149.

69. Levinus Lemnius, *The Touchstone of Complexions*, trans. Thomas Newton (London, 1581), fol. 19r. Hereafter cited parenthetically in the text.

70. Thomas Wright, *The Passions of the Minde in Generall* (1604), ed. Thomas O. Sloan (Urbana: University of Illinois Press, 1971), pp. lviii and lxi. Hereafter cited parenthetically in the text.

71. Roger Ascham, *The Scolemaster* (1570), facsimile edition (Menston, England: The Scolar Press Limited, 1967), fol. 25v. For a thorough survey of the varied responses to Ascham's censure of travel in the early modern period, see Warneke, *Images of the Educational Traveller*.

72. Ascham, *The Scolemaster*, fol. 26r.

73. Sir Thomas Palmer, *An Essay of the Meanes how to make our Travailes, into forraine Countries, the more profitable and honourable* (1606), quoted in Warneke, *Images of the Educational Traveller*, p. 243.

74. James Howell, *Instructions for Forreine Travell* (1642) in *English Reprints* (New York: AMS Press, 1966), IV, p. 68.

75. Edward Hyde, Earl of Clarendon, quoted in Warneke, *Images of the Educational Traveller*, p. 244.

76. Ascham, *The Scolemaster*, fol. 26r.

77. Frank Whigham, *Ambition and Privilege: The Social Tropes of Elizabethan Courtesy Theory* (Berkeley: University of California Press, 1984), p. 178.

78. Ascham, *The Scolemaster*, fol. 4v.

79. *Ibid.*, fols. 4v–5r.

80. Whigham, *Ambition and Privilege*, p. 179.

81. W. Rankins, *The English Ape, the Italian Imitation, the Footesteppes of Fraunce* (London, 1588), p. 3. Rankins also cites Boorde as the painter who "made the Englyshe naked, because hee knew not of what giuse to make the chaungeable variety of his attyre" (p. 21).

82. *Ibid.*, p. 3.

83. On the melancholic malcontent, see E. E. Stoll, "Shakespeare, Marston, and the Malcontent Type," *Modern Philology* 3 (1906): 281–303; Zera S. Fink, "Jacques and the Malcontent Traveler," *Philological Quarterly* 14 (1935): 237–52; Theodore Spencer, "The Elizabethan Malcontent," *Joseph Quincy Adams Memorial Studies* (Washington: Folger Shakespeare Library, 1948), pp. 523–35; Oscar James Campbell, *Shakespeare's Satire* (Hamden, Connecticut: Archon Books, reprinted 1963), pp. 45–56, 142–67. See Lawrence Babb, *The Elizabethan Malady: A Study of Melancholia in English Literature from 1580 to 1642* (East Lansing: Michigan State College Press, 1951) for a description of the stereotypical malcontent's clothing and behavior (pp. 73–101). As Malcolm's line to Macduff suggests ("What, man, ne'er pull your hat upon your brows. Give sorrow words" (*Macbeth*, 4. 3. 209–10), the visual signs of the mourner merged easily with that of the malcontent. See also Warneke's *Images of the Educational Traveller*, pp. 124–5; 128–30;

258, which extends Babb's observations to note the associations made between the Italianated English traveler, the machiavel, and the malcontent.

3 AN INSIDE STORY OF RACE: MELANCHOLY AND ETHNOLOGY

1. The most complete survey of the various formulations of melancholia in early modern England remains Lawrence Babb, *The Elizabethan Malady: A Study of Melancholia in English Literature from 1580 to 1642* (East Lansing: Michigan State College Press, 1951).
2. "Wit's Miserie," quoted in Zera Fink's "Jaques and the Malcontent Traveler," *Philological Quarterly* 14 (1935): 246. Citing Sir Robert Dallington, who said the traveler came home with "a leprous soule and a tainted body," Fink observes that "the traveler's melancholy and railing were not merely affected but real" (pp. 243–4).
3. Babb observes that the "immediate reason [for the vogue of melancholy in England] seems to have been the imitation of the Italian affectation of melancholy by travelers returned from the Continent (*Elizabethan Malady*, p. 73), thus agreeing with Fink's conclusion that melancholy in England was initially a "fashionable pose . . . an importation of the Italianated foreign traveler." "Jaques and the Malcontent Traveler," p. 242, n. 25. Fink does note that Italians were thought to be a melancholy race, but he does not discuss the English complexion or how the adoption of melancholy may be related to conceptions of Englishness.
4. On these characteristics of black bile, see Raymond Klibansky, Erwin Panofsky, and Fritz Saxl, *Saturn and Melancholy: Studies in the History of Natural Philosophy, Religion, and Art* (New York: Basic Books, 1964), p. 63.
5. Eric Lott, *Love and Theft: Blackface Minstrelsy and the American Working Class* (New York and Oxford: Oxford University Press, 1993), p. 8.
6. Levinus Lemnius, *The Touchstone of Complexions*, trans. Thomas Newton (London, 1581), fol. 16v. On these perceptions of melancholy, see Babb, *Elizabethan Malady*, pp. 76–91. L. C. Knights argues that the transitional "economic and social organization of the state in the early seventeenth century" produced a discontented class of men whose ambitions had been thwarted. "Seventeenth-Century Melancholy," *Drama and Society in the Age of Jonson* (London: Chatto & Windus, 1937), p. 331. George Williamson, on the other hand, connects the rise in melancholic discourse to the metaphysical concept that the world was decaying. "Mutability, Decay, and Seventeenth-Century Melancholy," *English Literary History* 2 (1935): 121–50. For a survey of early modern negative responses to genial melancholy, see Winfried Schleiner, *Melancholy, Genius, and Utopia in the Renaissance* (Wiesbaden: Otto Harrassowitz, 1991).
7. Jean Bodin, *Method for the Easy Comprehension of History*, trans. Beatrice Reynolds (New York: Columbia University Press, 1945), p. 103. Hereafter cited parenthetically in the text. Aristotle's *Problem* xxx reads: "Why is it that all those who have become eminent in philosophy or politics or poetry or the arts are clearly of an atrabilious temperament, and some of them to such an extent as to be affected by diseases caused by black bile . . . For many such persons have bodily afflictions as the result of this kind of temperament, while some of them obviously possess a natural inclination to affections of this kind; in a word, they all, as has been said, are naturally atrabilious . . . this humour, namely, the atrabilious, is originally mingled in the bodily nature, for it is a mixture of heat and cold, of which two things the bodily nature consists.

Black bile, therefore, becomes both very hot and very cold . . . In most people then black bile engendered from their daily nutriment does not change their character, but merely produces an atrabilious disease. But those who naturally possess an atrabilious temperament immediately develop diverse characters in accordance with their various temperaments; for example those who are originally full of cold black bile become dull and stupid, whereas those who possess a large quantity of hot black bile become frenzied or clever or erotic or easily moved to anger and desire . . . Many too, if this heat approaches the region of the intellect, are affected by diseases of frenzy and possession; and this is the origin of Sibyls and soothsayers and all inspired persons, when they are affected not by disease but by natural temperament . . . Those in whom the excessive heat dies down to a mean temperature are atrabilious, but they are cleverer and less eccentric and in many respects superior to others either in mental accomplishments in the arts or in public life." *Problemata* in *The Works of Aristotle*, trans. E. S. Forster, vol. VII (Oxford: Clarendon Press, 1927): 953a–954a.

Schleiner, *Melancholy, Genius and Utopia*, argues that most of the prose written on melancholy in the early modern period is "an attempt to make sense of" Aristotle's *Problem* XXX (p. 22).

8. Juliana Schiesari, *The Gendering of Melancholia: Feminism, Psychoanalysis, and the Symbolics of Loss in Renaissance Literature* (Ithaca: Cornell University Press, 1992), p. 4.

9. Juan Huarte, *The Examination of Men's Wits* (1594), trans. Richard Carew (Gainesville, Fla.: Scholars' Facsimiles & Reprints, 1959), p. 116. The northerners' white fleshiness is less favorable than the temperate Spanish body, for it is ideal to be "somewhat browne . . . have blacke haire, [and be] of meane stature" (p. 116).

10. Jean Bodin, *The Six Bookes of a Commonweale* (1606), trans. Richard Knolles, ed. Kenneth Douglas McRae (Cambridge, Mass.: Harvard University Press, 1962), p. 556. One of the many reformulations of the melancholic temperament is Avicenna's contention that when melancholy is combined with other humors, it produces various behavior: "If the black bile which causes melancholy be mixed with blood it will appear coupled with joy and laughter and not accompanied by deep sadness; but if it be mixed with phlegm, it is coupled with inertia, lack of movement, and quiet; if it be mixed with yellow bile its symptoms will be unrest, violence, and obsessions, and it is like frenzy. And if it be pure black bile, then there is very great thoughtfulness, and less agitation and frenzy except when the patient is provoked and quarrels, or nourishes a hatred which he cannot forget." Quoted in Klibansky *et al.*, *Saturn and Melancholy*, p. 89.

11. Bodin, *Method*, p. 114.

12. Pierre Charron, *Of Wisdome*, trans. Samson Lennard (London, 1612), p. 167. Bodin observes that northerners "accomplish everything by force of arms like slaves and in the way of wild beasts" (*Method*, p. 115).

13. Bodin, *Method*, p. 102. Sander Gilman observes that in classical Greek texts "the image of the melancholic seems to be that of the Black," but, he hastens to add, a modern reader making this connection would actually be confusing "two types of blackness, the racial and the humoral." To support his claim that there are "two types of blackness," Gilman quotes two passages from ancient Greek physiognomy; one describes the melancholic as "governed by black bile . . . indolent, timid, ailing, and, with regard to body, swarthy and black-haired," the other states that "Those who are

too swarthy are cowardly; this applies to Egyptians and Ethiopians ... Those with very wooly hair are cowardly; this applies to the Ethiopian." Sander L. Gilman, *On Blackness Without Blacks: Essays on the Image of the Black in Germany* (Boston: G. K. Hall, 1982), p. 16. Although Gilman insists that only the second description is one of racial difference, he provides no substantial evidence for making such a distinction.

14. Bodin, *Method*, p. 113.
15. Bodin, *Six Bookes*, p. 558.
16. Schiesari, *The Gendering of Melancholia*, p. 7.
17. Marsilio Ficino, *Marsilio Ficino, The Book of Life*, trans. Charles Boer (Irving, Texas: Spring Publications, 1980), p. 6. Cited parenthetically in the text.
18. Bodin, *Method*, pp. 106 and 113.
19. Bodin, *Six Bookes*, p. 560.
20. Bodin, *Method*, p. 110.
21. *The Battle of Alcazar* (1597) (London: Malone Society Reprints, 1907), line 1399.
22. See Wayne Shumaker's *The Occult Sciences in the Renaissance: A Study in Intellectual Patterns* (Berkeley: University of California Press, 1972), p. 229. Significantly, in "*Stobaeus* XXIV, 11, Horus asks his mother Isis, 'By what cause, Mother, do men who live outside our most holy place lack our quickness of apprehension?' " (Shumaker, *Occult Sciences*, p. 229).
23. Quoted in Klibansky *et al.*, *Saturn and Melancholy*, p. 258.
24. Schiesari, *The Gendering of Melancholia*, p. 7.
25. Ficino, *The Book of Life*, pp. 7–8; emphasis added.
26. Ficino's speech in "praise of medicine" observes that "The Pythagorean and Platonic philosophers ... emanated from the fount of philosophy, Hermes Trismegistus ... the Egyptians, most ancient of all races, whose priests, without exception, were outstanding physicians, as Homer, Euripides and Plato attest." *The Letters of Marsilio Ficino*, trans. Language Department of the School of Economic Science, London, vol. III (London: Shepheard-Walwyn, 1981), pp. 22–3.
27. Huarte, *The Examination of Men's Wits*, p. 57. Hereafter in this chapter, cited parenthetically in the text.
28. Charron, *Of Wisdome*, pp. 48–9. Hereafter cited parenthetically.
29. According to Eugene F. Rice, Jr., in *The Renaissance Idea of Wisdom* (Cambridge, Mass.: Harvard University Press, 1958), Charron strives to redefine the conventional interpretations of wisdom and completes the period's gradual "transformation of *sapientia* from contemplation to action and from knowledge to virtue" (p. 178).
30. Peter Erickson, "Can We Talk about Race in *Hamlet*?" *Hamlet: New Critical Essays*, ed. Arthur F. Kinney (New York: Routledge, 2002), pp. 207–13.
31. *The Problemes of Aristotle* (Edenborough [Edinburgh], 1595), sig. F8v. A cursory survey of the nationality of the writers cited in Lawrence Babb's study of melancholy suggests that negative responses toward melancholy emanate from nations located above the Alps, while the more positive responses issue from those below the Alps. Some of the more northern texts provide mixed reviews; however, the southern texts are markedly less negative. The most enthusiastic supporters of Ficinian melancholy include Vives, Fracastoro, and Silvaticus.
32. Thomas Walkington, *The Optick Glasse of Humors* (1631) (Delmar, New York: Scholars' Facsimiles & Reprints, 1981), pp. 128 and 130.

33. Timothie Bright, *A Treatise of Melancholie* (London, 1586), p. 125.
34. Bridget Gellert Lyons, *Voices of Melancholy; Studies in Literary Treatments of Melancholy in Renaissance England* (London: Routledge, 1971), p. 128.
35. As Lyons observes, "one of the main achievements of the *Anatomy* as a work of literature is to portray the melancholy mind in action, even while it is occupied with melancholy as a formal subject" (*Voices of Melancholy*, p. 114).
36. Robert Burton, *The Anatomy of Melancholy*, ed. Holbrook Jackson (London and Toronto: J. M. Dent & Sons Ltd., 1977) section 2, pp. 43–4. Hereafter in this chapter cited parenthetically.
37. Huarte, *The Examination of Men's Wits*, p. 116.
38. Lyons, *Voices of Melancholy*, p. 142. See Burton, *Anatomy*, section 1, p. 174.
39. Quoted in Lynda E. Boose, " 'The Getting of a Lawful Race,' Racial Discourse in Early Modern England and the Unrepresentable Black Woman," *Women, "Race," and Writing in Early Modern England*, ed. Margo Hendricks and Patricia Parker (London and New York: Routledge, 1994), p. 42.
40. Sir Francis Bacon, *Sylva Sylvarum* in *The Works of Francis Bacon*, ed. James Spedding, Robert Leslie Ellis, and Douglas Denon Heath, 15 vols. (Boston: Brown and Taggard, 1860–4), IV, pp. 851–2.
41. By suggesting that the sun's heat "concocteth" rather than "soaketh" the blood, Bacon is also contending that the blood is refined into a purer substance or energy; my thanks to Gail Kern Paster for this clarification.
42. Sir Thomas Browne, *Pseudodoxia Epidemica* in *The Works of Sir Thomas Browne*, ed. Geoffrey Keynes, vol. II (Chicago: University of Chicago Press, 1964), p. 469. Cited parenthetically in the text.
43. Leo Africanus, *The History and Description of Africa* (1600), trans. John Pory, 3 vols. (London: The Hakluyt Society, 1896), I, p. 802.
44. For seventeenth-century discussions of maternal imagination, see Ambroise Paré, *On Monsters and Marvels*, trans. Janis L. Pallister (Chicago: University of Chicago Press, 1982) and Helkiah Crooke, *Microcosmographia* (London, 1615). See also Marie-Hélène Huet's consideration of this notion, *Monstrous Imagination* (Cambridge, Mass.: Harvard University Press, 1993). The notorious impressionability of the female mind (due to her excessive moisture) was typically charged with producing irregularities in births. Early modern texts abound with references to the power of a mother's imagination during conception and pregnancy as explanations for birthmarks and the birth of monsters.
45. Kim F. Hall, *Things of Darkness: Economies of Race and Gender in Early Modern England* (Ithaca: Cornell University Press, 1995), p. 87. See also Dympna Callaghan, *Shakespeare Without Women: Representing Gender and Race on the Renaissance Stage* (London and New York: Routledge, 2000), pp. 75–96.
46. Hall, *Things of Darkness*, p. 87, and all of chapter two, "Fair Texts / Dark Ladies." Hall provides readings of Browne and John Bulwer on these issues, but from a different perspective than mine. On face painting, see Frances Dolan, "Taking the Pencil Out of God's Hand: Art, Nature, and the Face-Painting Debate in Early Modern England," *PMLA* 108 (1993): 224–39; Annette Drew-Bear, *Painted Faces on the Renaissance Stage: The Moral Significance of Face-Painting Conventions* (Lewisburg: Bucknell University Press, 1994).

47. Francis Beaumont and John Fletcher, *The Knight of Malta* in *The Dramatic Works in the Beaumont and Fletcher Canon*, ed. Fredson Bowers, vol. 8 (Cambridge: Cambridge University Press, 1966). The Queen of Fez in Thomas Heywood's *The Fair Maid of the West, Parts I and II*, ed. Robert K. Turner, Jr. (Lincoln: University of Nebraska, 1967) expresses amazement when she learns that Englishwomen change their faces. Her countrywomen wear no masks, "but that which nature hath bestowed on us and our births give us freely" (1. 1. 86–7). See also Aaron's criticism of the Goths' skin in *Titus Andronicus* as "whitelimed walls, ye alehouse painted signs, / Coal-black is better than another hue / In that it scorns to bear another hue" (4. 2. 97–9). Callaghan states that Aaron "counters the dominant idea of an originary whiteness." *Shakespeare Without Women*, p. 80.

48. On the masculine aspects of darkness, see Kim F. Hall, " 'These bastard signs of fair': Literary Whiteness in Shakespeare's Sonnets" in *Post-Colonial Shakespeares*, ed. Ania Loomba and Martin Orkin (London: Routledge, 1998), p. 74.

49. As one scholar has put it, "whether Germanic or not, barbarians were generally acknowledged to be handsome. They were blond and tall, although frightfully dirty and addicted to the most unusual habits of grooming." Herwig Wolfram, "Gothic History and Historical Ethnography," *Journal of Medieval History* 7 (1981): 315.

50. Thomas Wright, *The Passions of the Minde in Generall* (1604), ed. Thomas O. Sloan (Urbana: University of Illinois Press, 1971), pp. lix and lxii. On the effeminacy of whiteness, see Callaghan, *Shakespeare Without Women*, p. 80.

51. See T. D. Kendrick's paraphrase of John Twynne, *De Rebus Albionicis Britannicis atque Anglicis* (1590), in *British Antiquity* (London: Methuen, 1950), p. 107.

52. For a fine discussion of the ethnology in Bulwer's *Anthropometamorphosis*, see Mary Baine Campbell's *Wonder and Science: Imagining Worlds in Early Modern Europe* (Ithaca: Cornell University Press, 1999), pp. 221–56.

53. John Bulwer, *Anthropometamorphosis: Man Transform'd; Or, The Artificial Changeling* (London, 1650), p. 253. Hereafter cited parenthetically. Later editions of *Anthropometamorphosis* extend the main text beyond Bulwer's concluding words about the origins of blackness.

54. Browne, *Pseudodoxia*, p. 474.

55. Although writers throughout the seventeenth century disputed climate theory as an explanation of blackness, it remained a viable body of knowledge in Europe and the New World well into the eighteenth century. See Roxann Wheeler's *The Complexion of Race: Categories of Difference in Eighteenth-Century British Culture* (Philadelphia: University of Pennsylvania Press, 2000).

56. On the import of Linnaeus' classificatory system on ethnological thought, see Margaret T. Hodgen, *Early Anthropology in the Sixteenth and Seventeenth Centuries* (Philadelphia: University of Pennsylvania Press, 1964), pp. 424–6; Richard H. Popkin, "The Philosophical Bases of Modern Racism," *Philosophy and the Civilizing Arts: Essays Presented to Herbert W. Schneider*, ed. Craig Walton and John P. Anton (Athens: Ohio University Press, 1974), pp. 134–5; Michael Banton, *The Idea of Race* (London: Tavistock Press, 1977), p. 29; Henry Louis Gates, Jr., "Critical Remarks," *Anatomy of Racism*, ed. David Theo Goldberg (Minneapolis: University of Minnesota Press, 1990), p. 320; Ivan Hannaford, *Race: The History of an Idea in the West* (Baltimore: Johns Hopkins University Press, 1996), pp. 203–4 and *passim*.

57. Paula Findlen, "Jokes of Nature and Jokes of Knowledge: The Playfulness of Scientific Discourse in Early Modern Europe," *Renaissance Quarterly* 43 (1990): 325.
58. Quoted in Hodgen, *Early Anthropology*, p. 425.

4 TAMBURLAINE AND THE STAGING OF WHITE BARBARITY

1. On the reciprocal relationship between the Elizabethan theatre and Ortelian geography, see John Gillies' *Shakespeare and the Geography of Difference* (Cambridge: Cambridge University Press, 1994). Quotation on p. 76. See in particular Gillies' citation of early modern writers who treat the theatre "as a source of ethnographic information," or a place to learn, as Richard Edwardes puts it, "The manners of all Nations" (p. 93).
2. Emily C. Bartels, *Spectacles of Strangeness: Imperialism, Alienation, and Marlowe* (Philadelphia: University of Pennsylvania Press, 1993), p. 60.
3. Greenblatt argues that the "other world" depicted in *Tamburlaine* reflects the "acquisitive energies of English merchants, entrepreneurs, and adventurers, promoters alike of trading companies and theatrical companies." *Renaissance Self-Fashioning: From More to Shakespeare* (Chicago: University of Chicago Press, 1980, rpt. 1984), p. 194. Bartels maintains that Marlowe's plays consciously questioned English superiority by dramatizing "the means through which and the ends to which alien types and imperialist ideologies, and the self defined by both, were being fashioned" (*Spectacles of Strangeness*, p. xv).
4. Lisa Hopkins has acknowledged the possible correspondence between Tamburlaine's ethnicity and the Scythian-Irish, but she fails to historicize contemporary attitudes toward the "Scythian," concluding that the term "demarcated an absolute otherness, a being so sharply inferior to civilized Western man that his very membership of the same species was open to doubt." " 'And shall I die, and this unconquered?' : Marlowe's Inverted Colonialism," *Early Modern Literary Studies* 2. 2 (1996): 1. 2. Richard Wilson has suggested that Tamburlaine's Scythian identity may align him with Ivan the Terrible, whom the English viewed with ambivalence, as a "slave-born Muscovite" and one of a "race of 'false truce-breakers, subtle foxes, and ravenous wolves, barbarous, yet cunning and unfaithful.' " "Visible Bullets: Tamburlaine the Great and Ivan the Terrible," *English Literary History* 62. 1 (1995): 60.
5. Quoted in Neil Rhodes' discussion of Tamburlaine in *The Power of Eloquence and English Renaissance Literature* (New York: Harvester/Wheatsheaf, 1992), p. 100.
6. Graham Parry, *The Trophies of Time: English Antiquarians of the Seventeenth Century* (New York: Oxford University Press, 1995), p. 36.
7. Christopher Marlowe, *Tamburlaine Parts* I *and* II, ed. Anthony B. Dawson, New Mermaids's second edition (London: A & C Black, 1997). Hereafter parenthetical citations refer to this edition.
8. The story of Tamburlaine, or Timur Khan (1336–1405), would have been available to Marlowe in a variety of sources: among them, Petrus Perondinus' *Magni Tamerlanis Scytharum Imperatoris Vita* (1553), Thomas Fortescue's *The Forest or Collection of Histories* (translated from Pedro Mexía's *Silva de Varia Lección* [1542]), and George Whetstone's *The English Mirror* (1586). All are excerpted in *Christopher Marlowe: The Plays and their Sources*, ed. Vivien Thomas and William Tydeman (London and New York: Routledge, 1994).

9. See Harry Levin's classic study *The Overreacher: A Study of Christopher Marlowe* (Cambridge, Mass.: Harvard University Press, 1952). Thomas Cartelli argues that the "danger Tamburlaine courts in 'managing arms' against the reigning gods of this earth becomes a source of transgressive pleasure for an audience whose more mundane [class] ambitions are recast in the form of heroic aspiration." *Marlowe, Shakespeare and the Economy of Theatrical Experience* (Philadelphia: University of Pennsylvania Press, 1991), p. 67.

10. See my discussion of class and ethnicity in chapter 2.

11. Greenblatt, *Renaissance Self-Fashioning*, p. 211.

12. I see some sympathy between my contention that the play celebrates Tamburlaine's northern complexion and temperament and Eugene M. Waith's description of Tamburlaine's greatness as "Herculean" in that he recognizes that the Scythian's cruelty, primitive savagery, and physicality are what make him a "hero." *The Herculean Hero in Marlowe, Chapman, Shakespeare and Dryden* (London: Chatto & Windus, 1962), pp. 60–87.

13. Glossing these lines in the New Mermaids' edition, Anthony B. Dawson explains: "The 'accidental [abnormal] heat' has parched Tamburlaine's arteries and 'dried up in his blood the radical moisture (*humidum*) which is necessary for the preservation of his natural heat (*calor*)" (p. 168). It is interesting to note that the King of Soria predicts the humoral circumstances of Tamburlaine's death well before he has burned the Koran: "May never spirit, vein, or artier feed / The cursed substance of that cruel heart, / But, wanting moisture and remorseful blood, / Dry up with anger and consume with heat!" (II: 4. 1. 176–9).

14. For a discussion of Marlowe's sources on Tamburlaine as the scourge of God, see Roy W. Battenhouse's *Marlowe's Tamburlaine: A Study in Renaissance Moral Philosophy* (Nashville: Vanderbilt University Press, 1941). Attila's barbaric invasions of Rome, Battenhouse observes, anticipated Tamburlaine's actions as scourge (pp. 130–1).

15. See David Glimp, *Increase and Multiply: Governing Cultural Reproduction in Early Modern England* (Minneapolis: University of Minnesota Press, 2003), p. 95.

16. Edmund Spenser, *A View of the State of Ireland* (1633), ed. Andrew Hadfield and Willy Maley (Oxford: Blackwell, 1997), pp. 50–1.

17. Herwig Wolfram, "Gothic History and Historical Ethnography," *Journal of Medieval History* 7 (1981): 312.

18. Robert Burton, *The Anatomy of Melancholy*, ed. Holbrook Jackson (London and Toronto: J. M. Dent & Sons Ltd., 1977), section 1, pp. 212–13.

19. *Ibid.*, "Democritus to the Reader," p. 96. Attila and Hercules are the other "visitors" that Burton names.

20. Noting Tamburlaine's "insatiable desire for movement," Mark Thornton Burnett has suggested that the Scythian represents to a certain degree the wandering masterless men and vagabonds that alarmed authorities in Elizabethan England. "Tamburlaine: An Elizabethan Vagabond," *Studies in Philology* 84 (1987): 320. As tribes of people, Scythians and Tartars were both associated with a wandering pastoral life; see Spenser's *A View*, which cites Olaus Magnus and Boemus to draw a link between the Irish-Scythian custom of "boolying" and the "Tartarians and the people about the Caspian Sea, which are naturally Scythians, to live in heards as they call them, being the very same, that the Irish boolies are, driving their cattle continually . . ." (*A View*, p. 55).

21. Louis Le Roy, *Of Vicissitude, or the Variety of Things in the Universe* (1577), trans. Joseph H. McMahon (New Haven, Conn., 1961), p. 14. Levin cites Le Roy to note that Tamburlaine stood as "an exponent of the new age" (*The Overreacher*, p. 33).

22. Le Roy, *Of Vicissitude*, p. 17.

23. Samuel Daniel, *A Defence of Ryme* (1603) in *Poems and A Defence of Ryme*, ed. Arthur Colby Sprague (Cambridge, Mass.: Harvard University Press, 1930), p. 143. Daniel contends, "all our understandings are not to be built by the square of *Greece* and *Italie*. We are the children of nature as well as they, we are not so placed out of the way of judgement, but that the same Sunne of Discretion shineth uppon us, wee have our portion of the same vertues as well as of the same vices..." (p. 139).

24. *Ibid.*, p. 140.

25. *Ibid.*, p. 142.

26. For a summary of these issues, see Gillies, *Shakespeare and the Geography of Difference*, p. 56.

27. *Ibid.*, p. 57

28. On the Psalter map, John Block Friedman observes that "to the north and...located at the edge of the world is the land of the unclean peoples associated with the names of Gog and Magog." *The Monstrous Races in Medieval Art and Thought* (Cambridge, Mass.: Harvard University Press, 1981), p. 45. The Scythians, according to Josephus in his *Histories* and Isidore of Seville, were the sons of Magog. J. W. Johnson, "The Scythian: His Rise and Fall," *Journal of the History of Ideas* 20 (1959): 255. We should note as well that by following the new geography of Ortelius, Tamburlaine refutes the classical notion of the uninhabitability of certain climatic zones. On the ways in which the Ptolemaic maps did and did not shape Ortelius' geography, see Gillies, *Shakespeare and the Geography of Difference*, p. 165. Ethel Seaton traces Tamburlaine's reliance on Ortelius in "Marlowe's Map," *Essays and Studies* 10 (1924): 13–35.

29. It is Marlowe's original detail to make Tamburlaine's wife an Egyptian.

30. Quoted in Arthur F. Kinney's *Markets of Bawdrie: The Dramatic Criticism of Stephen Gosson* (Salzburg: Salzburg Studies in English Literature, 1974), p. 79.

31. Richard Helgerson, *Forms of Nationhood: The Elizabethan Writing of England* (Chicago: University of Chicago Press, 1992), pp. 25–40.

32. For the Greeks, *barbaros* at its most literal meant people who did not speak Greek. Anthony Pagden, *The Fall of Natural Man: The American Indian and the Origins of Comparative Ethnology* (Cambridge: Cambridge University Press, 1982), p. 16. Renaissance writers often equated barbarousness with ineloquence: see Ian Smith's "Barbarian Errors: Performing Race in Early Modern England," *Shakespeare Quarterly* 49 (1998): 169. Although it is a commonplace in *Tamburlaine* criticism to note that the Scythian's words are just as powerful as his sword, few critics pay much attention to the *contradiction* inherent in representing an eloquent barbarian. A notable exception is Neil Rhodes, *The Power of Eloquence and English Renaissance Literature* (New York: Harvester/Wheatsheaf, 1992), who concedes not only the oddity of Le Roy's portrait of Tamburlaine as a "patron of Humanist learning and Renaissance culture hero" but also cites it as a "significant precedent" for Marlowe's otherwise surprising portrait of Tamburlaine as a "master of eloquence" (p. 85). We should note that it is Marlowe's original contribution to the Tamburlaine story to make the Scythian so remarkably skilled in oratory.

Notable discussions of Tamburlaine's rhetorical strengths include David H. Thurn "Sights of Power in *Tamburlaine*," *English Literary Renaissance* 19 (1989): 3–21; Greenblatt, *Renaissance Self-Fashioning*, pp. 193–221; Helen Watson-Williams, "The Power of Words: A Reading of *Tamburlaine the Great, Part I*," *English* 22 (1973): 13–18; David Daiches, *More Literary Essays* (Chicago: University of Chicago Press, 1968), pp. 42–69; Donald Peet, "The Rhetoric of Tamburlaine," *English Literary History* 26 (1959): 137–55; Levin, *The Overreacher*, pp. 29–54.

33. Helgerson, *Forms of Nationhood*, p. 243.

34. *Ibid.*, p. 200.

35. Jean E. Howard has noted the repeated references to national degeneracy in the anti-theatrical texts and connected them to the "changes in social and economic relations in sixteenth-century England," in particular the rise in vagrants and masterless men, culminating in the Elizabethan Poor Laws. *The Stage and Social Struggle in Early Modern England* (London and New York: Routledge, 1994), p. 26.

36. Though no one has made an argument about the relationship between constructions of ethnicity in *Tamburlaine* and in the anti-theatrical writings, there are several significant discussions of the way in which *Tamburlaine* is engaged in the anti-theatrical controversies. See Katharine Maus' *Inwardness and Theater in the English Renaissance* (Chicago: University of Chicago Press, 1995), pp. 72–103; Jonathan V. Crewe, "The Theatre of the Idols: Marlowe, Rankins, and Theatrical Images," *Theatre Journal* 36 (1984): 321–33. See also T. M. Pearce, "Tamburlaine's 'Discipline to his Three Sonnes': An Interpretation of *Tamburlaine, Part II*," *Modern Language Quarterly* 15 (1954): 20–1.

37. Gosson, *The Schoole of Abuse* in *Markets of Bawdrie*, pp. 90–1. Emphasis added. In "Tamburlaine's 'Discipline,' " Pearce quotes this same passage to draw a correspondence between Tamburlaine's censure of his sons' effeminacy and the state of the nation's youth. He makes no mention, however, of Tamburlaine's Scythian origins and deletes Gosson's reference to Scythia from the quotation.

38. *Ibid.*, p. 91.

39. Paraphrased by Howard, *The Stage and Social Struggle*, p. 29.

40. William Rankins, *A Mirrour of Monsters* (1587) (New York: Garland Publishing, 1973), sig. D1.

41. Philip Stubbes, *Anatomy of the Abuses in England* (Vaduz: Kraus Reprint Ltd., 1965). On English strengths, see p. 23 and on their attachment to foreign "new fangles," see p. 32.

42. *Ibid.*, p. 103.

43. *Ibid.*, p. 54.

44. I am quoting Michael Schoenfeldt's *Bodies and Selves in Early Modern England: Physiology and Inwardness in Spenser, Shakespeare, Herbert, and Milton* (Cambridge: Cambridge University Press, 1999), p. 1. On the correspondences between the flesh – its relative hardness or softness – and temperament, see Juan Huarte's *The Examination of Men's Wits* (1594), trans. Richard Carew (Gainesville, Fla.: Scholars' Facsimiles & Reprints, 1959), p. 83. On Scythian characteristics, see F. G. Butler's "The Barbarous Scythian in 'King Lear,' " *English Studies in Africa* 28 (1985): 73–9.

45. Scythians and Goths are often admired for their capacity to withstand harsh environmental conditions. To substantiate the northerner's reputation for fortitude, Jean

Bodin states that when "hunger comes upon the Scythians, they cut the veins of horses under the ears, suck the blood, and feast on the flesh, as tradition reports about the army of Tamerlane. The southerners, however, are neat and elegant and cannot endure filth." *Method for the Easy Comprehension of History*, trans. Beatrice Reynolds (New York: Columbia University Press, 1945), p. 128.

46. Quoted in Butler, "The Barbarous Scythian," p. 78. See also *The Merchant of Venice* in which the "stubborn Turks and Tartars" are inured against pity by their "brassy bosoms and rough hearts of flint" (4. 1. 30–1). In *Titus Andronicus*, the Goths characterize Tamora's heart as "unrelenting flint" in its resistance to Lavinia's pitiable appeal (2. 3. 140–1).

47. I am quoting Stephen Gosson, *Plays Confuted in Five Actions* (1582), in Kinney's *Markets of Bawdrie*, p. 192.

48. Quoted in Arthur B. Ferguson, *Utter Antiquity: Perceptions of Prehistory in Renaissance England* (Durham, NC: Duke University Press, 1993), p. 68; emphasis added. Ferguson discusses the early modern perception, following the classical tradition, that poets were "civilizers who led mankind out of the woods and mountain fastnesses where they had lived 'vagrant and dispersed like wild beasts'" (p. 31).

49. Sir Philip Sidney, *An Apology for Poetry* (1595), ed. Geoffrey Shepherd (London: Thomas Nelson, 1965), p. 98. Robert Matz observes that "The 'primitive' cultures of Ireland and the New World might suggest England's own fading warrior traditions, particularly since Sidney's equation of masculine hardness with an unsophisticated past echoes similar equations in writers such as Gosson and Philip Stubbes." "Sidney's *Defence of Poesie*: The Politics of Pleasure," *English Literary Renaissance* 25 (1995): 144–5.

50. Joseph R. Roach, *The Player's Passion: Studies in the Science of Acting*, first published 1985 (Ann Arbor: University of Michigan Press, 1993), p. 27.

51. Sidney, *Apology*, p. 118.

52. Thomas Heywood, *An Apology for Actors* (1612), *The English Stage*, ed. Arthur Freeman (New York: Garland, 1973), B4r.
    Important work on the anti-theatricalists' fears includes Jonas A. Barish, *The Antitheatrical Prejudice* (Berkeley: University of California Press, 1981) and Laura Levine, *Men in Women's Clothing: Anti-Theatricality and Effeminization, 1579–1642* (Cambridge: Cambridge University Press, 1994).

53. Richard Levin provides these and other examples in "The Contemporary Perception of Marlowe's *Tamburlaine*," *Medieval and Renaissance Drama in England*, ed. J. Leeds Barroll III and Paul Werstine (New York: AMS Press, 1984), p. 63.

54. Bartels, *Spectacles of Strangeness*, p. 64.

55. This fits with Thurn's argument that it is Tamburlaine's "determination [throughout the play] to stage his power by making it fully visible" ("Sights of Power," p. 15).

56. Bodin, *Method*, p. 97. See also Louis Le Roy's discussion of similar ideas: "Among the Arcadians it was considered churlish to know nothing about music which they learned, not for pleasure and delight, but from necessity so that from its habit might be rendered sweet and gracious what nature had made rough in them because of the coldness of the climate (much like our own) in which they were born, as well as by the continuous working of the land and the general brutality of their lives." *Of Vicissitude*, pp. 10–11.

57. Thomas Proctor, *Of the Knowledge and Conducte of Warres* (London, 1578).

58. *Ibid.*, ¶ iii r.
59. *Ibid.*, ¶ iii v.
60. Proctor puts Tamburlaine in the same category as Alexander the Great and Henry V.
61. Proctor, *Of the Knowledge*, ¶ iv r.
62. See Levin's *The Overreacher*, for example, on the critical response to the last line's anti-climactic effect (pp. 38–9).
63. Levin, *The Overreacher*, p. 41.
64. Sidney, *Apology*, p. 98.
65. Though Tamburlaine may identify his power with Machiavellian *virtù*, this does not translate to mean that he "is a romanticized dramatization of the Florentine's ideal prince," as Claude J. Summers has proposed. *Christopher Marlowe and the Politics of Power* (Salzburg: Salzburg Studies in English Literature, 1974), p. 43. As Summers also acknowledges (citing Mario Praz's *The Flaming Heart*), "Tamburlaine's role as God's scourge is incompatible with Machiavelli's thought" (p. 67). For more on Machiavelli and Tamburlaine, see Battenhouse, *Marlowe's Tamburlaine*, pp. 206–16; Irving Ribner's "The Idea of History in Marlowe's *Tamburlaine*," *English Literary History* 20 (1953): 251–66; Ribner, "Marlowe and Machiavelli," *Comparative Literature* 6 (1954): 348–56; Antonio D'Andrea, "The Aspiring Mind: A Study of the Machiavellian Element in Marlowe's *Tamburlaine*," *Yearbook of Italian Studies* (1972): 51–77.
66. Thomas Fortescue asserts that the Scythian finally paid the "debt due unto Nature" when his two sons, who were "not such as was the father," lost his empire (p. 89) and George Whetstone finds that the sons, disappointingly, in "every way [were] far unlike their father" (p. 95). *Christopher Marlowe: The Plays and their Sources*, ed. Thomas and Tydeman.
67. For many critics, Tamburlaine's "former approach to conquest" in *Part II* has "become dulled and rigidified." Cartelli, *Marlowe, Shakespeare and the Economy*, p. 90. The play's shift in focus is noted by the frontispiece to the quarto, which informs us that we have left the battlefield behind to explore more familial issues: Tamburlaine's "impassionate fury" at Zenocrate's death, "his forme of exhortation and discipline to his three Sonnes," and the "manner" of his own demise.
68. Kenneth Friedenreich contrasts this speech with Menaphon's description of Tamburlaine in *Part I*, noting that the differences in hair color, humoral complexion, and strength underscores the boys' "effeminacy [which] prohibits their becoming anything but soft courtiers." " 'Huge Greatnessee' Overthrown: The Fall of the Empire in Marlowe's *Tamburlaine* Plays," *Clio* 1 (1972): 40.
69. In a similar vein, Friedenreich argues that "Tamburlaine is compelled to violently exorcise this coward because he correctly perceived in Calyphas the threat to his empire's future. Thus Tamburlaine is seen vainly attempting to dominate the future as well as the present, ironically in the light of an historical reality that Marlowe's audiences certainly knew – the empire, in spite of Tamburlaine's staged efforts to preserve it, vanished soon after he died." " 'Huge Greatnesse' Overthrown," p. 47.
70. Pearce, "Tamburlaine's 'Discipline to his Three Sonnes,' " p. 20.
71. Quoted in Pearce, "Tamburlaine's 'Discipline to his Three Sonnes,' " p. 24.
72. Gosson, *Playes Confuted in Five Actions* (1582) in *Markets of Bawdrie*, pp. 192–3. I have modernized some of the spelling for clarity's sake.

73. In the introduction to the New Mermaids' edition of *Tamburlaine Parts* I *and* II, Dawson suggests that this speech is representative of the way early modern "secular theatre [was] taking over certain ritual forms and practices and transmuting them into theatrical rather than religious events . . . by a peculiarly theatrical magic, the body of the actor, in the person of the character, participates in the process, imparting his flesh to the raucous spectators at the Rose in a temporary and secular reenactment of Eucharistic communality" (p. xxviii).

74. Quotations taken from Levin, "Contemporary Perception of Marlowe's *Tamburlaine*," pp. 53–4.

5 TEMPERATURE AND TEMPERANCE IN BEN JONSON'S *THE MASQUE OF BLACKNESS*

1. Jonas A. Barish, "Jonson and the Loathed Stage," *A Celebration of Ben Jonson*, ed. William Blissett, Julian Patrick, and R. W. Van Fossen (Toronto and Buffalo: University of Toronto Press, 1973), pp. 27–53 and Barish, *The Antitheatrical Prejudice* (Berkeley: University of California Press, 1981).

2. I am paraphrasing Jonson's statements made in the introduction to *Hymenaei* in *Ben Jonson: The Complete Masques*, ed. Stephen Orgel (New Haven: Yale University Press, 1969), p. 75.

3. For an insightful discussion of Jonson's paradoxical relationship with his audiences, see John Gordon Sweeney III, *Jonson and the Psychology of Public Theater: To Coin the Spirit, Spend the Soul* (Princeton: Princeton University Press, 1985). See also Richard Dutton's *Ben Jonson: Authority: Criticism* (London: Macmillan, 1996).

4. Prologue to *The Alchemist* in *The Alchemist and Other Plays*, ed. Gordon Campbell (Oxford: Oxford University Press, 1995).

5. See John J. Enck, *Jonson and the Comic Truth* (Madison: University of Wisconsin Press, 1957), pp. 44–69; James D. Redwine, Jr., "Beyond Psychology: The Moral Basis of Jonson's Theory of Humour Characterizations," *English Literary History* 28 (1961): 316–34; Dutton, *Ben Jonson*, pp. 115–23; Robert S. Miola's introduction to *Every Man in His Humour* (Manchester: Manchester University Press, 2000), pp. 12–15.

6. On "racialism" in *The Masque of Blackness*, see Kim F. Hall's "Sexual Politics and Cultural Identity in *The Masque of Blackness*," *The Performance of Power: Theatrical Discourse and Politics*, ed. Sue-Ellen Case and Janelle Reinelt (Iowa City: University of Iowa Press, 1991), pp. 3–18; Yumna Siddiqi, "Dark Incontinents: The Discourses of Race and Gender in Three Renaissance Masques," *Renaissance Drama* 23 (1992), pp. 139–63; Suzy Beemer, "Masks of Blackness, Masks of Whiteness: Coloring the (Sexual) Subject in Jonson, Cary, and Fletcher," *Thamyris* 4 (1997): 223–47; Mary Floyd-Wilson, "Temperature, Temperance, and Racial Difference in Ben Jonson's *The Masque of Blackness*," *English Literary Renaissance* 28 (1998): 183–209; Richmond Barbour, "Britain and the Great Beyond: *The Masque of Blackness* at Whitehall," *Playing the Globe: Genre and Geography in English Renaissance Drama*, ed. John Gillies and Virginia Mason Vaughan (London: Associated University Presses, 1998), pp. 129–53; Bernadette Andrea, "Black Skin, The Queen's Masques: Africanist Ambivalence and Feminine Author(ity) in the Masques of *Blackness* and *Beauty*," *English Literary Renaissance* 29 (1999): 246–81.

7. Ben Jonson, *Every Man Out of His Humour* (1600), *Ben Jonson*, ed. C. H. Herford and Percy Simpson, 11 vols. (Oxford: Clarendon Press, 1925–52 [1966]), vol. III.

8. On the "spirits" in the pre-Cartesian body, see John Sutton, *Philosophy and Memory Traces: Descartes to Connectionism* (Cambridge: Cambridge University Press, 1998), pp. 38–49.

9. Quoted in Robert Shenk's "The Habits and Ben Jonson's Humours," *The Journal of Medieval and Renaissance Studies* 8 (1978): 123. Though Shenk worries over "an excessive emphasis on physiology" (p. 116) in critics' readings of Jonson's humors, his own well-informed approach also implies that it is difficult to separate "habit" from its effects on the physiological: "the tendencies of the bodily complexion could be ruled and managed, suppressed and aroused, and generally disposed by the habits . . . The humours of the soul with which Ben Jonson is mainly concerned certainly affect physiology, but generally their cause can be located in human act, specifically, in human act as retained and embodied in the various moral habits" (p. 128).

10. I am quoting Cordatus' description of Carlo Buffone in *Every Man Out of His Humour* (line 366).

11. The "Palinode" (lines 1–2) of *Cynthia's Revels* (1601), *Ben Jonson*, ed. Herford and Simpson, vol. IV.

12. I am influenced here by Terrance Dunford's essay, "Consumption of the World: Reading, Eating, and Imitation in *Every Man Out of His Humour*," *English Literary Renaissance* 14 (1984): 131–47. Dunford writes, "Sordido's book is one of many guidebooks in the play that generate the rules of behaviour exhibited by the characters of *Every Man Out* . . . *Every Man Out* is an imitation within which characters imitate the language and actions of the books they read . . . Their habits (or pretending) become natural" (p. 134).

13. On the link between the physician and the satirist, see Mary Claire Randolph, "The Medical Concept in English Renaissance Satiric Theory: Its Possible Relationships and Implications," *Studies in Philology* 38 (1941): 125–57. On the use of physical cures for mental disorders in the early modern period, see Michael MacDonald's *Mystical Bedlam: Madness, Anxiety, and Healing in Seventeenth-Century England* (Cambridge: Cambridge University Press, 1981). Some early modern texts cite theatrical deception as a curative, hence physically transformative, practice. See Alan Walworth's " 'To Laugh with Open Throate': Mad Lovers, Theatrical Cures, and Gendered Bodies in Jacobean Drama," *Enacting Gender on the Renaissance Stage*, ed. Viviana Comensoli and Anne Russell (Urbana: University of Illinois Press, 1999), pp. 53–72; Carol Thomas Neely, " 'Documents in Madness': Reading Madness and Gender in Shakespeare's Tragedies and Early Modern Culture," *Shakespeare Quarterly* 42 (1991): 315–38; Winfried Schleiner, *Melancholy, Genius, and Utopia in the Renaissance* (Wiesbaden: Otto Harrassowitz, 1991), pp. 233–309; Donald A. Beecher, "Antiochus and Stratonice: The Heritage of a Medico-Literary Motif in the Theater of the English Renaissance," *Seventeenth Century* 5 (1990): 118–20.

14. Jonson, Induction to *Every Man Out of His Humour* (1600).

15. Helen M. Ostovich argues that the end of *Every Man Out of His Humour* takes the form of a masque in " 'So Sudden and Strange a Cure': A Rudimentary Masque in *Every Man Out of His Humour*," *English Literary Renaissance* 22 (1992): 315–32.

16. *Ibid.*, p. 331.

17. Stephen Orgel, *The Illusion of Power: Political Theater in the Renaissance* (Berkeley: University of California Press, 1975), p. 56.

18. For an insightful consideration of union politics, see *Scots and Britons: Scottish Political Thought and the Union of 1603*, ed. Roger A. Mason (Cambridge: Cambridge University Press, 1994), especially the essays by Mason, Jenny Wormald, Maurice Lee Jr., and Brian P. Levack. See also Bruce Galloway, *The Union of England and Scotland, 1603–1608* (Edinburgh: John Donald, 1986); *Scotland and England, 1286–1815*, ed. Mason (Edinburgh: John Donald, 1987); and Maurice Lee, Jr., *Great Britain's Solomon: James VI and I in His Three Kingdoms* (Urbana: University of Illinois Press, 1990).

19. Jenny Wormald, "The Union of 1603," in *Scots and Britons*, ed. Mason, p. 34.

20. Galloway, *The Union*, p. 36; and "Speech of 1603," *The Political Works of James I*, ed. Charles Howard McIlwain (New York: Russell and Russell, 1965), p. 271. Galloway observes that James I "evoked the revival of Britain and reconciliation of its peoples under a monarch of mixed blood"; the Great Seal, for example, conjoined "not only English and Scottish arms but also those of Cadwallader and Edward the Confessor – the last undisputed kings of Celtic Britain and Anglo-Saxon England" (Galloway, *The Union*, p. 16).

21. See Keith M. Brown, "The Vanishing Emperor: British Kingship and Its Decline, 1603–1707," in *Scots and Britons*, ed. Mason, p. 83; Martin Butler, "The Invention of Britain and the Early Stuart Masque," *The Stuart Court and Europe: Essays in Politics and Political Culture*, ed. Malcolm Smuts (Cambridge: Cambridge University Press, 1996), p. 74.

22. *The Political Works*, ed. McIlwain, pp. 271 and 273.

23. The phrase a "world divided from the world" is taken from Virgil's first eclogue and can be less flatteringly employed to stress Britain's isolation and removal from the center of civilization. Gerald M. Maclean explores the application of this phrase in early modern English literature in *Time's Witness: Historical Representation in English Poetry, 1603–1660* (Madison: University of Wisconsin Press, 1990), cited in Richard Helgerson's *Forms of Nationhood* (Chicago: University of Chicago Press, 1992), p. 308, n. 20.

24. Butler, "The Invention of Britain," p. 74.

25. John C. Meagher, *Method and Meaning in Jonson's Masques* (London: University of Notre Dame Press, 1966), p. 111 and Alexander Leggatt, *Ben Jonson: His Vision and His Art* (New York: Methuen & Co., 1981), p. 20.

26. Stephen Orgel, *The Jonsonian Masque* (Cambridge, Mass.: Harvard University Press, 1965), p. 124. Many also interpret James' light as engendering a "Christian transformation." Dolara Cunningham, "The Jonsonian Masque as a Literary Form," *English Literary History* 22 (1955): 123; Anthony Gerard Barthelemy, *Black Face Maligned Race: The Representation of Blacks in English Drama from Shakespeare to Southerne* (Baton Rouge: Louisiana State University Press, 1987), p. 25.

27. Quotations of Jonson's masques are taken from *Ben Jonson: The Complete Masques*, ed. Stephen Orgel (New Haven: Yale University Press, 1969), cited hereafter as *The Complete Masques* or by parenthetical references to line numbers.

28. The *Oxford English Dictionary*, second edn. (Oxford: Clarendon Press, 1989) defines "ward" or "black ward" in Scots law as "Tenure by military service." Citing Spelman and Coke, the *OED* defines "blanch" as "Law Rent paid in silver, instead

of service, labour, or produce; in Scottish writers extended to a merely nominal quit-rent, not only of money, as a silver penny, but of other things," such as are listed in the text.

29. *The Trew Law of Free Monarchies, The Political Works*, ed. McIlwain, p. 62. Emphasis added.

30. *Speech of 1603, The Political Works*, ed. McIlwain, p. 301.

31. For a discussion of the union in terms of law, see Galloway, *The Union*, pp. 38–41. King James also stressed that he was not "extinguishing the name of England, but adding to it by reviving an ancient title: Arthur was king of Great Britain." Lee, *Great Britain's Solomon*, p. 118.

32. *The Trew Law of Free Monarchies*, p. 63.

33. Quotation is from Orgel, *The Jonsonian Masque*, p. 128.

34. Orgel glosses "sciential" as "endowed with the powers of science." *The Complete Masques*, p. 56. In his study *The Renaissance Idea of Wisdom* (Cambridge, Mass.: Harvard University Press, 1958), Eugene F. Rice Jr. traces what he terms the "secularization" of wisdom throughout the early modern period. This secularization is suggested by the increased privileging of an active, prudent, worldly knowledge (most often associated with *scientia*), over more speculative, contemplative wisdom (identified as *sapientia*). Jonson may be privileging James' *"sciential"* wisdom over *sapientia*, which the neoplatonists traced to southern origins. Fittingly, James' symbolic role as the British Solomon characterizes him as wiser than the Egyptians.

35. Jean Bodin, *The Six Bookes of a Commonweale* (1606), trans. Richard Knolles, ed. Kenneth Douglas McRae (Cambridge, Mass.: Harvard University Press, 1962), p. 547.

36. *Basilikon Doron, The Political Works*, ed. McIlwain, pp. 22 and 27.

37. Arthur H. Williamson, "Scots, Indians, and Empire: The Scottish Politics of Civilization, 1519–1609," *Past and Present* 150 (1996): 64.

38. Jean Bodin, *Method for the Easy Comprehension of History*, trans. Beatrice Reynolds (New York: Columbia University Press, 1945), p. 99.

39. *Basilikon Doron*, p. 22.

40. Quotation is from Orgel, *The Jonsonian Masque*, p. 123.

41. Hall, "Sexual Politics," p. 6.

42. In his notes to *The Masque of Blackness*, Jonson glosses "Albion" as "white land." *The Complete Masques*, p. 511.

43. Juan Huarte, *The Examination of Men's Wits* (1594), trans. Richard Carew (Gainesville, Fla.: Scholars Facsimiles & Reprints, 1959), p. 116.

44. Orgel glosses the "triple world" as "heaven, earth, and the underworld" (*The Complete Masques*, 55), but this phrase can also be interpreted as Asia, Europe, and Africa, or as the northern, temperate, and southern regions.

45. Andrew Boorde, *The Fyrst Boke of the Introduction of Knowledge* (1547), ed. F. J. Furnivall (London: Early English Text Society, 1870), p. 136.

46. "A Discourse of Naturalisation," quoted in Galloway, *The Union*, pp. 71–2.

47. Edmund Spenser, *A View of the State of Ireland* (1633), ed. Andrew Hadfield and Willy Maley (Oxford: Blackwell, 1997), p. 63.

48. Samuel Kliger, *The Goths in England: A Study in Seventeenth- and Eighteenth-Century Thought* (Cambridge, Mass.: Harvard University Press, 1952), p. 244.

49. *Speech of 1607, The Political Works*, ed. McIlwain, p. 294.

50. *Ibid.*, pp. 294–5.

51. Francis Bacon, "The Union of the Two Kingdoms" (Edinburgh, 1670), sig. C2v.

52. Quoted in *Ben Jonson*, ed. Herford and Simpson, x, p. 448.

53. See Barbour, "Britain and the Great Beyond," pp. 140–1.

54. Hardin Aasand, " 'To blanch an Ethiop, and revive a corse': Queen Anne and *The Masque of Blackness*," *Studies in English Literature, 1500–1900* 32 (1992): 273.

55. Ann Cline Kelly maintains that the "Queen's proviso that the royal dancers . . . appear as 'blackamores at first'" presents Jonson with "two seemingly impossible problems": the unavoidable "negative connotations of *blackness*" and the impossibility of "removing the disguises so that the masquers and spectators could join as equals." "The Challenge of the Impossible: Ben Jonson's *Masque of Blackness*," *College Language Association Journal* 20 (1977): 341–2. The issue of artistic authority is a problematic one, considering not only the panegyric aim of court performances, but also Jonson's special contribution to modern conceptions of authorship through the publication of his *Works*. A fruitful approach to Queen Anne's involvement in the masques is Marion Wynne-Davies' "The Queen's Masque: Renaissance Women and the Seventeenth-Century Court Masque," in *Gloriana's Face: Women, Public and Private, in the English Renaissance*, ed. S.P. Cerasano and Marion Wynne-Davies (Detroit: Wayne State University Press, 1992), pp. 79–104. Wynne-Davies argues that the queen's "penetration into this exclusively masculine field disrupted the court, for the Queen's masque not only challenged the gendered preserves of authorship but questioned the legitimacy of absolute male power as symbolised by the Stuart King" (p. 80). See also Hall's discussion of Anne's role in "Sexual Politics," pp. 10–12.

56. Aasand, "To Blanch an Ethiop," p. 277 and Kelly, "The Challenge of the Impossible," p. 342.

57. As William C. Carroll writes, early modern Scotland was thought to be "inhabited by . . . a near-barbarous populace descended from the Picts – the ancient, savage peoples (named 'Picts,' presumably, for being 'painted' or tattooed) absorbed by the hardly-more-civilized invading Scots between the sixth and ninth centuries." *"Macbeth": Texts and Contexts* (Boston: Bedford / St. Martin's Press, 1999), p. 271.

58. Jonson's biographer David Riggs notes that William Camden influenced Jonson's work as his teacher at Westminster, and that *Britannia* was "instrumental in shaping [Jonson's] vision of an England where the classical world was vividly present in wood nymphs, river gods, architectural forms, and curious etymologies." *Ben Jonson: A Life* (Cambridge, Mass.: Harvard University Press, 1989), p. 14.

59. William Camden, *Britain*, trans. Philemon Holland (London, 1610), p. 27.

60. Camden, *Britain*, p. 26. In discussions of this masque that both appeared in 1998, Richmond Barbour and I independently came to the conclusion that Jonson drew on Camden's text for this particular passage. See Floyd-Wilson, "Temperature, Temperance, and Racial Difference," pp. 193–5 and Barbour, "Britain and the Great Beyond," pp. 147, 150, n. 19. As this chapter will bear out, I am sympathetic to Barbour's argument that "To identify Britain with Albion, that 'white land,' and to naturalize an equation of whiteness with beauty and civility, the poet must suppress powerful contestatory discourses, alternate histories, that Camden derives from the

name" (p. 147). Though he does not focus on the issue of coloration, Thomas Worden's "The Rhetoric of Place in Ben Jonson's 'Chorographical' Entertainments and Masques," *Renaissance Forum* 3 (1998), also notes Jonson's allusion to this passage in Camden.

61. Camden, *Britain*, p. 26.
62. Camden, *Britain*, p. 115. The subject of parliamentary meetings in 1604 was "the change of the name or style of England and Scotland into the name or style of Great Brittany." Galloway, *The Union*, p. 28.
63. Camden, *Britain*, p. 31. See Barbour, "Britain and the Great Beyond," p. 147.
64. For a discussion of the traditional associations made between effeminacy and artifice in the Middle Ages, see R. Howard Bloch, "Medieval Misogyny," *Representations* 20 (1987): 1–24. See also Frances Dolan, "Taking the Pencil Out of God's Hand: Art, Nature, and the Face-Painting Debate in Early Modern England," *PMLA* 108 (1993): 224–39. Hall discusses the "link among poetic discussions of blackness, racial difference, and beauty practices which recurs throughout Renaissance texts and reveals one way in which the discourse of racial blackness is continually gendered." "Sexual Politics," p. 6. For an important discussion of the implications of painting in early modern representations of "others," see Dympna Callaghan's *Shakespeare Without Women: Representing Gender and Race on the Renaissance Stage* (London and New York: Routledge, 2000), pp. 75–96.
65. Jodi Mikalachki, *The Legacy of Boadicea: Gender and Nation in Early Modern England* (London and New York: Routledge, 1998), p. 12.
66. For a different viewpoint, see Gail Kern Paster's "The Unbearable Coldness of Female Being: Women's Imperfection and the Humoral Economy," *English Literary Renaissance* 28 (1998): 437–9, which contends that the masque has "found an opportunity to reiterate gender boundaries and mark the temperamental difference of the sexes as more fundamental than any other [i.e. race]. The theory of climates yields to the theory of temperaments" (p. 439). Paster's essay, however, does not take into account the effeminate "imperfection" of the northern complexion, regardless of gender.
67. Andrew Hadfield, "Briton and Scythian: Tudor Representations of Irish Origins," *Irish Historical Studies* 112 (1993): 390–408; William Matthews,"The Egyptians in Scotland: the Political History of a Myth," *Viator: Medieval and Renaissance Studies* 1 (1970): 289–306.
68. Camden, *Britain*, p. 7.
69. Spenser, *A View*, p. 49.
70. "The Description of Scotland," in Raphael Holinshed, *The First and Second Volumes of Chronicles* (London, 1587), p. 21.
71. For a discussion of Jonson's use of hieroglyphics, see D. J. Gordon's "The Imagery of Ben Jonson's *Masques of Blackness and Beautie*," *The Renaissance Imagination*, ed. Stephen Orgel (Berkeley: University of California Press, 1975), pp. 140–1. In *The King's Entertainment* Jonson displays his admiration for hieroglyphic writing, which he sees as a symbol of obscure knowledge and uncommon understanding. *Ben Jonson*, ed. Herford and Simpson, VII, p. 91.
72. Printed in *The Frame of Order: An Outline of Elizabethan Belief Taken from Treatises of the Late Sixteenth Century*, ed. James Winny (New York: Macmillan Co., 1957), pp. 135–6.

73. See T. D. Kendrick's paraphrase of John Twynne's *De Rebus Albionicis Britannicis atque Anglicis* (1590) in *British Antiquity* (London: Methuen, 1950), p. 107.

74. Spenser, *A View*, p. 60. Spenser refers here to Richard Stanihurst who tells the Scota story in "The Description of Ireland" in Holinshed's *Chronicles* (1577).

75. Jean Bodin, *Method*, p. 102; emphasis, added.

76. Marsilio Ficino, *Marsilio Ficino: The Book of Life*, trans. Charles Boer (Irving, Texas: Spring Publication, 1980), p. 6. For another perspective on the neoplatonic elements of Jonson's masques, see Richard S. Peterson, "Icon and Mystery in Jonson's *Masque of Beautie*," *John Donne Journal* 5 (1986): 169–99.

77. Bodin, *Method*, p. 111.

78. These lines anticipate Enobarbus' description of Cleopatra: "Age cannot wither her, nor custom stale / Her infinite variety" (2. 2. 240–1).

79. Ficino, *The Book of Life*, p. 6.

80. Sir Walter Ralegh, *The History of the World* (1614), ed. C. A. Patrides (Philadelphia: Temple University Press, 1971), pp. 126–7.

81. Ann Cline Kelly has argued that by underlining the "venerability of Ethiopia and its civilization," Jonson draws on "Africa's associations with fertility and creation... to praise in general the vitality, enlightenment, and permanence of the English nation." "The Challenge of the Impossible," pp. 349 and 344. However, Kelly neglects to consider the environmental framework which links moisture, fertility, and the South's antiquity; in this context, these associations not only qualify the south, but they are also the direct inverse of the "northern" climate's attributes.

82. Timothie Bright, *A Treatise of Melancholy* (London, 1586), p. 40.

83. See Michael T. Ryan, "Assimilating New Worlds in the Sixteenth and Seventeenth Centuries," *Comparative Studies in Society and History* 23 (1981): 532.

84. In *The King's Entertainment*, Jonson associates subtlety with Theosophia or divine wisdom. *Ben Jonson*, ed. Herford and Simpson, VII, pp. 84–5. These positive associations are tempered, of course, by the craftiness of Subtle in *The Alchemist*.

85. Bright, *Treatise of Melancholy*, p. 126.

86. Pierre Charron, *Of Wisdome*, trans. Samson Lennard (London, 1612), p. 165.

87. See in particular Stephano's affectation of melancholy in *Every Man in His Humour* (1. 2. 115–17).

88. Jonson, *The Complete Masques*, p. 510.

89. *Diodorus of Sicily*, trans. C. H. Oldfather (Cambridge, Mass.: Harvard University Press, 1935), pp. 89, 91.

90. *Ibid.*, pp. 93–5.

91. *Ibid.*, p. 91.

92. Jonson, *The Complete Masques*, p. 510.

93. The correspondences between origins and flowing water are derived from the Latin *fontes*, which means both "water fountains" and "sources." Bodin writes of the south in general: "From these people letters, useful arts, virtues, training, philosophy, religion, and lastly *humanitas* itself flowed upon earth as from a fountain" (*Method*, p. 110).

94. Quoted in Arthur Ferguson's *Clio Unbound: Perception of the Social and Cultural Past in Renaissance England* (Durham, NC: Duke University Press, 1979), p. 302.

95. *Speech of 1603*, p. 273.

96. Quoted in *Dudley Carleton to John Chamberlain, 1603–1624: Jacobean Letters*, ed. Maurice Lee, Jr. (New Brunswick: Rutgers University Press, 1972), p. 68.
97. *Ibid.*, p. 64.
98. Galloway, *The Union*, pp. 73–6.
99. Galloway notes that "The Commission [on union] dissolved under the assumption of immediate action. An English parliament was scheduled for February 1605, to discuss the Instrument [they had composed]. It was however November 1606 before Union was actually considered in detail by either national parliament" (p. 79).
100. On Carleton's antipathy toward the idea of union, see Galloway, *The Union*, pp. 61, 72; Lee, *Great Britain's Solomon*, p. 143.
101. Lee, ed., *Dudley Carleton*, pp. 34–5.
102. *Ben Jonson*, ed. Herford and Simpson, x, p. 448.
103. Galloway, *The Union*, p. 58. For England's mistrust of France during the union negotiations, see p. 72. Quotation from *Ben Jonson*, ed. Herford and Simpson, x, p. 446.
104. *Dudley Carleton*, ed. Lee, p. 61.
105. Quoted in Wormald, "The Union of 1603," p. 20.

6 OTHELLO'S JEALOUSY

1. See Robert S. Miola's introduction to *Every Man in His Humour* (1601) (Manchester: Manchester University Press, 2000): "Shakespeare's experience acting in the original *EMI* bore fruit several years later in *Othello* (1604) – his tale of jealous husbands and innocent wives. Shakespeare remembers Thorello in his choice of name for Cinthio's Moor..." (p. 65).
2. For an excellent survey of the jealousy theme in early modern English drama, see Katharine Eisaman Maus' "Horns of Dilemma: Jealousy, Gender, and Spectatorship in English Renaissance Drama," *English Literary History* 54 (1987): 561–83. See also Mark Breitenberg, *Anxious Masculinity in Early Modern England* (Cambridge: Cambridge University Press, 1996), pp. 175–201. For a more general literary history of jealousy, see Paolo Cherchi, "A Dossier for the Study of Jealousy," *Eros and Anteros: The Medical Traditions of Love in the Renaissance*, ed. Donald A. Beecher and Massimo Ciavolella (Ottawa: Dovehouse Editions, 1992), pp. 123–34; Rosemary Lloyd, *Closer and Closer Apart: Jealousy in Literature* (Ithaca: Cornell University Press, 1995). On city comedy types, see Alexander Leggatt, *Citizen Comedy in the Age of Shakespeare* (Toronto: University of Toronto Press, 1973); Theodore Leinwand, *The City Staged: Jacobean Comedy, 1603–1613* (Madison: University of Wisconsin Press, 1986). Discussions of *Othello* as inverted comedy include Barbara H. C. de Mendonca, "*Othello*: A Tragedy Built on Comic Structure," *Shakespeare Survey* 21 (1968): 31–8; Susan Snyder, *The Comic Matrix of Shakespeare's Tragedies* (Princeton: Princeton University Press, 1979), pp. 70–90; Frances Teague, "*Othello* and New Comedy," *Comparative Drama* 20 (1986): 54–64; Michael D. Bristol, "Charivari and the Comedy of Abjection in *Othello*," *Renaissance Drama* 21 (1990): 3–21. See also Teresa Flaherty, "*Othello dell'arte*: The Presence of *commedia* in Shakespeare's Tragedy" *Theatre Journal* 43 (1991): 179–94.
3. In *Shakespeare's Tragic Heroes: Slaves of Passion* (New York: Barnes and Noble, rprinted 1952), Lily B. Campbell identifies *Othello* as "a study in jealousy and in

jealousy as it affects those of different races" (p. 148). For a representative view of Othello's jealousy as an exotic passion, see Virginia Mason Vaughan, *Othello: A Contextual History* (Cambridge: Cambridge University Press, 1984). In addition to Leo Africanus' *The History and Description of Africa* (1600), Vaughan cites the portrayals of jealousy in Richard Knolles' *The Generall Historie of the Turkes* and Geoffrey Fenton's *Certaine Tragical Discourses of Bandello*, texts widely recognized as possible sources for Shakespeare's play. Making an important distinction, Vaughan notes that in both Knolles and Fenton, it is the husband's "excessive and sensual desire for his wife [that] leads to obsessive jealousy," whereas Giraldi Cinthio "provided an outside instigator in the husband's jealousy" (pp. 82–3).

Studies of race in *Othello* are too numerous to be exhaustive here, but significant work includes Eldred D. Jones, *The Elizabethan Image of Africa* (Charlottesville: University of Virginia Press, 1971); Jones, *Othello's Countrymen: The African in English Renaissance Drama* (London: Oxford University Press, 1965); G. K. Hunter, "Othello and Colour Prejudice," *Dramatic Identities and Cultural Tradition: Studies in Shakespeare and his Contemporaries* (New York: Barnes and Noble, 1978), pp. 31–59; Eliot H. Tokson, *The Popular Image of the Black Man in English Drama, 1550–1688* (Boston: G. K. Hall, 1982); Ruth Cowig, "Blacks in English Renaissance Drama and the Role of Shakespeare's Othello," *The Black Presence in English Literature*, ed. David Dabydeen (Manchester: Manchester University Press, 1985), pp. 1–25; Anthony Gerard Barthelemy, *Black Face Maligned Race: The Representation of Blacks in English Drama from Shakespeare to Southerne* (Baton Rouge: Louisiana State University Press, 1987); Martin Orkin, "*Othello* and the 'plain face' of Racism," *Shakespeare Quarterly* 38 (1987): 166–88; Ania Loomba, *Gender, Race, Renaissance Drama* (Manchester: Manchester University Press, 1989); Michael Neill, "Unproper Beds: Race, Adultery, and the Hideous in *Othello*," *Shakespeare Quarterly* 40 (1989): 383–412; Emily C. Bartels, "Making More of the Moor: Aaron, Othello, and Renaissance Refashionings of Race," *Shakespeare Quarterly* 41 (1990): 433–54; Jack D'Amico, *The Moor in English Renaissance Drama* (Tampa: University of South Florida Press, 1991); Karen Newman, *Fashioning Femininity and English Renaissance Drama* (Chicago: University of Chicago Press, 1991), pp. 71–94; James R. Aubrey, "Race and the Spectacle of the Monstrous in *Othello*," *Clio* 22 (1993): 221–38; Arthur L. Little, Jr., " 'An essence that's not seen': The Primal Scene of Racism in *Othello*," *Shakespeare Quarterly* 44 (1993): 304–24; Patricia Parker "Fantasies of 'Race' and 'Gender': Africa, *Othello*, and Bringing to the Light," *Women, "Race," and Writing in the Early Modern Period*, ed. Margo Hendricks and Patricia Parker (New York: Routledge, 1994), pp. 84–100; Jyotsna Singh, "Othello's Identity, Postcolonial Theory, and Contemporary Rewritings of *Othello*," *Women, "Race," and Writing*, ed. Hendricks and Parker, pp. 287–99; Carol Thomas Neely, "Circumscriptions and Unhousedness: *Othello* in the Borderlands," *Shakespeare and Gender: A History*, ed. Deborah Barker and Ivo Kamps (London: Verso, 1995), pp. 302–15; Emily C. Bartels, "*Othello* and Africa: Postcolonialism Reconsidered," *William and Mary Quarterly* 54 (1997): 45–64; Julia Reinhard Lupton, "*Othello* Circumcised: Shakespeare and the Pauline Discourse of Nations," *Representations* 57 (1997): 73–89; Ian Smith, "Barbarian Errors: Performing Race in Early Modern England," *Shakespeare Quarterly* 49 (1998): 168–86; Michael Neill, " 'Mulattos,' 'Blacks,' and 'Indian Moors': *Othello* and Early Modern Constructions of Human

Difference," *Shakespeare Quarterly* 49 (1998): 362–74; Dympna Callaghan, *Shakespeare Without Women: Representing Gender and Race on the Renaissance Stage* (London and New York: Routledge, 2000), pp. 75–96; Peter Erickson, "Images of White Identity in *Othello*," *Othello: New Critical Essays*, ed. Philip Kolin (New York: Routledge, 2002), pp. 133–45.

4. Giraldi Cinthio's *Gli Heccatommithi* (1566) in Geoffrey Bullough's *Narrative and Dramatic Sources of Shakespeare*, vol. VII (London and Henley: Routledge and Kegan Paul, 1973), p. 245.

5. Leo Africanus, *The History and Description of Africa* (1600), trans. John Pory, 3 vols. (London: The Hakluyt Society, 1896), I, p. 183. On the influence of Leo Africanus' history on *Othello*, see Lois Whitney "Did Shakespeare Know Leo Africanus?" *PMLA* 37 (1922): 470–83; Jones, *The Elizabethan Image of Africa*; Rosalind R. Johnson, "African Presence in Shakespearean Drama: Parallels between Othello and the Historical Leo Africanus," *Journal of African Civilizations* 7 (1985): 276–87 and "Parallels between Othello and the Historical Leo Africanus," *Bim* 18 (1986): 9–34; Bartels, "Making More of the Moor"; Jonathan Burton, " 'A most wily bird': Leo Africanus, *Othello* and the trafficking in difference," *Post-Colonial Shakespeares*, ed. Ania Loomba and Martin Orkin (London: Routledge, 1998), pp. 43–63. On the translations and transmission of Leo's text, see Oumelbanine Zhiri, *L'Afrique au miroir de l'Europe: Fortunes de Jean Leon l'Africain a la Renaissance* (Geneva: Librairie Droz, 1991) and "Leo Africanus's Description of Africa," *Travel Knowledge: European 'Discoveries' in the Early Modern Period*, ed. Ivo Kamps and Jyotsna G. Singh (New York: Palgrave, 2001), pp. 258–66.

6. The question of whether the portrayal of Othello's jealousy is exotic or domestic in its origins is related to the critical discussion of whether the play's sexual anxieties are racialized or the product of a European Christian culture. On the latter perspective, see Edward A. Snow, "Sexual Anxiety and the Male Order of Things in *Othello*," *English Literary Renaissance* 10 (1980): 384–412; Stephen Greenblatt, *Renaissance Self-Fashioning* (Chicago: University of Chicago Press, 1980), pp. 222–54. On Italianate "hypercivility," see Ann Rosalind Jones, "Italians and Others' *The White Devil*," *Staging the Renaissance: Reinterpretations of Elizabethan and Jacobean Drama*, ed. David Scott Kastan and Peter Stallybrass (New York: Routledge, 1991): 251–62.

7. Though her interests in the play differ from mine, Gail Kern Paster has also read *Othello* with an aim towards historicizing emotion. She makes the astute argument that "What we have tended not to see is how early modern physiological discourse determines a universalized language of the natural passions in *Othello*, undergirding the play's construction of gender, racial, and ethnic differences with a discourse of embodied passions in which all the play's early modern bodies – black and white, male and female, Florentine and Venetian and Moor – participate because it is the discourse in which all these early modern subjects necessarily think about the psychological sources of their own and others' behavior." Stated in "The Clear Spirit Puddled: Physiological Tropes of Passion in *Othello*," delivered at the Shakespeare Association of America meeting in Montreal, 2000. I agree that a shared early modern discourse of passions – a discourse that had yet to make clear distinctions between the body, mind, and soul – undergirds the construction of all the bodies in the play. I would add, however, that this discourse is already inflected with ethnological differences and that

these differences prove unfamiliar to modern notions of passion and ethnicity. I am grateful to Paster for sharing her important paper with me.

8. I use "inwardness" here as Michael C. Schoenfeldt explains it in *Bodies and Selves in Early Modern England: Physiology and Inwardness in Spenser, Shakespeare, Herbert, and Milton* (Cambridge: Cambridge University Press, 1999). Schoenfeldt demonstrates how "bodily condition, subjective state, and psychological character" are "fully imbricated" in the early modern period (p. 1). See also David Hillman's discussion of corporeal/psychological interiority in "Visceral Knowledge: Shakespeare, Skepticism, and the Interior of the Early Modern Body," *The Body in Parts: Fantasies of Corporeality in Early Modern Europe*, ed. David Hillman and Carla Mazzio (London and New York: Routledge, 1997), pp. 81–105. Both Hillman and Schoenfeldt follow Gail Kern Paster's approach to reading early modern physiological discourse – an approach that resists "substitut[ing] figurative where literal meanings ought to remain" but also recognizes the discourse's "master tropes of early modern social narratives." Paster, "Nervous Tension: Networks of Blood and Spirit in the Early Modern Body," *Body in Parts*, ed. Hillman and Mazzir, pp. 110–11. These discussions of embodied interiority move in a different direction from Katharine Eisaman Maus' important study *Inwardness and Theater in the English Renaissance* (Chicago: University of Chicago Press, 1995), which examines the rhetoric of inwardness in early modern legal, religious, and political discourses. Maus' work is a response to the critical movement in the mid-1980s (Francis Barker; Catherine Belsey), which had insisted that notions of "bourgeois subjectivity" or "interiority" were anachronistically imposed on Renaissance drama. Maus, *Inwardness*, p. 2. My understanding of Italian inwardness, in particular, as both corrupt and shaped by the climate has also been informed by Thomas George Olsen's dissertation, "Circe's Court: Italy and Cultural Politics in English Writing, 1530–1615" (Ohio State University, 1997).

9. I seek to reverse, for example, Ian Smith's contention that "Iago is invested with the notoriously 'Moor-like' quality of jealousy." "Barbarian Errors," p. 180.

10. Maus, "Horns of Dilemma," p. 562.

11. Quotation from Miola's edition. Miola notes that this speech is quoted in Robert Allot's *England's Parnassus* (1600, p. 143) "under the heading 'Jealousy' " (p. 121).

12. Jealousy is sometimes identified as a species of melancholy. See Robert Burton's *The Anatomy of Melancholy*, ed. Holbrook Jackson (London: J. M. Dent and Sons, 1977), section 3, pp. 257–311.

13. This speech is often praised for its "realism." In the introduction to the Mermaids' edition of *Every Man in His Humour*, editor Martin Seymour-Smith insists that "there is no more precisely drawn character in English drama (outside Shakespeare) before 1598." *Every Man in His Humour* (New York: W. W. Norton, 1992), p. xxii.

14. Nicholas Breton, "Pasquil's Mistress; Or the Worthie and Unworthie Woman. With his description of that Furie, Jealousie" (London, 1600), sigs. F4-F4v.

15. I am thinking in particular of Allwit in Thomas Middleton's *A Chaste Maid in Cheapside* (1630). In one late sixteenth-century tract, the author advises cuckolds to keep the knowledge of their wives' infidelity to themselves and "make the best of it," for it is better to "choose to diet her in his owne house, then to pay for the boord of her and her lover in a strange place" (sig. C2). *Tell-Trothes New-Yeares Gift: Beeing Robin Good-Fellowes newes out of those Countries, where inhabites neither Charity*

nor honesty. With his owne Invective against Jelosy (London, 1593). Although cuckolds abound in early modern literature, I should note here that playwrights seem especially fascinated with jealous men and innocent women (*Every Man in His Humour; 1 The Fair Maid of the West; The Merry Wives of Windsor; Westward Ho; Northward Ho; Volpone; Much Ado About Nothing; The Winter's Tale; Cymbeline*).

16. On cuckoldry and class issues, see Douglas Bruster, "The Horn of Plenty: Cuckoldry and Capital in the Drama of the Age of Shakespeare," *Studies in English Literature, 1500–1900* 30 (1990): 195–215.

17. See Linda Woodbridge, *Women and the English Renaissance: Literature and the Nature of Womankind, 1540–1620* (Urbana: University of Illinois Press, 1984), pp. 171–3, 177–81, on the freedom of English city wives. The wives' presence in shops and on the streets as laborers and consumers underscored not only the liminal position of merchants and shopkeepers but also became the focus of the husbands' fears of loss and social failure.

18. I believe that the citizens' contradictory position – excluded from the elite's codification of violent and erotic impulses and estranged monetarily from the impetuous multitude – makes them a persistent focus of England's concerns regarding the nation's internationally marginalized status. See my discussion of how class distinctions inform ethnological discourse in chapter 2.

19. Burton, *The Anatomy of Melancholy*, section 3, p. 271.

20. William Harrison, *The Description of Britaine* in *The First and Second Volumes of Chronicles* (London, 1587), p. 114.

21. *Ibid.*, p. 115.

22. Thomas Wright, *The Passions of the Minde in Generall* (1604), ed. Thomas O. Sloan (Urbana: University of Illinois Press, 1971), p. lix.

23. On English views of Italian behavior, see Felix Raab, *The English Face of Machiavelli: A Changing Interpretation, 1500–1700* (London: Routledge, 1964); Mario Praz, *The Flaming Heart* (Gloucester, Mass.: Peter Smith, 1966), pp. 91–135; G. K. Hunter, *Dramatic Identities and Cultural Tradition: Studies in Shakespeare and His Contemporaries* (Liverpool: Liverpool University Press, 1978), pp. 3–30, 103–32; David C. McPherson, *Shakespeare, Jonson, and the Myth of Venice* (Newark: University of Delaware Press, 1990); Vaughan, *Othello: A Contextual History*, pp. 13–34; *Shakespeare and Italy*, ed. Holger Klein and Michele Marrapodi (Lewiston, New York: Edwin Mellen Press, 1999). Though her argument moves in a different direction than mine, Carol Thomas Neely also considers the humoral complexion of the Italians in "Hot Blood: Estranging Mediterranean Bodies in Early Modern Medical and Dramatic Texts," a paper delivered at the World Shakespeare Conference in Valencia, Spain (April 2001). My gratitude to Neely for allowing me to see her work in manuscript.

24. Levinus Lemnius, *The Touchstone of Complexions*, trans. Thomas Newton (London, 1581), fol. 17v.

25. Sara Warneke, *Images of the Educational Traveller in Early Modern England* (Leiden: E. J. Brill, 1995), p. 113.

26. Schoenfeldt, *Bodies and Selves*, p. 15.

27. William Harrison, *The Description of England* in *The First and Second Volumes of Chronicles* (London, 1587), p. 168. See Olsen, "Circe's Court," p. 109.

28. Lemnius, *The Touchstone of Complexions*, fol. 36r.

29. Edward Reynolds, *A Treatise of the Passions and Faculties of the Soule of Man* (London, 1640), pp. 59–60. See Schoenfeldt's discussion of this quotation in "'Commotion Strange': Passion in *Paradise Lost*," forthcoming in *Reading the Early Modern Passions*, ed. Mary Floyd-Wilson, Gail Kern Paster, and Katherine Rowe (Philadelphia: University of Pennsylvania Press). Schoenfeldt observes that "Stoic apathy is for Reynolds not a state of mental calm and moral constancy but rather a cesspool of fetid muck; it is by contrast the subject suffused by vigorous desires who is clear, quick, fresh, and healthy, like a mountain stream." My understanding of the general correspondences between puddle imagery, "cognitive confusion," and internal corruption has been informed by Paster's "The Clear Spirit Puddled."

30. Sincerity is often identified as a natural English trait. See Olsen's "Circe's Court" and Steven Shapin, *A Social History of Truth: Civility and Science in Seventeenth-Century England* (Chicago: University of Chicago Press, 1994).

31. Wright, *The Passions of the Minde*, p. lxii.

32. Thomas Dekker and John Webster, *Westward Ho* in *The Dramatic Works of Thomas Dekker*, ed. Fredson Bowers, vol. II (Cambridge: Cambridge University Press, 1955).

33. Benedetto Varchi, *The Blazon of Jealousie*, trans. R. T. (London, 1615), p. 21.

34. James Howell, *Instructions for Forreine Travell* (1642) in *English Reprints* (New York: AMS Press, 1966), IV, p. 68.

35. Nicolas Coeffeteau, *A Table of Humane Passions*, trans. Edmond Grimeston (London, 1621), p. 178.

36. *Tell-Trothes*, sig. E2r.

37. Varchi, *The Blazon of Jealousie*, p. 24.

38. Early modern jealousy appears to modern readers as an incipient form of skepticism. On Othello's skepticism, see Stanley Cavell, *Disowning Knowledge: In Six Plays of Shakespeare* (Cambridge: Cambridge University Press, 1987), pp. 125–42; Cavell, *The Claim of Reason* (Oxford: Oxford University Press, 1979), pp. 481–96. In *The Body in Parts*, David Hillman's discussion in "Visceral Knowledge" locates the "skeptical impulse to access the interior of the body" within the "pre-Cartesian belief systems of the period" (pp. 90, 83). As will become evident, my argument about jealousy in *Othello* corresponds with Hillman's conclusions about Shakespeare's anti-skeptical bent: "[In Shakespeare a] primary narcissism that refuses acknowledgement of the other as other is . . . akin to a steeling of the body, a refusal to take something or someone into it; accepting the fact of the outside world is imagined as taking that world (and in particular, its inhabitants) into one's body. (We might here ask whether Cartesian skepticism is not always akin to a refusal to be corporeally inhabited by knowledge; whether, in fact, this dynamic lies somewhere about the heart of Cartesian mind-body dualism)." (p. 96) Fittingly, Hillman describes the jealous Leontes in *The Winter's Tale* as "Caught in the web of his skepticism" (p. 94).

39. See Praz's chapter "The Politic Brain" in *The Flaming Heart*, which discusses the climate theory at work in the late sixteenth-century pamphlet, *Discovery of the Great Subtiltie and Wonderful Wisedome of the Italians* (1591): "The author draws from the first a distinction between the Septentrional and Occidental peoples and the Meridional nations: all the advantages possessed by the latter, chiefly as regards statecraft, are traced to the subtlety of the air. The former, on the other hand, are

described as labouring under 'a grosse humour ingendred in them, by reason of the grosnes and coldnes of the aier' " (p. 91).

40. George Chapman, *The Widow's Tears* (1612), ed. Ethel M. Smeak (Lincoln: University of Nebraska Press, 1966). Smeak notes that most scholars date the play's composition in 1605 or 1606.

41. On the controversies over the detrimental effects of traveling to Italy, see Sara Warneke's *Images of the Educational Traveller*.

42. Maus notes that the jealous man's "marginality confers a compensatory form of potency: the power of superior discernment. He comprehends more than his oblivious beloved and rival." "Horns of Dilemma," p. 571.

43. As Ian Smith observes, "Othello does not betray any signs of jealousy until act 3, when Iago begins his deliberate work of destruction. Rather, Shakespeare foregrounds Iago's jealousy for the entire first half of the play ... In addition, the exact nature of [Iago's] jealousy has been the subject of much critical speculation, notably summarized in Coleridge's phrase 'motiveless malignity': (a) Is it the job promotion? (b) Does he really believe that Othello has been sexually involved with his wife? (c) Does he desire Desdemona for himself? (d) Does he really suspect Cassio of being involved with Emilia, too? (e) Or, is there just sheer hate of Othello?" "Barbarian Errors," pp. 180–1.

44. Smith, "Barbarian Errors," p. 179.

45. Burton, *The Anatomy of Melancholy*, section 3, p. 264. As we observed in chapter 1, Bodin does not, in fact, describe Africans as "hot."

46. In "African Presence" Rosalind R. Johnson argues that Leo's text is a direct challenge to the early modern period's misconceptions about Africa and Africans. Jonathan Burton writes that "unlike other travelers of the period, Africanus refuses to rehearse the fantastic and preposterous material African historiography had inherited from Herodotus, Pliny and Mandeville" ("A most wily bird," p. 47), and in a footnote he observes that "Some material of this sort, including descriptions of dragons and hydras, was later inserted in the text by Pory" (p. 61, n. 6). However, celebrating Leo's history as an eyewitness account may be a modern presumption. His false report that the Niger "flows westward into the ocean ... we navigated it with the current from Timbuktu to Jenn and Mali" casts doubt on the eyewitness status of other segments of his text. According to E. W. Bovill, this erroneous assertion is most likely derived from a twelfth-century Arabic writer of geography El-Edrisi. E. W. Bovill, *The Golden Trade of the Moors* (London: Oxford University Press, 1958), p. 131.

47. Leo Africanus, *History*, 1, 183. I have discerned Pory's interpolation by comparing this section with Zhiri's translation of the same passage in "Leo Africanus's Description of Africa," *Travel Knowledge*, pp. 258–66.

48. Leo Africanus, *History*, 1. 183.

49. *Ibid.*, 1.187.

50. Even Pliny praises the Africans' mental strengths: "the Ethiopians are burnt by the heat of the heavenly body near them, and are born with a scorched appearance, with curly beard and hair, and ... [they prove] wise because of the mobility" of their climate. *Natural History*, trans. H. Rackham, vol. 1 (Cambridge, Mass.: Harvard University Press, 1938), pp. 321–3. See chapter 1 for a survey of the pertinent classical texts.

51. As Bernard Lewis has shown in *Race and Color in Islam* (New York: Harper and Row, 1971) color prejudice in Muslim culture is traceable to the Arabs' early enslavement of Africans (p. 27). Moreover, Islamic texts locate the terms of their color prejudice within climatic discourse; like the Greeks and Romans, they denigrate white northerners and black southerners (pp. 9; 28). However, their determinations suggest a climatic tradition contrary to the dominant counteractive theory in the west. In the Arabic texts, southerners possess fiery humors, which make them fickle and ignorant; the northerners have frigid humors, and they prove dull and ignorant (p. 36). Leo Africanus' history draws heavily on Ibn Khaldun, an important Arab historian and climate theorist. Zhiri, "Leo Africanus," p. 257.

52. Samuel Purchas, for example, writes that the Africans "lived, *saith* Leo, like beasts, without King, Lord, Commonwealth, or any government, scarse knowing to sowe their grounds: cladde in skinnes of beasts: not having any peculiar wife, but lie ten or twelve men and women together, each man chusing which he best liked." Quoted in Barthelemy, *Black Face*, p. 5.

53. Bodin, *Method*, p. 105. Emphasis added.

54. *Ibid.*, p. 102.

55. Giovanni Botero, *Relations of the Most Famous Kingdomes and Common-wealths thorowout the World*, trans. R. I. (London, 1630), p. 14.

56. Bernard Spivack, *Shakespeare and the Allegory of Evil: The History of a Metaphor in Relation to his Major Villains* (New York: Columbia University Press, 1958), p. 7.

57. Noting that "Roderigo" is a Spanish name and that Iago's name may be derived from Santiago Matamoros, St. James the Moorslayer, several critics have suggested that Iago may be Spanish rather than Italian. See Barbara Everett, " 'Spanish' Othello: the Making of Shakespeare's Moor," *Shakespeare and Race*, ed. Catherine M. S. Alexander and Stanley Wells (Cambridge: Cambridge University Press, 2000), pp. 64–81 and Eric Griffin, "Un-Sainting James: Or, *Othello* and the 'Spanish Spirits' of Shakespeare's Globe," *Representations* 62 (1998): 58–99. Griffin's essay, quite compellingly, notes that the Spaniards' stereotypical "humors" marked them as lustful (pp. 71–2) and perfidious (p. 79). And as we have seen from Thomas Wright's discussion above, there was a tendency among the early modern English to equate Spanish and Italian dispositions, especially since they shared a warm Mediterranean climate. Intriguingly, James Howell maintained that Spanish subtlety had its roots in Italy: "*Italy* hath beene always accounted the Nurse of *Policy, Learning, Musique, Architecture*, and *Limning*, with other perfections, which she disperseth to the rest of *Europe*, nor was the *Spaniard* but a dunce, till he had taken footing in her, and so grew subtilized by co-alition with her people" (*Instructions for Forreine Travell*, 42).

   I do, however, take Iago at his word when he identifies himself as a Venetian, who believes he understands the sexual mores of Italian culture in a way that Othello cannot: "I know our country disposition well. / In Venice they do let God see the pranks / They dare not show their husbands" (3. 3. 205–7).

58. For a good survey of approaches to Iago, see Marvin Rosenberg, "In Defense of Iago" *Shakespeare Quarterly* 6 (1955): 145–58. On Iago as a Machiavel, see E. E. Stoll, *Othello: An Historical and Comparative Study* (Minneapolis: University

of Minnesota Press, 1915); Stanley Edgar Hyman, *Iago: Some Approaches to the Illusion of His Motivation* (New York: Atheneum, 1970).

59. Iago later contrasts Venetian secrecy with those "knaves ... abroad, / Who having by their own importunate suit / Or voluntary dotage of some mistress, / Convinced or supplied them, cannot choose / But they must blab–" (4. 1. 25–9).

60. Janet Adelman, "Iago's Alter Ego: Race as Projection in *Othello*," *Shakespeare Quarterly* 48 (1997): 131.

61. On the garden speech, Adelman writes, "This is not, presumably, his experience of his own body's interior or of his management of it; it seems rather a defensive fantasy." "Iago's Alter Ego," p. 132.

62. Even Adelman, who takes Iago's emotional state seriously, does not believe he represents the feelings of "jealousy" *per se*: "Iago's words here, like Emilia's at 3. 4. 157–60, refer explicitly to *jealousy* but nonetheless define the self-referential qualities of *envy* ... [he] repeatedly comes up with narratives of jealousy as though to justify his intolerable envy to himself ... narratives of jealousy are far more legible and recognizably 'human' than the envy represented through Iago and dismissed in him as unrecognizable, inhuman, or demonic" ("Iago's Alter Ego," p. 138). Yet these distinctions between "envy" and "jealousy" neglect to take into account the bizarre early modern conception of jealousy-as-suspicion and internal corruption that I have been tracing here.

63. In "Changing Places in *Othello*," Michael Neill argues that Iago's motives are all "rationalizations for an attitude towards the world whose real origins lie much deeper ... Indeed I take it to be profoundly true of emotions like resentment, envy, and jealousy that they are in some sense *their own motive*." *Shakespeare Survey* 37 (1984): 121.

64. Adelman observes,"Split himself, Iago is a master at splitting others: his seduction of Othello works by inscribing in Othello the sense of dangerous interior spaces – thoughts that cannot be known, monsters in the mind – which Othello seems to lack, introducing him to the world of self-alienation that Iago inhabits." "Iago's Alter Ego," p. 128.

65. The commonplace perspective is represented here by Jonathan Burton in "A most wily bird": "when Othello first appears before the audience, his impeccable behavior reveals him to be, in some ways, more like the idealized New World savage (tractable but noble) who gratefully embraces Christianity" (p. 56). Of course, "Othello" is the product of "Western" culture; the play tells a story of English projections onto Africa and Africans. However, it is my contention that what modern critics perceive to be Othello's cloak of European "civility," early modern English audiences would have readily ascribed to a southern climate and culture.

66. James L. Calderwood calls this speech "puritanical" in *The Properties of Othello* (Amherst: University of Massachusetts Press, 1989), p. 29. For arguments suggesting that Othello's behavior stems from sexual repression, see Snow, "Sexual Anxiety" and Greenblatt, *Renaissance Self-Fashioning*, p. 233. Others have suggested that sexual repression informs the entire play. Little, "An essence that's not seen"; Neill, "Unproper Beds."

67. It is a commonplace in humoral discourse that one becomes cooler and drier with age.

68. See Valerie Traub's argument "Jewels, Statues, and Corpses: Containment of Female Erotic Power in Shakespeare's Plays," that "Othello associates romantic love with calm and 'content[ment]' and ... the loss of that love with chaos ... Othello also equates Desdemona's sexuality with chaos and violence." *Shakespeare Studies* 20 (1987): 224.

69. In *A Midsummer Night's Dream*, the organ is the eye (3. 2. 177).

70. Summarizing Pierre Janton's argument in "Othello's Weak Function," *Cahiers Elisabéthains*, 7 (1975): 43–50, Little identifies this line as important to the debate over the consummation of Othello and Desdemona's marriage: " 'Othello's libidinous aggressivity' remains unchanneled because of Othello's impotence." "An essence that's not seen," p. 321, n. 50. Janton's convoluted conclusion recalls Bodin's and Botero's efforts to reconcile the African's lack of internal heat with the emergent charges of lasciviousness.

71. The Quarto edition reads "My heart's subdued / Even to the utmost pleasure of my lord" (1. 3. 249–50).

72. See Sara Warneke, "A Taste for Newfangledness: The Destructive Potential of Novelty in Early Modern England," *The Sixteenth Century Journal* 26 (1995): 881–96.

73. John Davies of Hereford, *Microcosmos* in *The Complete Works of John Davies of Hereford*, ed. Alexander B. Grosart, vol. 1 (Edinburgh: Edinburgh University Press, 1878), p. 31.

74. This is, of course, a familiar plot, replayed again and again in modern situation comedies. However, the early modern representation of this emotional transformation indicates that the passions are not always awakened or stirred or repressed; they can also be planted or newly created by another's manipulation or intervention.

75. There has been, of course, a long critical tradition of questioning Othello's self-assessment as "one not easily jealous," most notably T. S. Eliot's contention that when Othello identifies himself as such, he is "cheering himself up." "Shakespeare and the Stoicism of Seneca," *Selected Essays* (New York: Harcourt, Brace & World, Inc., 1950), p. 111. I mention Leontes here as someone easily jealous in part because he either begins the play already jealous, or it takes no more than his observation of Hermione and Polixenes conversing together to raise his suspicions. When critics consider Leontes' jealousy in relation to *Othello*, they tend to look for correspondences between him and Othello, but a more fruitful comparison might be Iago and Leontes. Indeed, Leontes echoes Iago when he reads lechery in "paddling palms, and pinching fingers" (1. 2. 117). It is suggestive as well that Shakespeare departs from his source, Robert Greene's *Pandosto*, in making Leontes the King of Sicily, instead of Bohemia. As J. H. P. Pafford observes in the introduction to the Arden edition, "In *Pandosto* the onset of jealousy was slow." "Introduction," *The Winter's Tale* (London and New York: Routledge, 1966), p. lvii.

76. See Wright's discussion of how reason may stir the passions, especially through the power of oratory (*The Passions of the Minde*, p. 184).

77. We should compare Iago's single statement regarding the nature of Othello's changeability with his repeated references to Desdemona's supposedly inconstant disposition. To persuade Roderigo that Desdemona's marriage to the Moor is doomed, Iago relies on the stereotype of female inconstancy: "She must change for youth" (1. 3. 342); "Her eye must be fed ... Very nature will instruct her in it and compel her to some second choice" (2. 1. 220, 227–9). Once jealous, Othello adopts

the same language: "she can turn, and turn, and yet go on / And turn again..."
(4. 1. 250–1).

78. In *Othello: A Contextual History*, for example, Vaughan writes: "Iago also per-
petuates the myth of Moors having promiscuous sexual appetites: 'These Moors
are changeable in their wills' " (p. 66). See also Smith, "Barbarian Errors,"
p. 180.

79. Natural philosophers located the "will" in the rational soul and identified it as a
mediator between human reason and the senses; the will is "the means by which
man exerts his rational control over the data of sense, for the object of will is 'the
good which reason doth lead us to seek.' " Herschel Baker, *The Image of Man: A
Study of the Idea of Human Dignity in Classical Antiquity, the Middle Ages, and the
Renaissance* (New York: Harper and Row, 1947), p. 290.

80. Quotation from Wright, *The Passions of the Minde*, p. 32. For more on the status of
the "will," see the introduction to Wright's text, especially p. xxxi.

81. When trying to determine why Othello is so violent, Lodovico wonders "did the
letters work upon his blood / And new-create his fault?" (4. 1. 272–3).

82. See Robert Ralston Cawley, *The Voyagers and Elizabethan Drama* (London: Oxford
University Press, 1938), pp. 131–2.

83. Seneca, *Natural Questions*, trans. Thomas H. Corcoran, vol. II (Cambridge, Mass.:
Harvard University Press, 1972), pp. 41–3.

84. On epilepsy and melancholy, see Burton, *The Anatomy of Melancholy*, pp. 408, 430.

85. Christian patience is akin to moisture; Brabantio in act 1 notes that to "pay grief,"
which dries the body, he "must of poor patience borrow," implying a need for the
moisture of patience (1. 3. 214). Othello tells "Patience" to "turn thy complexion
there," as if to ask whether moist, young, and rose-lipped patience could withstand
Desdemona's dry and darkened interior space.

86. See Sir Thomas Browne's *Pseudodoxia Epidemica* on the spontaneous generation
of frogs from putrefaction in *The Works of Sir Thomas Browne*, ed. Geoffrey Keynes,
vol. III (Chicago: University of Chicago Press, 1964), pp. 200–1.

87. Traub notes that "Just prior to the murder, Desdemona's moistness and heat are
replaced in Othello's imagination by the cool, dry, immobile image of 'monumental
alabaster.' " "Jewels, Statues, and Corpses," p. 226.

88. Adelman, "Iago's Alter Ego," p. 128.

89. On the role of the Turks in the play, see Daniel Vitkus, "Turning Turk in *Othello*:
The Conversion and Damnation of the Moor," *Shakespeare Quarterly* 48 (1997):
145–76.

90. Jean Bodin, *The Six Bookes of a Commonweale* (1606), trans. Richard Knoles,
ed. Kenneth Douglas McRae (Cambridge, Mass.: Harvard University Press, 1962),
p. 557.

91. Varchi, *The Blazon of Jealousie*, p. 23.

92. Thomas Dekker and John Webster, *Northward Ho* (1607) in *The Dramatic Works
of Thomas Dekker*, vol. II.

93. Wright, *Passions of the Minde*, p. 334.

94. Fascinatingly, when Jonson revises *Every Man in His Humour*, making Thorello
into the English Kitely, he also changes the last three lines of his jealous soliloquy
to "Ah, but what miserie' is it, to know this? / Or, knowing it, to want the mind's
erection, / In such extremes?" (New Mermaids' edition [1966], 2. 1. 232–4). Where

the Italian is predestined to be jealous (lacking the free election of the soul), the Englishman's deficiencies appear to be more physiologically oriented.

95. Wright, *The Passions of the Minde*, p. lix.

7 CYMBELINE'S ANGELS

1. Leah S. Marcus, *Puzzling Shakespeare: Local Reading and Its Discontents* (Berkeley: University of California Press, 1988), pp. 106–48. Other notable readings of the play's union sentiments include Emrys Jones, "Stuart *Cymbeline*," *Essays in Criticism* 11 (1961): 84–99; Glynne Wickham, "Riddle and Emblem: A Study in the Dramatic Structure of *Cymbeline*," *English Renaissance Studies* (Oxford: Clarendon Press, 1980), pp. 94–113; Constance Jordan, *Shakespeare's Monarchies: Ruler and Subject in the Romances* (Ithaca and London: Cornell University Press, 1997), pp. 69–106; Michael J. Redmond, "'My Lord, I fear has forgot Britain': Rome, Italy, and the (Re)construction of British National Identity," *Shakespeare and Italy*, ed. Holger Klein and Michele Marrapodi (Lewiston, New York: Edwin Mellen Press, 1999), pp. 297–316.

2. On the correspondences between *Cymbeline*'s representation of Roman Britain and Camden's *Britannia*, see John E. Curran, Jr.'s "Royalty Unlearned, Honor Untaught: British Savages and Historiographical Change in *Cymbeline*," *Comparative Drama* 31 (1997): 277–303. See also Garrett A. Sullivan, Jr.'s *The Drama of Landscape: Land, Property, and Social Relations on the Early Modern Stage* (Stanford: Stanford University Press, 1998), pp. 150–8. Thomas G. Olsen, who also attends to the play's climatic and ethnological discourse, has argued that the Giacomo plot in particular plays out the "unwanted excesses of a civilizing process which, according to one historiographical tradition [Camden] in early modern England, the Roman conquerors initiated." "Iachimo's 'Drug–Damn'd Italy' and the Problem of British National Character in *Cymbeline*," *Shakespeare and Italy*, ed. Klein and Marrapodi p. 270. I discuss Camden's influence and the play's representation of Britain's degree of civility in "*Cymbeline*, the Scots, and the English Race," *British Identities and English Renaissance Literature*, ed. David Baker and Willy Maley (Cambridge: Cambridge University Press, 2002), pp. 101–15, and I presented an early version of this chapter in the seminar "The English and the Scots," directed by Rebecca Bushnell, at the 1997 Shakespeare Association of America meeting in Washington DC. Though she does not focus on Camden, Jodi Mikalachki has read the play as concerned with purging the effeminate savagery of England's early history in "The Masculine Romance of Roman Britain: *Cymbeline* and Early Modern Nationalism," *Shakespeare Quarterly* 46 (1995): 301–22. Peter Parolin also attends to the play's representation of "Britain's efforts to banish its own potential barbarism," in "Anachronistic Italy: Cultural Alliances and National Identity in *Cymbeline*," *Shakespeare Studies* (in press).

3. On England's degeneracy, see, for example, Sir Thomas Craig, *De Unione Regnorum Britanniæ Tractatus* (1606) (Edinburgh: Scottish History Society, 1909), pp. 414–15. For a survey of the issues in the union tracts, see the introduction to *The Jacobean Union: Six Tracts of 1604*, ed. Bruce R. Galloway and Brian P. Levack (Edinburgh: Scottish History Society, 1985).

4. In "Questioning History in *Cymbeline*," *Studies in English Literature* 41 (2001), J. Clinton Crumley has made the argument that the play "demonstrates awareness

that it occupies a space between history and romance, and that it uses romance to question history" (p. 298). Crumley's essay was published after the composition of this chapter; however, his perspective on the play's complex use of history is consonant with mine.

5. In a reading that is sympathetic with my own and Thomas G. Olsen's, Parolin has argued that *Cymbeline* "continually reminds audiences that imperial Rome degenerated into contemporary Italy . . . Britain achieves its civility . . . but at the cost of the very alignment with Italy that the play had been seeking to avoid" ("Anachronistic Italy").

6. Graham Parry, *The Trophies of Time: English Antiquarians of the Seventeenth Century* (Oxford: Oxford University Press, 1995), p. 45.

7. William Camden, *Remains Concerning Britain*, ed. R. D. Dunn (Toronto: University of Toronto Press, 1984), p. 16.

8. Parry, *Trophies of Time*, p. 37.

9. See my discussion of Robert Burton and the early modern racialist interpretations of northern migrations in chapter 4 above.

10. Camden, *Remains*, p. 24.

11. Parry notes of Camden that "By 1607 . . . when the last revised edition [of *Britannia*] appeared, he had grown more sympathetic, and the account of the Saxons had been much enlarged" (*Trophies of Time*, p. 37).

12. In his discussion of the antiquarians' interest in Saxon language studies, R. F. Jones has observed that the heavy reliance on Tacitus infused much of this work with a proto-racialist tinge. *The Triumph of the English Language* (Stanford: Stanford University Press, 1953), pp. 214–15.

13. In the notes to the *Remains*, R. D. Dunn states that "There are some strikingly similar ideas in Verstegan's *Restitution of Decayed Intelligence* and it is possible that the appearance of Verstegan's book in 1605 prompted Camden to revise his own discussion of the Germanic element in English" (p. 372). On the significance of Verstegan's text to racialism in England, see Hugh A. MacDougall, *Racial Myth in English History: Trojans, Teutons, and Anglo-Saxons* (Montreal: Harvest House, 1982), pp. 47–9; Kwame Anthony Appiah's entry "Race" in *Critical Terms for Literary Study*, ed. Frank Lentricchia and Thomas McLaughlin (Chicago: University of Chicago Press, 1995), p. 283.

14. On the study of Anglo-Saxon language roots, see R. F. Jones, *The Triumph of the English Language*. On the controversies over law, see J. G. A. Pocock, *The Ancient Constitution and the Feudal Law: A Study of English Historical Thought in the Seventeenth Century* (Cambridge: Cambridge University Press, 1957). See also Arthur B. Ferguson, *Clio Unbound: Perception of the Social and Cultural Past in Renaissance England* (Durham, NC: Duke University Press, 1979); on law, pp. 259–311; on language, pp. 312–45.

15. MacDougall, *Racial Myth*, p. 129.

16. Richard Verstegan, *A Restitution of Decayed Intelligence* (1605) (London: Scolar Press, 1976), pp. 42–50. Verstegan is able to dismiss the potentially contaminating influences of the Danish and Norman invasions by arguing that they too are issued from the Germans.

17. *Ibid.*, p. 50.

18. *Ibid.*, pp. 51–2. See the introduction for a more complete discussion of Verstegan's dismissal of climate theory.

19. On degeneration in Polybius, see Charles William Fornara's *The Nature of History in Ancient Greece and Rome* (Berkeley: University of California Press, 1983), pp. 83–6.

20. I am quoting R. F. Brinkley's reference to Geoffrey of Monmouth as it appears in Emrys Jones' "Stuart *Cymbeline*," p. 90.

21. See Marcus, *Puzzling Shakespeare*, for example, pp. 134–5.

22. Mikalachki notes that the "display of pseudo-etymology recalls the involved and equally fanciful antiquarian derivations of the name *Britain*" in Camden's *Britannia* ("The Masculine Romance," p. 320).

23. In her reading of *Cymbeline*, Constance Jordan has demonstrated how the "language of arboriculture was current in defenses of the Union of England and Scotland" (*Shakespeare's Monarchies*, p. 82); however, none of the examples she cites has the verbal echoes of Camden's *Remains*.

24. As I discuss in the *Tamburlaine* chapter, the early moderns often equated the acquisition of civility with softening or mollifying.

25. I am quoting Curran, "Royalty Unlearned," p. 286. On the brothers' "Briton" identity, see Marcus, *Puzzling Shakespeare*, p. 134. See also Ronald J. Boling, who contends that Arviragus and Guiderius are representative of Wales and its historical subjection to an anglicizing and civilizing process. "Anglo-Welsh Relations in *Cymbeline*" *Shakespeare Quarterly* 51 (2000): 33–66.

26. Curran, "Royalty Unlearned," pp. 286–7.

27. Mikalachki, "The Masculine Romance," p. 313.

28. Sullivan, *The Drama of Landscape*, p. 146.

29. On the brothers' "exclusion from history," see Mikalachki, "The Masculine Romance," p. 314.

30. Acknowledging the play's indebtedness to early modern climate theory, Jean Feerick has read *Cymbeline* in relation to England's colonizing ventures in the New World: "Retrieving the Barbarian: The Western Translation of Masculinity in *Cymbeline*" (presented in the seminar "Shakespeare and the Nature of Barbarism," directed by Mary Floyd-Wilson, at the 1999 Shakespeare Association of America meeting in San Francisco). Feerick makes the argument that Arviragus and Guiderius are not only meant to recall the ancient Britons but also the new men surviving the harsh climates in "Nova Britannia."

31. Raphael Holinshed, *The First and Second Volumes of Chronicles* (London, 1587); "Historie of England," pp. 159–64. Hereafter, references to the English and Scottish chronicles are cited parenthetically in the text. The "Historie of England" is designated by "*E*" and the "Historie of Scotland" by "*S*."

32. In Holinshed, they intervene by sending the cowardly Scots back into battle, leaving the Scots to choose whether they "would be slaine of their own fellowes coming to their aid, or to returne againe to fight with the enimies." Thus, the Danes believe that the returning Scots are a "new power of Scotishmen" (*S*, 155).

33. Camden, *Remains*, p. 16. For an extended version of the Venerable Bede's story, see also Verstegan, *Restitution*, pp. 140–1.

34. Heather James, *Shakespeare's Troy: Drama, Politics, and the Translation of Empire* (Cambridge: Cambridge University Press, 1997), p. 154.

35. Verstegan, *Restitution*, p. v. Though Verstegan blames "Divers forreyn writers" for misrepresenting the English people's origins, it is significant that he explicitly

names "*John Bodin*" as "blame woorthy." Craig also cites the Britons' polyandry as evidence of their barbarous past (*De Unione Regnorum*, p. 389).

36. James, *Shakespeare's Troy*, pp. 155–6.
37. Parolin, "Anachronistic Italy."
38. Mikalachki, "The Masculine Romance," p. 322.
39. Parolin, "Anachronistic Italy."
40. I am quoting Stephanie H. Jed, *Chaste Thinking: The Rape of Lucretia and the Birth of Humanism* (Bloomington: Indiana University Press, 1989), p. 2. On the symbolism of Cleopatra, see Mary Nyquist, " 'Profuse, proud Cleopatra': 'Barbarism' and Female Rule in Early Modern Republicanism," *Women's Studies* 24 (1994): 85–130.
41. D. R. Woolf, *The Idea of History in Early Stuart England* (Toronto: University of Toronto Press, 1990), p. 59.
42. John Russell, *A Treatise of the Happie and Blissed Unioun* (*c.* 1604/5), *The Jacobean Union*, ed. Galloway and Levack, p. 84.
43. Roger A. Mason, "Scotching the Brut: Politics, History and National Myth in Sixteenth-Century Britain," *Scotland and England 1286–1815*, ed. Roger A. Mason (Edinburgh: John Donald, 1987), p. 64.
44. John [Mair] Major, *A History of Greater Britain* (1521), trans. and ed. Archibald Constable (Edinburgh: Edinburgh University Press for the Scottish History Society, 1892), p. 18.
45. Edmund Bolton in *Hypercritica* (1618), quoted in MacDougall, *Racial Myth*, p. 23. Indeed, the ethnological identity of the Britons becomes a major point of contention in the Jacobean union debates, as controversialists discussed whom the ancients, the Romans, the Scots, and the English each meant when they referred to "Britannia." See for example, "Of the Union" by Sir Henry Spelman (*The Jacobean Union*, ed. Galloway and Levack, p. 168).
46. Geoffrey of Monmouth, *Histories of the Kings of Britain* (London: J. M. Dent, 1911), p. 65.
47. Homer Nearing, Jr., "The Legend of Julius Caesar's British Conquest," *PMLA* 64 (1949): 921. Holinshed refutes those "Scotish writers [who] report, that the Britains, after the Romans were the first time repelled . . . refused to receive aid of the Scotish men the second time, and so were vanquished" (*E*, 31).
48. On Scottish claims to independence, see Mason, "Scotching the Brut," p. 64. See also Craig, *De Unione Regnorum*, pp. 463–4.
49. "A Treatise About the Union of England and Scotland," p. 49.
50. Craig, *De Unione Regnorum*, pp. 414–5.
51. Spelman, "Of the Union," p. 170. Galloway and Levack speculate that "many sections of Spelman's tract reflect Camden's views" of the union controversy (*The Jacobean Union*, p. lxix).
52. Camden, *Remains*, p. 16.
53. William Camden, *Britain*, trans. Philemon Holland (London, 1610), p. 119.
54. Roger A. Mason, "The Scottish Reformation and the Origins of Anglo-British Imperialism," *Scots and Britons: Scottish Political Thought and the Union of 1603*, ed. Roger A. Mason (Cambridge: Cambridge University Press, 1994), p. 186. In a paper entitled "Saxons, Britons, and the Jacobean Union," delivered in "The English and Scots" seminar at the 1997 meeting of the Shakespeare Association of America, Christopher Highley detects anti-Scottish sentiment in Richard Verstegan's *A Restitution of Decayed Intelligence*. Although Verstegan claims that James

is descended from English-Saxon kings, he is much more ambiguous about the racial status of the Scots themselves.

55. Mikalachki, "The Masculine Romance," p. 309.

56. In his astute discussion of how decadent Italy haunts Britain's "nationalistic narrative," Parolin has shown how *Cymbeline*'s anachronisms put "different historical moments into active engagement with each other." Since, as he observes, "historical moments carry powerful symbolic charge, to evoke a new historical moment inevitably deploys a new set of symbolic meanings" ("Anachronistic Italy"). And while the temporal gap between ancient Rome and contemporary Italy is the widest that the play represents, it is only one example of the play's historiographical self-consciousness.

57. Jones, "Stuart *Cymbeline*," p. 88.

58. I refer to Joan Warchol Rossi's characterization of the play's criticism a generation ago in "*Cymbeline*'s Debt to Holinshed: The Richness of III.i," *Shakespeare's Romances Reconsidered*, ed. Carol McGinnis Kay and Henry E. Jacobs (Lincoln and London: University of Nebraska Press, 1978), p. 104.

59. Holinshed is more definitive about Theomantius, but on Cymbeline he writes: "But, whether this controversie which appeareth to fall forth betwixt the Britains and Augustus, was occasioned by Kymbeline, or some other prince of the Britains, I have not to avouch" (*E*, 33). Crumley also makes this point, observing that "Holinshed's text here focuses on what the Roman historians have to say about international politics during Cymbeline's reign" ("Questioning History," p. 301).

60. On the collaborative authorship of Holinshed's *Chronicles*, see Annabel Patterson's *Reading Holinshed's Chronicles* (Chicago: University of Chicago Press, 1994). John Bellenden's translation of Hector Boece's *Scotorum Historia* is presumed to be the primary source of Holinshed's *Historie of Scotland*. On the Scottish history's sources and authorship, see Sally Mapstone, "Shakespeare and Scottish Kingship: a Case History," *The Rose and the Thistle: Essays on the Culture of Late Medieval and Renaissance Scotland*, ed. Sally Mapstone and Juliette Wood (East Linton, Edinburgh: Tuckwell Press, 1998), pp. 160–1.

61. It is customarily presumed that the play's singular debt to Holinshed's "Historie of Scotland" is the refrain in act 5 "Two boys, and old man twice a boy, a lane" (5. 3. 57). Rossi appears to be alone in her acknowledgement that other portions of the play may also be derived from the Scottish chronicles ("*Cymbeline*'s Debt to Holinshed," p. 111).

62. Though Arviragus eventually renounces Genissa, the Romans ultimately prevail by "fortune" (*S*, 47–8).

63. As we have already discussed, Mikalachki identifies Cymbeline's queen with the Boadicea of Holinshed's *Historie of England*. Though Mikalachki makes no direct reference to the Scottish *Chronicles*, she does note that John Fletcher's *Bonduca* drew on the Scottish "account of Voada, a northern queen" ("The Masculine Romance," p. 311, n. 32).

64. On this scene as a critical "stumbling block," see Mikalachki, "The Masculine Romance," pp. 303–5.

65. Curran, "Royalty Unlearned," p. 289.

66. Olsen characterizes the queen as a "subtle Machiavel" and Cloten as the "English ape" ("Iachimo's 'Drug-Damn'd Italy,' " p. 289). On Cloten, he writes, "Though

dull-witted and therefore subjected to Northern climatic influences, Cloten nonetheless is obsessed by false appearances in a manner Shakespeare's contemporaries would have expected of Iachimo and his countrymen, or of those unfortunate Italianate Englishmen who came under their sway" (pp. 289–90). As G. Wilson Knight observed, Cloten's "worst qualities" are "habitually associated by Shakespeare with foreign travel or foreign birth." *The Crown of Life* (London: Methuen, 1958), pp. 136–7. See also Parolin, "Anachronistic Italy"; James, *Shakespeare's Troy*, p. 159. By portraying these characters as superficially refined, Shakespeare further underscores their affiliation with Scots, whose close ties with France made them more cosmopolitan than the English in certain ways. On Scottish cosmopolitanism, see J. G. A. Pocock, "Two Kingdoms and three histories? Political thought in British contexts," *Scots and Britons*, ed. Mason, p. 305.

67. See my discussion in chapter 2 on the relationship between being conquered and cultural degeneration.

68. I am quoting Heather James here, who notes that "Cloten is the model of cultural degeneration that the play offers first as Posthumus' foil and double" (*Shakespeare's Troy*, p. 159). Identifying Cloten as Posthumus' double is a commonplace of *Cymbeline* criticism; see for example, Joan Hartwig, "Cloten, Autolycus, and Caliban: Bearers of Parodic Burdens," *Shakespeare's Romances Reconsidered*, ed. Mcginnis and Jacobs, pp. 91–103.

69. Marcus contends that Posthumus represents the "Post Nati" – James' Scottish subjects born after his accession to England's throne, who in the 1608 legal case were "declared citizens, entitled to recourse at English law" (*Puzzling Shakespeare*, p. 124).

70. On Posthumus as the *inglese italianato*, see Parolin ("Anachronistic Italy") and Olsen ("Iachimo's 'Drug-Damn'd Italy,' " p. 285).

71. See Patricia Parker, "Romance and Empire: Anachronistic *Cymbeline*," *Unfolded Tales: Essays on Renaissance Romance*, ed. George M. Logan and Gordon Teskey (Ithaca: Cornell University Press, 1989), pp. 189–207.

72. Camden, *Britain*, p. 88.

73. I have changed the Norton's "wing-led" at line 24 to the Second Folio (1632) emendation of "mingled." "Mingled" connotes, in an ethnological sense, the tempering quality that Caesar's civilizing "discipline" presumably brought to the Britons' heated and unruly "courage."

74. Innogen's references to the "jay[s] of Italy" (3. 4. 48) implies that she would agree with Iago's assessment of his country's "disposition."

75. We should recall here that in *A View* Spenser's Eudoxus conflates forgetting one's nation with cultural degeneration: "And is it possible that an Englishman, brought up in such sweet civility as England affords, should find such likeing in that barbarous rudenes, that he should forget his owne nature, and forgoe his owne nation!" Edmund Spenser, *A View of the State of Ireland* (1633), ed. Andrew Hadfield and Willy Maley (Oxford: Blackwell, 1997), p. 54. See my discussion of *A View* in chapter 2.

76. Jean Bodin, *Method for the Easy Comprehension of History* (1566), trans. Beatrice Reynolds (New York: Columbia University Press, 1945), p. 97. For another reading of Giacomo's appeal to climate theory, see Olsen, "Iachimo's 'Drug-Damn'd Italy,' " pp. 286–7.

Index